GW01080972

THE WORLD'S CLASSICS

133

THE
GOLDEN TREASURY
OF THE BEST SONGS AND
LYRICAL POEMS IN
THE ENGLISH LANGUAGE

With a Fifth Book

Oxford University Press, Walton Street, Oxford OX2 6DP

OXFORD LONDON GLASGOW
NEW YORK TORONTO MELBOURNE WELLINGTON
KUALA LUMPUR SINGAPORE JAKARTA HONG KONG TOKYO
DELHI BOMBAY CALCUTTA MADRAS KARACHI
IBADAN NAIROBI DAR ES SALAAM CAPE TOWN

THE
GOLDEN TREASURY

OF THE BEST SONGS AND LYRICAL POEMS IN THE ENGLISH LANGUAGE

Selected and arranged by

FRANCIS TURNER PALGRAVE

—

WITH A FIFTH BOOK

selected by

JOHN PRESS

OXFORD
OXFORD UNIVERSITY PRESS
LONDON NEW YORK TORONTO

FRANCIS TURNER PALGRAVE

Born, Great Yarmouth, 28 September 1824
Died, London, 24 October 1897

The Golden Treasury of the best Songs and Lyrical Poems in the English Language *was first published in 1861. In* The World's Classics *it was first published, with additional Poems, in 1907 and reprinted six times. New edition 1914, reprinted eighteen times. Enlarged edition, with poems by contemporary writers, 1928, reprinted eight times. Further poems (bringing the additions up to the date of publication) were included in 1941; reprinted ten times and again in 1959, 1960, and 1963. New edition (with a new Fifth Book) 1965, reprinted in 1968, 1974, and 1978.*

ISBN 0 19 250900 4

This selection
© OXFORD UNIVERSITY PRESS 1964

*Printed in Great Britain
at the University Press, Oxford
by Vivian Ridler
Printer to the University*

CONTENTS

Εἰς τὸν λειμῶνα καθίσας,
ἔδρεπεν ἕτερον ἐφ' ἑτέρῳ
αἱρόμενος ἄγρευμ' ἀνθέων
ἁδομένᾳ ψυχᾷ

[Eurip. *frag.* 754]

['He sat in the meadow and plucked with glad
heart the spoil of the flowers, gathering them
one by one']

TO ALFRED TENNYSON

POET LAUREATE

THIS book in its progress has recalled often to my memory a man with whose friendship we were once honoured, to whom no region of English Literature was unfamiliar, and who, whilst rich in all the noble gifts of Nature, was most eminently distinguished by the noblest and the rarest,—just judgement and high-hearted patriotism. It would have been hence a peculiar pleasure and pride to dedicate what I have endeavoured to make a true national Anthology of three centuries to Henry Hallam. But he is beyond the reach of any human tokens of love and reverence; and I desire therefore to place before it a name united with his by associations which, whilst Poetry retains her hold on the minds of Englishmen, are not likely to be forgotten.

Your encouragement, given while traversing the wild scenery of Treryn Dinas, led me to begin the work; and it has been completed under your advice and assistance. For the favour now asked I have thus a second reason: and to this I may add, the homage which is your right as Poet, and the gratitude due to a Friend, whose regard I rate at no common value.

Permit me then to inscribe to yourself a book which, I hope, may be found by many a lifelong fountain of innocent and exalted pleasure; a source of animation to friends when they meet; and able to sweeten solitude itself with best society,—with the companionship of the wise and the good, with the beauty which the eye cannot see, and the music only heard in silence. If this Collection proves a storehouse of delight to Labour and to Poverty,—if it teaches those indifferent to the Poets to love them, and those who love them to love them more, the aim and the desire entertained in framing it will be fully accomplished.

F. T. P.

May 1861

PREFACE

THIS little Collection differs, it is believed, from others in the attempt made to include in it all the best original Lyrical pieces and Songs in our language,—by writers not living,—and none beside the best. Many familiar verses will hence be met with; many also which should be familiar:—the Editor will regard as his fittest readers those who love Poetry so well that he can offer them nothing not already known and valued.

The Editor is acquainted with no strict and exhaustive definition of Lyrical Poetry; but he has found the task of practical decision increase in clearness and in facility as he advanced with the work, whilst keeping in view a few simple principles. Lyrical has been here held essentially to imply that each Poem shall turn on some single thought, feeling, or situation. In accordance with this, narrative, descriptive, and didactic poems—unless accompanied by rapidity of movement, brevity, and the colouring of human passion—have been excluded. Humorous poetry, except in the very unfrequent instances where a truly poetical tone pervades the whole, with what is strictly personal, occasional, and religious, has been considered foreign to the idea of the book. Blank verse and the ten-syllable couplet, with all pieces markedly dramatic, have been rejected as alien from what is commonly understood by Song, and rarely conforming to Lyrical conditions in treatment. But it is not anticipated, nor is it possible, that all readers shall think the line accurately drawn. Some poems, as Gray's *Elegy*, the *Allegro* and *Penseroso*, Wordsworth's *Ruth* or Campbell's *Lord Ullin*, might be claimed with perhaps equal justice for a narrative or descriptive selection: whilst with reference especially to Ballads and Sonnets, the Editor can only state that he has taken his utmost pains to decide without caprice or partiality.

This also is all he can plead in regard to a point even more liable to question;—what degree of merit should give rank among the Best. That a Poem shall be worthy of the writer's genius,—that it shall reach a perfection commensurate with its aim,—that we should require finish in proportion to brevity,—that passion, colour, and originality cannot atone for serious imperfections in clearness, unity, or truth,—that a few good lines do not make a good poem,—that popular estimate is serviceable as a guidepost more than as a compass,—above all, that Excellence should be looked for rather in the Whole than in the Parts,—such and other such canons have been always steadily regarded. He may however add that the pieces chosen, and a far larger number rejected, have been carefully and repeatedly considered; and that he has been aided throughout by two friends of independent and exercised judgement, besides the distinguished person addressed in the Dedication. It is hoped that by this procedure the volume has been freed from that one-sidedness which must beset individual decisions:—but for the final choice the Editor is alone responsible.

It would obviously have been invidious to apply the standard aimed at in this Collection to the Living. Nor, even in the cases where this might be done without offence, does it appear wise to attempt to anticipate the verdict of the Future on our contemporaries. Should the book last, poems by Tennyson, Bryant, Clare, Lowell, and others, will no doubt claim and obtain their place among the best. But the Editor trusts that this will be effected by other hands, and in days far distant.

Chalmers' vast collection, with the whole works of all accessible poets not contained in it, and the best Anthologies of different periods, have been twice systematically read through; and it is hence improbable that any omissions which may be regretted are due to oversight. The poems are printed entire, except in a very few instances (specified in the notes) where a stanza has been omitted. The omissions have been risked only when the piece could be thus brought to a closer lyrical unity: and, as essentially opposed to this unity, extracts, obviously such, are excluded. In regard to the text, the purpose of the book has appeared to justify the choice of the most poetical version, wherever more than one exists: and much labour has been given to present each poem, in

PREFACE

disposition, spelling, and punctuation, to the greatest advantage.

For the permission under which the copyright pieces are inserted, thanks are due to the respective Proprietors, without whose liberal concurrence the scheme of the collection would have been defeated.

In the arrangement the most poetically-effective order has been attempted. The English mind has passed through phases of thought and cultivation so various and so opposed during these three centuries of Poetry, that a rapid passage between Old and New, like rapid alteration of the eye's focus in looking at the landscape, will always be wearisome and hurtful to the sense of Beauty. The poems have been therefore distributed into Books corresponding, I to the ninety years closing about 1616, II thence to 1700, III to 1800, IV to the half century just ended. Or, looking at the Poets who more or less give each portion its distinctive character, they might be called the Books of Shakespeare, Milton, Gray, and Wordsworth. The volume, in this respect, so far as the limitations of its range allow, accurately reflects the natural growth and evolution of our Poetry. A rigidly chronological sequence, however, rather fits a collection aiming at instruction than at pleasure, and the Wisdom which comes through Pleasure:—within each book the pieces have therefore been arranged in gradations of feeling or subject. The development of the symphonies of Mozart and Beethoven has been here thought of as a model, and nothing placed without careful consideration. And it is hoped that the contents of this Anthology will thus be found to present a certain unity, 'as episodes', in the noble language of Shelley, 'to that great Poem which all poets, like the co-operating thoughts of one great mind, have built up since the beginning of the world'.

As he closes his long survey, the Editor trusts he may add without egotism, that he has found the vague general verdict of popular Fame more just than those have thought, who, with too severe a criticism, would confine judgements on Poetry to 'the selected few of many generations'. Not many appear to have gained reputation without some gift or performance that, in due degree, deserved it: and if no verses by certain writers who show less strength than sweetness, or more thought than mastery in expression, are printed in this volume, it should not be imagined that they have been excluded without much hesitation and regret,—far less that they have been slighted. Throughout this vast and pathetic array of Singers now silent, few have been honoured with the name Poet, and have not possessed a skill in words, a sympathy with beauty, a tenderness of feeling, or seriousness in reflection, which render their works, although never perhaps attaining that loftier and finer excellence here required, better worth reading than much of what fills the scanty hours that most men spare for self-improvement, or for pleasure in any of its more elevated and permanent forms.— And if this be true of even mediocre poetry, for how much more are we indebted to the best! Like the fabled fountain of the Azores, but with a more various power, the magic of this Art can confer on each period of life its appropriate blessing: on early years Experience, on maturity Calm, on age, Youthfulness. Poetry gives treasures 'more golden than gold', leading us in higher and healthier ways than those of the world, and interpreting to us the lessons of Nature. But she speaks best for herself. Her true accents, if the plan has been executed with success, may be heard throughout the following pages:—wherever the Poets of England are honoured, wherever the dominant language of the world is spoken, it is hoped that they will find fit audience.

1861

PREFACE TO THE FIFTH EDITION

WHEN the first edition of Palgrave's *Golden Treasury* was published in 1861 it included no poems by living authors. The Fifth Book of the present edition contains work by poets who were alive in 1861, and by those born after that date. Living poets are represented by poems drawn from books published before the autumn of 1962, when the final choice was made.

The hundred years which have passed since the publication of the *Golden Treasury* have seen the flowering of poetry written in English in the United States and in the lands of the British Commonwealth. The Fifth Book confines itself to poems by British and by Irish poets. In deciding borderline cases I have been guided by common sense rather than by legalism or by logic. Thus I have counted both W. H. Auden and T. S. Eliot as British poets, but Ezra Pound as an American poet; I have included poems by Roy Campbell and by F. T. Prince, but have reluctantly omitted poems by A. D. Hope; and I have felt no scruples about regarding Demetrios Capetanakis as eligible for inclusion in this anthology.

I was unable to obtain permission to print any poems by Kathleen Raine, whom I wished to represent by 'Spell of Creation'; or to include Kipling's 'Gehazi' or Siegfried Sassoon's 'Blighters'.

JOHN PRESS

1964

ACKNOWLEDGEMENTS

FOR permission to include poems of which they control the copyright, grateful acknowledgement is made to the following:

George Allen & Unwin Ltd. for Alun Lewis's 'All Day It Has Rained' and 'Postscript for Gweno' from *Raiders' Dawn*;

Curtis Brown Ltd. and the Roy Campbell Estate for Roy Campbell's 'The Serf', 'Horses on the Camargue', 'Autumn', 'On Professor Drennan's Verse', and 'On Certain South African Novelists' from *Adamastor*;

Jonathan Cape Ltd., the authors and Mrs. H. M. Davies for W. H. Davies's 'The Inquest' from *Poems*; C. Day Lewis's 'O Dreams, O Destinations (9)' and 'Emily Brontë' from *Collected Poems*; and Henry Reed's 'Judging Distances' from *A Map of Verona*;

Chatto & Windus Ltd. for William Empson's 'To an Old Lady' and 'This Last Pain' from *Collected Poems*; Wilfred Owen's 'Greater Love', 'Futility', 'Anthem for Doomed Youth', 'Spring Offensive', and 'Strange Meeting' from *Collected Poems*; Isaac Rosenberg's 'Break of Day in the Trenches' and 'Dead Man's Dump' from *Collected Works*; Jon Silkin's 'Death of a Son' from *The Peaceable Kingdom*; and Edward Lowbury's 'Swan' from *Time for Sale*;

J. M. Dent & Sons Ltd. for Dylan Thomas's 'The Conversation of Prayer', 'A Refusal to Mourn the Death, by Fire, of a Child in London', 'In my Craft or Sullen Art', and 'Fern Hill' from *Collected Poems*;

André Deutsch Ltd. for Stevie Smith's 'Not Waving but Drowning' from *Not Waving but Drowning*; and Roy Fuller's 'The Image' and 'Mythological Sonnets VIII' from *Collected Poems*;

The Dolmen Press, Dublin, for Austin Clarke's 'Penal Law' and 'Marriage' from *Later Poems*; and Thomas Kinsella's 'Mirror in February' from *Downstream*;

Mrs. Marie J. Douglas for Keith Douglas's 'Vergissmeinnicht' from *Collected Poems*;

Faber & Faber Ltd. for W. H. Auden's 'Chorus' ('The Wanderers'), 'Seascape' ('Look, Stranger'), and 'Musée des Beaux Arts' from *Collected Shorter Poems*, 'Song' from *Nones*,

ACKNOWLEDGEMENTS

and 'The Shield of Achilles' from *The Shield of Achilles*; George Barker's 'Channel Crossing' from *Collected Poems*; Lawrence Durrell's 'Nemea' and 'Sarajevo' from *Collected Poems*; T. S. Eliot's 'Gerontion', 'Marina', and 'Landscapes: I. New Hampshire' from *Collected Poems*, and 'Little Gidding' from *Four Quartets*; Thom Gunn's 'To Yvor Winters, 1955' from *The Sense of Movement* and 'In Santa Maria del Popolo' from *My Sad Captains*; Ted Hughes's 'Hawk Roosting' and 'November' from *Lupercal*; Louis MacNeice's 'The Sunlight on the Garden', 'Bagpipe Music', and 'Prayer Before Birth' from *Collected Poems*; Edwin Muir's 'The Face', 'The Child Dying', 'The Brothers', 'For Ann Scott-Moncrieff (1914–1943)', and 'One Foot in Eden' from *Collected Poems*; Stephen Spender's 'Ice' and 'Missing My Daughter' from *Collected Poems*; and Vernon Watkins's 'The Heron' from *The Death Bell* and 'Peace in the Welsh Hills' from *Cypress and Acacia*;

Rupert Hart-Davis Ltd. and the authors for Charles Causley's 'Innocent's Song' from *Johnny Alleluia*; F. T. Prince's 'The Question' and 'Soldiers Bathing' from *The Doors of Stone*; R. S. Thomas's 'The Hill Farmer Speaks' from *Song at the Year's Turning*, 'The Country Clergy' from *Poetry for Supper*, and 'Here' from *Tares*; Laurence Whistler's 'A Portrait in the Guards' and 'A Form of Epitaph' from *Audible Silence*; and Andrew Young's 'Wiltshire Downs', 'A Dead Mole', 'Culbin Sands', and 'Field-Glasses' from *Collected Poems*;

David Higham Associates Ltd. and the Scorpion Press for David Gascoyne's 'Ex Nihilo', 'Winter Garden', and 'Eve' from *Poems 1937–1942*; David Higham Associates Ltd., Macmillan & Co. Ltd., and the Vanguard Press Inc., New York, for Edith Sitwell's 'Hornpipe' and 'Most Lovely Shade' from *The Collected Poems of Edith Sitwell* (© 1949, 1954, by Edith Sitwell);

The Hogarth Press Ltd. for Norman Cameron's 'The Thespians at Thermopylae', 'The Compassionate Fool', 'Forgive Me, Sire', and 'Three Love Poems' from *Collected Poems*; Norman MacCaig's 'Too Bright a Day' and 'Ego' from *The Sinai Sort*, and 'Spate in Winter Midnight' from *A Common Grace*; and Terence Tiller's 'Reading a Medal' and 'Street Performers, 1851' from *Reading a Medal*;

Mr. John Lehmann and The Devin-Adair Company, New York, for Demetrios Capetanakis's 'Abel' and 'The Isles of Greece' from *Demetrios Capetanakis: A Greek Poet in England* (U.S. title: *The Shores of Darkness*);

ACKNOWLEDGEMENTS

Longmans, Green & Co. Ltd. and the author for Patrick Kavanagh's 'October' and 'To the Man After the Harrow' from *Come Dance With Kitty Stobling and Other Poems*;

Macmillan & Co. Ltd., The Macmillan Company of Canada Ltd., The Macmillan Company, New York, and the Trustees of the Hardy Estate for Thomas Hardy's 'Friends Beyond', 'Drummer Hodge', 'To an Unborn Pauper Child', 'The Voice', 'After a Journey', 'At Castle Boterel', 'Great Things', 'The Five Students', 'During Wind and Rain', 'Afterwards', and 'An Ancient to Ancients' from *The Collected Poems of Thomas Hardy*;

Macmillan & Co. Ltd., The Macmillan Company of Canada Ltd., St. Martin's Press, Inc., New York, and Mrs. Ralph Hodgson for Ralph Hodgson's 'Time' from *Collected Poems* (first published in *The Skylark and Other Poems*);

The Marvell Press, Hessle, Yorkshire, for Philip Larkin's 'Wants', 'Maiden Name', 'Deceptions', and 'Church Going' from *The Less Deceived*;

Methuen & Co. Ltd. for Jack Clemo's 'Christ in the Clay-Pit' from *The Map of Clay*;

John Murray Ltd. and Houghton Mifflin Company, Boston, Mass. for John Betjeman's 'Ireland With Emily' and 'The Cottage Hospital' from *Collected Poems*;

Oliver & Boyd Ltd., Edinburgh, for Hugh MacDiarmid's 'O Wha's the Bride?' and 'At My Father's Grave' from *Collected Poems*;

A. D. Peters and William Collins Sons & Co. Ltd. for Edmund Blunden's 'The Midnight Skaters', 'Report on Experience', and 'At the Great Wall of China' from *Poems of Many Years*;

Laurence Pollinger Ltd., the Estate of the late Mrs. Frieda Lawrence, and William Heinemann Ltd. for D. H. Lawrence's 'Sorrow', 'Piano', 'Song of a Man Who Has Come Through', 'Bat', 'Red Geranium and Godly Mignonette', 'Bavarian Gentians', and 'The Ship of Death' from *The Complete Poems of D. H. Lawrence*;

Putnam & Co. Ltd. for Thomas Blackburn's 'The Lucky Marriage' and 'Hospital for Defectives' from *The Next Word*;

School of Fine Art, University of Reading, for Bernard Spencer's 'A Spring Wind' and 'The Rendezvous' from *The Twist in the Plotting*;

ACKNOWLEDGEMENTS

Routledge & Kegan Paul Ltd. for T. E. Hulme's 'Above the Dock' and 'The Embankment' from *Speculations*; and Donald Davie's 'The Fountain' and 'Hearing Russian Spoken' from *A Winter Talent*;

The author and The Viking Press, Inc., New York, for Siegfried Sassoon's 'Everyone Sang' and 'At the Grave of Henry Vaughan' from *Collected Poems* (© 1920 by E. P. Dutton & Co., 1948 by Siegfried Sassoon);

Martin Secker & Warburg Ltd. for W. R. Rodgers's 'Life's Circumnavigators' from *Awake!*;

Sidgwick & Jackson Ltd. for Ronald Bottrall's 'Icarus' from *The Collected Poems of Ronald Bottrall*;

The Society of Authors as the literary representative of the Estate of the late Laurence Binyon for Laurence Binyon's 'The Burning of the Leaves' from *The Burning of the Leaves*; the Literary Trustees of Walter de la Mare and The Society of Authors as their representative for Walter de la Mare's 'Reserved', 'Fare Well', 'At Ease', and 'The Old Summerhouse' from *Collected Poems*; The Society of Authors as the literary representative of the Estate of the late A. E. Housman, and Jonathan Cape Ltd. for A. E. Housman's 'On Wenlock Edge', 'Tell me not here', 'Crossing alone the nighted ferry', and 'The stars have not dealt me' from *Collected Poems*; The Society of Authors and Dr. John Masefield, O.M. for John Masefield's 'The Dead Knight' from *Collected Poems*;

Mrs. Helen Thomas and Faber & Faber Ltd. for Edward Thomas's 'Tears', 'The Owl', 'As the Team's Head-Brass', 'Thaw', 'The Combe', 'In Memoriam (Easter, 1915)', 'Cock-Crow', 'A Private', and 'Out in the Dark' from *Collected Poems*;

Mr. Milton Waldman, Literary Executor, and Wm. Collins Sons & Co. Ltd. for Robert Nichols's 'The Sprig of Lime' from *Such Was My Singing*;

International Authors N.V. for Robert Graves's 'Love Without Hope', 'The Cool Web', 'Vanity', 'Pure Death', 'Sick Love', 'Certain Mercies', 'The Thieves', 'Counting the Beats', and 'A Plea to Boys and Girls' from *Collected Poems* (Cassell & Co. Ltd., London, and Doubleday & Co. Inc., New York);

Mrs. W. B. Yeats, Macmillan & Co. Ltd., and The Macmillan Company, New York, for W. B. Yeats's 'No Second Troy' (© 1912 by The Macmillan Company, renewed 1940 by Bertha Georgie Yeats), 'September 1913' (© 1916 by The Macmillan Company,

ACKNOWLEDGEMENTS

renewed 1944 by Bertha Georgie Yeats), 'The Cold Heaven' (© 1912 by The Macmillan Company, renewed 1940 by Bertha Georgie Yeats), 'An Irish Airman Foresees His Death' (© 1919 by The Macmillan Company, renewed 1946 by Bertha Georgie Yeats), 'The Second Coming' (© 1924 by The Macmillan Company, renewed 1952 by Bertha Georgie Yeats), 'Sailing to Byzantium' (© 1928 by The Macmillan Company, renewed 1956 by Georgie Yeats), 'The Stare's Nest by My Window' (© 1928 by The Macmillan Company, renewed 1956 by Georgie Yeats), 'The Wheel' (© 1928 by The Macmillan Company, renewed 1956 by Georgie Yeats), 'The New Faces' (© 1928 by The Macmillan Company, renewed 1956 by Georgie Yeats), 'Leda and the Swan' (© 1928 by The Macmillan Company, renewed 1956 by Georgie Yeats), 'Among School Children' (© 1928 by The Macmillan Company, renewed 1956 by Georgie Yeats), 'Coole Park and Ballylee, 1931' (© 1933 by The Macmillan Company, renewed 1961 by Bertha Georgie Yeats), 'Before the World Was Made' (© 1933 by The Macmillan Company, renewed 1961 by Bertha Georgie Yeats), 'The Gyres' (© 1940 by Georgie Yeats), and 'The Municipal Gallery Revisited' (© 1940 by Georgie Yeats) from *The Collected Poems of W. B. Yeats*;

The Macmillan Company, New York, for Hugh MacDiarmid's 'O Wha's the Bride?' (© 1932 by Christopher Murray Grieve) and 'At My Father's Grave' (© 1962 by Christopher Murray Grieve) from *Collected Poems*; and John Masefield's 'The Dead Knight' (© 1912 by The Macmillan Company, renewed 1940 by John Masefield) from *The Story of the Round House*;

Mrs. George Bambridge, Methuen & Co. Ltd., and The Macmillan Company of Canada Ltd. for Rudyard Kipling's 'Danny Deever' from *Barrack Room Ballads*; Mrs. Bambridge, Macmillan & Co. Ltd., and The Macmillan Company of Canada Ltd. for Kipling's 'Song of the Galley-Slaves' from *Many Inventions*; Mrs. Bambridge and Doubleday & Co. Inc., New York, for U.S. rights in the two poems, where their source is *Rudyard Kipling's Verse, Definitive Edition*;

E. P. Dutton & Co. Inc., New York, for Lawrence Durrell's 'Nemea' and 'Sarajevo' from *Collected Poems* (© 1956, 1960 by Lawrence Durrell);

Grove Press Inc., New York, for Edwin Muir's 'The Face', 'The Child Dying', 'For Ann Scott-Moncrieff (1914–1943)', and 'One Foot in Eden' from *Collected Poems 1921–1915* (© 1957 by Edwin Muir);

ACKNOWLEDGEMENTS

Harcourt, Brace & World, Inc., New York, for T. S. Eliot's 'Gerontion', 'Marina', 'Landscapes: I. New Hampshire' from *Collected Poems 1909–1962* (© 1936 by Harcourt, Brace & World, Inc.; © 1963 by T. S. Eliot) and 'Little Gidding' from *Four Quartets* in *Collected Poems 1909–1962* (© 1936 by Harcourt, Brace & World, Inc.; © 1963 by T. S. Eliot); and William Empson's 'To an Old Lady' and 'This Last Pain' from *Collected Poems of William Empson* (© 1949 by William Empson);

Harper & Row, Publishers, Inc., New York, for Ted Hughes's 'Hawk Roosting' (© 1959 by Ted Hughes) and 'November' (© 1960 by Ted Hughes) from *Lupercal*;

Holt, Rinehart and Winston, Inc., Publishers, New York, for A. E. Housman's 'On Wenlock Edge' from 'A Shropshire Lad', Authorized Edition, from *Complete Poems* (© 1959 by Holt, Rinehart and Winston, Inc.); and A. E. Housman's 'Tell me not here, it needs not saying' and 'Crossing alone the nighted ferry' from *Complete Poems* (© 1922 by Holt, Rinehart and Winston, Inc.; © 1936 by Barclays Bank Ltd.; © renewed 1950 by Barclays Bank Ltd.);

New Directions, Publishers, New York, for Wilfred Owen's 'Greater Love', 'Futility', 'Anthem for Doomed Youth', 'Spring Offensive', and 'Strange Meeting' from *The Poems of Wilfred Owen*, ed. by Edmund Blunden (all rights reserved); Dylan Thomas's 'The Conversation of Prayer', 'A Refusal to Mourn the Death, by Fire, of a Child in London', 'In my Craft or Sullen Art', and 'Fern Hill' from *The Collected Poems of Dylan Thomas* (© 1957 by New Directions); and Vernon Watkins's 'The Heron' from *The Death Bell* (all rights reserved) and 'Peace in the Welsh Hills' from *Cypress and Acacia* (© 1959 by Vernon Watkins);

Oxford University Press, Inc., New York, for Louis MacNeice's 'The Sunlight on the Garden', 'Bagpipe Music', and 'Prayer Before Birth' from *Eighty-Five Poems* (© Louis MacNeice 1959);

Random House, Inc., New York, for W. H. Auden's 'Doom is dark and deeper'—also entitled 'The Wanderers'—(© 1934, renewed 1961 by W. H. Auden), 'Look, stranger, on this island now' (© 1937 by W. H. Auden), and 'Musée des Beaux Arts' (© 1940 by W. H. Auden) from *The Collected Poetry of W. H. Auden*; 'Song' (© 1939 by W. H. Auden) from *Nones*; 'The Shield of Achilles' (© 1952 by W. H. Auden) from *The Shield of Achilles*; Stephen Spender's 'Ice' (© 1949 by Stephen Spender) from *The Edge of Being*; and 'Missing My Daughter' (© 1955 by Stephen Spender) from *Collected Poems 1928–1953*;

ACKNOWLEDGEMENTS

Schocken Books Inc., New York, for Isaac Rosenberg's 'Break of Day in the Trenches' and 'Dead Man's Dump' from *The Collected Poems of Isaac Rosenberg*, edited by Gordon Bottomley and Denys Harding (© 1949 by Schocken Books Inc.);

Charles Scribner's Sons, New York, for A. E. Housman's 'The stars have not dealt me' from *My Brother, A. E. Housman: Personal Recollections Together with Thirty Hitherto Unpublished Poems* by Laurence Housman (© 1937, 1938 Laurence Housman);

The University of Chicago Press for Thom Gunn's 'To Yvor Winters, 1955' from *The Sense of Movement* (© 1959 by Thompson William Gunn) and 'In Santa Maria del Popolo' from *My Sad Captains* (© 1961 by Thompson William Gunn).

The following copyright poems are published by the Oxford University Press: Gerard Manley Hopkins's 'The Windhover', 'Pied Beauty', 'Duns Scotus's Oxford', 'Peace', 'Felix Randal', 'The Leaden Echo and the Golden Echo', 'No worst there is none', 'I wake and feel the fell of dark, not day', and 'That Nature is a Heraclitean Fire' in *Poems of Gerard Manley Hopkins*, edited by W. H. Gardner; John Heath-Stubbs's 'Titus and Berenice' in *The Blue Fly in his Head*; and Charles Tomlinson's 'Icos', 'Tramontana at Lerici', and 'Farewell to Van Gogh' in *Seeing is Believing*. The Clarendon Press, Oxford, controls the copyright in Robert Bridges's 'London Snow', 'Awake, my heart, to be loved', and 'The storm is over, the land hushes to rest':

THE GOLDEN TREASURY

BOOK FIRST

═══════════

1

SPRING

Spring, the sweet Spring, is the year's pleasant king;
Then blooms each thing, then maids dance in a ring,
Cold doth not sting, the pretty birds do sing,
   Cuckoo, jug-jug, pu-we, to-witta-woo!

The palm and may make country houses gay,
Lambs frisk and play, the shepherds pipe all day,
And we hear aye birds tune this merry lay,
   Cuckoo, jug-jug, pu-we, to-witta-woo!

The fields breathe sweet, the daisies kiss our feet,
Young lovers meet, old wives a-sunning sit,
In every street these tunes our ears do greet,
   Cuckoo, jug-jug, pu-we, to-witta-woo!
      Spring! the sweet Spring!

T. NASH

2

SUMMONS TO LOVE

Phoebus, arise!
And paint the sable skies
With azure, white, and red:
Rouse Memnon's mother from her Tithon's bed
That she may thy career with roses spread:
The nightingales thy coming each where sing:

Make an eternal spring!
Give life to this dark world which lieth dead;
Spread forth thy golden hair
In larger locks than thou wast wont before,
And emperor-like decore
With diadem of pearl thy temples fair:
Chase hence the ugly night
Which serves but to make dear thy glorious light.

—This is that happy morn,
That day, long-wishéd day
Of all my life so dark,
(If cruel stars have not my ruin sworn
And fates my hopes betray),
Which, purely white, deserves
An everlasting diamond should it mark.
This is the morn should bring unto this grove
My Love, to hear and recompense my love.
Fair King, who all preserves,
But show thy blushing beams,
And thou two sweeter eyes
Shalt see than those which by Penéus' streams
Did once thy heart surprise.
Now, Flora, deck thyself in fairest guise:
If that ye winds would hear
A voice surpassing far Amphion's lyre,
Your furious chiding stay;
Let Zephyr only breathe,
And with her tresses play.
—The winds all silent are,
And Phoebus in his chair
Ensaffroning sea and air
Makes vanish every star:
Night like a drunkard reels
Beyond the hills, to shun his flaming wheels:
The fields with flowers are deck'd in every hue,
The clouds with orient gold spangle their blue;
Here is the pleasant place—
And nothing wanting is, save She, alas!

W. DRUMMOND OF HAWTHORNDEN

2

3

TIME AND LOVE

I

WHEN I have seen by Time's fell hand defaced
The rich proud cost of out-worn buried age;
When sometime lofty towers I see down-razed,
And brass eternal slave to mortal rage;

When I have seen the hungry ocean gain
Advantage on the kingdom of the shore,
And the firm soil win of the watery main,
Increasing store with loss, and loss with store;

When I have seen such interchange of state,
Or state itself confounded to decay,
Ruin hath taught me thus to ruminate—
That Time will come and take my Love away:

—This thought is as a death, which cannot choose
But weep to have that which it fears to lose.

W. SHAKESPEARE

4

II

SINCE brass, nor stone, nor earth, nor boundless sea,
But sad mortality o'ersways their power,
How with this rage shall beauty hold a plea,
Whose action is no stronger than a flower?

O how shall summer's honey breath hold out
Against the wreckful siege of battering days,
When rocks impregnable are not so stout
Nor gates of steel so strong, but time decays?

O fearful meditation! where, alack!
Shall Time's best jewel from Time's chest lie hid?
Or what strong hand can hold his swift foot back,
Or who his spoil of beauty can forbid?

O! none, unless this miracle have might,
That in black ink my love may still shine bright.

W. SHAKESPEARE

5

THE PASSIONATE SHEPHERD TO HIS LOVE

COME live with me and be my Love,
And we will all the pleasures prove
That hills and valleys, dale and field,
And all the craggy mountains yield.

There will we sit upon the rocks
And see the shepherds feed their flocks,
By shallow rivers, to whose falls
Melodious birds sing madrigals.

There will I make thee beds of roses
And a thousand fragrant posies,
A cap of flowers, and a kirtle
Embroider'd all with leaves of myrtle.

A gown made of the finest wool,
Which from our pretty lambs we pull,
Fair linéd slippers for the cold,
With buckles of the purest gold.

A belt of straw and ivy buds
With coral clasps and amber studs:
And if these pleasures may thee move,
Come live with me and be my Love.

Thy silver dishes for thy meat
As precious as the gods do eat,
Shall on an ivory table be
Prepared each day for thee and me.

The shepherd swains shall dance and sing
For thy delight each May-morning:
If these delights thy mind may move,
Then live with me and be my Love.

C. MARLOWE

6

A MADRIGAL

CRABBED Age and Youth
Cannot live together:
Youth is full of pleasance,
Age is full of care;
Youth like summer morn,
Age like winter weather,
Youth like summer brave,
Age like winter bare:
Youth is full of sport,
Age's breath is short,
Youth is nimble, Age is lame:
Youth is hot and bold,
Age is weak and cold,
Youth is wild, and Age is tame:—
Age, I do abhor thee;
Youth, I do adore thee;
O! my Love, my Love is young!
Age, I do defy thee—
O sweet shepherd, hie thee,
For methinks thou stay'st too long.

W. SHAKESPEARE

7

UNDER the greenwood tree
Who loves to lie with me,
And tune his merry note
Unto the sweet bird's throat—
Come hither, come hither, come hither!
Here shall he see
No enemy
But winter and rough weather.

Who doth ambition shun
And loves to live i' the sun,

Seeking the food he eats
  And pleased with what he gets—
Come hither, come hither, come hither!
    Here shall he see
      No enemy
But winter and rough weather.

W. SHAKESPEARE

8

IT was a lover and his lass
  With a hey and a ho, and a hey-nonino!
That o'er the green cornfield did pass
In the spring time, the only pretty ring time,
When birds do sing hey ding a ding:
  Sweet lovers love the Spring.

Between the acres of the rye
These pretty country folks would lie:

This carol they began that hour,
How that life was but a flower:

And therefore take the present time
  With a hey and a ho, and a hey-nonino!
For love is crownéd with the prime
In spring time, the only pretty ring time,
When birds do sing hey ding a ding:
  Sweet lovers love the Spring.

W. SHAKESPEARE

9

PRESENT IN ABSENCE

ABSENCE, hear thou my protestation
    Against thy strength,
    Distance, and length;
Do what thou canst for alteration:

For hearts of truest mettle
Absence doth join, and Time doth settle.

Who loves a mistress of such quality,
    He soon hath found
    Affection's ground
Beyond time, place, and all mortality.
    To hearts that cannot vary
    Absence is Presence, Time doth tarry.

By absence this good means I gain,
    That I can catch her,
    Where none can watch her,
In some close corner of my brain:
    There I embrace and kiss her;
    And so I both enjoy and miss her.

ANON.

10

ABSENCE

BEING your slave, what should I do but tend
Upon the hours and times of your desire?
I have no precious time at all to spend
Nor services to do, till you require:

Nor dare I chide the world-without-end hour
Whilst I, my sovereign, watch the clock for you,
Nor think the bitterness of absence sour
When you have bid your servant once adieu:

Nor dare I question with my jealous thought
Where you may be, or your affairs suppose,
But like a sad slave, stay and think of nought
Save, where you are, how happy you make those;—

So true a fool is love, that in your will
Though you do anything, he thinks no ill.

W. SHAKESPEARE

11

How like a winter hath my absence been
From Thee, the pleasure of the fleeting year!
What freezings have I felt, what dark days seen,
What old December's bareness everywhere!

And yet this time removed was summer's time:
The teeming autumn, big with rich increase,
Bearing the wanton burden of the prime
Like widow'd wombs after their lords' decease:

Yet this abundant issue seem'd to me
But hope of orphans, and unfather'd fruit;
For summer and his pleasures wait on thee,
And, thou away, the very birds are mute;

Or if they sing, 'tis with so dull a cheer,
That leaves look pale, dreading the winter's near.

W. SHAKESPEARE

12

A CONSOLATION

When in disgrace with fortune and men's eyes
I all alone beweep my outcast state,
And trouble deaf heaven with my bootless cries,
And look upon myself, and curse my fate;

Wishing me like to one more rich in hope,
Featured like him, like him with friends possest,
Desiring this man's art, and that man's scope,
With what I most enjoy contented least;

Yet in these thoughts myself almost despising,
Haply I think on Thee—and then my state,
Like to the lark at break of day arising
From sullen earth, sings hymns at heaven's gate;

For thy sweet love remember'd, such wealth brings,
That then I scorn to change my state with kings.

W. SHAKESPEARE

13

THE UNCHANGEABLE

O NEVER say that I was false of heart,
Though absence seem'd my flame to qualify:
As easy might I from myself depart
As from my soul, which in thy breast doth lie;

That is my home of love; if I have ranged,
Like him that travels, I return again,
Just to the time, not with the time exchanged,
So that myself bring water for my stain.

Never believe, though in my nature reign'd
All frailties that besiege all kinds of blood,
That it could so preposterously be stain'd
To leave for nothing all thy sum of good:

For nothing this wide universe I call,
Save thou, my rose: in it thou art my all.
                              W. SHAKESPEARE

14

To me, fair Friend, you never can be old,
For as you were when first your eye I eyed
Such seems your beauty still. Three winters cold
Have from the forests shook three summers' pride;

Three beauteous springs to yellow autumn turn'd
In process of the seasons have I seen,
Three April perfumes in three hot Junes burn'd,
Since first I saw you fresh, which yet are green.

Ah! yet doth beauty, like a dial-hand,
Steal from his figure, and no pace perceived;
So your sweet hue, which methinks still doth stand,
Hath motion, and mine eye may be deceived:

For fear of which, hear this, thou age unbred,—
Ere you were born, was beauty's summer dead.
                              W. SHAKESPEARE

15

DIAPHENIA

DIAPHENIA like the daffadowndilly,
White as the sun, fair as the lily,
Heigh ho, how I do love thee!
  I do love thee as my lambs
  Are belovéd of their dams;
How blest were I if thou would'st prove me.

Diaphenia like the spreading roses,
  That in thy sweets all sweets encloses,
Fair sweet, how I do love thee!
  I do love thee as each flower
  Loves the sun's life-giving power;
For dead, thy breath to life might move me.

Diaphenia like to all things blesséd
When all thy praises are expresséd,
Dear joy, how I do love thee!
  As the birds do love the spring,
  Or the bees their careful king:
Then in requite, sweet virgin, love me!

H. CONSTABLE

16

ROSALINE

LIKE to the clear in highest sphere
Where all imperial glory shines,
Of selfsame colour is her hair
Whether unfolded, or in twines:
    Heigh ho, fair Rosaline!
Her eyes are sapphires set in snow,
Resembling heaven by every wink;
The Gods do fear whenas they glow,
And I do tremble when I think
    Heigh ho, would she were mine!

Her cheeks are like the blushing cloud
That beautifies Aurora's face,
Or like the silver crimson shroud
That Phoebus' smiling looks doth grace;
    Heigh ho, fair Rosaline!
Her lips are like two budded roses
Whom ranks of lilies neighbour nigh,
Within which bounds she balm encloses
Apt to entice a deity:
    Heigh ho, would she were mine!

Her neck is like a stately tower,
Where Love himself imprison'd lies,
To watch for glances every hour
From her divine and sacred eyes:
    Heigh ho, for Rosaline!
Her paps are centres of delight,
Her breasts are orbs of heavenly frame,
Where Nature moulds the dew of light
To feed perfection with the same:
    Heigh ho, would she were mine!

With orient pearl, with ruby red,
With marble white, with sapphire blue
Her body everyway is fed,
Yet soft in touch and sweet in view:
    Heigh ho, fair Rosaline!
Nature herself her shape admires;
The Gods are wounded in her sight;
And Love forsakes his heavenly fires
And at her eyes his brand does light:
    Heigh ho, would she were mine!

Then muse not, Nymphs, though I bemoan
The absence of fair Rosaline,
Since for a fair there's fairer none,
Nor for her virtues so divine:
    Heigh ho, fair Rosaline;
Heigh ho, my heart! would God that she were mine!

T. LODGE

11   B

17

COLIN

BEAUTY sat bathing by a spring
　　Where fairest shades did hide her;
The winds blew calm, the birds did sing,
　　The cool streams ran beside her.
My wanton thoughts enticed mine eye
　　To see what was forbidden:
But better memory said, fie!
　　So vain desire was chidden:—
　　　　Hey nonny nonny O!
　　　　Hey nonny nonny!

Into a slumber then I fell,
　　When fond imagination
Seeméd to see, but could not tell
　　Her feature or her fashion.
But ev'n as babes in dreams do smile,
　　And sometimes fall a-weeping,
So I awaked, as wise this while
　　As when I fell a-sleeping:—
　　　　Hey nonny nonny O!
　　　　Hey nonny nonny!

THE SHEPHERD TONIE

18

TO HIS LOVE

SHALL I compare thee to a summer's day?
Thou art more lovely and more temperate:
Rough winds do shake the darling buds of May,
And summer's lease hath all too short a date:

Sometime too hot the eye of heaven shines,
And often is his gold complexion dimm'd:
And every fair from fair sometime declines,
By chance, or nature's changing course, untrimm'd.

But thy eternal summer shall not fade
Nor lose possession of that fair thou owest;
Nor shall death brag thou wanderest in his shade,
When in eternal lines to time thou growest;

So long as men can breathe, or eyes can see,
So long lives this, and this gives life to thee.

W. SHAKESPEARE

19

TO HIS LOVE

WHEN in the chronicle of wasted time
I see descriptions of the fairest wights,
And beauty making beautiful old rhyme
In praise of ladies dead, and lovely knights;

Then in the blazon of sweet beauty's best
Of hand, of foot, of lip, of eye, of brow,
I see their antique pen would have exprest
Ev'n such a beauty as you master now.

So all their praises are but prophecies
Of this our time, all, you prefiguring;
And for they look'd but with divining eyes,
They had not skill enough your worth to sing:

For we, which now behold these present days,
Have eyes to wonder, but lack tongues to praise.

W. SHAKESPEARE

20

LOVE'S PERJURIES

ON a day, alack the day!
Love, whose month is ever May,
Spied a blossom passing fair
Playing in the wanton air:
Through the velvet leaves the wind,
All unseen, 'gan passage find;

13

That the lover, sick to death,
Wish'd himself the heaven's breath.
Air, quoth he, thy cheeks may blow;
Air, would I might triumph so!
But, alack, my hand is sworn
Ne'er to pluck thee from thy thorn:
Vow, alack, for youth unmeet;
Youth so apt to pluck a sweet.
Do not call it sin in me
That I am forsworn for thee:
Thou for whom e'en Jove would swear
Juno but an Ethiope were,
And deny himself for Jove,
Turning mortal for thy love.

W. SHAKESPEARE

21

A SUPPLICATION

FORGET not yet the tried intent
Of such a truth as I have meant;
My great travail so gladly spent,
   Forget not yet!

Forget not yet when first began
The weary life ye know, since whan
The suit, the service none tell can;
   Forget not yet!

Forget not yet the great assays,
The cruel wrong, the scornful ways,
The painful patience in delays,
   Forget not yet!

Forget not! O, forget not this,
How long ago hath been, and is
The mind that never meant amiss—
   Forget not yet!

Forget not then thine own approved
The which so long hath thee so loved,
Whose steadfast faith yet never moved—
Forget not this!

SIR T. WYAT

22

TO AURORA

O IF thou knew'st how thou thyself dost harm,
And dost prejudge thy bliss, and spoil my rest;
Then thou would'st melt the ice out of thy breast
And thy relenting heart would kindly warm.

O if thy pride did not our joys controul,
What world of loving wonders should'st thou see!
For if I saw thee once transform'd in me,
Then in thy bosom I would pour my soul;

Then all my thoughts should in thy visage shine,
And if that aught mischanced thou should'st not moan
Nor bear the burthen of thy griefs alone;
No, I would have my share in what were thine:

And whilst we thus should make our sorrows one,
This happy harmony would make them none.

W. ALEXANDER, EARL OF STERLINE

23

TRUE LOVE

LET me not to the marriage of true minds
Admit impediments. Love is not love
Which alters when it alteration finds,
Or bends with the remover to remove:—

O no! it is an ever-fixéd mark
That looks on tempests, and is never shaken;
It is the star to every wandering bark,
Whose worth's unknown, although his height be taken.

Love's not Time's fool, though rosy lips and cheeks
Within his bending sickle's compass come;
Love alters not with his brief hours and weeks,
But bears it out ev'n to the edge of doom:—

If this be error, and upon me proved,
I never writ, nor no man ever loved.

W. SHAKESPEARE

24

A DITTY

My true-love hath my heart, and I have his,
By just exchange one to the other given:
I hold his dear, and mine he cannot miss,
There never was a better bargain driven:
   My true-love hath my heart, and I have his.

His heart in me keeps him and me in one,
My heart in him his thoughts and senses guides:
He loves my heart, for once it was his own,
I cherish his because in me it bides:
   My true-love hath my heart, and I have his.

SIR P. SIDNEY

25

LOVE'S OMNIPRESENCE

Were I as base as is the lowly plain,
And you, my Love, as high as heaven above,
Yet should the thoughts of me your humble swain
Ascend to heaven, in honour of my Love.

Were I as high as heaven above the plain,
And you, my Love, as humble and as low
As are the deepest bottoms of the main,
Whereso'er you were, with you my love should go.

Were you the earth, dear Love, and I the skies,
My love should shine on you like to the sun,
And look upon you with ten thousand eyes
Till heaven wax'd blind, and till the world were done.

Whereso'er I am, below, or else above you,
Whereso'er you are, my heart shall truly love you.

J. SYLVESTER

26

CARPE DIEM

O MISTRESS mine, where are you roaming?
O stay and hear! your true-love's coming
    That can sing both high and low;
Trip no further, pretty sweeting,
Journeys end in lovers' meeting—
    Every wise man's son doth know.

What is love? 'tis not hereafter;
Present mirth hath present laughter;
    What's to come is still unsure:
In delay there lies no plenty,—
Then come kiss me, Sweet-and-twenty,
    Youth's a stuff will not endure.

W. SHAKESPEARE

27

WINTER

WHEN icicles hang by the wall
    And Dick the shepherd blows his nail,
And Tom bears logs into the hall,
    And milk comes frozen home in pail;
When blood is nipt, and ways be foul,
Then nightly sings the staring owl
        Tuwhoo!
Tuwhit! tuwhoo! A merry note!
While greasy Joan doth keel the pot.

When all around the wind doth blow,
 And coughing drowns the parson's saw,
And birds sit brooding in the snow,
 And Marian's nose looks red and raw;
When roasted crabs hiss in the bowl—
Then nightly sings the staring owl
  Tuwhoo!
Tuwhit! tuwhoo! A merry note!
While greasy Joan doth keel the pot.

W. SHAKESPEARE

28

THAT time of year thou may'st in me behold
When yellow leaves, or none, or few, do hang
Upon those boughs which shake against the cold,
Bare ruin'd choirs, where late the sweet birds sang.

In me thou see'st the twilight of such day
As after sunset fadeth in the west,
Which by and by black night doth take away,
Death's second self, that seals up all in rest.

In me thou see'st the glowing of such fire,
That on the ashes of his youth doth lie
As the death-bed whereon it must expire,
Consumed with that which it was nourish'd by:

—This thou perceiv'st, which makes thy love more strong,
To love that well which thou must leave ere long.

W. SHAKESPEARE

29

REMEMBRANCE

WHEN to the sessions of sweet silent thought
I summon up remembrance of things past,
I sigh the lack of many a thing I sought,
And with old woes new wail my dear time's waste:

Then can I drown an eye, unused to flow,
For precious friends hid in death's dateless night,
And weep afresh love's long-since-cancell'd woe,
And moan the expense of many a vanish'd sight.

Then can I grieve at grievances foregone,
And heavily from woe to woe tell o'er
The sad account of fore-bemoanéd moan,
Which I new pay as if not paid before:

—But if the while I think on thee, dear friend,
All losses are restored, and sorrows end.

W. SHAKESPEARE

30

REVOLUTIONS

LIKE as the waves make towards the pebbled shore
So do our minutes hasten to their end;
Each changing place with that which goes before,
In sequent toil all forwards do contend.

Nativity, once in the main of light,
Crawls to maturity, wherewith being crown'd,
Crooked eclipses 'gainst his glory fight,
And Time that gave, doth now his gift confound.

Time doth transfix the flourish set on youth,
And delves the parallels in beauty's brow;
Feeds on the rarities of nature's truth,
And nothing stands but for his scythe to mow:

And yet, to times in hope, my verse shall stand
Praising Thy worth, despite his cruel hand.

W. SHAKESPEARE

31

FAREWELL! thou art too dear for my possessing,
And like enough thou know'st thy estimate:
The charter of thy worth gives thee releasing;
My bonds in thee are all determinate.

For how do I hold thee but by thy granting?
And for that riches where is my deserving?
The cause of this fair gift in me is wanting,
And so my patent back again is swerving.

Thyself thou gav'st, thy own worth then not knowing,
Or me, to whom thou gav'st it, else mistaking;
So thy great gift, upon misprision growing,
Comes home again, on better judgement making.

Thus have I had thee as a dream doth flatter;
In sleep, a king; but waking, no such matter.

W. SHAKESPEARE

32

THE LIFE WITHOUT PASSION

THEY that have power to hurt, and will do none,
That do not do the thing they most do show,
Who, moving others, are themselves as stone,
Unmovéd, cold, and to temptation slow,—

They rightly do inherit Heaven's graces,
And husband nature's riches from expense;
They are the lords and owners of their faces,
Others, but stewards of their excellence.

The summer's flower is to the summer sweet,
Though to itself it only live and die;
But if that flower with base infection meet,
The basest weed outbraves his dignity:

For sweetest things turn sourest by their deeds;
Lilies that fester smell far worse than weeds.

W. SHAKESPEARE

33

THE LOVER'S APPEAL

AND wilt thou leave me thus?
Say nay! say nay! for shame,
To save thee from the blame
Of all my grief and grame.
And wilt thou leave me thus?
Say nay! say nay!

And wilt thou leave me thus?
That hath loved thee so long
In wealth and woe among:
And is thy heart so strong
As for to leave me thus?
Say nay! say nay!

And wilt thou leave me thus,
That hath given thee my heart
Never for to depart
Neither for pain nor smart:
And wilt thou leave me thus?
Say nay! say nay!

And wilt thou leave me thus,
And have no more pity
Of him that loveth thee?
Alas! thy cruelty!
And wilt thou leave me thus?
Say nay! say nay!

SIR T. WYAT

34

THE NIGHTINGALE

As it fell upon a day
In the merry month of May,
Sitting in a pleasant shade
Which a grove of myrtles made,

Beasts did leap and birds did sing,
Trees did grow and plants did spring,
Everything did banish moan
Save the Nightingale alone.
She, poor bird, as all forlorn,
Lean'd her breast against a thorn,
And there sung the dolefull'st ditty
That to hear it was great pity.
Fie, fie, fie, now would she cry;
Tereu, tereu, by and by:
That to hear her so complain
Scarce I could from tears refrain;
For her griefs so lively shown
Made me think upon mine own.
—Ah, thought I, thou mourn'st in vain,
None takes pity on thy pain:
Senseless trees, they cannot hear thee,
Ruthless beasts, they will not cheer thee;
King Pandion, he is dead,
All thy friends are lapp'd in lead:
All thy fellow birds do sing
Careless of thy sorrowing:
Even so, poor bird, like thee
None alive will pity me.

R. BARNEFIELD

35

CARE-CHARMER Sleep, son of the sable Night,
Brother to Death, in silent darkness born,
Relieve my languish, and restore the light;
With dark forgetting of my care return.

And let the day be time enough to mourn
The shipwreck of my ill adventured youth:
Let waking eyes suffice to wail their scorn,
Without the torment of the night's untruth.

Cease, dreams, the images of day-desires,
To model forth the passions of the morrow;

Never let rising Sun approve you liars
To add more grief to aggravate my sorrow:

Still let me sleep, embracing clouds in vain,
And never wake to feel the day's disdain.

S. DANIEL

36

MADRIGAL

TAKE, O take those lips away
That so sweetly were forsworn,
And those eyes, the break of day,
Lights that do mislead the morn:
But my kisses bring again,
Bring again—
Seals of love, but seal'd in vain,
Seal'd in vain!

W. SHAKESPEARE

37

LOVE'S FAREWELL

SINCE there's no help, come let us kiss and part,—
Nay I have done, you get no more of me;
And I am glad, yea, glad with all my heart,
That thus so cleanly I myself can free;

Shake hands for ever, cancel all our vows,
And when we meet at any time again,
Be it not seen in either of our brows
That we one jot of former love retain.

Now at the last gasp of love's latest breath,
When his pulse failing, passion speechless lies,
When faith is kneeling by his bed of death,
And innocence is closing up his eyes,

—Now if thou would'st, when all have given him over,
From death to life thou might'st him yet recover!

M. DRAYTON

38

TO HIS LUTE

My lute, be as thou wert when thou didst grow
With thy green mother in some shady grove,
When immelodious winds but made thee move,
And birds their ramage did on thee bestow.

Since that dear Voice which did thy sounds approve,
Which wont in such harmonious strains to flow,
Is reft from Earth to tune those spheres above,
What art thou but a harbinger of woe?

Thy pleasing notes be pleasing notes no more,
But orphans' wailings to the fainting ear;
Each stroke a sigh, each sound draws forth a tear;
For which be silent as in woods before:

Or if that any hand to touch thee deign,
Like widow'd turtle still her loss complain.

W. DRUMMOND

39

BLIND LOVE

O me! what eyes hath love put in my head
Which have no correspondence with true sight:
Or if they have, where is my judgement fled
That censures falsely what they see aright?

If that be fair whereon my false eyes dote,
What means the world to say it is not so?
If it be not, then love doth well denote
Love's eye is not so true as all men's: No,

How can it? O how can love's eye be true,
That is so vex'd with watching and with tears?
No marvel then though I mistake my view:
The sun itself sees not till heaven clears.

O cunning Love! with tears thou keep'st me blind,
Lest eyes well-seeing thy foul faults should find!

W. SHAKESPEARE

40

THE UNFAITHFUL SHEPHERDESS

WHILE that the sun with his beams hot
Scorchèd the fruits in vale and mountain,
Philon the shepherd, late forgot,
Sitting beside a crystal fountain,
   In shadow of a green oak-tree
   Upon his pipe this song play'd he:
Adieu Love, adieu Love, untrue Love,
Untrue Love, untrue Love, adieu Love;
Your mind is light, soon lost for new love.

So long as I was in your sight
I was your heart, your soul, and treasure;
And evermore you sobb'd and sigh'd
Burning in flames beyond all measure:
   —Three days endured your love to me,
   And it was lost in other three!
Adieu Love, adieu Love, untrue Love,
Untrue Love, untrue Love, adieu Love;
Your mind is light, soon lost for new love.

Another Shepherd you did see
To whom your heart was soon enchainèd;
Full soon your love was leapt from me,
Full soon my place he had obtainèd.
   Soon came a third, your love to win,
   And we were out and he was in.
Adieu Love, adieu Love, untrue Love,
Untrue Love, untrue Love, adieu Love;
Your mind is light, soon lost for new love.

Sure you have made me passing glad
That you your mind so soon removèd,
Before that I the leisure had
To choose you for my best belovèd:

For all your love was past and done
Two days before it was begun:—
Adieu Love, adieu Love, untrue Love,
Untrue Love, untrue Love, adieu Love;
Your mind is light, soon lost for new love.

ANON.

41

A RENUNCIATION

IF women could be fair, and yet not fond,
Or that their love were firm, not fickle still,
I would not marvel that they make men bond
By service long to purchase their goodwill;
But when I see how frail those creatures are,
I muse that men forget themselves so far.

To mark the choice they make, and how they change,
How oft from Phoebus they do flee to Pan;
Unsettled still, like haggards wild they range,
These gentle birds that fly from man to man;
Who would not scorn and shake them from the fist,
And let them fly, fair fools, which way they list?

Yet for disport we fawn and flatter both,
To pass the time when nothing else can please,
And train them to our lure with subtle oath,
Till, weary of their wiles, ourselves we ease;
And then we say when we their fancy try,
To play with fools, O what a fool was I!

E. VERE, EARL OF OXFORD

42

BLOW, blow, thou winter wind,
Thou art not so unkind
As man's ingratitude;
Thy tooth is not so keen
Because thou art not seen
Although thy breath be rude.

Heigh ho! sing heigh ho! unto the green holly:
Most friendship is feigning, most loving mere folly:
       Then, heigh ho! the holly!
       This life is most jolly.

       Freeze, freeze, thou bitter sky,
       Thou dost not bite so nigh
       As benefits forgot:
       Though thou the waters warp,
       Thy sting is not so sharp
       As friend remember'd not.
Heigh ho! sing heigh ho! unto the green holly:
Most friendship is feigning, most loving mere folly:
       Then, heigh ho! the holly!
       This life is most jolly.

W. SHAKESPEARE

43

MADRIGAL

MY thoughts hold mortal strife;
I do detest my life,
And with lamenting cries
Peace to my soul to bring
Oft call that prince which here doth monarchize:
—But he, grim grinning King,
Who caitiffs scorns, and doth the blest surprise,
Late having deck'd with beauty's rose his tomb,
Disdains to crop a weed, and will not come.

W. DRUMMOND

44

DIRGE OF LOVE

COME away, come away, Death,
And in sad cypres let me be laid;
Fly away, fly away, breath;
I am slain by a fair cruel maid.

My shroud of white, stuck all with yew,
   O prepare it!
My part of death, no one so true
   Did share it.

Not a flower, not a flower sweet
On my black coffin let there be strown;
 Not a friend, not a friend greet
My poor corpse, where my bones shall be thrown:
   A thousand thousand sighs to save,
    Lay me, O where
Sad true lover never find my grave,
    To weep there.

W. SHAKESPEARE

45

FIDELE

FEAR no more the heat o' the sun
  Nor the furious winter's rages;
Thou thy worldly task. hast done,
  Home art gone and ta'en thy wages:
Golden lads and girls all must,
As chimney-sweepers, come to dust.

Fear no more the frown o' the great,
  Thou art past the tyrant's stroke;
Care no more to clothe and eat;
  To thee the reed is as the oak:
The sceptre, learning, physic, must
All follow this, and come to dust.

Fear no more the lightning-flash
  Nor the all-dreaded thunder-stone;
Fear not slander, censure rash;
  Thou hast finish'd joy and moan:
All lovers young, all lovers must
Consign to thee, and come to dust.

W. SHAKESPEARE

46

A SEA DIRGE

FULL fathom five thy father lies:
　　Of his bones are coral made;
Those are pearls that were his eyes:
　　Nothing of him that doth fade,
But doth suffer a sea-change
Into something rich and strange.
Sea-nymphs hourly ring his knell:
Hark! now I hear them,—
　　Ding, dong, bell.

W. SHAKESPEARE

47

A LAND DIRGE

CALL for the robin redbreast and the wren,
Since o'er shady groves they hover
And with leaves and flowers do cover
The friendless bodies of unburied men.
Call unto his funeral dole
The ant, the field-mouse, and the mole
To rear him hillocks that shall keep him warm
And (when gay tombs are robb'd) sustain no harm;
But keep the wolf far thence, that's foe to men,
For with his nails he'll dig them up again.

J. WEBSTER

48

POST MORTEM

IF thou survive my well-contented day
When that churl Death my bones with dust shall cover,
And shalt by fortune once more re-survey
These poor rude lines of thy deceaséd lover;

Compare them with the bettering of the time,
And though they be outstripp'd by every pen,
Reserve them for my love, not for their rhyme
Exceeded by the height of happier men.

O then vouchsafe me but this loving thought—
'Had my friend's muse grown with this growing age,
A dearer birth than this his love had brought,
To march in ranks of better equipage:

But since he died, and poets better prove,
Theirs for their style I'll read, his for his love.'

W. SHAKESPEARE

49

THE TRIUMPH OF DEATH

No longer mourn for me when I am dead
Than you shall hear the surly sullen bell
Give warning to the world, that I am fled
From this vile world, with vilest worms to dwell;

Nay, if you read this line, remember not
The hand that writ it; for I love you so,
That I in your sweet thoughts would be forgot,
If thinking on me then should make you woe.

O if, I say, you look upon this verse
When I perhaps compounded am with clay,
Do not so much as my poor name rehearse,
But let your love even with my life decay;

Lest the wise world should look into your moan,
And mock you with me after I am gone.

W. SHAKESPEARE

50

MADRIGAL

Tell me where is Fancy bred,
Or in the heart, or in the head?
How begot, how nourishéd?
Reply, reply.

It is engender'd in the eyes,
With gazing fed; and Fancy dies
In the cradle where it lies:
Let us all ring Fancy's knell;
I'll begin it,—Ding, dong, bell.
—Ding, dong, bell.

W. SHAKESPEARE

51

CUPID AND CAMPASPE

CUPID and my Campaspe play'd
At cards for kisses; Cupid paid:
He stakes his quiver, bow, and arrows,
His mother's doves, and team of sparrows;
Loses them too; then down he throws
The coral of his lip, the rose
Growing on's cheek (but none knows how);
With these, the crystal of his brow,
And then the dimple on his chin;
All these did my Campaspe win:
At last he set her both his eyes—
She won, and Cupid blind did rise.
    O Love! has she done this to thee?
    What shall, alas! become of me?

J. LYLYE

52

PACK, clouds, away, and welcome day,
    With night we banish sorrow;
Sweet air blow soft, mount larks aloft
    To give my Love good-morrow!
Wings from the wind to please her mind
    Notes from the lark I'll borrow;
Bird prune thy wing, nightingale sing,
    To give my Love good-morrow;
        To give my Love good-morrow
        Notes from them both I'll borrow.

31

Wake from thy nest, robin redbreast,
  Sing birds in every furrow;
And from each hill, let music shrill
  Give my fair Love good-morrow!
Blackbird and thrush in every bush,
  Stare, linnet, and cock-sparrow!
You pretty elves, amongst yourselves
  Sing my fair Love good-morrow;
    To give my Love good-morrow
    Sing birds in every furrow!

T. HEYWOOD

53

PROTHALAMION

CALM was the day, and through the trembling **air**
Sweet-breathing Zephyrus did softly play—
A gentle spirit, that lightly did delay
Hot Titan's beams, which then did glister fair;
When I (whom sullen care,
Through discontent of my long fruitless stay
In princes' court, and expectation vain
Of idle hopes, which still do fly away,
Like empty shadows, did afflict my brain),
Walk'd forth to ease my pain
Along the shore of silver-streaming Thames;
Whose rutty bank, the which his river hems,
Was painted all with variable flowers,
And all the meads adorn'd with dainty gems
Fit to deck maidens' bowers,
And crown their paramours
Against the bridal day, which is not long:
  Sweet Thames! run softly, till I end my song.

There in a meadow by the river's side
A flock of nymphs I chancéd to espy,
All lovely daughters of the flood thereby,
With goodly greenish locks all loose untied
As each had been a bride;

And each one had a little wicker basket
Made of fine twigs, entrailéd curiously,
In which they gather'd flowers to fill their flasket,
And with fine fingers cropt full feateously
The tender stalks on high.
Of every sort which in that meadow grew
They gather'd some; the violet, pallid blue,
The little daisy that at evening closes,
The virgin lily and the primrose true:
With store of vermeil roses,
To deck their bridegrooms' posies
Against the bridal day, which was not long:
 Sweet Thames! run softly, till I end my song.

With that I saw two swans of goodly hue
Come softly swimming down along the lee;
Two fairer birds I yet did never see;
The snow which doth the top of Pindus strow
Did never whiter show,
Nor Jove himself, when he a swan would be
For love of Leda, whiter did appear;
Yet Leda was (they say) as white as he,
Yet not so white as these, nor nothing near;
So purely white they were
That even the gentle stream, the which them bare,
Seem'd foul to them, and bade his billows spare
To wet their silken feathers, lest they might
Soil their fair plumes with water not so fair,
And mar their beauties bright
That shone as Heaven's light
Against their bridal day, which was not long:
 Sweet Thames! run softly, till I end my song.

Eftsoons the nymphs, which now had flowers their fill,
Ran all in haste to see that silver brood
As they came floating on the crystal flood;
Whom when they saw, they stood amazéd still,
Their wondering eyes to fill;
Them seem'd they never saw a sight so fair
Of fowls, so lovely, that they sure did deem
Them heavenly born, or to be that same pair

Which through the sky draw Venus' silver team;
For sure they did not seem
To be begot of any earthly seed,
But rather angels, or of angels' breed;
Yet were they bred of summer's heat, they say,
In sweetest season, when each flower and weed
The earth did fresh array;
So fresh they seem'd as day,
Even as their bridal day, which was not long:
   Sweet Thames! run softly, till I end my song.

Then forth they all out of their baskets drew
Great store of flowers, the honour of the field,
That to the sense did fragrant odours yield,
All which upon those goodly birds they threw
And all the waves did strew,
That like old Peneus' waters they did seem
When down along by pleasant Tempe's shore
Scatter'd with flowers, through Thessaly they stream,
That they appear, through lilies' plenteous store,
Like a bride's chamber-floor.
Two of those nymphs meanwhile two garlands bound
Of freshest flowers which in that mead they found,
The which presenting all in trim array,
Their snowy foreheads therewithal they crown'd;
Whilst one did sing this lay
Prepared against that day,
Against their bridal day, which was not long:
   Sweet Thames! run softly, till I end my song.

'Ye gentle birds! the world's fair ornament,
And Heaven's glory, whom this happy hour
Doth lead unto your lovers' blissful bower,
Joy may you have, and gentle heart's content
Of your love's complement;
And let fair Venus, that is queen of love,
With her heart-quelling son upon you smile,
Whose smile, they say, hath virtue to remove
All love's dislike, and friendship's faulty guile
For ever to assoil.

Let endless peace your steadfast hearts accord,
And blessed plenty wait upon your board;
And let your bed with pleasures chaste abound,
That fruitful issue may to you afford
Which may your foes confound,
And make your joys redound
Upon your bridal day, which is not long:
 Sweet Thames! run softly, till I end my song.'

So ended she; and all the rest around
To her redoubled that her undersong,
Which said their bridal day should not be long:
And gentle Echo from the neighbour ground
Their accents did resound.
So forth those joyous birds did pass along
Adown the lee that to them murmur'd low,
As he would speak but that he lack'd a tongue,
Yet did by signs his glad affection show,
Making his stream run slow.
And all the fowl which in his flood did dwell
'Gan flock about these twain, that did excel
The rest, so far as Cynthia doth shend
The lesser stars. So they, enrangéd well,
Did on those two attend,
And their best service lend
Against their wedding day, which was not long:
 Sweet Thames! run softly, till I end my song.

At length they all to merry London came,
To merry London, my most kindly nurse,
That to me gave this life's first native source,
Though from another place I take my name,
An house of ancient fame:
There when they came whereas those bricky towers
The which on Thames' broad aged back do ride,
Where now the studious lawyers have their bowers,
There whilome wont the Templar-knights to bide,
Till they decay'd through pride;
Next whereunto there stands a stately place,
Where oft I gainéd gifts and goodly grace

35

Of that great lord, which therein wont to dwell,
Whose want too well now feels my friendless case;
But ah! here fits not well
Old woes, but joys to tell
Against the bridal day, which is not long:
　　Sweet Thames! run softly, till I end my song.

Yet therein now doth lodge a noble peer,
Great England's glory and the world's wide wonder,
Whose dreadful name late thro' all Spain did thunder,
And Hercules' two pillars standing near
Did make to quake and fear:
Fair branch of honour, flower of chivalry!
That fillest England with thy triumphs' fame
Joy have thou of thy noble victory,
And endless happiness of thine own name
That promiseth the same;
That through thy prowess and victorious arms
Thy country may be freed from foreign harms,
And great Eliza's glorious name may ring
Through all the world, fill'd with thy wide alarms
Which some brave Muse may sing
To ages following,
Upon the bridal day, which is not long:
　　Sweet Thames! run softly, till I end my song.

From those high towers this noble lord issuing
Like radiant Hesper, when his golden hair
In th' ocean billows he hath bathéd fair,
Descended to the river's open viewing
With a great train ensuing.
Above the rest were goodly to be seen
Two gentle knights of lovely face and feature,
Beseeming well the bower of any queen,
With gifts of wit and ornaments of nature,
Fit for so goodly stature,
That like the twins of Jove they seem'd in sight
Which deck the baldric of the Heavens bright;
They two, forth pacing to the river's side,
Received those two fair brides, their love's delight;

Which, at th' appointed tide,
Each one did make his bride
Against their bridal day, which is not long:
   Sweet Thames! run softly, till I end my song.

E. SPENSER

54

THE HAPPY HEART

ART thou poor, yet hast thou golden slumbers?
     O sweet content!
Art thou rich, yet is thy mind perplexéd?
     O punishment!
Dost thou laugh to see how fools are vexéd
To add to golden numbers, golden numbers?
O sweet content! O sweet, O sweet content!
  Work apace, apace, apace, apace;
  Honest labour bears a lovely face;
Then hey nonny nonny, hey nonny nonny!

Canst drink the waters of the crispéd spring?
     O sweet content!
Swimm'st thou in wealth, yet sink'st in thine own tears?
     O punishment!
Then he that patiently want's burden bears
No burden bears, but is a king, a king!
O sweet content! O sweet, O sweet content!
  Work apace, apace, apace, apace;
  Honest labour bears a lovely face;
Then hey nonny nonny, hey nonny nonny!

T. DEKKER

55

THIS Life, which seems so fair,
Is like a bubble blown up in the air
By sporting children's breath,
Who chase it everywhere
And strive who can most motion it bequeath.
And though it sometimes seem of its own might

Like to an eye of gold to be fix'd there,
And firm to hover in that empty height,
That only is because it is so light.
—But in that pomp it doth not long appear;
For when 'tis most admired, in a thought,
Because it erst was nought, it turns to nought.

W. DRUMMOND

56

SOUL AND BODY

POOR Soul, the centre of my sinful earth,
Fool'd by those rebel powers that thee array,
Why dost thou pine within, and suffer dearth,
Painting thy outward walls so costly gay?

Why so large cost, having so short a lease,
Dost thou upon thy fading mansion spend?
Shall worms, inheritors of this excess,
Eat up thy charge? is this thy body's end?

Then, Soul, live thou upon thy servant's loss,
And let that pine to aggravate thy store;
Buy terms divine in selling hours of dross;
Within be fed, without be rich no more:—

So shalt thou feed on death, that feeds on men,
And death once dead, there's no more dying then.

W. SHAKESPEARE

57

LIFE

THE World's a bubble, and the Life of Man
　　　　Less than a span:
In his conception wretched, from the womb
　　　　So to the tomb;
Curst from his cradle, and brought up to years
　　　　With cares and fears.
Who then to frail mortality shall trust,
But limns on water, or but writes in dust.

Yet whilst with sorrow here we live opprest,
    What life is best?
Courts are but only superficial schools
    To dandle fools:
The rural parts are turn'd into a den
    Of savage men:
And where's a city from foul vice so free,
But may be term'd the worst of all the three?

Domestic cares afflict the husband's bed,
    Or pains his head:
Those that live single, take it for a curse,
    Or do things worse:
Some would have children: those that have them moan
    Or wish them gone:
What is it, then, to have, or have no wife,
But single thraldom, or a double strife?

Our own affections still at home to please
    Is a disease:
To cross the seas to any foreign soil,
    Peril and toil:
Wars with their noise affright us; when they cease,
    We are worse in peace;—
What then remains, but that we still should cry
For being born, or, being born, to die?

LORD BACON

58

THE LESSONS OF NATURE

Of this fair volume which we World do name
If we the sheets and leaves could turn with care,
Of Him who it corrects, and did it frame,
We clear might read the art and wisdom rare:

Find out His power which wildest powers doth tame,
His providence extending everywhere,
His justice which proud rebels doth not spare,
In every page, no period of the same,

But silly we, like foolish children, rest
Well pleased with colour'd vellum, leaves of gold,
Fair dangling ribbands, leaving what is best,
On the great Writer's sense ne'er taking hold;

Or if by chance we stay our minds on aught,
It is some picture on the margin wrought.

W. DRUMMOND

59

DOTH then the World go thus, doth all thus move?
Is this the justice which on Earth we find?
Is this that firm decree which all doth bind?
Are these your influences, Powers above?

Those souls which vice's moody mists doth blind,
Blind Fortune, blindly, most their friend doth prove;
And they who thee, poor idol Virtue! love,
Ply like a feather toss'd by storm and wind.

Ah! if a Providence doth sway this all
Why should best minds groan under most distress?
Or why should pride humility make thrall,
And injuries the innocent oppress?

Heavens! hinder, stop this fate; or grant a time
When good may have, as well as bad, their prime!

W. DRUMMOND

60

THE WORLD'S WAY

TIRED with all these, for restful death I cry—
As, to behold desert a beggar born
And needy nothing trimm'd in jollity,
And purest faith unhappily forsworn,

And gilded honour shamefully misplaced,
And maiden virtue rudely strumpeted,
And right perfection wrongfully disgraced,
And strength by limping sway disabled,

And art made tongue-tied by authority,
And folly, doctor-like, controlling skill,
And simple truth miscall'd simplicity,
And captive Good attending captain Ill:—

—Tired with all these, from these would I be gone,
Save that, to die, I leave my Love alone.

W. SHAKESPEARE

61

SAINT JOHN BAPTIST

THE last and greatest Herald of Heaven's King
Girt with rough skins, hies to the deserts wild,
Among that savage brood the woods forth bring,
Which he more harmless found than man, and mild.

His food was locusts, and what there doth spring,
With honey that from virgin hives distill'd;
Parch'd body, hollow eyes, some uncouth thing
Made him appear, long since from earth exiled.

There burst he forth: All ye whose hopes rely
On God, with me amidst these deserts mourn,
Repent, repent, and from old errors turn!
—Who listen'd to his voice, obey'd his cry?

Only the echoes, which he made relent,
Rung from their flinty caves, Repent! Repent!

W. DRUMMOND

62

ODE ON THE
MORNING OF CHRIST'S NATIVITY

THIS is the month, and this the happy morn
Wherein the Son of Heaven's Eternal King
Of wedded maid and virgin mother born,
Our great redemption from above did bring;
For so the holy sages once did sing
That He our deadly forfeit should release,
And with His Father work us a perpetual peace.

That glorious Form, that Light unsufferable,
And that far-beaming blaze of Majesty
Wherewith He wont at Heaven's high council-table
To sit the midst of Trinal Unity,
He laid aside; and, here with us to be,
Forsook the courts of everlasting day,
And chose with us a darksome house of mortal clay.

Say, heavenly Muse, shall not thy sacred vein
Afford a present to the Infant God?
Hast thou no verse, no hymn, or solemn strain
To welcome Him to this His new abode,
Now while the heaven, by the sun's team untrod,
Hath took no print of the approaching light,
And all the spangled host keep watch in squadrons bright?

See how from far, upon the eastern road,
The star-led wizards haste with odours sweet:
O run, prevent them with thy humble ode
And lay it lowly at His blessed feet;

Have thou the honour first thy Lord to greet,
And join thy voice unto the angel quire
From out His secret altar touch'd with hallow'd fire.

THE HYMN

It was the winter wild
While the heaven-born Child
All meanly wrapt in the rude manger lies;
Nature in awe to Him
Had doff'd her gaudy trim,
With her great Master so to sympathize:
It was no season then for her
To wanton with the sun, her lusty paramour.

Only with speeches fair
She woos the gentle air
To hide her guilty front with innocent snow;
And on her naked shame,
Pollute with sinful blame,
The saintly veil of maiden white to throw;
Confounded, that her Maker's eyes
Should look so near upon her foul deformities.

But He, her fears to cease,
Sent down the meek-eyed Peace;
She, crown'd with olive green, came softly sliding
Down through the turning sphere,
His ready harbinger,
With turtle wing the amorous clouds dividing;
And waving wide her myrtle wand,
She strikes a universal peace through sea and land.

No war, or battle's sound
Was heard the world around:
The idle spear and shield were high uphung;
The hookéd chariot stood
Unstain'd with hostile blood;
The trumpet spake not to the arméd throng;
And kings sat still with awful eye,
As if they surely knew their sovran Lord was by.

43

But peaceful was the night
Wherein the Prince of Light
His reign of peace upon the earth began:
The winds, with wonder whist,
Smoothly the waters kist
Whispering new joys to the mild oceán—
Who now hath quite forgot to rave,
While birds of calm sit brooding on the charméd wave.

The stars, with deep amaze,
Stand fix'd in steadfast gaze,
Bending one way their precious influence;
And will not take their flight
For all the morning light,
Or Lucifer that often warn'd them thence;
But in their glimmering orbs did glow
Until their Lord Himself bespake, and bid them go.

And though the shady gloom
Had given day her room,
The sun himself withheld his wonted speed,
And hid his head for shame,
As his inferior flame
The new-enlighten'd world no more should need:
He saw a greater Sun appear
Than his bright throne, or burning axletree, could bear.

The shepherds on the lawn
Or ere the point of dawn
Sate simply chatting in a rustic row;
Full little thought they then
That the mighty Pan
Was kindly come to live with them below;
Perhaps their loves, or else their sheep
Was all that did their silly thoughts so busy keep.

When such music sweet
Their hearts and ears did greet
As never was by mortal finger strook—
Divinely-warbled voice
Answering the stringéd noise,
As all their souls in blissful rapture took:

The air, such pleasure loth to lose,
With thousand echoes still prolongs each heavenly close.

Nature that heard such sound
Beneath the hollow round
Of Cynthia's seat the airy region thrilling,
Now was almost won
To think her part was done,
And that her reign had here its last fulfilling;
She knew such harmony alone
Could hold all heaven and earth in happier union.

At last surrounds their sight
A globe of circular light
That with long beams the shamefaced night array'd;
The helmèd Cherubim
And sworded Seraphim
Are seen in glittering ranks with wings display'd,
Harping in loud and solemn quire
With unexpressive notes, to Heaven's new-born Heir.

Such music (as 'tis said)
Before was never made
But when of old the sons of morning sung,
While the Creator great
His constellations set
And the well-balanced world on hinges hung;
And cast the dark foundations deep,
And bid the weltering waves their oozy channel keep.

Ring out, ye crystal spheres!
Once bless our human ears,
If ye have power to touch our senses so;
And let your silver chime
Move in melodious time;
And let the base of heaven's deep organ blow;
And with your ninefold harmony
Make up full consort to the angelic symphony.

For if such holy song
Enwrap our fancy long,

Time will run back, and fetch the age of gold;
And speckled vanity
Will sicken soon and die,
And leprous sin will melt from earthly mould;
And Hell itself will pass away,
And leave her dolorous mansions to the peering day.

Yea, Truth and Justice then
Will down return to men,
Orb'd in a rainbow; and, like glories wearing,
Mercy will sit between
Throned in celestial sheen,
With radiant feet the tissued clouds down steering;
And Heaven, as at some festival,
Will open wide the gates of her high palace hall.

But wisest Fate says No;
This must not yet be so;
The Babe yet lies in smiling infancy
That on the bitter cross
Must redeem our loss;
So both Himself and us to glorify:
Yet first, to those ychain'd in sleep
The wakeful trump of doom must thunder through the deep;

With such a horrid clang
As on mount Sinai rang
While the red fire and smouldering clouds outbrake:
The aged Earth aghast
With terror of that blast
Shall from the surface to the centre shake,
When, at the world's last sessión,
The dreadful Judge in middle air shall spread His throne.

And then at last our bliss
Full and perfect is,
But now begins; for from this happy day
The old Dragon under ground,
In straiter limits bound,
Not half so far casts his usurpéd sway;
And, wroth to see his kingdom fail,
Swinges the scaly horror of his folded tail.

The oracles are dumb;
No voice or hideous hum
Runs through the archéd roof in words deceiving:
Apollo from his shrine
Can no more divine,
With hollow shriek the steep of Delphos leaving:
No nightly trance or breathéd spell
Inspires the pale-eyed priest from the prophetic cell.

The lonely mountains o'er
And the resounding shore
A voice of weeping heard, and loud lament;
From haunted spring and dale
Edged with popular pale
The parting Genius is with sighing sent;
With flower-inwoven tresses torn
The nymphs in twilight shade of tangled thickets mourn.

In consecrated earth
And on the holy hearth
The Lars and Lemurés moan with midnight plaint;
In urns and altars round
A drear and dying sound
Affrights the Flamens at their service quaint;
And the chill marble seems to sweat,
While each peculiar Power forgoes his wonted seat.

Peor and Baalim
Forsake their temples dim,
With that twice-batter'd god of Palestine;
And moonéd Ashtaroth
Heaven's queen and mother both,
Now sits not girt with tapers' holy shine;
The Lybic Hammon shrinks his horn,
In vain the Tyrian maids their wounded Thammuz mourn.

And sullen Moloch, fled,
Hath left in shadows dread
His burning idol all of blackest hue;
In vain with cymbals' ring
They call the grisly king,
In dismal dance about the furnace blue;

47

The brutish gods of Nile as fast,
Isis, and Orus, and the dog Anubis, haste.

Nor is Osiris seen
In Memphian grove, or green,
Trampling the unshower'd grass with lowings loud:
Nor can he be at rest
Within his sacred chest;
Nought but profoundest hell can be his shroud;
In vain with timbrell'd anthems dark
The sable stoléd sorcerers bear his worshipt ark.

He feels from Juda's land
The dreaded infant's hand;
The rays of Bethlehem blind his dusky eyn;
Nor all the gods beside
Longer dare abide,
Nor Typhon huge ending in snaky twine:
Our Babe, to show his Godhead true,
Can in His swaddling bands control the damnéd crew.

So, when the sun in bed
Curtain'd with cloudy red
Pillows his chin upon an orient wave,
The flocking shadows pale
Troop to the infernal jail,
Each fetter'd ghost slips to his several grave;
And the yellow-skirted fays
Fly after the night-steeds, leaving their moon-loved maze.

But see, the Virgin blest
Hath laid her Babe to rest;
Time is, our tedious song should here have ending:
Heaven's youngest-teeméd star
Hath fix'd her polish'd car,
Her sleeping Lord with hand-maid lamp attending:
And all about the courtly stable
Bright-harness'd angels sit in order serviceable.

J. MILTON

63

SONG FOR SAINT CECILIA'S DAY, 1687

FROM Harmony, from heavenly Harmony
    This universal frame began:
    When Nature underneath a heap
      Of jarring atoms lay
    And could not heave her head,
The tuneful voice was heard from high
      Arise, ye more than dead!
Then cold, and hot, and moist, and dry
In order to their stations leap,
    And Music's power obey.
From harmony, from heavenly harmony
    This universal frame began:
    From harmony to harmony
Through all the compass of the notes it ran,
The diapason closing full in Man.

What passion cannot Music raise and quell?
    When Jubal struck the chorded shell
  His listening brethren stood around,
    And, wondering, on their faces fell
    To worship that celestial sound.
Less than a god they thought there could not dwell
    Within the hollow of that shell
    That spoke so sweetly and so well.
What passion cannot Music raise and quell?

    The trumpet's loud clangor
      Excites us to arms,
  With shrill notes of anger
    And mortal alarms.
    The double double double beat
    Of the thundering drum
Cries 'Hark! the foes come;
Charge, charge, 'tis too late to retreat!'

The soft complaining flute
In dying notes discovers
  The woes of hopeless lovers,
Whose dirge is whisper'd by the warbling lute.

  Sharp violins proclaim
Their jealous pangs and desperation,
Fury, frantic indignation,
Depth of pains, and height of passion
  For the fair disdainful dame.

But oh! what art can teach,
What human voice can reach
  The sacred organ's praise?
Notes inspiring holy love,
Notes that wing their heavenly ways
  To mend the choirs above.

Orpheus could lead the savage race,
And trees uprooted left their place
  Sequacious of the lyre:
But bright Cecilia raised the wonder higher:
When to her Organ vocal breath was given
An Angel heard, and straight appear'd—
  Mistaking Earth for Heaven!

Grand Chorus

As from the power of sacred lays
  The spheres began to move,
And sung the great Creator's praise
  To all the blest above;
So when the last and dreadful hour
This crumbling pageant shall devour,
The trumpet shall be heard on high,
The dead shall live, the living die,
And Music shall untune the sky.

J. DRYDEN

64

ON THE LATE MASSACRE IN PIEMONT

AVENGE, O Lord! Thy slaughter'd Saints, whose bones
Lie scatter'd on the Alpine mountains cold;
Even them who kept Thy truth so pure of old
When all our fathers worship stocks and stones
Forget not: In Thy book record their groans
Who were Thy sheep, and in their ancient fold
Slain by the bloody Piemontese, that roll'd
Mother with infant down the rocks. Their moans

The vales redoubled to the hills, and they
To Heaven. Their martyr'd blood and ashes sow
O'er all the Italian fields, where still doth sway
The triple tyrant: that from these may grow
A hundred-fold, who, having learnt Thy way,
Early may fly the Babylonian woe.

J. MILTON

65

HORATIAN ODE UPON CROMWELL'S RETURN FROM IRELAND

THE forward youth that would appear,
Must now forsake his Muses dear,
    Nor in the shadows sing
    His numbers languishing.

'Tis time to leave the books in dust,
And oil the unused armour's rust,
    Removing from the wall
    The corslet of the hall.

So restless Cromwell could not cease
In the inglorious arts of peace,
    But through adventurous war
    Urgéd his active star:

And like the three-fork'd lightning first,
Breaking the clouds where it was nurst,
 Did thorough his own side
 His fiery way divide:

For 'tis all one to courage high
The emulous, or enemy;
 And with such, to enclose
 Is more than to oppose.

Then burning through the air he went
And palaces and temples rent;
 And Caesar's head at last
 Did through his laurels blast.

'Tis madness to resist or blame
The face of angry heaven's flame;
 And if we would speak true,
 Much to the Man is due

Who, from his private gardens, where
He lived reservéd and austere
 (As if his highest plot
 To plant the bergamot),

Could by industrious valour climb
To ruin the great work of time,
 And cast the Kingdoms old
 Into another mould.

Though Justice against Fate complain,
And plead the ancient Rights in vain—
 But those do hold or break
 As men are strong or weak.

Nature, that hateth emptiness,
Allows of penetration less,
 And therefore must make room
 Where greater spirits come.

What field of all the civil war
Where his were not the deepest scar?
 And Hampton shows what part
 He had of wiser art,

Where, twining subtle fears with hope,
He wove a net of such a scope
    That Charles himself might chase
    To Carisbrook's narrow case;

That thence the Royal actor borne
The tragic scaffold might adorn:
    While round the arméd bands
    Did clap their bloody hands;

He nothing common did or mean
Upon that memorable scene,
    But with his keener eye
    The axe's edge did try;

Nor call'd the Gods, with vulgar spite,
To vindicate his helpless right;
    But bow'd his comely head
    Down, as upon a bed.

—This was that memorable hour
Which first assured the forcéd power:
    So when they did design
    The Capitol's first line.

A Bleeding Head, where they begun,
Did fright the architects to run;
    And yet in that the State
    Foresaw its happy fate!

And now the Irish are ashamed
To see themselves in one year tamed:
    So much one man can do
    That does both act and know.

They can affirm his praises best,
And have, though overcome, confest
    How good he is, how just
    And fit for highest trust;

Nor yet grown stiffer with command,
But still in the Republic's hand—
    How fit he is to sway
    That can so well obey!

He to the Commons' feet presents
A Kingdom for his first year's rents.
    And (what he may) forbears
    His fame, to make it theirs:

And has his sword and spoils ungirt
To lay them at the Public's skirt.
    So when the falcon high
    Falls heavy from the sky,

She, having kill'd, no more does search
But on the next green bough to perch,
    Where, when he first does lure,
    The falconer has her sure.

—What may not then our Isle presume
While victory his crest does plume?
    What may not others fear
    If thus he crowns each year!

As Caesar he, ere long, to Gaul,
To Italy an Hannibal,
    And to all states not free
    Shall climacteric be.

The Pict no shelter now shall find
Within his parti-colour'd mind,
    But from this valour, sad
    Shrink underneath the plaid—

Happy, if in the tufted brake
The English hunter him mistake,
    Nor lay his hounds in near
    The Caledonian deer.

But Thou, the War's and Fortune's son,
March indefatigably on;
    And for the last effect
    Still keep the sword erect:

Besides the force it has to fright
The spirits of the shady night,
    The same arts that did gain
    A power, must it maintain.

A. MARVELL

LYCIDAS

Elegy on a Friend drowned in the Irish Channel

YET once more, O ye laurels, and once more
Ye myrtles brown, with ivy never sere,
I come to pluck your berries harsh and crude,
And with forced fingers rude
Shatter your leaves before the mellowing year.
Bitter constraint, and sad occasion dear
Compels me to disturb your season due,
For Lycidas is dead, dead ere his prime,
Young Lycidas, and hath not left his peer:
Who would not sing for Lycidas? he knew
Himself to sing, and build the lofty rhyme.
He must not float upon his watery bier
Unwept, and welter to the parching wind,
Without the meed of some melodious tear.

Begin then, Sisters of the sacred well
That from beneath the seat of Jove doth spring,
Begin, and somewhat loudly sweep the string.
Hence with denial vain and coy excuse:
So may some gentle Muse
With lucky words favour my destined urn;
And as he passes, turn
And bid fair peace be to my sable shroud.

For we were nursed upon the selfsame hill,
Fed the same flock by fountain, shade, and rill.
Together both, ere the high lawns appear'd
Under the opening eye-lids of the morn,
We drove a-field, and both together heard
What time the gray-fly winds her sultry horn,
Battening our flocks with the fresh dews of night,
Oft till the star, that rose at evening bright,
Towards heaven's descent had sloped his westering **wheel.**
Meanwhile the rural ditties were not mute,
Temper'd to the oaten flute;
Rough Satyrs danced, and Fauns with cloven **heel**

From the glad sound would not be absent long;
And old Damoetas loved to hear our song.

But, O the heavy change, now thou art gone,
Now thou art gone, and never must return!
Thee, Shepherd, thee the woods, and desert caves
With wild thyme and the gadding vine o'ergrown,
And all their echoes, mourn:
The willows and the hazel copses green
Shall now no more be seen
Fanning their joyous leaves to thy soft lays:—
As killing as the canker to the rose,
Or taint-worm to the weanling herds that graze,
Or frost to flowers, that their gay wardrobe wear
When first the white-thorn blows;
Such, Lycidas, thy loss to shepherd's ear.

Where were ye, Nymphs, when the remorseless deep
Closed o'er the head of your loved Lycidas?
For neither were ye playing on the steep
Where your old bards, the famous Druids, lie,
Nor on the shaggy top of Mona high,
Nor yet where Deva spreads her wizard stream:
Ay me! I fondly dream—
Had ye been there—for what could that have done?
What could the Muse herself that Orpheus bore,
The Muse herself, for her enchanting son,
Whom universal nature did lament,
When by the rout that made the hideous roar
His gory visage down the stream was sent,
Down the swift Hebrus to the Lesbian shore?

Alas! what boots it with uncessant care
To tend the homely, slighted, shepherd's trade
And strictly meditate the thankless Muse?
Were it not better done, as others use,
To sport with Amaryllis in the shade.
Or with the tangles of Neaera's hair?
Fame is the spur that the clear spirit doth raise
(That last infirmity of noble mind)
To scorn delights, and live laborious days:
But the fair guerdon when we hope to find,

And think to burst out into sudden blaze,
Comes the blind Fury with the abhorréd shears
And slits the thin-spun life. 'But not the praise'
Phoebus replied, and touch'd my trembling ears;
'Fame is no plant that grows on mortal soil,
Nor in the glistering foil
Set off to the world, nor in broad rumour lies:
But lives and spreads aloft by those pure eyes
And perfect witness of all-judging Jove;
As he pronounces lastly on each deed,
Of so much fame in heaven expect thy meed.

O fountain Arethuse, and thou honour'd flood,
Smooth-sliding Mincius, crown'd with vocal reeds,
That strain I heard was of a higher mood:
But now my oat proceeds,
And listens to the herald of the sea
That came in Neptune's plea:
He ask'd the waves, and ask'd the felon winds,
What hard mishap hath doom'd this gentle swain?
And question'd every gust of rugged wings
That blows from off each beakéd promontory:
They knew not of his story;
And sage Hippotadés their answer brings,
That not a blast was from his dungeon stray'd;
The air was calm, and on the level brine
Sleek Panopé with all her sisters play'd.
It was that fatal and perfidious bark
Built in the eclipse, and rigg'd with curses dark,
That sunk so low that sacred head of thine.

Next Camus, reverend sire, went footing slow,
His mantle hairy, and his bonnet sedge
Inwrought with figures dim, and on the edge
Like to that sanguine flower inscribed with woe:
'Ah! who hath reft,' quoth he, 'my dearest pledge!'
Last came, and last did go
The pilot of the Galilean lake;
Two massy keys he bore of metals twain
(The golden opes, the iron shuts amain);
He shook his mitred locks, and stern bespake:

'How well could I have spared for thee, young swain,
Enow of such, as for their bellies' sake
Creep and intrude and climb into the fold!
Of other care they little reckoning make
Than how to scramble at the shearers' feast,
And shove away the worthy bidden guest.
Blind mouths! that scarce themselves know how to hold
A sheep-hook, or have learn'd aught else the least
That to the faithful herdman's art belongs!
What recks it them? What need they? They are sped;
And when they list, their lean and flashy songs
Grate on their scrannel pipes of wretched straw:
The hungry sheep look up, and are not fed,
But swoln with wind and the rank mist they draw
Rot inwardly, and foul contagion spread:
Besides what the grim wolf with privy paw
Daily devours apace, and nothing said:
—But that two-handed engine at the door
Stands ready to smite once, and smite no more.'

Return, Alphéus, the dread voice is past
That shrunk thy streams; return, Sicilian Muse,
And call the vales, and bid them hither cast
Their bells and flowerets of a thousand hues.
Ye valleys low, where the mild whispers use
Of shades, and wanton winds, and gushing brooks
On whose fresh lap the swart star sparely looks;
Throw hither all your quaint enamell'd eyes
That on the green turf suck the honey'd showers
And purple all the ground with vernal flowers.
Bring the rathe primrose that forsaken dies,
The tufted crow-toe, and pale jessamine,
The white pink, and the pansy freak'd with jet,
The glowing violet,
The musk-rose, and the well-attired woodbine,
With cowslips wan that hang the pensive head,
And every flower that sad embroidery wears:
Bid Amaranthus all his beauty shed,
And daffodillies fill their cups with tears
To strew the laureat hearse where Lycid lies.

For so to interpose a little ease,
Let our frail thoughts dally with false surmise;
Ay me! whilst thee the shores and sounding seas
Wash far away,—where'er thy bones are hurl'd,
Whether beyond the stormy Hebrides
Where thou perhaps, under the whelming tide,
Visitest the bottom of the monstrous world;
Or whether thou, to our moist vows denied,
Sleep'st by the fable of Bellerus old,
Where the great Vision of the guarded mount
Looks towards Namancos and Bayona's hold,
—Look homeward, Angel, now, and melt with ruth:
—And, O ye dolphins, waft the hapless youth!

Weep no more, woful shepherds, weep no more,
For Lycidas, your sorrow, is not dead,
Sunk though he be beneath the watery floor;
So sinks the day-star in the ocean-bed,
And yet anon repairs his drooping head
And tricks his beams, and with new-spangled ore
Flames in the forehead of the morning sky:
So Lycidas sunk low, but mounted high
Through the dear might of Him that walk'd the waves;
Where, other groves and other streams along,
With nectar pure his oozy locks he laves,
And hears the unexpressive nuptial song
In the blest kingdoms meek of joy and love.
There entertain him all the saints above
In solemn troops, and sweet societies,
That sing, and singing, in their glory move,
And wipe the tears for ever from his eyes.
Now, Lycidas, the shepherds weep no more;
Henceforth thou art the Genius of the shore
In thy large recompense, and shalt be good
To all that wander in that perilous flood.

Thus sang the uncouth swain to the oaks and rills,
While the still morn went out with sandals grey;
He touch'd the tender stops of various quills,
With eager thought warbling his Doric lay:

And now the sun had stretch'd out all the hills,
    And now was dropt into the western bay:
At last he rose, and twitch'd his mantle blue:
    Tomorrow to fresh woods, and pastures new.

J. MILTON

67

ON THE TOMBS IN WESTMINSTER ABBEY

MORTALITY, behold and fear
What a change of flesh is here!
Think how many royal bones
Sleep within these heaps of stones;
Here they lie, had realms and lands,
Who now want strength to stir their hands,
Where from their pulpits seal'd with dust
They preach, 'In greatness is no trust.'
Here's an acre sown indeed
With the richest royallest seed
That the earth did e'er suck in
Since the first man died for sin:
Here the bones of birth have cried
'Though gods they were, as men they died!'
Here are sands, ignoble things,
Dropt from the ruin'd sides of kings;
Here's a world of pomp and state
Buried in dust, once dead by fate.

F. BEAUMONT

68

THE LAST CONQUEROR

VICTORIOUS men of earth, no more
    Proclaim how wide your empires are;
Though you bind-in every shore
    And your triumphs reach as far
        As night or day,
    Yet you, proud monarchs, must obey
And mingle with forgotten ashes, when
Death calls ye to the crowd of common men.

Devouring Famine, Plague, and War,
    Each able to undo mankind,
Death's servile emissaries are;
    Nor to these alone confined,
        He hath at will
    More quaint and subtle ways to kill;
A smile or kiss, as he will use the art,
Shall have the cunning skill to break a heart.

                         J. SHIRLEY

69

DEATH THE LEVELLER

THE glories of our blood and state
    Are shadows, not substantial things;
There is no armour against fate;
    Death lays his icy hand on kings:
        Sceptre and Crown
        Must tumble down,
And in the dust be equal made
With the poor crooked scythe and spade.

Some men with swords may reap the field,
    And plant fresh laurels where they kill:
But their strong nerves at last must yield;
    They tame but one another still:
        Early or late
        They stoop to fate,
And must give up their murmuring breath
When they, pale captives, creep to death.

The garlands wither on your brow;
    Then boast no more your mighty deeds;
Upon Death's purple altar now
    See where the victor-victim bleeds:
        Your heads must come
        To the cold tomb;
Only the actions of the just
Smell sweet, and blossom in their dust.

                         J. SHIRLEY

70

WHEN THE ASSAULT WAS INTENDED TO THE CITY

CAPTAIN, or Colonel, or Knight in arms,
Whose chance on these defenceless doors may seize,
If deed of honour did thee ever please,
Guard them, and him within protect from harms.

He can requite thee; for he knows the charms
That call fame on such gentle acts as these,
And he can spread thy name o'er lands and seas,
Whatever clime the sun's bright circle warms.

Lift not thy spear against the Muses' bower:
The great Emathian conqueror did spare
The house of Pindarus, when temple and tower
Went to the ground: and the repeated air
Of sad Electra's poet had the power
To save the Athenian walls from ruin bare.

J. MILTON

71

ON HIS BLINDNESS

WHEN I consider how my light is spent
Ere half my days, in this dark world and wide,
And that one talent which is death to hide
Lodged with me useless, though my soul more bent

To serve therewith my Maker, and present
My true account, lest He returning chide,—
Doth God exact day-labour, light denied?
I fondly ask:—But Patience, to prevent

That murmur, soon replies; God doth not need
Either man's work, or His own gifts: who best
Bear His mild yoke, they serve Him best: His state

Is kingly; thousands at His bidding speed
And post o'er land and ocean without rest:—
They also serve who only stand and wait.

J. MILTON

72

CHARACTER OF A HAPPY LIFE

How happy is he born and taught
That serveth not another's will:
Whose armour is his honest thought
And simple truth his utmost skill!

Whose passions not his masters are,
Whose soul is still prepared for death,
Not tied unto the world with care
Of public fame, or private breath;

Who envies none that chance doth raise
Or vice; Who never understood
How deepest wounds are given by praise;
Nor rules of state, but rules of good;

Who hath his life from rumours freed,
Whose conscience is his strong retreat;
Whose state can neither flatterers feed,
Nor ruin make accusers great;

Who God doth late and early pray
More of His grace than gifts to lend;
And entertains the harmless day
With a well-chosen book or friend;

—This man is freed from servile bands
Of hope to rise, or fear to fall;
Lord of himself, though not of lands;
And have nothing, yet hath all.

SIR H. WOTTON

73

THE NOBLE NATURE

It is not growing like a tree
In bulk, doth make Man better be;
Or standing long an oak, three hundred year,
To fall a log at last, dry, bald, and sere:

A lily of a day
Is fairer far in May,
Although it fall and die that night—
It was the plant and flower of Light.
In small proportions we just beauties see:
And in short measures life may perfect be.

B. JONSON

74

THE GIFTS OF GOD

WHEN God at first made Man,
Having a glass of blessings standing by;
Let us (said He) pour on him all we can:
Let the world's riches, which dispersèd lie,
Contract into a span.

So strength first made a way;
Then beauty flow'd, then wisdom, honour, pleasure:
When almost all was out, God made a stay,
Perceiving that alone, of all His treasure,
Rest in the bottom lay.

For if I should (said He)
Bestow this jewel also on my creature,
He would adore My gifts instead of Me,
And rest in Nature, not the God of Nature:
So both should losers be.

Yet let him keep the rest,
But keep them with repining restlessness:
Let him be rich and weary, that at least,
If goodness lead him not, yet weariness
May toss him to My breast.

G. HERBERT

75

THE RETREAT

HAPPY those early days, when I
Shined in my Angel-infancy!
Before I understood this place
Appointed for my second race,
Or taught my soul to fancy aught
But a white, celestial thought;
When yet I had not walk'd above
A mile or two from my first Love,
And looking back, at that short space
Could see a glimpse of His bright face;
When on some gilded cloud or flower
My gazing soul would dwell an hour,
And in those weaker glories spy
Some shadows of eternity;
Before I taught my tongue to wound
My conscience with a sinful sound,
Or had the black art to dispense
A several sin to every sense,
But felt through all this fleshly dress
Bright shoots of everlastingness.

O how I long to travel back,
And tread again that ancient track!
That I once more might reach that plain,
Where first I left my glorious train;
From whence th' enlighten'd spirit sees
That shady City of Palm-trees!
But ah! my soul with too much stay
Is drunk, and staggers in the way:—
Some men a forward motion love,
But I by backward steps would move;
And when this dust falls to the urn,
In that state I came, return.

H. VAUGHAN

76

TO MR. LAWRENCE

LAWRENCE, of virtuous father virtuous son,
Now that the fields are dank and ways are mire,
Where shall we sometimes meet, and by the fire
Help waste a sullen day, what may be won

From the hard season gaining? Time will run
On smoother, till Favonius re-inspire
The frozen earth, and clothe in fresh attire
The lily and rose, that neither sow'd nor spun.

What neat repast shall feast us, light and choice,
Of Attic taste, with wine, whence we may rise
To hear the lute well touch'd, or artful voice

Warble immortal notes and Tuscan air?
He who of those delights can judge, and spare
To interpose them oft, is not unwise.

J. MILTON

77

TO CYRIACK SKINNER

CYRIACK, whose grandsire, on the royal bench
Of British Themis, with no mean applause
Pronounced, and in his volumes taught, our laws,
Which others at their bar so often wrench;

Today deep thoughts resolve with me to drench
In mirth, that after no repenting draws;
Let Euclid rest, and Archimedes pause,
And what the Swede intend, and what the French.

To measure life learn thou betimes, and know
Toward solid good what leads the nearest way;
For other things mild Heaven a time ordains,

And disapproves that care, though wise in show,
That with superfluous burden loads the day,
And, when God sends a cheerful hour, refrains.

J. MILTON

78

HYMN TO DIANA

Queen and Huntress, chaste and fair,
  Now the sun is laid to sleep,
Seated in thy silver chair
    State in wonted manner keep:
        Hesperus entreats thy light,
        Goddess excellently bright.

Earth, let not thy envious shade
  Dare itself to interpose;
Cynthia's shining orb was made
    Heaven to clear when day did close:
        Bless us then with wishéd sight,
        Goddess excellently bright.

Lay thy bow of pearl apart
  And thy crystal-shining quiver;
Give unto the flying hart
    Space to breathe, how short soever:
        Thou that mak'st a day of night,
        Goddess excellently bright!

                                    B. JONSON

79

WISHES FOR THE SUPPOSED MISTRESS

Whoe'er she be,
That not impossible She
That shall command my heart and me;

Where'er she lie,
Lock'd up from mortal eye
In shady leaves of destiny:

Till that ripe birth
Of studied Fate stand forth,
And teach her fair steps to our earth;

Till that divine
Idea take a shrine
Of crystal flesh, through which to shine:

—Meet you her, my Wishes,
Bespeak her to my blisses,
And be ye call'd, my absent kisses.

I wish her beauty
That owes not all its duty
To gaudy tire, or glist'ring shoe-tie:

Something more than
Taffata or tissue can,
Or rampant feather, or rich fan.

A face that's best
By its own beauty drest,
And can alone command the rest:

A face made up
Out of no other shop
Than what Nature's white hand sets ope.

Sidneian showers
Of sweet discourse, whose powers
Can crown old Winter's head with flowers.

Whate'er delight
Can make day's forehead bright
Or give down to the wings of night.

Soft silken hours,
Open suns, shady bowers;
'Bove all, nothing within that lowers.

Days, that need borrow
No part of their good morrow
From a fore-spent night of sorrow:

Days, that in spite
Of darkness, by the light
Of a clear mind are day all night.

Life, that dares send
A challenge to his end,
And when it comes, say, 'Welcome, friend.'

I wish her store
Of worth may leave her poor
Of wishes; and I wish——no more.

—Now, if Time knows
That Her, whose radiant brows
Weave them a garland of my vows;

Her that dares be
What these lines wish to see:
I seek no further, it is She.

'Tis She, and here
Lo! I unclothe and clear
My wishes' cloudy character.

Such worth as this is
Shall fix my flying wishes,
And determine them to kisses.

Let her full glory,
My fancies, fly before ye;
Be ye my fictions:—but her story.

R. CRASHAW

80

THE GREAT ADVENTURER

OVER the mountains
And over the waves,
Under the fountains,
And under the graves;
Under floods that are deepest,
While Neptune obey;
Over rocks that are steepest
Love will find out the way.

Where there is no place
For the glow-worm to lie;
Where there is no space
For receipt of a fly;
Where the midge dares not venture
Lest herself fast she lay;
If love come, he will enter
And soon find out the way.

You may esteem him
A child for his might;
Or you may deem him
A coward from his flight;
But if she whom love doth honour
Be conceal'd from the day,
Set a thousand guards upon her,
Love will find out the way.

Some think to lose him
By having him confined;
And some do suppose him,
Poor thing, to be blind;
But if ne'er so close ye wall him.
Do the best that you may,
Blind love, if so ye call him,
Will find out his way.

You may train the eagle
To stoop to your fist;
Or you may inveigle
The phoenix of the east;
The lioness, ye may move her
To give o'er her prey;
But you'll ne'er stop a lover:
He will find out his way.

ANON.

81

CHILD AND MAIDEN

AH, Chloris! could I now but sit
  As unconcern'd as when
Your infant beauty could beget
  No happiness or pain!
When I the dawn used to admire,
  And praised the coming day,
I little thought the rising fire
  Would take my rest away.

Your charms in harmless childhood lay
  Like metals in a mine;
Age from no face takes more away
  Than youth conceal'd in thine.
But as your charms insensibly
  To their perfection prest,
So love as unperceived did fly,
  And center'd in my breast.

My passion with your beauty grew,
  While Cupid at my heart
Still as his mother favour'd you
  Threw a new flaming dart:
Each gloried in their wanton part;
  To make a lover, he
Employ'd the utmost of his art—
  To make a beauty, she.

SIR C. SEDLEY

82

COUNSEL TO GIRLS

GATHER ye rose-buds while ye may,
  Old Time is still a-flying:
And this same flower that smiles today,
  Tomorrow will be dying.

The glorious Lamp of Heaven, the Sun,
   The higher he's a-getting
The sooner will his race be run,
   And nearer he's to setting.

That age is best which is the first,
   When youth and blood are warmer:
But being spent, the worse, and worst
   Times, will succeed the former.

Then be not coy, but use your time;
   And while ye may, go marry:
For having lost but once your prime,
   You may for ever tarry.

R. HERRICK

83

TO LUCASTA, ON GOING TO THE WARS

TELL me not, Sweet, I am unkind
   That from the nunnery
Of thy chaste breast and quiet mind,
   To war and arms I fly.

True, a new mistress now I chase,
   The first foe in the field;
And with a stronger faith embrace
   A sword, a horse, a shield.

Yet this inconstancy is such
   As you too shall adore;
I could not love thee, Dear, so much,
   Loved I not Honour more.

COLONEL LOVELACE

84

ELIZABETH OF BOHEMIA

You meaner beauties of the night,
  Which poorly satisfy our eyes
More by your number than your light,
  You common people of the skies,
What are you, when the Moon shall rise?

Ye violets that first appear,
  By your pure purple mantles known
Like the proud virgins of the year
  As if the spring were all your own,—
What are you, when the Rose is blown?

Ye curious chanters of the wood
  That warble forth dame Nature's lays,
Thinking your passions understood
  By your weak accents; what's your praise
When Philomel her voice doth raise?

So when my Mistress shall be seen
  In sweetness of her looks and mind,
By virtue first, then choice, a Queen,
  Tell me, if she were not design'd
Th' eclipse and glory of her kind?

SIR H. WOTTON

85

TO THE LADY MARGARET LEY

DAUGHTER to that good Earl, once President
Of England's Council and her Treasury,
Who lived in both, unstain'd with gold or fee,
And left them both, more in himself content.

Till the sad breaking of that Parliament
Broke him, as that dishonest victory
At Chaeronea, fatal to liberty,
Kill'd with report that old man eloquent;—

Though later born than to have known the days
Wherein your father flourish'd, yet by you,
Madam, methinks I see him living yet;

So well your words his noble virtues praise,
That all both judge you to relate them true,
And to possess them, honour'd Margaret.

J. MILTON

86

THE LOVELINESS OF LOVE

It is not Beauty I demand,
A crystal brow, the moon's despair,
Nor the snow's daughter, a white hand,
Nor mermaid's yellow pride of hair:

Tell me not of your starry eyes,
Your lips that seem on roses fed,
Your breasts, where Cupid tumbling lies
Nor sleeps for kissing of his bed:—

A bloomy pair of vermeil cheeks
Like Hebe's in her ruddiest hours,
A breath that softer music speaks
Than summer winds a-wooing flowers.

These are but gauds: nay what are lips?
Coral beneath the ocean-stream,
Whose brink when your adventurer slips
Full oft he perisheth on them.

And what are cheeks, but ensigns oft
That wave hot youth to fields of blood?
Did Helen's breast, though ne'er so soft,
Do Greece or Illium any good?

Eyes can with baleful ardour burn;
Poison can breath, that erst perfumed;
There's many a white hand holds an urn
With lovers' hearts to dust consumed.

For crystal brows there's nought within;
They are but empty cells for pride;
He who the Syren's hair would win
Is mostly strangled in the tide.

Give me, instead of Beauty's bust,
A tender heart, a loyal mind
Which with temptation I would trust,
Yet never link'd with error find,—

One in whose gentle bosom I
Could pour my secret heart of woes,
Like the care-burthen'd honey-fly
That hides his murmurs in the rose,—

My earthly Comforter! whose love
So indefeasible might be
That, when my spirit wonn'd above,
Hers could not stay, for sympathy.

G. DARLEY

87

THE TRUE BEAUTY

HE that loves a rosy cheek
    Or a coral lip admires,
Or from starlike eyes doth seek
    Fuel to maintain his fires;
As old Time makes these decay,
So his flames must waste away.

But a smooth and steadfast mind,
    Gentle thoughts, and calm desires,
Hearts with equal love combined,
    Kindle never-dying fires:—
Where these are not, I despise
Lovely cheeks or lips or eyes.

T. CAREW

88

TO DIANEME

SWEET, be not proud of those two eyes
Which starlike sparkle in their skies;
Nor be you proud, that you can see
All hearts your captives; yours yet free:
Be you not proud of that rich hair
Which wantons with the lovesick air;
Whenas that ruby which you wear,
Sunk from the tip of your soft ear,
Will last to be a precious stone
When all your world of beauty's gone.

R. HERRICK

89

Go, lovely Rose!
Tell her, that wastes her time and me,
　　That now she knows,
When I resemble her to thee,
How sweet and fair she seems to be.

Tell her that's young
And shuns to have her graces spied,
　　That hadst thou sprung
In deserts, where no men abide,
Thou must have uncommended died.

Small is the worth
Of beauty from the light retired;
　　Bid her come forth,
Suffer herself to be desired,
And not blush so to be admired.

Then die! that she
The common fate of all things rare
　　May read in thee:
How small a part of time they share
That are so wondrous sweet and fair!

E. WALLER

76

90

TO CELIA

DRINK to me only with thine eyes,
    And I will pledge with mine;
Or leave a kiss but in the cup
    And I'll not look for wine.
The thirst that from the soul doth rise
    Doth ask a drink divine;
But might I of Jove's nectar sup,
    I would not change for thine.

I sent thee late a rosy wreath,
    Not so much honouring thee
As giving it a hope that there
    It could not wither'd be;
But thou thereon didst only breathe
    And sent'st it back to me;
Since when it grows, and smells, I swear,
    Not of itself but thee!

B. JONSON

91

CHERRY-RIPE

THERE is a garden in her face
    Where roses and white lilies blow;
A heavenly paradise is that place,
    Wherein all pleasant fruits do grow;
There cherries grow that none may buy,
Till Cherry-Ripe themselves do cry.

Those cherries fairly do enclose
    Of orient pearl a double row,
Which when her lovely laughter shows,
    They look like rose-buds fill'd with snow:
Yet them no peer nor prince may buy,
Till Cherry-Ripe themselves do cry.

Her eyes like angels watch them still;
   Her brows like bended bows do stand,
Threat'ning with piercing frowns to kill
   All that approach with eye or hand
These sacred cherries to come nigh,
—Till Cherry-Ripe themselves do cry!

92

THE POETRY OF DRESS

I

A SWEET disorder in the dress
Kindles in clothes a wantonness:—
A lawn about the shoulders thrown
Into a fine distractión,—
An erring lace, which here and there
Enthrals the crimson stomacher,—
A cuff neglectful, and thereby
Ribbands to flow confusedly,—
A winning wave, deserving note,
In the tempestuous petticoat,—
A careless shoe-string, in whose tie
I see a wild civility,—
Do more bewitch me, than when art
Is too precise in every part.

R. HERRICK

93

II

WHENAS in silks my Julia goes
Then, then (methinks) how sweetly flows
That liquefaction of her clothes.

Next, when I cast mine eyes and see
That brave vibration each way free;
O how that glittering taketh me!

R. HERRICK

94

III

MY Love in her attire doth shew her wit,
    It doth so well become her:
For every season she hath dressings fit,
    For Winter, Spring, and Summer.
    No beauty she doth miss
    When all her robes are on:
    But Beauty's self she is
    When all her robes are gone.

ANON.

95

ON A GIRDLE

THAT which her slender waist confined
Shall now my joyful temples bind:
No monarch but would give his crown
His arms might do what this has done.

It was my Heaven's extremest sphere,
The pale which held that lovely deer:
My joy, my grief, my hope, my love
Did all within this circle move.

A narrow compass! and yet there
Dwelt all that's good, and all that's fair:
Give me but what this ribband bound,
Take all the rest the Sun goes round.

E. WALLER

96

TO ANTHEA WHO MAY COMMAND HIM ANYTHING

BID me to live, and I will live,
    Thy Protestant to be:
Or bid me love, and I will give
    A loving heart to thee.

A heart as soft, a heart as kind,
    A heart as sound and free
As in the whole world thou canst find,
    That heart I'll give to thee.

Bid that heart stay, and it will stay,
    To honour thy decree:
Or bid it languish quite away,
    And't shall do so for thee.

Bid me to weep, and I will weep
    While I have eyes to see:
And having none, yet I will keep
    A heart to weep for thee.

Bid me despair, and I'll despair,
    Under that cypress tree:
Or bid me die, and I will dare
    E'en Death, to die for thee.

Thou art my life, my love, my heart,
    The very eyes of me,
And hast command of every part,
    To live and die for thee.

R. HERRICK

97

Love not me for comely grace,
For my pleasing eye or face,
Nor for any outward part,
No, nor for my constant heart,—
    For those may fail, or turn to ill,
    So thou and I shall sever:
Keep therefore a true woman's eye,
And love me still, but know not why—
    So hast thou the same reason still
    To doat upon me ever!

ANON.

98

NOT, Celia, that I juster am
  Or better than the rest;
For I would change each hour, like them,
  Were not my heart at rest.

But I am tied to very thee
  By every thought I have;
Thy face I only care to see,
  Thy heart I only crave.

All that in woman is adored
  In thy dear self I find—
For the whole sex can but afford
  The handsome and the kind.

Why then should I seek further store,
  And still make love anew?
When change itself can give no more,
  'Tis easy to be true.

SIR C. SEDLEY

99

TO ALTHEA FROM PRISON

WHEN Love with unconfinéd wings
  Hovers within my gates,
And my divine Althea brings
  To whisper at the grates;
When I lie tangled in her hair
  And fetter'd to her eye,
The gods that wanton in the air
  Know no such liberty.

When flowing cups run swiftly round
  With no allaying Thames,
Our careless heads with roses crown'd,
  Our hearts with loyal flames;

When thirsty grief in wine we steep,
  When healths and draughts go free—
Fishes that tipple in the deep
  Know no such liberty.

When, linnet-like confinéd, I
  With shriller throat shall sing
The sweetness, mercy, majesty
  And glories of my King;
When I shall voice aloud how good
  He is, how great should be,
Enlargéd winds, that curl the flood,
  Know no such liberty.

Stone walls do not a prison make,
  Nor iron bars a cage;
Minds innocent and quiet take
  That for an hermitage:
If I have freedom in my love
  And in my soul am free,
Angels alone, that soar above,
  Enjoy such liberty.

COLONEL LOVELACE

100

TO LUCASTA, ON GOING BEYOND THE SEAS

If to be absent were to be
  Away from thee;
  Or that when I am gone
  You or I were alone;
Then, my Lucasta, might I crave
Pity from blustering wind, or swallowing wave.

Though seas and land betwixt us both,
    Our faith and troth,
      Like separated souls,
    All time and space controls:
Above the highest sphere we meet
Unseen, unknown, and greet as Angels greet.

So then we do anticipate
    Our after-fate,
      And are alive i' the skies,
    If thus our lips and eyes
Can speak like spirits unconfined
In Heaven, their earthy bodies left behind.
                 COLONEL LOVELACE

101

ENCOURAGEMENTS TO A LOVER

WHY so pale and wan, fond lover?
    Prythee, why so pale?
Will, if looking well can't move her,
      Looking ill prevail?
    Prythee, why so pale?

Why so dull and mute, young sinner?
    Prythee, why so mute?
Will, when speaking well can't win her,
      Saying nothing do't?
    Prythee, why so mute?

Quit, quit, for shame! this will not move,
    This cannot take her;
If of herself she will not love,
      Nothing can make her:
    The D—l take her!
                 SIR J. SUCKLING

102

A SUPPLICATION

AWAKE, awake, my Lyre!
And tell thy silent master's humble tale
     In sounds that may prevail;
   Sounds that gentle thoughts inspire:
     Though so exalted she
     And I so lowly be
Tell her, such different notes make all thy harmony.

     Hark! how the strings awake:
And, though the moving hand approach not near,
     Themselves with awful fear
   A kind of numerous trembling make.
     Now all thy forces try.
     Now all thy charms apply;
Revenge upon her ear the conquests of her eye.

     Weak Lyre! thy virtue sure
Is useless here, since thou art only found
     To cure, but not to wound,
   And she to wound, but not to cure,
     Too weak too wilt thou prove
     My passion to remove;
Physic to other ills, thou'rt nourishment to love.

     Sleep, sleep again, my Lyre!
For thou canst never tell my humble tale
     In sounds that will prevail,
   Nor gentle thoughts in her inspire;
     All thy vain mirth lay by,
     Bid thy strings silent lie,
Sleep, sleep again, my Lyre, and let thy master die.
                                      A. COWLEY

84

THE MANLY HEART

SHALL I, wasting in despair,
Die because a woman's fair?
Or my cheeks make pale with care
'Cause another's rosy are?
Be she fairer than the day
Or the flowery meads in May—
  If she be not so to me
  What care I how fair she be?

Shall my foolish heart be pined
'Cause I see a woman kind;
Or a well disposéd nature
Joinéd with a lovely feature?
Be she meeker, kinder, than
Turtle-dove or pelican,
  If she be not so to me
  What care I how kind she be?

Shall a woman's virtues move
Me to perish for her love?
Or her merit's value known
Make me quite forget mine own?
Be she with that goodness blest
Which may gain her name of Best;
  If she seem not such to me,
  What care I how good she be?

'Cause her fortune seems too high,
Shall I play the fool and die?
Those that bear a noble mind
Where they want of riches find,
Think what with them they would do
Who without them dare to woo;
  And unless that mind I see,
  What care I though great she be?

Great or good, or kind or fair,
I will ne'er the more despair;
If she love me, this believe,
I will die ere she shall grieve;
If she slight me when I woo,
I can scorn and let her go;
  For if she be not for me,
  What care I for whom she be?
G. WITHER

104

MELANCHOLY

HENCE, all you vain delights,
As short as are the nights
Wherein you spend your folly:
There's nought in this life sweet
If man were wise to see 't,
But our melancholy,
O sweetest Melancholy!
Welcome, folded arms, and fixéd eyes,
A sigh that piercing mortifies,
A look that's fasten'd to the ground,
A tongue chain'd up without a sound!
Fountain heads and pathless groves,
Places which pale passion loves!
Moonlight walks, when all the fowls
Are warmly housed save bats and owls!
A midnight bell, a parting groan!
These are the sounds we feed upon;
Then stretch our bones in a still gloomy valley;
Nothing's so dainty sweet as lovely melancholy.
J. FLETCHER

105

TO A LOCK OF HAIR

THY hue, dear pledge, is pure and bright
As in that well-remember'd night
When first thy mystic braid was wove,
And first my Agnes whisper'd love.

Since then how often hast thou prest
The torrid zone of this wild breast,
Whose wrath and hate have sworn to dwell
With the first sin that peopled hell;
A breast whose blood's a troubled ocean,
Each throb the earthquake's wild commotion!
O if such clime thou canst endure
Yet keep thy hue unstain'd and pure,
What conquest o'er each erring thought
Of that fierce realm had Agnes wrought!
I had not wander'd far and wide
With such an angel for my guide;
Nor heaven nor earth could then reprove me
If she had lived, and lived to love me.

Not then this world's wild joys had been
To me one savage hunting scene,
My sole delight the headlong race
And frantic hurry of the chase;
To start, pursue, and bring to bay,
Rush in, drag down, and rend my prey,
Then—from the carcass turn away!
Mine ireful mood had sweetness tamed,
And soothed each wound which pride inflamed:—
Yes, God and man might now approve me
If thou hadst lived, and lived to love me!

SIR W. SCOTT

106

THE FORSAKEN BRIDE

O WALY waly up the bank,
    And waly waly down the brae,
And waly waly yon burn-side
    Where I and my Love wont to gae!
I leant my back unto an aik,
    I thought it was a trusty tree;
But first it bow'd, and syne it brak,
    Sae my true Love did lichtly me.

O waly waly, but love be bonny
    A little time while it is new;
But when 'tis auld, it waxeth cauld
    And fades awa' like morning dew.
O wherefore should I busk my head?
    Or wherefore should I kame my hair?
For my true Love has me forsook,
    And says he'll never loe me mair.

Now Arthur-seat sall be my bed;
    The sheets shall ne'er be prest by me:
Saint Anton's well sall be my drink,
    Since my true Love has forsaken me.
Marti'mas wind, when wilt thou blaw
    And shake the green leaves aff the tree?
O gentle Death, when wilt thou come?
    For of my life I am wearíe.

'Tis not the frost, that freezes fell,
    Nor blawing snaw's inclemencie;
'Tis not sic cauld that makes me cry,
    But my Love's heart grown cauld to me.
When we came in by Glasgow town
    We were a comely sight to see;
My Love was clad in the black velvét,
    And I myself in cramasie.

But had I wist, before I kist,
    That love had been sae ill to win;
I had lockt my heart in a case of gowd
    And pinn'd it with a siller pin.
And, O! if my young babe were born,
    And set upon the nurse's knee.
And I mysell were dead and gane,
    And the green grass growing over me!
                ANON.

107

FAIR HELEN

I WISH I were where Helen lies;
Night and day on me she cries;
O that I were where Helen lies
    On fair Kirconnell lea!

Curst be the heart that thought the thought,
And curst the hand that fired the shot,
When in my arms burd Helen dropt,
    And died to succour me!

O think na but my heart was sair
When my Love dropt down and spak nae mair!
I laid her down wi' meikle care
    On fair Kirconnell lea.

As I went down the water-side,
None but my foe to be my guide,
None but my foe to be my guide,
    On fair Kirconnell lea;

I lighted down my sword to draw,
I hackéd him in pieces sma',
I hackéd him in pieces sma',
    For her sake that died for me.

O Helen fair, beyond compare!
I'll make a garland of thy hair
Shall bind my heart for evermair
    Until the day I die.

O that I were where Helen lies!
Night and day on me she cries;
Out of my bed she bids me rise,
    Says, 'Haste and come to me!'

O Helen fair! O Helen chaste!
If I were with thee, I were blest,
Where thou lies low and takes thy rest
    On fair Kirconnell lea.

I wish my grave were growing green,
A winding-sheet drawn ower my een,
And I in Helen's arms lying,
    On fair Kirconnell lea.

I wish I were where Helen lies;
Night and day on me she cries;
And I am weary of the skies,
    Since my Love died for me.

                    ANON.

108

THE TWA CORBIES

As I was walking all alane
I heard twa corbies making a mane;
The tane unto the t'other say,
'Where sall we gang and dine today?'

'—In behint yon auld fail dyke,
I wot there lies a new-slain Knight;
And naebody kens that he lies there,
But his hawk, his hound, and lady fair.

'His hound is to the hunting gane,
His hawk to fetch the wild-fowl hame,
His lady's ta'en another mate,
So we may mak our dinner sweet.

'Ye'll sit on his white hause-bane,
And I'll pick out his bonny blue een:
Wi' ae lock o' his gowden hair
We'll theek our nest when it grows bare.

'Mony a one for him makes mane,
But nane sall ken where he is gane;
O'er his white banes, when they are bare,
The wind sall blaw for evermair.'

                    ANON.

109

TO BLOSSOMS

FAIR pledges of a fruitful tree,
　　　Why do ye fall so fast?
　　　Your date is not so past,
But you may stay yet here awhile
　　　To blush and gently smile,
　　　　　And go at last.

What, were ye born to be
　　　An hour or half's delight,
　　　And so to bid good-night?
'Twas pity Nature brought ye forth
　　　Merely to show your worth,
　　　　　And lose you quite.

But you are lovely leaves, where we
　　　May read how soon things have
　　　Their end, though ne'er so brave:
And after they have shown their pride
　　　Like you, awhile, they glide
　　　　　Into the grave.

　　　　　　　　　　R. HERRICK

110

TO DAFFODILS

FAIR Daffodils, we weep to see
　　　You haste away so soon:
As yet the early-rising Sun
　　　Has not attain'd his noon.
　　　　Stay, stay,
　　　Until the hasting day
　　　　Has run
　　　But to the even-song;
And, having pray'd together, we
　　　Will go with you along.

We have short time to stay, as you,
    We have as short a Spring;
As quick a growth to meet decay
    As you, or any thing.
      We die,
    As your hours do, and dry
      Away
    Like to the Summer's rain;
Or as the pearls of morning's dew
    Ne'er to be found again.

R. HERRICK

111

THOUGHTS IN A GARDEN

How vainly men themselves amaze
To win the palm, the oak, or bays,
And their incessant labours see
Crown'd from some single herb or tree,
Whose short and narrow-vergéd shade
Does prudently their toils upbraid;
While all the flowers and trees do close
To weave the garlands of Repose.

Fair Quiet, have I found thee here,
And Innocence thy sister dear?
Mistaken long, I sought you then
In busy companies of men:
Your sacred plants, if here below,
Only among the plants will grow:
Society is all but rude
To this delicious solitude.

No white nor red was ever seen
So amorous as this lovely green.
Fond lovers, cruel as their flame,
Cut in these trees their mistress' name:
Little, alas, they know or heed
How far these beauties her exceed!
Fair trees! where'er your barks I wound,
No name shall but your own be found.

When we have run our passion's heat
Love hither makes his best retreat:
The gods, who mortal beauty chase,
Still in a tree did end their race:
Apollo hunted Daphne so
Only that she might laurel grow:
And Pan did after Syrinx speed
Not as a nymph, but for a reed.

What wondrous life is this I lead!
Ripe apples drop about my head;
The luscious clusters of the vine
Upon my mouth do crush their wine;
The nectarine and curious peach
Into my hands themselves do reach;
Stumbling on melons, as I pass,
Ensnared with flowers, I fall on grass.

Meanwhile the mind from pleasure less
Withdraws into its happiness;
The mind, that ocean where each kind
Does straight its own resemblance find;
Yet it creates, transcending these,
Far other worlds, and other seas;
Annihilating all that's made
To a green thought in a green shade.

Here at the fountain's sliding foot
Or at some fruit-tree's mossy root,
Casting the body's vest aside
My soul into the boughs does glide;
There, like a bird, it sits and sings,
Then whets and claps its silver wings,
And, till prepared for longer flight,
Waves in its plumes the various light.

Such was that happy Garden-state
While man there walk'd without a mate:
After a place so pure and sweet,
What other help could yet be meet!
But 'twas beyond a mortal's share
To wander solitary there:

Two paradises 'twere in one,
To live in Paradise alone.

How well the skilful gardener drew
Of flowers and herbs this dial new!
Where, from above, the milder sun
Does through a fragrant zodiac run:
And, as it works, th' industrious bee
Computes its time as well as we.
How could such sweet and wholesome hours
Be reckon'd, but with herbs and flowers!

A. MARVELL

112

L'ALLÉGRO

HENCE, loathèd Melancholy,
  Of Cerberus and blackest Midnight born
  In Stygian cave forlorn
  'Mongst horrid shapes, and shrieks, and sights unholy!
Find out some uncouth cell
  Where brooding Darkness spreads his jealous wings
And the night-raven sings;
  There under ebon shades, and low-brow'd rocks
As ragged as thy locks,
  In dark Cimmerian desert ever dwell.

  But come, thou Goddess fair and free,
  In heaven yclep'd Euphrosyne,
  And by men, heart-easing Mirth,
  Whom lovely Venus at a birth
  With two sister Graces more
  To ivy-crownèd Bacchus bore
  Or whether (as some sager sing)
  The frolic wind that breathes the spring
  Zephyr, with Aurora playing,
  As he met her once a-Maying—
  There on beds of violets blue
  And fresh-blown roses wash'd in dew
  Fill'd her with thee, a daughter fair,
  So buxom, blithe, and debonair.

94

Haste thee, Nymph, and bring with thee
Jest, and youthful jollity,
Quips, and cranks, and wanton wiles,
Nods, and becks, and wreathéd smiles
Such as hang on Hebe's cheek,
And love to live in dimple sleek;
Sport that wrinkled Care derides,
And Laughter holding both his sides:—
Come, and trip it as you go
On the light fantastic toe;
And in thy right hand lead with thee
The mountain nymph, sweet Liberty;
And if I give thee honour due
Mirth, admit me of thy crew,
To live with her, and live with thee
In unreprovéd pleasures free;
To hear the lark begin his flight
And singing startle the dull night
From his watch-tower in the skies,
Till the dappled dawn doth rise;
Then to come, in spite of sorrow,
And at my window bid good-morrow
Through the sweetbriar, or the vine,
Or the twisted eglantine:
While the cock with lively din
Scatters the rear of darkness thin,
And to the stack, or the barn-door,
Stoutly struts his dames before:
Oft listening how the hounds and horn
Cheerly rouse the slumbering morn,
From the side of some hoar hill,
Through the high wood echoing shrill.
Sometime walking, not unseen,
By hedge-row elms, on hillocks green,
Right against the eastern gate
Where the great Sun begins his state
Robed in flames and amber light,
The clouds in thousand liveries dight,
While the ploughman, near at hand,
Whistles o'er the furrow'd land,

And the milkmaid singeth blithe,
And the mower whets his scythe,
And every shepherd tells his tale
Under the hawthorn in the dale.

Straight mine eye hath caught new pleasures
Whilst the landscape round it measures;
Russet lawns, and fallows grey,
Where the nibbling flocks do stray;
Mountains, on whose barren breast
The labouring clouds do often rest;
Meadows trim with daisies pied,
Shallow brooks and rivers wide;
Towers and battlements it sees
Bosom'd high in tufted trees,
Where perhaps some Beauty lies,
The Cynosure of neighbouring eyes.

Hard by, a cottage chimney smokes
From betwixt two aged oaks,
Where Corydon and Thyrsis, met,
Are at their savoury dinner set
Of herbs, and other country messes
Which the neat-handed Phillis dresses;
And then in haste her bower she leaves
With Thestylis to bind the sheaves;
Or, if the earlier season lead,
To the tann'd haycock in the mead.

Sometimes with secure delight
The upland hamlets will invite,
When the merry bells ring round,
And the jocund rebecks sound
To many a youth and many a maid,
Dancing in the chequer'd shade;
And young and old come forth to play
On a sun-shine holy-day,
Till the live-long day-light fail:
Then to the spicy nut-brown ale,
With stories told of many a feat,
How Faery Mab the junkets eat;
She was pinch'd, and pull'd, she said;
And he, by Friar's lantern led;

Tells how the drudging Goblin sweat
To earn his cream-bowl duly set,
When in one night, ere glimpse of morn,
His shadowy flail hath thresh'd the corn
That ten day-labourers could not end;
Then lies him down the lubber fiend,
And, stretch'd out all the chimney's length,
Basks at the fire his hairy strength;
And crop-full out of doors he flings,
Ere the first cock his matin rings.
   Thus done the tales, to bed they creep,
By whispering winds soon lull'd asleep.
   Tower'd cities please us then
And the busy hum of men,
Where throngs of knights and barons bold,
In weeds of peace high triumphs hold,
With store of ladies, whose bright eyes
Rain influence, and judge the prize
Of wit or arms, while both contend
To win her grace, whom all commend.
There let Hymen oft appear
In saffron robe, with taper clear,
And pomp, and feast, and revelry,
With mask, and antique pageantry;
Such sights as youthful poets dream
On summer eves by haunted stream.
Then to the well-trod stage anon,
If Jonson's learned sock be on,
Or sweetest Shakespeare, Fancy's child,
Warble his native wood-notes wild.
   And ever against eating cares
Lap me in soft Lydian airs
Married to immortal verse,
Such as the meeting soul may pierce
In notes, with many a winding bout
Of linkéd sweetness long drawn out,
With wanton heed and giddy cunning,
The melting voice through mazes running,
Untwisting all the chains that tie
The hidden soul of harmony;

That Orpheus' self may heave his head
From golden slumber, on a bed
Of heap'd Elysian flowers, and hear
Such strains as would have won the ear
Of Pluto, to have quite set free
His half-regain'd Eurydice.

These delights if thou canst give,
Mirth, with thee I mean to live.

J. MILTON

113

IL PENSEROSO

HENCE, vain deluding Joys,
   The brood of Folly without father bred!
How little you bestead
   Or fill the fixéd mind with all your toys!
Dwell in some idle brain,
   And fancies fond with gaudy shapes possess
As thick and numberless
   As the gay motes that people the sunbeams,
Or likest hovering dreams,
   The fickle pensioners of Morpheus' train.

   But hail, thou goddess sage and holy,
   Hail, divinest Melancholy!
Whose saintly visage is too bright
To hit the sense of human sight,
And therefore to our weaker view
O'erlaid with black, staid Wisdom's hue;
Black, but such as in esteem
Prince Memnon's sister might beseem,
Or that starr'd Ethiop queen that strove
To set her beauty's praise above
The sea-nymphs, and their powers offended:
Yet thou art higher far descended:

Thee bright-hair'd Vesta, long of yore,
To solitary Saturn bore;
His daughter she; in Saturn's reign
Such mixture was not held a stain:
Oft in glimmering bowers and glades
He met her, and in secret shades
Of woody Ida's inmost grove,
While yet there was no fear of Jove.

Come, pensive nun, devout and pure,
Sober, steadfast, and demure,
All in a robe of darkest grain
Flowing with majestic train,
And sable stole of cypres lawn
Over thy decent shoulders drawn:
Come, but keep thy wonted state,
With even step, and musing gait,
And looks commercing with the skies,
Thy rapt soul sitting in thine eyes:
There, held in holy passion still,
Forget thyself to marble, till
With a sad leaden downward cast
Thou fix them on the earth as fast:
And join with thee calm Peace, and Quiet,
Spare Fast, that oft with gods doth diet,
And hears the Muses in a ring
Ay round about Jove's altar sing;
And add to these retired Leisure
That in trim gardens takes his pleasure:—
But first, and chiefest, with thee bring
Him that yon soars on golden wing
Guiding the fiery-wheeléd throne,
The cherub Contemplatión;
And the mute Silence hist along,
'Less Philomel will deign a song
In her sweetest saddest plight,
Smoothing the rugged brow of Night,
While Cynthia checks her dragon yoke
Gently o'er the accustom'd oak.
—Sweet bird, that shunn'st the noise of folly
Most musical, most melancholy!

Thee, chauntress, oft, the woods among
I woo, to hear thy even-song;
And missing thee, I walk unseen
On the dry smooth-shaven green,
To behold the wandering Moon
Riding near her highest noon,
Like one that had been led astray
Through the heaven's wide pathless way,
And oft, as if her head she bow'd,
Stooping through a fleecy cloud.

　　Oft, on a plat of rising ground
I hear the far-off curfeu sound
Over some wide-water'd shore,
Swinging slow with sullen roar:
Or, if the air will not permit,
Some still removéd place will fit,
Where glowing embers through the room
Teach light to counterfeit a gloom;
Far from all resort of mirth,
Save the cricket on the hearth,
Or the bellman's drowsy charm
To bless the doors from nightly harm.

　　Or let my lamp at midnight hour
Be seen in some high lonely tower,
Where I may oft out-watch the Bear
With thrice-great Hermes, or unsphere
The spirit of Plato, to unfold
What worlds or what vast regions hold
The immortal mind, that hath forsook
Her mansion in this fleshly nook:
And of those demons that are found
In fire, air, flood, or under ground,
Whose power hath a true consent
With planet, or with element.
Sometime let gorgeous Tragedy
In scepter'd pall come sweeping by,
Presenting Thebes, or Pelops' line,
Or the tale of Troy divine;
Or what (though rare) of later age
Ennobled hath the buskin'd stage.

But, O sad Virgin, that thy power
Might raise Musaeus from his bower,
Or bid the soul of Orpheus sing
Such notes as, warbled to the string,
Drew iron tears down Pluto's cheek
And made Hell grant what Love did seek!
Or call up him that left half-told
The story of Cambuscan bold,
Of Camball, and of Algarsife,
And who had Canacé to wife,
That own'd the virtuous ring and glass,
And of the wondrous horse of brass
On which the Tartar king did ride:
And if aught else great bards beside
In sage and solemn tunes have sung
Of turneys, and of trophies hung,
Of forests and enchantments drear,
Where more is meant than meets the ear.
    Thus, Night, oft see me in thy pale career,
Till civil-suited Morn appear,
Not trick'd and frounced as she was wont
With the Attic Boy to hunt,
But kercheft in a comely cloud
While rocking winds are piping loud,
Or usher'd with a shower still,
When the gust hath blown his fill,
Ending on the rustling leaves
With minute drops from off the eaves.
And when the sun begins to fling
His flaring beams, me, goddess, bring
To archéd walks of twilight groves,
And shadows brown, that Sylvan loves,
Of pine, or monumental oak,
Where the rude axe, with heavéd stroke,
Was never heard the nymphs to daunt
Or fright them from their hallow'd haunt.
There in close covert by some brook
Where no profaner eye may look,
Hide me from day's garish eye,
While the bee with honey'd thigh

That at her flowery work doth sing,
And the waters murmuring,
With such consort as they keep
Entice the dewy-feather'd Sleep;
And let some strange mysterious dream
Wave at his wings in airy stream
Of lively portraiture display'd,
Softly on my eyelids laid:
And, as I wake, sweet music breathe
Above, about, or underneath,
Sent by some Spirit to mortals good,
Or the unseen Genius of the wood.
　　But let my due feet never fail
To walk the studious cloister's pale,
And love the high-embowéd roof,
With antique pillars massy proof,
And storied windows richly dight
Casting a dim religious light:
There let the pealing organ blow
To the full-voiced quire below
In service high and anthems clear,
As may with sweetness, through mine ear,
Dissolve me into ecstasies,
And bring all Heaven before mine eyes.
　　And may at last my weary age
Find out the peaceful hermitage,
The hairy gown and mossy cell
Where I may sit and rightly spell
Of every star that heaven doth show,
And every herb that sips the dew:
Till old experience do attain
To something like prophetic strain.

　　These pleasures, Melancholy, give,
And I with thee will choose to live.
J. MILTON

114

SONG OF THE EMIGRANTS
IN BERMUDA

WHERE the remote Bermudas ride
In the ocean's bosom unespied,
From a small boat that row'd along
The listening winds received this song.
    'What should we do but sing His praise
That led us through the watery maze
Where He the huge sea-monsters wracks,
That lift the deep upon their backs,
Unto an isle so long unknown,
And yet far kinder than our own?
He lands us on a grassy stage,
Safe from the storms, and prelate's rage:
He gave us this eternal spring
Which here enamels everything,
And sends the fowls to us in care
On daily visits through the air.
He hangs in shades the orange bright
Like golden lamps in a green night,
And does in the pomegranates close
Jewels more rich than Ormus shows:
He makes the figs our mouths to meet,
And throws the melons at our feet;
But apples plants of such a price,
No tree could ever bear them twice.
With cedars chosen by His hand
From Lebanon He stores the land;
And makes the hollow seas that roar
Proclaim the ambergris on shore.
He cast (of which we rather boast)
The Gospel's pearl upon our coast;
And in these rocks for us did frame
A temple where to sound His name.
O let our voice His praise exalt
Till it arrive at Heaven's vault,
Which then perhaps rebounding may
Echo beyond the Mexique bay!'

—Thus sung they in the English boat
A holy and a cheerful note:
And all the way, to guide their chime,
With falling oars they kept the time.

A. MARVELL

115

AT A SOLEMN MUSIC

BLEST pair of Sirens, pledges of Heaven's joy,
Sphere-born harmonious Sisters, Voice and Verse!
Wed your divine sounds, and mixt power employ
Dead things with inbreathed sense able to pierce;
And to our high-raised phantasy present
That undisturbéd Song of pure concent
Ay sung before the sapphire-colour'd throne
　　　To Him that sits thereon,
With saintly shout and solemn jubilee;
Where the bright Seraphim in burning row
Their loud uplifted angel-trumpets blow;
And the Cherubic host in thousand quires
Touch their immortal harps of golden wires,
With those just Spirits that wear victorious palms,
　　　Hymns devout and holy psalms
　　　Singing everlastingly:
Thus we on earth, with undiscording voice
May rightly answer that melodious noise;
As once we did, till disproportion'd sin
Jarr'd against nature's chime, and with harsh din
Broke the fair music that all creatures made
To their great Lord, whose love their motion sway'd
In perfect diapason, whilst they stood
In first obedience, and their state of good.
　　O may we soon again renew that Song,
　　And keep in tune with Heaven, till God ere long
　　　To His celestial concert us unite,
To live with Him, and sing in endless morn of light!

J. MILTON

116

ALEXANDER'S FEAST; OR, THE POWER OF MUSIC

'TWAS at the royal feast for Persia won
    By Philip's warlike son—
    Aloft in awful state
    The godlike hero sate
    On his imperial throne;
    His valiant peers were placed around,
    Their brows with roses and with myrtles bound
    (So should desert in arms be crown'd);
    The lovely Thais by his side
    Sate like a blooming eastern bride
    In flower of youth and beauty's pride:—
    Happy, happy, happy pair!
    None but the brave
    None but the brave
    None but the brave deserves the fair!

  Timotheus placed on high
Amid the tuneful quire
With flying fingers touch'd the lyre:
The trembling notes ascend the sky
And heavenly joys inspire.
The song began from Jove
Who left his blissful seats above—
Such is the power of mighty love!
A dragon's fiery form belied the god;
Sublime on radiant spires he rode
When he to fair Olympia prest,
And while he sought her snowy breast,
Then round her slender waist he curl'd,
And stamp'd an image of himself, a sovereign of the world.
—The listening crowd admire the lofty sound!
A present deity! they shout around:
A present deity! the vaulted roofs rebound!

With ravish'd ears
The monarch hears,
Assumes the god;
Affects to nod
And seems to shake the spheres.

The praise of Bacchus then the sweet musician sung,
Of Bacchus ever fair and ever young:
The jolly god in triumph comes!
Sound the trumpets, beat the drums!
Flush'd with a purple grace
He shows his honest face:
Now give the hautboys breath; he comes, he comes!
Bacchus, ever fair and young,
Drinking joys did first ordain;
Bacchus' blessings are a treasure,
Drinking is the soldier's pleasure:
Rich the treasure,
Sweet the pleasure,
Sweet is pleasure after pain.

Soothed with the sound, the king grew vain;
Fought all his battles o'er again,
And thrice he routed all his foes, and thrice he slew the slain!
The master saw the madness rise,
His glowing cheeks, his ardent eyes;
And while he Heaven and Earth defied
Changed his hand and check'd his pride.
He chose a mournful Muse
Soft pity to infuse:
He sung Darius great and good,
By too severe a fate
Fallen, fallen, fallen, fallen,
Fallen from his high estate,
And weltering in his blood;
Deserted, at his utmost need,
By those his former bounty fed;
On the bare earth exposed he lies
With not a friend to close his eyes.
—With downcast looks the joyless victor sate,

Revolving in his alter'd soul
The various turns of Chance below;
And now and then a sigh he stole,
And tears began to flow.

The mighty master smiled to see
That love was in the next degree;
'Twas but a kindred sound to move,
For pity melts the mind to love.
Softly sweet, in Lydian measures
Soon he soothed his soul to pleasures.
War, he sung, is toil and trouble,
Honour but an empty bubble;
Never ending, still beginning,
Fighting still, and still destroying;
If the world be worth thy winning,
Think, O think, it worth enjoying:
Lovely Thais sits beside thee,
Take the good the gods provide thee!
—The many rend the skies with loud applause;
So Love was crown'd, but Music won the cause.
The prince, unable to conceal his pain,
Gazed on the fair
Who caused his care,
And sigh'd and look'd, sigh'd and look'd,
Sigh'd and look'd, and sigh'd again:
At length with love and wine at once opprest
The vanquish'd victor sunk upon her breast.

Now strike the golden lyre again:
A louder yet, and yet a louder strain
Break his bands of sleep asunder
And rouse him like a rattling peal of thunder.
Hark, hark! the horrid sound
Has raised up his head:
As awaked from the dead
And amazed he stares around.
Revenge, revenge, Timotheus cries,
See the Furies arise!
See the snakes that they rear
How they hiss in their hair,

And the sparkles that flash from their eyes!
Behold a ghastly band,
Each a torch in his hand!
Those are Grecian ghosts, that in battle were slain
And unburied remain
Inglorious on the plain:
Give the vengeance due
To the valiant crew!
Behold how they toss their torches on high
How they point to the Persian abodes
And glittering temples of their hostile gods.
—The princes applaud with a furious joy:
And the King seized a flambeau with zeal to destroy;
Thais led the way
To light him to his prey,
And like another Helen, fired another Troy!

—Thus, long ago,
Ere heaving bellows learn'd to blow
While organs yet were mute,
Timotheus, to his breathing flute
And sounding lyre
Could swell the soul to rage, or kindle soft desire.
At last divine Cecilia came,
Inventress of the vocal frame;
The sweet enthusiast from her sacred store
Enlarged the former narrow bounds,
And added length to solemn sounds,
With Nature's mother-wit, and arts unknown before.
—Let old Timotheus yield the prize
Or both divide the crown;
He raised a mortal to the skies;
She drew an angel down!

J. DRYDEN

117

ODE ON THE PLEASURE ARISING FROM VICISSITUDE

Now the golden Morn aloft
   Waves her dew-bespangled wing,
With vermeil cheek and whisper soft
   She wooes the tardy Spring:
Till April starts, and calls around
The sleeping fragrance from the ground,
And lightly o'er the living scene
Scatters his freshest, tenderest green.

New-born flocks in rustic dance,
   Frisking ply their feeble feet;
Forgetful of their wintry trance
   The birds his presence greet:
But chief, the skylark warbles high
His trembling thrilling ecstasy;
And lessening from the dazzled sight,
Melts into air and liquid light.

Yesterday the sullen year
   Saw the snowy whirlwind fly;
Mute was the music of the air,
   The herd stood drooping by:
Their raptures now that wildly flow
No yesterday nor morrow know;
'Tis Man alone that joy descries
With forward and reverted eyes.

Smiles on past Misfortune's brow
   Soft Reflection's hand can trace,
And o'er the cheek of Sorrow throw
   A melancholy grace;
While Hope prolongs our happier hour,
Or deepest shades, that dimly lour
And blacken round our weary way,
Gilds with a gleam of distant day.

Still, where rosy Pleasure leads,
   See a kindred Grief pursue;
Behind the steps that Misery treads
   Approaching Comfort view:
The hues of bliss more brightly glow
Chastised by sabler tints of woe,
And blended form, with artful strife,
The strength and harmony of life.

See the wretch that long has tost
   On the thorny bed of pain,
At length repair his vigour lost
   And breathe and walk again:
The meanest floweret of the vale,
The simplest note that swells the gale,
The common sun, the air, the skies,
To him are opening Paradise.

T. GRAY

118

THE QUIET LIFE

HAPPY the man, whose wish and care
A few paternal acres bound,
Content to breathe his native air
       In his own ground.

Whose herds with milk, whose fields with bread,
Whose flocks supply him with attire;
Whose trees in summer yield him shade,
       In winter, fire.

Blest, who can unconcern'dly find
Hours, days, and years, slide soft away
In health of body, peace of mind,
        Quiet by day,

Sound sleep by night; study and ease
Together mix'd; sweet recreation,
And innocence, which most does please
        With meditation.

Thus let me live, unseen, unknown;
Thus unlamented let me die;
Steal from the world, and not a stone
        Tell where I lie.

A. POPE

119

THE BLIND BOY

O SAY what is that thing call'd Light,
   Which I must ne'er enjoy;
What are the blessings of the sight,
   O tell your poor blind boy!

You talk of wondrous things you see,
   You say the sun shines bright;
I feel him warm, but how can he
   Or make it day or night?

My day or night myself I make
   Whene'er I sleep or play;
And could I ever keep awake
   With me 'twere always day.

With heavy sighs I often hear
   You mourn my hapless woe;
But sure with patience I can bear
   A loss I ne'er can know.

Then let not what I cannot have
  My cheer of mind destroy:
Whilst thus I sing, I am a king,
  Although a poor blind boy.
C. CIBBER

120

ON A FAVOURITE CAT, DROWNED IN A TUB OF GOLD FISHES

'Twas on a lofty vase's side
Where China's gayest art had dyed
  The azure flowers that blow,
Demurest of the tabby kind
The pensive Selima, reclined,
  Gazed on the lake below.

Her conscious tail her joy declared:
The fair round face, the snowy beard,
  The velvet of her paws,
Her coat that with the tortoise vies,
Her ears of jet, and emerald eyes—
  She saw, and purr'd applause.

Still had she gazed, but 'midst the tide
Two angel forms were seen to glide,
  The Genii of the stream:
Their scaly armour's Tyrian hue
Through richest purple, to the view
  Betray'd a golden gleam.

The hapless Nymph with wonder saw:
A whisker first, and then a claw
  With many an ardent wish
She stretch'd, in vain, to reach the prize—
What female heart can gold despise?
  What Cat's averse to Fish?

Presumptuous maid! with looks intent
Again she stretch'd, again she bent,
Nor knew the gulf between—
Malignant Fate sat by and smiled—
The slippery verge her feet beguiled;
She tumbled headlong in!

Eight times emerging from the flood
She mew'd to every watery God
Some speedy aid to send:—
No Dolphin came, no Nereid stirr'd,
Nor cruel Tom nor Susan heard—
A favourite has no friend!

From hence, ye Beauties! undeceived
Know one false step is ne'er retrieved,
And be with caution bold:
Not all that tempts your wandering eyes
And heedless hearts, is lawful prize,
Not all that glisters, gold!

T. GRAY

121

TO CHARLOTTE PULTENEY

TIMELY blossom, Infant fair,
Fondling of a happy pair,
Every morn and every night
Their solicitous delight,
Sleeping, waking, still at ease,
Pleasing, without skill to please;
Little gossip, blithe and hale,
Tattling many a broken tale,
Singing many a tuneless song,
Lavish of a heedless tongue;
Simple maiden, void of art,
Babbling out the very heart,
Yet abandon'd to thy will,
Yet imagining no ill,

Yet too innocent to blush;
Like the linnet in the bush
To the mother-linnet's note
Moduling her slender throat;
Chirping forth thy petty joys,
Wanton in the change of toys,
Like the linnet green, in May
Flitting to each bloomy spray;
Wearied then and glad of rest,
Like the linnet in the nest:—
This thy present happy lot
This, in time will be forgot:
Other pleasures, other cares,
Ever-busy Time prepares;
And thou shalt in thy daughter see,
This picture, once, resembled thee.

A. PHILIPS

122

RULE, BRITANNIA

WHEN Britain first at Heaven's command
    Arose from out the azure main,
This was the charter of her land,
    And guardian angels sung the strain:
Rule, Britannia! Britannia, rule the waves!
    Britons never shall be slaves.

The nations not so blest as thee
    Must in their turn to tyrants fall,
Whilst thou shalt flourish great and free,
    The dread and envy of them all.

Still more majestic shalt thou rise,
    More dreadful from each foreign stroke;
As the loud blast that tears the skies
    Serves but to root thy native oak.

Thee haughty tyrants ne'er shall tame;
    All their attempts to bend thee down
Will but arouse thy generous flame,
    And work their woe and thy renown.

To thee belongs the rural reign;
   Thy cities shall with commerce shine;
All thine shall be the subject main,
   And every shore it circles thine!

The Muses, still with Freedom found,
   Shall to thy happy coast repair;
Blest Isle, with matchless beauty crown'd,
   And manly hearts to guard the fair:—
Rule, Britannia! Britannia rules the waves!
    Britons never shall be slaves!

J. THOMSON

123

THE BARD

Pindaric Ode

'RUIN seize thee, ruthless King!
  Confusion on thy banners wait!
Tho' fann'd by Conquest's crimson wing
  They mock the air with idle state.
Helm, nor hauberk's twisted mail,
Nor e'en thy virtues, tyrant, shall avail
To save thy secret soul from nightly fears,
From Cambria's curse, from Cambria's tears!
—Such were the sounds that o'er the crested pride
  Of the first Edward scatter'd wild dismay,
As down the steep of Snowdon's shaggy side
  He wound with toilsome march his long array:—
Stout Glo'ster stood aghast in speechless trance;
'To arms!' cried Mortimer, and couch'd his quivering lance.

On a rock, whose haughty brow
Frowns o'er old Conway's foaming flood,
  Robed in the sable garb of woe
With haggard eyes the Poet stood;
(Loose his beard and hoary hair
Stream'd like a meteor to the troubled air)
And with a master's hand and prophet's fire
Struck the deep sorrows of his lyre:

'Hark, how each giant oak and desert-cave
  Sighs to the torrent's awful voice beneath!
O'er thee, O King! their hundred arms they wave,
  Revenge on thee in hoarser murmurs breathe:
Vocal no more, since Cambria's fatal day,
To high-born Hoel's harp, or soft Llewellyn's lay.

'Cold is Cadwallo's tongue,
  That hush'd the stormy main:
Brave Urien sleeps upon his craggy bed:
  Mountains, ye mourn in vain
  Modred, whose magic song
Made huge Plinlimmon bow his cloud-topt head.
  On dreary Arvon's shore they lie
Smear'd with gore and ghastly pale:
  Far, far aloof the affrighted ravens sail;
  The famish'd eagle screams, and passes by.
Dear lost companions of my tuneful art,
  Dear as the light that visits these sad eyes,
Dear as the ruddy drops that warm my heart,
  Ye died amidst your dying country's cries—
No more I weep; They do not sleep;
  On yonder cliffs, a griesly band,
I see them sit; They linger yet,
  Avengers of their native land:
With me in dreadful harmony they join,
And weave with bloody hands the tissue of thy line.

'Weave the warp and weave the woof
  The winding sheet of Edward's race:
Give ample room and verge enough
  The characters of hell to trace.
Mark the year and mark the night
When Severn shall re-echo with affright
The shrieks of death thro' Berkley's roof that ring,
Shrieks of an agonizing king!
  She-wolf of France, with unrelenting fangs
That tear'st the bowels of thy mangled mate,
  From thee be born, who o'er thy country hangs
The scourge of Heaven! What terrors round him wait!

Amazement in his van, with Flight combined,
And Sorrow's faded form, and Solitude behind.

'Mighty victor, mighty lord,
 Low on his funeral couch he lies!
No pitying heart, no eye, afford
 A tear to grace his obsequies.
Is the sable warrior fled?
Thy son is gone. He rests among the dead.
The swarm that in thy noon-tide beam were born?
—Gone to salute the rising morn.
Fair laughs the Morn, and soft the zephyr blows,
 While proudly riding o'er the azure realm
In gallant trim the gilded Vessel goes:
 Youth on the prow, and Pleasure at the helm:
Regardless of the sweeping Whirlwind's sway,
That hush'd in grim repose expects his evening prey.

 'Fill high the sparkling bowl,
The rich repast prepare;
 Reft of a crown, he yet may share the feast:
Close by the regal chair
 Fell Thirst and Famine scowl
A baleful smile upon their baffled guest.
Heard ye the din of battle bray,
 Lance to lance, and horse to horse?
Long years of havoc urge their destined course,
And thro' the kindred squadrons mow their way.
 Ye towers of Julius, London's lasting shame,
With many a foul and midnight murder fed,
 Revere his Consort's faith, his Father's fame,
And spare the meek usurper's holy head!
Above, below, the rose of snow,
 Twined with her blushing foe, we spread:
The bristled boar in infant-gore
 Wallows beneath the thorny shade.
Now, brothers, bending o'er the accursèd loom,
Stamp we our vengeance deep, and ratify his doom.

 'Edward, lo! to sudden fate
 (Weave we the woof; The thread is spun;)

117

Half of thy heart we consecrate.
  (The web is wove; The work is done;)
Stay, O stay! nor thus forlorn
Leave me unbless'd, unpitied, here to mourn:
In yon bright track that fires the western skies
They melt, they vanish from my eyes.
But O! what solemn scenes on Snowdon's height
  Descending slow their glittering skirts unroll?
Visions of glory, spare my aching sight,
  Ye unborn ages, crowd not on my soul
No more our long-lost Arthur we bewail:—
All hail, ye genuine kings! Britannia's issue, hail!

  'Girt with many a baron bold
Sublime their starry fronts they rear;
  And gorgeous dames, and statesmen old
In bearded majesty, appear.
  In the midst a form divine!
Her eye proclaims her of the Briton-Line:
Her lion-port, her awe-commanding face
Attemper'd sweet to virgin grace.
What strings symphonious tremble in the air,
  What strains of vocal transport round her play?
Hear from the grave, great Taliessin, hear;
  They breathe a soul to animate thy clay.
Bright Rapture calls, and soaring as she sings,
Waves in the eye of Heaven her many-colour'd wings.

  'The verse adorn again
Fierce War, and faithful Love,
And Truth severe, by fairy Fiction drest.
  In buskin'd measures move
Pale Grief, and pleasing Pain,
With Horror, tyrant of the throbbing breast.
A voice as of the cherub-choir
  Gales from blooming Eden bear,
  And distant warblings lessen on my ear
That lost in long futurity expire.
Fond impious man, think'st thou yon sanguine cloud
  Raised by thy breath, has quench'd the orb of day?

Tomorrow he repairs the golden flood
  And warms the nations with redoubled ray.
Enough for me: with joy I see
  The different doom our fates assign:
Be thine Despair and sceptred Care;
  To triumph and to die are mine.'
—He spoke, and headlong from the mountain's height
Deep in the roaring tide he plunged to endless night.

T. GRAY

124

ODE WRITTEN IN MDCCXLVI

How sleep the Brave who sink to rest
By all their Country's wishes blest!
When Spring, with dewy fingers cold,
Returns to deck their hallow'd mould,
She there shall dress a sweeter sod
Than Fancy's feet have ever trod.

By fairy hands their knell is rung,
By forms unseen their dirge is sung:
There Honour comes, a pilgrim grey,
To bless the turf that wraps their clay;
And Freedom shall awhile repair
To dwell a weeping hermit there!

W. COLLINS

125

LAMENT FOR CULLODEN

The lovely lass o' Inverness,
Nae joy nor pleasure can she see;
For e'en and morn she cries, Alas!
And ay the saut tear blin's her e'e:
Drumossie moor—Drumossie day—
A waefu' day it was to me!
For there I lost my father dear,
My father dear, and brethren three.

Their winding-sheet the bluidy clay,
Their graves are growing green to see:
And by them lies the dearest lad
That ever blest a woman's e'e!
Now wae to thee, thou cruel lord,
A bluidy man I trow thou be;
For mony a heart thou hast made sair
That ne'er did wrong to thine or thee.

R. BURNS

126

LAMENT FOR FLODDEN

I've heard them lilting at our ewe-milking,
    Lasses a' lilting before dawn o' day;
But now they are moaning on ilka green loaning—
    The Flowers of the Forest are a' wede away.

At bughts, in the morning, nae blythe lads are scorning,
    Lasses are lonely and dowie and wae;
Nae daffin', nae gabbin', but sighing and sabbing,
    Ilk ane lifts her leglin and hies her away.

In har'st, at the shearing, nae youths now are jeering,
    Bandsters are lyart, and runkled, and grey;
At fair or at preaching, nae wooing, nae fleeching—
    The Flowers of the Forest are a' wede away.

At e'en, in the gloaming, nae younkers are roaming
    'Bout stacks wi' the lasses at bogle to play;
But ilk ane sits drearie, lamenting her dearie—
    The Flowers of the Forest are weded away.

Dool and wae for the order, sent our lads to the Border!
    The English, for ance, by guile wan the day;
The Flowers of the Forest, that fought ay the foremost,
    The prime of our land, are cauld in the clay.

We'll hear nae mair lilting at the ewe-milking;
    Women and bairns are heartless and wae;
Sighing and moaning on ilka green loaning—
    The Flowers of the Forest are a' wede away.

J. ELLIOTT

127

THE BRAES OF YARROW

Thy braes were bonny, Yarrow stream.
When first on them I met my lover;
Thy braes how dreary, Yarrow stream,
When now thy waves his body cover!
For ever now, O Yarrow stream!
Thou art to me a stream of sorrow;
For never on thy banks shall I
Behold my Love, the flower of Yarrow.

He promised me a milk-white steed
To bear me to his father's bowers;
He promised me a little page
To squire me to his father's towers;
He promised me a wedding-ring,—
The wedding day was fix'd tomorrow;—
Now he is wedded to his grave,
Alas, his watery grave, in Yarrow!

Sweet were his words when last we met;
My passion I as freely told him;
Clasp'd in his arms, I little thought
That I should never more behold him!
Scarce was he gone, I saw his ghost;
It vanish'd with a shriek of sorrow;
Thrice did the water-wraith ascend,
And gave a doleful groan thro' Yarrow.

His mother from the window look'd
With all the longing of a mother;
His little sister weeping walk'd
The green-wood path to meet her brother;
They sought him east, they sought him west,
They sought him all the forest thorough;
They only saw the cloud of night,
They only heard the roar of Yarrow.

No longer from thy window look—
Thou hast no son, thou tender mother.
No longer walk, thou lovely maid;
Alas, thou hast no more a brother!
No longer seek him east or west
And search no more the forest thorough;
For, wandering in the night so dark,
He fell a lifeless corpse in Yarrow.

The tear shall never leave my cheek,
No other youth shall be my marrow—
I'll seek thy body in the stream,
And then with thee I'll sleep in Yarrow.
—The tear did never leave her cheek,
No other youth became her marrow;
She found his body in the stream,
And now with him she sleeps in Yarrow.

J. LOGAN

128

WILLY DROWNED IN YARROW

Down in yon garden sweet and gay
    Where bonnie grows the lily,
I heard a fair maid sighing say,
    'My wish be wi' sweet Willie!

'Willie's rare, and Willie's fair,
    And Willie's wondrous bonny;
And Willie hecht to marry me
    Gin e'er he married ony.

'O gentle wind, that bloweth south
    From where my Love repaireth,
Convey a kiss frae his dear mouth
    And tell me how he fareth!

'O tell sweet Willie to come doun
    And hear the mavis singing,
And see the birds on ilka bush
    And leaves around them hinging.

'The lav'rock there, wi' her white breast
    And gentle throat sae narrow;
There's sport eneuch for gentlemen
    On Leader haughs and Yarrow.

'O Leader haughs are wide and braid
    And Yarrow haughs are bonny;
There Willie hecht to marry me
    If e'er he married ony.

'But Willie's gone, whom I thought on,
    And does not hear me weeping;
Draws many a tear frae true love's e'e
    When other maids are sleeping.

'Yestreen I made my bed fu' braid,
    The night I'll mak' it narrow,
For a' the live-lang winter night
    I lie twined o' my marrow.

'O came ye by yon water-side?
    Pou'd you the rose or lily?
Or came you by yon meadow green,
    Or saw you my sweet Willie?'

She sought him up, she sought him down,
    She sought him braid and narrow;
Syne, in the cleaving of a craig,
    She found him drown'd in Yarrow!

ANON.

129

LOSS OF THE ROYAL GEORGE

TOLL for the Brave!
The brave that are no more!
All sunk beneath the wave
Fast by their native shore!
Eight hundred of the brave
Whose courage well was tried,

Had made the vessel heel
And laid her on her side.
A land-breeze shook the shrouds
And she was overset;
Down went the Royal George,
With all her crew complete.

Toll for the brave!
Brave Kempenfelt is gone;
His last sea-fight is fought,
His work of glory done.
It was not in the battle;
No tempest gave the shock;
She sprang no fatal leak,
She ran upon no rock.
His sword was in its sheath,
His fingers held the pen,
When Kempenfelt went down
With twice four hundred men.

Weigh the vessel up
Once dreaded by our foes!
And mingle with our cup
The tears that England owes.
Her timbers yet are sound,
And she may float again
Full charged with England's thunder,
And plough the distant main:
But Kempenfelt is gone,
His victories are o'er;
And he and his eight hundred
Shall plough the wave no more.

W. COWPER

130

BLACK-EYED SUSAN

ALL in the Downs the fleet was moor'd,
  The streamers waving in the wind,
When black-eyed Susan came aboard;
  'O! where shall I my true-love find?

Tell me, ye jovial sailors, tell me true
If my sweet William sails among the crew.'

William, who high upon the yard
  Rock'd with the billow to and fro,
Soon as her well-known voice he heard
  He sigh'd, and cast his eyes below:
The cord slides swiftly through his glowing hands,
And quick as lightning on the deck he stands.

So the sweet lark, high poised in air,
  Shuts close his pinions to his breast
If chance his mate's shrill call he hear,
  And drops at once into her nest:—
The noblest captain in the British fleet
Might envy William's lip those kisses sweet.

'O Susan, Susan, lovely dear,
  My vows shall ever true remain;
Let me kiss off that falling tear;
  We only part to meet again.
Change as ye list, ye winds; my heart shall be
The faithful compass that still points to thee.

'Believe not what the landmen say
  Who tempt with doubts thy constant mind:
They'll tell thee, sailors, when away,
  In every port a mistress find:
Yes, yes, believe them when they tell thee so,
For Thou art present wheresoe'er I go.

'If to fair India's coast we sail,
  Thy eyes are seen in diamonds bright,
Thy breath is Afric's spicy gale,
  Thy skin is ivory so white.
Thus every beauteous object that I view
Wakes in my soul some charm of lovely Sue.

'Though battle call me from thy arms
  Let not my pretty Susan mourn;
Though cannons roar, yet safe from harms
  William shall to his Dear return.
Love turns aside the balls that round me fly,
Lest precious tears should drop from Susan's eye.'

The boatswain gave the dreadful word,
  The sails their swelling bosom spread;
No longer must she stay aboard;
  They kiss'd, she sigh'd, he hung his head.
Her lessening boat unwilling rows to land;
'Adieu!' she cries; and waved her lily hand.

J. GAY

131

SALLY IN OUR ALLEY

OF all the girls that are so smart
  There's none like pretty Sally;
She is the darling of my heart,
  And she lives in our alley.
There is no lady in the land
  Is half so sweet as Sally;
She is the darling of my heart,
  And she lives in our alley.

Her father he makes cabbage-nets
  And through the streets does cry 'em;
Her mother she sells laces long
  To such as please to buy 'em:
But sure such folks could ne'er beget
  So sweet a girl as Sally!
She is the darling of my heart,
  And she lives in our alley.

When she is by, I leave my work,
  I love her so sincerely;
My master comes like any Turk,
  And bangs me most severely—
But let him bang his bellyful,
  I'll bear it all for Sally;
She is the darling of my heart,
  And she lives in our alley.

Of all the days that's in the week
  I dearly love but one day—

And that's the day that comes betwixt
    A Saturday and Monday;
For then I'm drest all in my best
    To walk abroad with Sally;
She is the darling of my heart,
    And she lives in our alley.

My master carries me to church,
    And often am I blamed
Because I leave him in the lurch
    As soon as text is named;
I leave the church in sermon-time
    And slink away to Sally;
She is the darling of my heart,
    And she lives in our alley.

When Christmas comes about again
    O then I shall have money;
I'll hoard it up, and box it all,
    I'll give it to my honey:
I would it were ten thousand pound,
    I'd give it all to Sally;
She is the darling of my heart,
    And she lives in our alley.

My master and the neighbours all
    Make game of me and Sally,
And, but for her, I'd better be
    A slave and row a galley;
But when my seven long years are out
    O then I'll marry Sally,—
O then we'll wed, and then we'll bed,
    But not in our alley!

H. CAREY

132

A FAREWELL

Go fetch to me a pint o' wine,
    An' fill it in a silver tassie;
That I may drink before I go
    A service to my bonnie lassie;

BURNS

The boat rocks at the pier o' Leith,
    Fu' loud the wind blaws frae the Ferry,
The ship rides by the Berwick-law,
    And I maun leave my bonnie Mary.

The trumpets sound, the banners fly,
    The glittering spears are rankéd ready;
The shouts o' war are heard afar,
    The battle closes thick and bloody;
But it's not the roar o' sea or shore
    Wad make me langer wish to tarry;
Nor shout o' war that's heard afar—
    It's leaving thee, my bonnie Mary.

R. BURNS

133

IF doughty deeds my lady please
    Right soon I'll mount my steed;
And strong his arm, and fast his seat
    That bears frae me the meed.
I'll wear thy colours in my cap,
    Thy picture at my heart;
And he that bends not to thine eye
    Shall rue it to his smart!
        Then tell me how to woo thee, Love;
        O tell me how to woo thee!
        For thy dear sake, nae care I'll take
        Tho' ne'er another trow me.

If gay attire delight thine eye
    I'll dight me in array;
I'll tend thy chamber door all night,
    And squire thee all the day.
If sweetest sounds can win thine ear,
    These sounds I'll strive to catch;
Thy voice I'll steal to woo thysell,
    That voice that nane can match.

But if fond love thy heart can gain,
    I never broke a vow;

Nae maiden lays her skaith to me,
   I never loved but you.
For you alone I ride the ring,
   For you I wear the blue;
For you alone I strive to sing,
   O tell me how to woo!
      Then tell me how to woo thee, Love;
        O tell me how to woo thee!
      For thy dear sake, nae care I'll take,
        Tho' ne'er another trow me.
GRAHAM OF GARTMORE

134

TO A YOUNG LADY

SWEET stream, that winds through yonder glade,
Apt emblem of a virtuous maid—
Silent and chaste she steals along,
Far from the world's gay busy throng:
With gentle yet prevailing force,
Intent upon her destined course;
Graceful and useful all she does,
Blessing and blest where'er she goes;
Pure-bosom'd as that watery glass,
And Heaven reflected in her face.
W. COWPER

135

THE SLEEPING BEAUTY

SLEEP on, and dream of Heaven awhile—
Tho' shut so close thy laughing eyes,
Thy rosy lips still wear a smile
And move, and breathe delicious sighs!

Ah, now soft blushes tinge her cheeks
And mantle o'er her neck of snow:
Ah, now she murmurs, now she speaks
What most I wish—and fear to know!

She starts, she trembles, and she weeps!
Her fair hands folded on her breast:
—And now, how like a saint she sleeps!
A seraph in the realms of rest!

Sleep on secure! Above control
Thy thoughts belong to Heaven and thee:
And may the secret of thy soul
Remain within its sanctuary!

S. ROGERS

136

FOR ever, Fortune, wilt thou prove
An unrelenting foe to Love,
And when we meet a mutual heart
Come in between, and bid us part?

Bid us sigh on from day to day,
And wish and wish the soul away;
Till youth and genial years are flown,
And all the life of life is gone?

But busy, busy, still art thou,
To bind the loveless joyless vow,
The heart from pleasure to delude,
To join the gentle to the rude.

For once, O Fortune, hear my prayer,
And I absolve thy future care;
All other blessings I resign,
Make but the dear Amanda mine.

J. THOMSON

137

THE merchant, to secure his treasure,
Conveys it in a borrow'd name:
Euphelia serves to grace my measure,
But Cloe is my real flame.

GOLDSMITH

My softest verse, my darling lyre
Upon Euphelia's toilet lay—
When Cloe noted her desire
That I should sing, that I should play.

My lyre I tune, my voice I raise,
But with my numbers mix my sighs;
And whilst I sing Euphelia's praise,
I fix my soul on Cloe's eyes.

Fair Cloe blush'd: Euphelia frown'd:
I sung, and gazed; I play'd, and trembled:
And Venus to the Loves around
Remark'd how ill we all dissembled.

M. PRIOR

138

WHEN lovely woman stoops to folly
And finds too late that men betray,—
What charm can soothe her melancholy,
What art can wash her guilt away?

The only art her guilt to cover,
To hide her shame from every eye
To give repentance to her lover
And wring his bosom, is—to die.

O. GOLDSMITH

139

YE banks and braes o' bonnie Doon
    How can ye bloom sae fair!
How can ye chant, ye little birds,
    And I sae fu' o' care!

Thou'll break my heart, thou bonnie bird
    That sings upon the bough;
Thou minds me o' the happy days
    When my fause Luve was true.

Thou'll break my heart, thou bonnie bird
  That sings beside thy mate;
For sae I sat, and sae I sang,
  And wist na o' my fate.

Aft hae I roved by bonnie Doon
  To see the woodbine twine,
And ilka bird sang o' its love;
  And sae did I o' mine.

Wi' lightsome heart I pu'd a rose,
  Frae aff its thorny tree;
And my fause luver staw the rose,
  But left the thorn wi' me.

R. BURNS

140

THE PROGRESS OF POESY

A *Pindaric Ode*

AWAKE, Aeolian lyre, awake,
And give to rapture all thy trembling strings.
From Helicon's harmonious springs
  A thousand rills their mazy progress take:
The laughing flowers that round them blow
Drink life and fragrance as they flow.
Now the rich stream of Music winds along
Deep, majestic, smooth, and strong,
Through verdant vales, and Ceres' golden reign;
Now rolling down the steep amain
Headlong, impetuous, see it pour:
The rocks and nodding groves re-bellow to the roar.

O Sovereign of the willing soul,
Parent of sweet and solemn-breathing airs,
Enchanting shell! the sullen Cares
  And frantic passions hear thy soft control.
On Thracia's hills the Lord of War
Has curb'd the fury of his car

And dropt his thirsty lance at thy command
Perching on the sceptred hand
Of Jove, thy magic lulls the feather'd king
With ruffled plumes, and flagging wing:
Quench'd in dark clouds of slumber lie
The terror of his beak, and lightnings of his eye.

Thee the voice, the dance, obey
Temper'd to thy warbled lay.
O'er Idalia's velvet-green
The rosy-crownéd Loves are seen
On Cytherea's day,
With antic Sport, and blue-eyed Pleasures,
Frisking light in frolic measures;
Now pursuing, now retreating,
   Now in circling troops they meet:
To brisk notes in cadence beating
   Glance their many-twinkling feet.
Slow melting strains their Queen's approach declare:
   Where'er she turns the Graces homage pay:
With arms sublime that float upon the air
   In gliding state she wins her easy way:
O'er her warm cheek and rising bosom move
The bloom of young Desire and purple light of Love.

   Man's feeble race what ills await!
Labour, and Penury, the racks of Pain,
Disease, and Sorrow's weeping train,
   And Death, sad refuge from the storms of Fate!
The fond complaint, my song, disprove,
And justify the laws of Jove.
Say, has he given in vain the heavenly Muse?
Night, and all her sickly dews,
Her sceptres wan, and birds of boding cry
He gives to range the dreary sky;
Till down the eastern cliffs afar
Hyperion's march they spy, and glittering shafts of war.

   In climes beyond the solar road
Where shaggy forms o'er ice-built mountains roam,
The Muse has broke the twilight gloom

To cheer the shivering native's dull abode,
And oft, beneath the odorous shade
Of Chili's boundless forests laid,
She deigns to hear the savage youth repeat
In loose numbers wildly sweet
Their feather-cinctured chiefs, and dusky loves.
Her track, where'er the Goddess roves,
Glory pursue, and generous Shame,
Th' unconquerable Mind, and Freedom's holy flame.

Woods, that wave o'er Delphi's steep,
Isles, that crown th' Aegean deep,
Fields that cool Ilissus laves,
Or where Maeander's amber waves
In lingering lab'rinths creep,
How do your tuneful echoes languish,
Mute, but to the voice of anguish!
Where each old poetic mountain
  Inspiration breathed around;
Every shade and hallow'd fountain
  Murmur'd deep a solemn sound:
Till the sad Nine, in Greece's evil hour
  Left their Parnassus for the Latian plains.
Alike they scorn the pomp of tyrant Power,
  And coward Vice, that revels in her chains.
When Latium had her lofty spirit lost,
They sought, O Albion! next, thy sea-encircled coast.

Far from the sun and summer-gale
In thy green lap was Nature's Darling laid,
What time, where lucid Avon stray'd,
  To him the mighty mother did unveil
Her awful face: the dauntless Child
Stretch'd forth his little arms, and smiled.
This pencil take (she said), whose colours clear
Richly paint the vernal year:
Thine, too, these golden keys, immortal Boy!
This can unlock the gates of Joy;
Of Horror that, and thrilling Fears,
Or ope the sacred source of sympathetic Tears.

Nor second He, that rode sublime
Upon the seraph-wings of Ecstasy
The secrets of the Abyss to spy:
    He pass'd the flaming bounds of Place and Time:
The living Throne, the sapphire-blaze
Where Angels tremble while they gaze,
He saw; but blasted with excess of light,
Closed his eyes in endless night.
Behold where Dryden's less presumptuous car
Wide o'er the fields of Glory bear
Two coursers of ethereal race
With necks in thunder clothed, and long-resounding pace.

Hark, his hands the lyre explore!
Bright-eyed Fancy, hovering o'er,
Scatters from her pictured urn
Thoughts that breathe, and words that burn.
But ah! 'tis heard no more——
O! Lyre divine, what daring Spirit
Wakes thee now! Tho' he inherit
Nor the pride, nor ample pinion,
    That the Theban Eagle bear,
Sailing with supreme dominion
    Thro' the azure deep of air:
Yet oft before his infant eyes would run
    Such forms as glitter in the Muse's ray
With orient hues, unborrow'd of the sun:
    Yet shall he mount, and keep his distant way
Beyond the limits of a vulgar fate:
Beneath the Good how far—but far above the Great.

T. GRAY

141

THE PASSIONS

An Ode for Music

WHEN Music, heavenly maid, was young,
While yet in early Greece she sung,
The Passions oft, to hear her shell,
Throng'd around her magic cell.
Exulting, trembling, raging, fainting,
Possest beyond the Muse's painting;
By turns they felt the glowing mind
Disturb'd, delighted, raised, refined:
'Till once, 'tis said, when all were fired,
Fill'd with fury, rapt, inspired,
From the supporting myrtles round
They snatch'd her instruments of sound,
And, as they oft had heard apart
Sweet lessons of her forceful art,
Each, for Madness ruled the hour,
Would prove his own expressive power.

First Fear his hand, its skill to try,
    Amid the chords bewilder'd laid,
And back recoil'd, he knew not why,
    E'en at the sound himself had made.

Next Anger rush'd, his eyes on fire,
    In lightnings own'd his secret stings;
In one rude clash he struck the lyre
    And swept with hurried hand the strings.

With woful measures wan Despair—
    Low sullen sounds his grief beguiled,
A solemn, strange, and mingled air,
    'Twas sad by fits, by starts 'twas wild.

But thou, O Hope, with eyes so fair,
    What was thy delightful measure?
Still it whisper'd promised pleasure
    And bade the lovely scenes at distance hail!

Still would her touch the strain prolong;
    And from the rocks, the woods, the vale
She call'd on Echo still through all the song;
    And, where her sweetest theme she chose,
    A soft responsive voice was heard at every close;
And Hope enchanted smiled, and waved her golden hair;—

And longer had she sung:—but with a frown
    Revenge impatient rose:
He threw his blood-stain'd sword in thunder down;
    And with a withering look
    The war-denouncing trumpet took
And blew a blast so loud and dread,
Were ne'er prophetic sounds so full of woe!
    And ever and anon he beat
    The doubling drum with furious heat;
And, though sometimes, each dreary pause between,
    Dejected Pity at his side
    Her soul-subduing voice applied,
Yet still he kept his wild unalter'd mien,
While each strain'd ball of sight seem'd bursting from his
    head.
Thy numbers, Jealousy, to nought were fix'd:
    Sad proof of thy distressful state!
Of differing themes the veering song was mix'd;
    And now it courted Love, now raving call'd on Hate.

With eyes up-raised, as one inspired,
Pale Melancholy sat retired;
And from her wild sequester'd seat,
In notes by distance made more sweet,
Pour'd through the mellow horn her pensive soul:
    And dashing soft from rocks around
    Bubbling runnels join'd the sound;
Through glades and glooms the mingled measure stole,
    Or, o'er some haunted stream, with fond delay,
    Round an holy calm diffusing,
    Love of peace, and lonely musing,
In hollow murmurs died away.

But O! how alter'd was its sprightlier tone
When Cheerfulness, a nymph of healthiest hue,
 Her bow across her shoulder flung,
 Her buskins gemm'd with morning dew,
Blew an inspiring air, that dale and thicket rung,
 The hunter's call to Faun and Dryad known!
The oak-crown'd Sisters and their chaste-eyed Queen,
 Satyrs and Sylvan Boys, were seen
 Peeping from forth their alleys green:
Brown Exercise rejoiced to hear;
 And Sport leapt up, and seized his beechen spear.

Last came Joy's ecstatic trial:
He, with viny crown advancing,
 First to the lively pipe his hand addrest:
But soon he saw the brisk awakening viol
 Whose sweet entrancing voice he loved the best:
They would have thought who heard the strain
 They saw, in Tempe's vale, her native maids
 Amidst the festal-sounding shades
To some unwearied minstrel dancing;
 While, as his flying fingers kiss'd the strings,
Love framed with Mirth a gay fantastic round:
Loose were her tresses seen, her zone unbound;
 And he, amidst his frolic play,
 As if he would the charming air repay,
Shook thousand odours from his dewy wings.

O Music! sphere-descended maid,
Friend of Pleasure, Wisdom's aid!
Why, goddess, why, to us denied,
Lay'st thou thy ancient lyre aside?
As in that loved Athenian bower
You learn'd an all-commanding power,
Thy mimic soul, O nymph endear'd!
Can well recall what then it heard,
Where is thy native simple heart
Devote to Virtue, Fancy, Art?
Arise, as in that elder time,
Warm, energic, chaste, sublime!

Thy wonders, in that god-like age,
  Fill thy recording Sister's page;—
'Tis sad, and I believe the tale,
Thy humblest reed could more prevail
Had more of strength, diviner rage,
Than all which charms this laggard age,
  E'en all at once together found
Cecilia's mingled world of sound:—
O bid our vain endeavours cease:
Revive the just designs of Greece:
Return in all thy simple state!
Confirm the tales her sons relate!

W. COLLINS

142

ODE ON THE SPRING

Lo! where the rosy-bosom'd Hours,
  Fair Venus' train, appear,
Disclose the long-expecting flowers
  And wake the purple year!
The Attic warbler pours her throat
Responsive to the cuckoo's note,
The untaught harmony of Spring:
While, whispering pleasure as they fly,
Cool Zephyrs thro' the clear blue sky
  Their gather'd fragrance fling.

Where'er the oak's thick branches stretch
  A broader, browner shade,
Where'er the rude and moss-grown beech
  O'er-canopies the glade,
Beside some water's rushy brink
With me the Muse shall sit, and think
(At ease reclined in rustic state)
How vain the ardour of the Crowd,
How low, how little are the Proud,
  How indigent the Great!

Still is the toiling hand of Care;
  The panting herds repose:
Yet hark, how thro' the peopled air
  The busy murmur glows!
The insect youth are on the wing,
Eager to taste the honied spring
And float amid the liquid noon:
Some lightly o'er the current skim,
Some show their gaily-gilded trim
  Quick-glancing to the sun.

To Contemplation's sober eye
  Such is the race of Man:
And they that creep, and they that fly,
  Shall end where they began.
Alike the busy and the gay
But flutter thro' life's little day,
In Fortune's varying colours drest:
Brush'd by the hand of rough Mischance,
Or chill'd by Age, their airy dance
  They leave, in dust to rest.

Methinks I hear in accents low
  The sportive kind reply:
Poor moralist! and what art thou?
  A solitary fly!
Thy joys no glittering female meets,
No hive hast thou of hoarded sweets,
No painted plumage to display:
On hasty wings thy youth is flown;
Thy sun is set, thy spring is gone—
  We frolic while 'tis May.

T. GRAY

143

THE POPLAR FIELD

THE poplars are fell'd, farewell to the shade
And the whispering sound of the cool colonnade:
The winds play no longer and sing in the leaves,
Nor Ouse on his bosom their image receives.

Twelve years have elapsed since I first took a view
Of my favourite field, and the bank where they grew:
And now in the grass behold they are laid,
And the tree is my seat that once lent me a shade.

The blackbird has fled to another retreat
Where the hazels afford him a screen from the heat;
And the scene where his melody charm'd me before
Resounds with his sweet-flowing ditty no more.

My fugitive years are all hasting away,
And I must ere long lie as lowly as they,
With a turf on my breast and a stone at my head,
Ere another such grove shall arise in its stead.

'Tis a sight to engage me, if anything can,
To muse on the perishing pleasures of man;
Short-lived as we are, our enjoyments, I see,
Have a still shorter date, and die sooner than we.

W. COWPER

144

TO A FIELD MOUSE

WEE, sleekit, cow'rin', tim'rous beastie,
O what a panic's in thy breastie!
Thou need na start awa sae hasty,
Wi' bickering brattle!
I wad be laith to rin an' chase thee
Wi' murd'ring pattle!

I'm truly sorry man's dominion
Has broken nature's social union,
An' justifies that ill opinion
Which makes thee startle
At me, thy poor earth-born companion,
An' fellow-mortal!

I doubt na, whiles, but thou may thieve;
What then? poor beastie, thou maun live!

BURNS

A daimen-icker in a thrave
'S a sma' request:
I'll get a blessin' wi' the lave,
And never miss't!

Thy wee bit housie, too, in ruin!
Its silly wa's the win's are strewin':
And naething, now, to big a new ane,
O' foggage green!
An' bleak December's winds ensuin'
Baith snell an' keen!

Thou saw the fields laid bare and waste
An' weary winter comin' fast,
An' cozie here, beneath the blast,
Thou thought to dwell,
Till, crash! the cruel coulter past
Out thro' thy cell.

That wee bit heap o' leaves an' stibble
Has cost thee mony a weary nibble!
Now thou's turn'd out, for a' thy trouble,
But house or hald,
To thole the winter's sleety dribble
An' cranreuch cauld!

But, Mousie, thou art no thy lane
In proving foresight may be vain:
The best laid schemes o' mice an' men
Gang aft a-gley,
An' lea'e us nought but grief an' pain,
For promised joy.

Still thou art blest, compared wi' me!
The present only toucheth thee:
But, oh! I backward cast my e'e
On prospects drear!
An' forward, tho' I canna see,
I guess an' fear!

R. BURNS

145

A WISH

Mine be a cot beside the hill;
A bee-hive's hum shall soothe my ear;
A willowy brook that turns a mill,
With many a fall shall linger near.

The swallow, oft, beneath my thatch
Shall twitter from her clay-built nest;
Oft shall the pilgrim lift the latch,
And share my meal, a welcome guest.

Around my ivied porch shall spring
Each fragrant flower that drinks the dew;
And Lucy, at her wheel, shall sing
In russet-gown and apron blue.

The village-church among the trees,
Where first our marriage-vows were given,
With merry peals shall swell the breeze
And point with taper spire to Heaven.

S. ROGERS

146

TO EVENING

If aught of oaten stop or pastoral song
May hope, chaste Eve, to soothe thy modest ear
    Like thy own solemn springs,
    Thy springs, and dying gales;

O Nymph reserved,—while now the bright-hair'd sun
Sits in yon western tent, whose cloudy skirts,
    With brede ethereal wove,
    O'erhang his wavy bed,

Now air is hush'd, save where the weak-eyed bat
With short shrill shriek flits by on leathern wing,
    Or where the beetle winds
    His small but sullen horn,

As oft he rises 'midst the twilight path,
Against the pilgrim borne in heedless hum,—
　　　　Now teach me, maid composed,
　　　　To breathe some soften'd strain

Whose numbers, stealing through thy dark'ning vale,
May not unseemly with its stillness suit;
　　　　As musing slow I hail
　　　　Thy genial loved return.

For when thy folding-star arising shows
His paly circlet, at his warning lamp
　　　　The fragrant Hours, and Elves
　　　　Who slept in buds the day,

And many a Nymph who wreathes her brows with sedge
And sheds the freshening dew, and lovelier still
　　　　The pensive Pleasures sweet,
　　　　Prepare thy shadowy car.

Then let me rove some wild and heathy scene;
Or find some ruin midst its dreary dells,
　　　　Whose walls more awful nod
　　　　By thy religious gleams.

Or if chill blustering winds or driving rain
Prevent my willing feet, be mine the hut
　　　　That, from the mountain's side,
　　　　Views wilds and swelling floods,

And hamlets brown, and dim-discover'd spires;
And hears their simple bell; and marks o'er all
　　　　Thy dewy fingers draw
　　　　The gradual dusky veil.

While Spring shall pour his showers, as oft he wont,
And bathe thy breathing tresses, meekest Eve!
　　　　While Summer loves to sport
　　　　Beneath thy lingering light;

While sallow Autumn fills thy lap with leaves;
Or Winter, yelling through the troublous air,
　　　　Affrights thy shrinking train
　　　　And rudely rends thy robes;

So long, regardful of thy quiet rule,
Shall Fancy, Friendship, Science, smiling Peace,
   Thy gentlest influence own,
   And love thy favourite name!

W. COLLINS

147

ELEGY

WRITTEN IN A COUNTRY CHURCH-YARD

THE curfew tolls the knell of parting day,
The lowing herd wind slowly o'er the lea,
The ploughman homeward plods his weary way,
And leaves the world to darkness and to me.

Now fades the glimmering landscape on the sight,
And all the air a solemn stillness holds,
Save where the beetle wheels his droning flight,
And drowsy tinklings lull the distant folds:

Save that from yonder ivy-mantled tower
The moping owl does to the moon complain
Of such as, wandering near her secret bower,
Molest her ancient solitary reign.

Beneath those rugged elms, that yew-tree's shade
Where heaves the turf in many a mouldering heap,
Each in his narrow cell for ever laid,
The rude Forefathers of the hamlet sleep.

The breezy call of incense-breathing morn,
The swallow twittering from the straw-built shed,
The cock's shrill clarion, or the echoing horn,
No more shall rouse them from their lowly bed.

For them no more the blazing hearth shall burn
Or busy housewife ply her evening care:
No children run to lisp their sire's return,
Or climb his knees the envied kiss to share.

Oft did the harvest to their sickle yield,
Their furrow oft the stubborn glebe has broke;
How jocund did they drive their team afield!
How bow'd the woods beneath their sturdy stroke!

Let not Ambition mock their useful toil,
Their homely joys, and destiny obscure;
Nor Grandeur hear with a disdainful smile
The short and simple annals of the Poor.

The boast of heraldry, the pomp of power,
And all that beauty, all that wealth e'er gave,
Awaits alike th' inevitable hour:—
The paths of glory lead but to the grave.

Nor you, ye Proud, impute to these the fault
If Memory o'er their tomb no trophies raise,
Where through the long-drawn aisle and fretted vault
The pealing anthem swells the note of praise.

Can storied urn or animated bust
Back to its mansion call the fleeting breath?
Can Honour's voice provoke the silent dust,
Or Flattery soothe the dull cold ear of Death?

Perhaps in this neglected spot is laid
Some heart once pregnant with celestial fire;
Hands, that the rod of empire might have sway'd,
Or waked to ecstasy the living lyre:

But Knowledge to their eyes her ample page
Rich with the spoils of time, did ne'er unroll;
Chill Penury repress'd their noble rage,
And froze the genial current of the soul.

Full many a gem of purest ray serene
The dark unfathom'd caves of ocean bear:
Full many a flower is born to blush unseen,
And waste its sweetness on the desert air.

Some village-Hampden, that with dauntless breast
The little tyrant of his fields withstood,
Some mute inglorious Milton here may rest,
Some Cromwell, guiltless of his country's blood.

Th' applause of list'ning senates to command,
The threats of pain and ruin to despise,
To scatter plenty o'er a smiling land,
And read their history in a nation's eyes

Their lot forbade: nor circumscribed alone
Their growing virtues, but their crimes confined;
Forbade to wade through slaughter to a throne,
And shut the gates of mercy on mankind;

The struggling pangs of conscious truth to hide,
To quench the blushes of ingenuous shame,
Or heap the shrine of Luxury and Pride
With incense kindled at the Muse's flame.

Far from the madding crowd's ignoble strife
Their sober wishes never learn'd to stray;
Along the cool sequester'd vale of life
They kept the noiseless tenor of their way.

Yet e'en these bones from insult to protect
Some frail memorial still erected nigh,
With uncouth rhymes and shapeless sculpture deck'd,
Implores the passing tribute of a sigh.

Their name, their years, spelt by th' unletter'd Muse,
The place of fame and elegy supply:
And many a holy text around she strews
That teach the rustic moralist to die.

For who, to dumb forgetfulness a prey,
This pleasing anxious being e'er resign'd,
Left the warm precincts of the cheerful day,
Nor cast one longing lingering look behind?

On some fond breast the parting soul relies,
Some pious drops the closing eye requires;
E'en from the tomb the voice of Nature cries,
E'en in our ashes live their wonted fires.

For thee, who, mindful of th' unhonour'd dead,
Dost in these lines their artless tale relate;
If chance, by lonely Contemplation led,
Some kindred spirit shall inquire thy fate,—

Haply some hoary-headed swain may say,
Oft have we seen him at the peep of dawn
Brushing with hasty steps the dews away,
To meet the sun upon the upland lawn;

GRAY

There at the foot of yonder nodding beech
That wreathes its old fantastic roots so high,
His listless length at noon-tide would he stretch,
And pore upon the brook that babbles by.

Hard by yon wood, now smiling as in scorn,
Muttering his wayward fancies he would rove;
Now drooping, woful-wan, like one forlorn,
Or crazed with care, or cross'd in hopeless love.

One morn I miss'd him on the custom'd hill,
Along the heath, and near his favourite tree;
Another came; nor yet beside the rill,
Nor up the lawn, nor at the wood was he;

The next with dirges due in sad array
Slow through the church-way path we saw him borne,—
Approach and read (for thou canst read) the lay
Graved on the stone beneath yon aged thorn.

THE EPITAPH

Here rests his head upon the lap of Earth
A Youth, to Fortune and to Fame unknown;
Fair Science frown'd not on his humble birth,
And Melancholy mark'd him for her own.

Large was his bounty, and his soul sincere;
Heaven did a recompense as largely send:
He gave to Misery all he had, a tear,
He gain'd from Heaven, 'twas all he wish'd, a friend.

No farther seek his merits to disclose,
Or draw his frailties from their dread abode,
(There they alike in trembling hope repose,)
The bosom of his Father and his God.

T. GRAY

148

MARY MORISON

O MARY, at thy window be,
It is the wish'd, the trysted hour!
Those smiles and glances let me see
That make the miser's treasure poor:
How blythely wad I bide the stoure,
A weary slave frae sun to sun,
Could I the rich reward secure,
The lovely Mary Morison.

Yestreen when to the trembling string
The dance gaed thro' the lighted ha',
To thee my fancy took its wing,—
I sat, but neither heard nor saw:
Tho' this was fair, and that was braw,
And yon the toast of a' the town,
I sigh'd, and said amang them a',
'Ye are na Mary Morison.'

O Mary, canst thou wreck his peace
Wha for thy sake wad gladly dee?
Or canst thou break that heart of his,
Whase only faut is loving thee?
If love for love thou wilt na gie,
At least be pity to me shown;
A thought ungentle canna be
The thought o' Mary Morison.

R. BURNS

149

BONNIE LESLEY

O SAW ye bonnie Lesley
As she gaed o'er the border?
She's gane, like Alexander,
To spread her conquests farther.

To see her is to love her,
    And love but her for ever;
'For nature made her what she is,
    And ne'er made sic anither!

Thou art a queen, fair Lesley,
    Thy subjects we, before thee;
Thou art divine, fair Lesley,
    The hearts o' men adore thee.

The deil he could na scaith thee,
    Or aught that wad belang thee;
He'd look into thy bonnie face,
    And say 'I canna wrang thee!'

The Powers aboon will tent thee;
    Misfortune sha' na steer thee;
Thou'rt like themselves sae lovely
    That ill they'll ne'er let near thee.

Return again, fair Lesley,
    Return to Caledonie!
That we may brag we hae a lass
    There's nane again sae bonnie.

                R. BURNS

150

O MY Luve's like a red, red rose
    That's newly sprung in June:
O my Luve's like the melodie
    That's sweetly play'd in tune.

As fair art thou, my bonnie lass,
    So deep in luve am I:
And I will luve thee still, my dear,
    Till a' the seas gang dry:

Till a' the seas gang dry, my dear,
    And the rocks melt wi' the sun;
I will luve thee still, my dear,
    While the sands o' life shall run.

And fare thee weel, my only Luve
    And fare thee weel awhile!
And I will come again, my Luve,
    Tho' it were ten thousand mile.

R. BURNS

151

HIGHLAND MARY

YE banks and braes and streams around
    The castle o' Montgomery,
Green be your woods, and fair your flowers,
    Your waters never drumlie!
There simmer first unfauld her robes,
    And there the langest tarry;
For there I took the last fareweel
    O' my sweet Highland Mary.

How sweetly bloom'd the gay green birk,
    How rich the hawthorn's blossom,
As underneath their fragrant shade
    I clasp'd her to my bosom!
The golden hours on angel wings
    Flew o'er me and my dearie;
For dear to me as light and life
    Was my sweet Highland Mary.

Wi' mony a vow and lock'd embrace
    Our parting was fu' tender;
And pledging aft to meet again,
    We tore oursels asunder;
But, O! fell Death's untimely frost,
    That nipt my flower sae early!
Now green's the sod, and cauld's the clay,
    That wraps my Highland Mary!

O pale, pale now, those rosy lips,
    I aft hae kiss'd sae fondly!
And closed for ay the sparkling glance
    That dwelt on me sae kindly;

And mouldering now in silent dust
 That heart that lo'ed me dearly;
But still within my bosom's core
 Shall live my Highland Mary.
R. BURNS

152

AULD ROBIN GRAY

WHEN the sheep are in the fauld, and the kye at hame,
And a' the warld to rest are gane,
The waes o' my heart fa' in showers frae my e'e,
While my gudeman lies sound by me.

Young Jamie lo'ed me weel, and sought me for his bride;
But saving a croun he had naething else beside:
To make the croun a pund, young Jamie gaed to sea;
And the croun and the pund were baith for me.

He hadna been awa' a week but only twa,
When my father brak his arm, and the cow was stown awa;
My mother she fell sick, and my Jamie at the sea—
And auld Robin Gray came a-courtin' me.

My father couldna work, and my mother couldna spin;
I toil'd day and night, but their bread I couldna win;
Auld Rob maintain'd them baith, and wi' tears in his e'e
Said, Jennie, for their sakes, O, marry me!

My heart it said nay; I look'd for Jamie back;
But the wind it blew high, and the ship it was a wrack;
His ship it was a wrack—why didna Jamie dee?
Or why do I live to cry, Wae's me?

My father urgit sair: my mother didna speak;
But she look'd in my face till my heart was like to break:
They gi'ed him my hand, but my heart was at the sea,
Sae auld Robin Gray he was gudeman to me.

I hadna been a wife a week but only four,
When mournfu' as I sat on the stane at the door,
I saw my Jamie's wraith, for I couldna think it he—
Till he said, I'm come hame to marry thee.

O sair, sair did we greet, and muckle did we say;
We took but ae kiss, and I bade him gang away:
I wish that I were dead, but I'm no like to dee;
And why was I born to say, Wae's me!

I gang like a ghaist, and I carena to spin;
I daurna think on Jamie, for that wad be a sin;
But I'll do my best a gude wife ay to be,
For auld Robin Gray he is kind unto me.

LADY A. LINDSAY

153

DUNCAN GRAY

Duncan Gray cam here to woo,
    Ha, ha, the wooing o't;
On blythe Yule night when we were fou,
    Ha, ha, the wooing o't:
Maggie coost her head fu' high,
Look'd asklent and unco skeigh,
Gart poor Duncan stand abeigh;
    Ha, ha, the wooing o't!

Duncan fleech'd, and Duncan pray'd;
Meg was deaf as Ailsa Craig;
Duncan sigh'd baith out and in,
Grat his een baith bleer't and blin',
Spak o' lowpin ower a linn!

Time and chance are but a tide,
Slighted love is sair to bide;
Shall I, like a fool, quoth he,
For a haughty hizzie dee?
She may gae to—France for me!

How it comes let doctors tell,
Meg grew sick—as he grew haill;
Something in her bosom wrings,
For relief a sigh she brings;
And O, her een, they spak sic things!

Duncan was a lad o' grace;
Maggie's was a piteous case;
Duncan couldna be her death,
Swelling pity smoor'd his wrath;
Now they're crouse and canty baith:
    Ha, ha, the wooing o't!

R. BURNS

154

THE SAILOR'S WIFE

AND are ye sure the news is true?
    And are ye sure he's weel?
Is this a time to think o' wark?
    Ye jades, lay by your wheel;
Is this the time to spin a thread,
    When Colin's at the door?
Reach down my cloak, I'll to the quay,
    And see him come ashore.
For there's nae luck about the house,
    There's nae luck at a';
There's little pleasure in the house
    When our gudeman's awa'.

And gie to me my bigonet,
    My bishop's satin gown;
For I maun tell the baillie's wife
    That Colin's in the town.
My Turkey slippers maun gae on,
    My stockins pearly blue;
It's a' to pleasure our gudeman,
    For he's baith leal and true.

MICKLE

Rise, lass, and mak a clean fireside,
   Put on the muckle pot;
Gie little Kate her button gown
   And Jock his Sunday coat;
And mak their shoon as black as slaes,
   Their hose as white as snaw;
It's a' to please my ain gudeman,
   For he's been long awa'.

There's twa fat hens upo' the coop
   Been fed this month and mair;
Mak haste and thraw their necks about,
   That Colin weel may fare;
And spread the table neat and clean,
   Gar ilka thing look braw,
For wha can tell how Colin fared
   When he was far awa'?

Sae true his heart, sae smooth his speech,
   His breath like caller air;
His very foot has music in't
   As he comes up the stair—
And will I see his face again?
   And will I hear him speak?
I'm downright dizzy wi' the thought,
   In troth I'm like to greet!

If Colin's weel, and weel content,
   I hae nae mair to crave:
And gin I live to keep him sae,
   I'm blest aboon the lave:
And will I see his face again,
   And will I hear him speak?
I'm downright dizzy wi' the thought,
   In troth I'm like to greet.
For there's nae luck about the house,
   There's nae luck at a';
There's little pleasure in the house
   When our gudeman's awa'.

                                    W. J. MICKLE

155

JEAN

Of a' the airts the wind can blaw
    I dearly like the West,
For there the bonnie lassie lives,
    The lassie I lo'e best:
There wild woods grow, and rivers row,
    And mony a hill between;
But day and night my fancy's flight
    Is ever wi' my Jean.

I see her in the dewy flowers,
    I see her sweet and fair:
I hear her in the tunefu' birds,
    I hear her charm the air:
There's not a bonnie flower that springs
    By fountain, shaw, or green,
There's not a bonnie bird that sings
    But minds me o' my Jean.

O blaw ye westlin winds, blaw saft
    Amang the leafy trees;
Wi' balmy gale, frae hill and dale
    Bring hame the laden bees;
And bring the lassie back to me
    That's ay sae neat and clean;
Ae smile o' her wad banish care,
    Sae charming is my Jean.

What sighs and vows amang the knowes
    Hae pass'd atween us twa!
How fond to meet, how wae to part
    That night she gaed awa!
The Powers aboon can only ken,
    To whom the heart is seen,
That nane can be sae dear to me
    As my sweet lovely Jean!

R. BURNS

156

JOHN ANDERSON

John Anderson my jo, John,
When we were first acquent
Your locks were like the raven,
Your bonnie brow was brent;
But now your brow is bald, John,
Your locks are like the snow;
But blessings on your frosty pow,
John Anderson my jo.

John Anderson my jo, John,
We clamb the hill thegither,
And mony a canty day, John,
We've had wi' ane anither:
Now we maun totter down, John,
But hand in hand we'll go,
And sleep thegither at the foot,
John Anderson my jo.

R. BURNS

157

THE LAND O' THE LEAL

I'm wearing awa', Jean,
Like snaw when its thaw, Jean,
I'm wearing awa'
   To the land o' the leal.
There's nae sorrow there, Jean,
There's neither cauld nor care, Jean,
The day is ay fair
   In the land o' the leal.

Ye were ay leal and true, Jean,
Your task's ended noo, Jean,
And I'll welcome you
   To the land o' the leal.

Our bonnie bairn's there, Jean,
　She was baith guid and fair, Jean;
O we grudged her right sair
　　To the land o' the leal!

Then dry that tearfu' e'e, Jean,
My soul langs to be free, Jean,
And angels wait on me
　　To the land o' the leal.
Now fare ye weel, my ain Jean,
This warld's care is vain, Jean;
We'll meet and ay be fain
　　In the land o' the leal.

LADY NAIRN

158

ODE ON A DISTANT PROSPECT OF ETON COLLEGE

YE distant spires, ye antique towers
　That crown the watery glade,
Where grateful Science still adores
　Her Henry's holy shade;
And ye, that from the stately brow
Of Windsor's heights th' expanse below
Of grove, of lawn, of mead survey,
Whose turf, whose shade, whose flowers among
Wanders the hoary Thames along
　His silver-winding way:

Ah happy hills! ah pleasing shade!
　Ah fields beloved in vain!
Where once my careless childhood stray'd,
　A stranger yet to pain!
I feel the gales that from ye blow
A momentary bliss bestow,
As waving fresh their gladsome wing
My weary soul they seem to soothe,
And, redolent of joy and youth,
　To breathe a second spring.

158

Say, Father Thames, for thou hast seen
   Full many a sprightly race
Disporting on thy margent green
   The paths of pleasure trace;
Who foremost now delight to cleave
With pliant arm, thy glassy wave
The captive linnet which enthral?
What idle progeny succeed
To chase the rolling circle's speed
   Or urge the flying ball?

While some on earnest business bent
   Their murmuring labours ply
'Gainst graver hours, that bring constraint
   To sweeten liberty:
Some bold adventurers disdain
The limits of their little reign
And unknown regions dare descry:
Still as they run they look behind,
They hear a voice in every wind
   And snatch a fearful joy.

Gay Hope is theirs by fancy fed,
   Less pleasing when possest;
The tear forgot as soon as shed,
   The sunshine of the breast:
Theirs buxom Health, of rosy hue,
Wild Wit, Invention ever new,
And lively Cheer, of Vigour born;
The thoughtless day, the easy night,
The spirits pure, the slumbers light
   That fly th' approach of morn.

Alas! regardless of their doom
   The little victims play!
No sense have they of ills to come
   Nor care beyond today:
Yet see how all around them wait
The ministers of human fate
And black Misfortune's baleful train!

Ah show them where in ambush stand
To seize their prey, the murderous band!
    Ah, tell them they are men!

These shall the fury Passions tear,
    The vultures of the mind,
Disdainful Anger, pallid Fear,
    And Shame that skulks behind;
Or pining Love shall waste their youth,
Or Jealousy with rankling tooth
That inly gnaws the secret heart,
And Envy wan, and faded Care,
Grim-visaged comfortless Despair,
    And Sorrow's piercing dart.

Ambition this shall tempt to rise,
    Then whirl the wretch from high
To bitter Scorn a sacrifice
    And grinning Infamy.
The stings of Falsehood those shall try,
And hard Unkindness' alter'd eye,
That mocks the tear it forced to flow;
And keen Remorse with blood defiled,
And moody Madness laughing wild
    Amid severest woe.

Lo, in the Vale of Years beneath
    A griesly troop are seen,
The painful family of Death
    More hideous than their Queen:
This racks the joints, this fires the veins,
That every labouring sinew strains,
Those in the deeper vitals rage:
Lo, Poverty, to fill the band,
That numbs the soul with icy hand,
    And slow-consuming Age.

To each his sufferings: all are men,
    Condemn'd alike to groan;
The tender for another's pain,
    Th' unfeeling for his own.

Yet, ah! why should they know their fate,
Since sorrow never comes too late,
And happiness too swiftly flies?
Thought would destroy their paradise!
No more;—where ignorance is bliss,
   'Tis folly to be wise.

T. GRAY

159

HYMN TO ADVERSITY

DAUGHTER of Jove, relentless power,
   Thou tamer of the human breast,
Whose iron scourge and torturing hour
   The bad affright, afflict the best!
Bound in thy adamantine chain
The proud are taught to taste of pain,
And purple tyrants vainly groan
With pangs unfelt before, unpitied and alone.

When first thy Sire to send on earth
   Virtue, his darling child, design'd,
To thee he gave the heavenly birth
   And bade to form her infant mind.
Stern, rugged Nurse! thy rigid lore
With patience many a year she bore:
What sorrow was, thou bad'st her know,
And from her own she learn'd to melt at others' woe.

Scared at thy frown terrific, fly
   Self-pleasing Folly's idle brood,
Wild Laughter, Noise, and thoughtless Joy,
   And leave us leisure to be good.
Light they disperse, and with them go
The summer Friend, the flattering Foe;
By vain Prosperity received,
To her they vow their truth, and are again believed.

Wisdom in sable garb array'd
   Immersed in rapturous thought profound,
And Melancholy, silent maid,
   With leaden eye, that loves the ground,

Still on thy solemn steps attend:
Warm Charity, the general friend,
   With Justice, to herself severe,
And Pity dropping soft the sadly-pleasing tear.

O, gently on thy suppliant's head
   Dread Goddess, lay thy chastening hand!
Not in thy Gorgon terrors clad,
   Not circled with the vengeful band
   (As by the impious thou art seen)
With thundering voice, and threatening mien,
With screaming Horror's funeral cry,
Despair, and fell Disease, and ghastly Poverty:

Thy form benign, O Goddess, wear,
   Thy milder influence impart,
Thy philosophic train be there
   To soften, not to wound my heart.
The generous spark extinct revive,
Teach me to love and to forgive,
Exact my own defects to scan,
What others are to feel, and know myself a Man.

                       T. GRAY

160

THE SOLITUDE OF
ALEXANDER SELKIRK

I AM monarch of all I survey;
  My right there is none to dispute;
From the centre all round to the sea
  I am lord of the fowl and the brute.
O Solitude! where are the charms
  That sages have seen in thy face?
Better dwell in the midst of alarms
  Than reign in this horrible place.

I am out of humanity's reach,
  I must finish my journey alone,
Never hear the sweet music of speech;
  I start at the sound of my own.

The beasts that roam over the plain
My form with indifference see;
They are so unacquainted with man,
Their tameness is shocking to me.

Society, Friendship, and Love
Divinely bestow'd upon man,
O had I the wings of a dove
How soon would I taste you again!
My sorrows I then might assuage
In the ways of religion and truth,
Might learn from the wisdom of age,
And be cheer'd by the sallies of youth.

Religion! what treasure untold
Resides in that heavenly word!
More precious than silver or gold,
Or all that this earth can afford.
But the sound of the church-going bell
These vallies and rocks never heard,
Ne'er sigh'd at the sound of a knell,
Or smil'd when a sabbath appear'd.

Ye winds that have made me your sport,
Convey to this desolate shore
Some cordial endearing report
Of a land I shall visit no more:
My friends, do they now and then send
A wish or a thought after me?
O tell me I yet have a friend,
Though a friend I am never to see.

How fleet is a glance of the mind!
Compared with the speed of its flight,
The tempest itself lags behind,
And the swift-wingéd arrows of light.
When I think of my own native land
In a moment I seem to be there;
But alas! recollection at hand
Soon hurries me back to despair.

But the seafowl is gone to her nest,
The beast is laid down in his lair;
Even here is a season of rest,
And I to my cabin repair.
There's mercy in every place,
And mercy, encouraging thought!
Gives even affliction a grace
And reconciles man to his lot.

W. COWPER

161

TO MARY UNWIN

MARY! I want a lyre with other strings,
Such aid from heaven as some have feign'd they drew,
An eloquence scarce given to mortals, new
And undebased by praise of meaner things,

That ere through age or woe I shed my wings
I may record thy worth with honour due,
In verse as musical as thou art true
And that immortalizes whom it sings:—

But thou hast little need. There is a Book
By seraphs writ with beams of heavenly light,
On which the eyes of God not rarely look,

A chronicle of actions just and bright—
There all thy deeds, my faithful Mary, shine;
And since thou own'st that praise, I spare thee mine.

W. COWPER

162

TO THE SAME

THE twentieth year is wellnigh past
Since first our sky was overcast;
Ah would that this might be the last!
My Mary!

Thy spirits have a fainter flow,
I see thee daily weaker grow—
'Twas my distress that brought thee low,
    My Mary!

Thy needles, once a shining store,
For my sake restless heretofore,
Now rust disused, and shine no more;
    My Mary!

For though thou gladly wouldst fulfil
The same kind office for me still,
Thy sight now seconds not thy will,
    My Mary!

But well thou play'dst the housewife's part,
And all thy threads with magic art
Have wound themselves about this heart,
    My Mary!

Thy indistinct expressions seem
Like language utter'd in a dream;
Yet me they charm, whate'er the theme,
    My Mary!

Thy silver locks, once auburn bright,
Are still more lovely in my sight
Than golden beams of orient light,
    My Mary!

For could I view nor them nor thee,
What sight worth seeing could I see?
The sun would rise in vain for me,
    My Mary!

Partakers of thy sad decline
Thy hands their little force resign;
Yet gently press'd, press gently mine,
    My Mary!

Such feebleness of limbs thou prov'st
That now at every step thou mov'st
Upheld by two; yet still thou lov'st,
    My Mary!

And still to love, though press'd with ill,
In wintry age to feel no chill,
With me is to be lovely still,
  My Mary!

But ah! by constant heed I know
How oft the sadness that I show
Transforms thy smiles to looks of woe,
  My Mary!

And should my future lot be cast
With much resemblance of the past,
Thy worn-out heart will break at last—
  My Mary!

     W. COWPER

163

THE DYING MAN IN HIS GARDEN

Why, Damon, with the forward day
Dost thou thy little spot survey,
From tree to tree, with doubtful cheer,
Pursue the progress of the year,
What winds arise, what rains descend,
When thou before that year shalt end?

What do thy noontide walks avail,
To clear the leaf, and pick the snail,
Then wantonly to death decree
An insect usefuller than thee?
Thou and the worm are brother-kind,
As low, as earthy, and as blind.

Vain wretch! canst thou expect to see
The downy peach make court to thee?
Or that thy sense shall ever meet
The bean-flower's deep-embosom'd sweet
Exhaling with an evening blast?
Thy evenings then will all be past!

Thy narrow pride, thy fancied green
(For vanity's in little seen),
All must be left when Death appears,
In spite of wishes, groans, and tears;
Nor one of all thy plants that grow
But Rosemary will with thee go.

G. SEWELL

164

TOMORROW

IN the downhill of life, when I find I'm declining,
  May my lot no less fortunate be
Than a snug elbow-chair can afford for reclining,
  And a cot that o'erlooks the wide sea;
With an ambling pad-pony to pace o'er the lawn,
  While I carol away idle sorrow,
And blithe as the lark that each day hails the dawn
  Look forward with hope for tomorrow.

With a porch at my door, both for shelter and shade too,
  As the sunshine or rain may prevail;
And a small spot of ground for the use of the spade too,
  With a barn for the use of the flail:
A cow for my dairy, a dog for my game,
  And a purse when a friend wants to borrow;
I'll envy no nabob his riches or fame,
  Nor what honours await him tomorrow.

From the bleak northern blast may my cot be completely
  Secured by a neighbouring hill;
And at night may repose steal upon me more sweetly
  By the sound of a murmuring rill:
And while peace and plenty I find at my board,
  With a heart free from sickness and sorrow,
With my friends may I share what today may afford,
  And let them spread the table tomorrow.

And when I at last must throw off this frail covering
    Which I've worn for threescore years and ten,
On the brink of the grave I'll not seek to keep hovering,
    Nor my thread wish to spin o'er again:
But my face in the glass I'll serenely survey,
    And with smiles count each wrinkle and furrow;
As this old worn-out stuff, which is threadbare today,
    May become everlasting tomorrow.

J. COLLINS

165

Life! I know not what thou art,
But know that thou and I must part;
And when, or how, or where we met
I own to me's a secret yet.

Life! we've been long together
Through pleasant and through cloudy weather;
'Tis hard to part when friends are dear—
Perhaps 'twill cost a sigh, a tear;
—Then steal away, give little warning,
    Choose thine own time;
Say not Good Night,—but in some brighter clime
    Bid me Good Morning.

A. L. BARBAULD

166

ON FIRST LOOKING INTO CHAPMAN'S HOMER

MUCH have I travell'd in the realms of gold
And many goodly states and kingdoms seen;
Round many western islands have I been
Which bards in fealty to Apollo hold.

Oft of one wide expanse had I been told
That deep-brow'd Homer ruled as his demesne:
Yet did I never breathe its pure serene
Till I heard Chapman speak out loud and bold:

—Then felt I like some watcher of the skies
When a new planet swims into his ken;
Or like stout Cortez—when with eagle eyes

He stared at the Pacific, and all his men
Look'd at each other with a wild surmise—
Silent, upon a peak in Darien.

J. KEATS

167

ODE ON THE POETS

BARDS of Passion and of Mirth
Ye have left your souls on earth!
Have ye souls in heaven too,
Double-lived in regions new?

—Yes, and those of heaven commune
With the spheres of sun and moon;
With the noise of fountains wonderous
And the parle of voices thunderous;
With the whisper of heaven's trees
And one another, in soft ease
Seated on Elysian lawns
Browsed by none but Dian's fawns;
Underneath large blue bells tented,
Where the daisies are rose-scented,
And the rose herself has got
Perfume which on earth is not;
Where the nightingale doth sing
Not a senseless, trancéd thing,
But divine melodious truth;
Philosophic numbers smooth;
Tales and golden histories
Of heaven and its mysteries.

Thus ye live on high, and then
On the earth ye live again;
And the souls ye left behind you
Teach us, here, the way to find you,
Where your other souls are joying,
Never slumber'd, never cloying.
Here, your earth-born souls still speak
To mortals, of their little week;
Of their sorrows and delights;
Of their passions and their spites;
Of their glory and their shame;
What doth strengthen and what maim:—
Thus ye teach us, everyday,
Wisdom, though fled far away.

Bards of Passion and of Mirth
Ye have left your souls on earth!
Ye have souls in heaven too,
Double-lived in regions new!

J. KEATS

168

LOVE

ALL thoughts, all passions, all delights,
Whatever stirs this mortal frame,
Are all but ministers of Love,
    And feed his sacred flame.

Oft in my waking dreams do I
Live o'er again that happy hour,
When midway on the mount I lay
    Beside the ruin'd tower.

The moonshine stealing o'er the scene
Had blended with the lights of eve;
And she was there, my hope, my joy,
    My own dear Genevieve!

She lean'd against the arméd man,
The statue of the arméd knight;
She stood and listen'd to my lay,
    Amid the lingering light.

Few sorrows hath she of her own,
My hope! my joy! my Genevieve!
She loves me best, whene'er I sing
    The songs that make her grieve.

I play'd a soft and doleful air,
I sang an old and moving story—
An old rude song, that suited well
    That ruin wild and hoary.

She listen'd with a flitting blush,
With downcast eyes and modest grace;
For well she knew, I could not choose
    But gaze upon her face.

I told her of the Knight that wore
Upon his shield a burning brand;
And that for ten long years he woo'd
    The Lady of the Land.

I told her how he pined: and ah!
The deep, the low, the pleading tone
With which I sang another's love
    Interpreted my own.

She listen'd with a flitting blush,
With downcast eyes, and modest grace;
And she forgave me, that I gazed
    Too fondly on her face.

But when I told the cruel scorn
That crazed that bold and lovely Knight,
And that he cross'd the mountain-woods,
    Nor rested day nor night;

That sometimes from the savage den,
And sometimes from the darksome shade,
And sometimes starting up at once
    In green and sunny glade

There came and look'd him in the face
An angel beautiful and bright;
And that he knew it was a Fiend,
    This miserable Knight!

And that unknowing what he did,
He leap'd amid a murderous band,
And saved from outrage worse than death
    The Lady of the Land;

And how she wept, and clasp'd his knees
And how she tended him in vain;
And ever strove to expiate
    The scorn that crazed his brain:

And that she nursed him in a cave,
And how his madness went away,
When on the yellow forest-leaves
    A dying man he lay;

—His dying words—but when I reach'd
That tenderest strain of all the ditty,
My faltering voice and pausing harp
    Disturb'd her soul with pity!

All impulses of soul and sense
Had thrill'd my guileless Genevieve;
The music and the doleful tale,
　　The rich and balmy eve;

And hopes, and fears that kindle hope,
An undistinguishable throng,
And gentle wishes long subdued,
　　Subdued and cherish'd long!

She wept with pity and delight,
She blush'd with love, and virgin shame;
And like the murmur of a dream,
　　I heard her breathe my name.

Her bosom heaved—she stepp'd aside,
As conscious of my look she stept—
Then suddenly, with timorous eye
　　She fled to me and wept.

She half enclosed me with her arms,
She press'd me with a meek embrace;
And bending back her head, look'd up,
　　And gazed upon my face.

'Twas partly love, and partly fear,
And partly 'twas a bashful art
That I might rather feel, than see,
　　The swelling of her heart.

I calm'd her fears, and she was calm
And told her love with virgin pride;
And so I won my Genevieve,
　　My bright and beauteous Bride.

S. T. COLERIDGE

169

ALL FOR LOVE

O TALK not to me of a name great in story;
The days of our youth are the days of our glory;
And the myrtle and ivy of sweet two-and-twenty
Are worth all your laurels, though ever so plenty.

What are garlands and crowns to the brow that is wrinkled?
'Tis but as a dead flower with May-dew besprinkled:
Then away with all such from the head that is hoary—
What care I for the wreaths that can only give glory?

O Fame!—if I e'er took delight in thy praises,
'Twas less for the sake of thy high-sounding phrases,
Than to see the bright eyes of the dear one discover
She thought that I was not unworthy to love her.

There chiefly I sought thee, there only I found thee;
Her glance was the best of the rays that surround thee;
When it sparkled o'er aught that was bright in my story,
I knew it was love, and I felt it was glory.

LORD BYRON

170

THE OUTLAW

O BRIGNALL banks are wild and fair,
    And Greta woods are green,
And you may gather garlands there
    Would grace a summer-queen.
And as I rode by Dalton-Hall
    Beneath the turrets high,
A Maiden on the castle-wall
    Was singing merrily:
'O Brignall Banks are fresh and fair,
    And Greta woods are green;
I'd rather rove with Edmund there
    Than reign our English queen.'

'If, Maiden, thou wouldst wend with me,
    To leave both tower and town,
Thou first must guess what life lead we
    That dwell by dale and down.
And if thou canst that riddle read,
    As read full well you may,
Then to the greenwood shalt thou speed
    As blithe as Queen of May.'

Yet sung she, 'Brignall banks are fair,
   And Greta woods are green;
I'd rather rove with Edmund there
   Than reign our English queen.

'I read you by your bugle-horn
   And by your palfrey good,
I read you for a ranger sworn
   To keep the king's greenwood.'
'A Ranger, lady, winds his horn,
   And 'tis at peep of light;
His blast is heard at merry morn,
   And mine at dead of night.'
Yet sung she, 'Brignall banks are fair,
   And Greta woods are gay;
I would I were with Edmund there
   To reign his Queen of May!

'With burnish'd brand and musketoon
   So gallantly you come,
I read you for a bold Dragoon
   That lists the tuck of drum.'
'I list no more the tuck of drum,
   No more the trumpet hear;
But when the beetle sounds his hum
   My comrades take the spear.
And O! though Brignall banks be fair
   And Greta woods be gay,
Yet mickle must the maiden dare
   Would reign my Queen of May!

'Maiden! a nameless life I lead,
   A nameless death I'll die!
The fiend whose lantern lights the mead
   Were better mate than I!
And when I'm with my comrades met
   Beneath the greenwood bough,—
What once we were we all forget,
   Nor think what we are now.'

Chorus

Yet Brignall banks are fresh and fair,
  And Greta woods are green,
And you may gather garlands there
  Would grace a summer-queen.

SIR W. SCOTT

171

THERE be none of Beauty's daughters
  With a magic like Thee;
And like music on the waters
  Is thy sweet voice to me:
When, as if its sound were causing
The charméd ocean's pausing,
The waves lie still and gleaming,
And the lull'd winds seem dreaming:

And the midnight moon is weaving
  Her bright chain o'er the deep,
Whose breast is gently heaving
  As an infant's asleep:
So the spirit bows before thee
To listen and adore thee;
With a full but soft emotion,
Like the swell of Summer's ocean.

LORD BYRON

172

LINES TO AN INDIAN AIR

I ARISE from dreams of Thee
In the first sweet sleep of night,
When the winds are breathing low
And the stars are shining bright:
I arise from dreams of thee,
And a spirit in my feet
Has led me—who knows how?
To thy chamber-window, Sweet!

The wandering airs they faint
On the dark, the silent stream—
The champak odours fail
Like sweet thoughts in a dream;
The nightingale's complaint
It dies upon her heart,
As I must die on thine
O belovéd as thou art!

O lift me from the grass!
I die, I faint, I fail!
Let thy love in kisses rain
On my lips and eyelids pale.
My cheek is cold and white, alas!
My heart beats loud and fast;
O! press it close to thine again
Where it will break at last.

P. B. SHELLEY

173

SHE walks in beauty, like the night
Of cloudless climes and starry skies,
And all that's best of dark and bright
Meets in her aspect and her eyes,
Thus mellow'd to that tender light
Which heaven to gaudy day denies.

One shade the more, one ray the less
Had half impair'd the nameless grace
Which waves in every raven tress
Or softly lightens o'er her face,
Where thoughts serenely sweet express
How pure, how dear their dwelling-place.

And on that cheek and o'er that brow
So soft, so calm, yet eloquent,
The smiles that win, the tints that glow
But tell of days in goodness spent,—
A mind at peace with all below,
A heart whose love is innocent.

LORD BYRON

174

SHE was a phantom of delight
When first she gleam'd upon my sight:
A lovely apparition, sent
To be a moment's ornament;
Her eyes as stars of twilight fair;
Like Twilight's, too, her dusky hair;
But all things else about her drawn
From May-time and the cheerful dawn;
A dancing shape, an image gay,
To haunt, to startle, and waylay.

I saw her upon nearer view,
A spirit, yet a woman too!
Her household motions light and free,
And steps of virgin-liberty;
A countenance in which did meet
Sweet records, promises as sweet;
A creature not too bright or good
For human nature's daily food,
For transient sorrows, simple wiles,
Praise, blame, love, kisses, tears, and smiles.

And now I see with eye serene
The very pulse of the machine;
A being breathing thoughtful breath,
A traveller between life and death:
The reason firm, the temperate will,
Endurance, foresight, strength, and skill;
A perfect woman, nobly plann'd
To warn, to comfort, and command;
And yet a Spirit still, and bright
With something of an angel-light.

W. WORDSWORTH

175

SHE is not fair to outward view
    As many maidens be;
Her loveliness I never knew
    Until she smiled on me.

O then I saw her eye was bright,
A well of love, a spring of light.

But now her looks are coy and cold,
   To mine they ne'er reply,
And yet I cease not to behold
   The love-light in her eye:
Her very frowns are fairer far
Than smiles of other maidens are.

H. COLERIDGE

176

I FEAR thy kisses, gentle maiden;
Thou needest not fear mine;
My spirit is too deeply laden
Ever to burthen thine.

I fear thy mien, thy tones, thy motion;
Thou needest not fear mine;
Innocent is the heart's devotion
With which I worship thine.

P. B. SHELLEY

177

THE LOST LOVE

SHE dwelt among the untrodden ways
   Beside the springs of Dove;
A maid whom there were none to praise,
   And very few to love.

A violet by a mossy stone
   Half-hidden from the eye!
—Fair as a star, when only one
   Is shining in the sky.

She lived unknown, and few could know
   When Lucy ceased to be;
But she is in her grave, and O!
   The difference to me!

W. WORDSWORTH

178

I TRAVELL'D among unknown men
   In lands beyond the sea;
Nor, England! did I know till then
   What love I bore to thee.

'Tis past, that melancholy dream!
   Nor will I quit thy shore
A second time, for still I seem
   To love thee more and more.

Among thy mountains did I feel
   The joy of my desire;
And she I cherish'd turn'd her wheel
   Beside an English fire.

Thy mornings show'd, thy nights conceal'd
   The bowers where Lucy play'd;
And thine too is the last green field
   That Lucy's eyes survey'd.

W. WORDSWORTH

179

THE EDUCATION OF NATURE

THREE years she grew in sun and shower;
Then Nature said, 'A lovelier flower
On earth was never sown:
This child I to myself will take;
She shall be mine, and I will make
A lady of my own.

'Myself will to my darling be
Both law and impulse: and with me
The girl, in rock and plain,
In earth and heaven, in glade and bower,
Shall feel an overseeing power
To kindle or restrain.

'She shall be sportive as the fawn
That wild with glee across the lawn
  Or up the mountain springs;
And her's shall be the breathing balm,
And her's the silence and the calm
  Of mute insensate things.

'The floating clouds their state shall lend
To her; for her the willow bend;
  Nor shall she fail to see
E'en in the motions of the storm
Grace that shall mould the maiden's form
  By silent sympathy.

'The stars of midnight shall be dear
To her; and she shall lean her ear
  In many a secret place
Where rivulets dance their wayward round,
And beauty born of murmuring sound
  Shall pass into her face.

'And vital feelings of delight
Shall rear her form to stately height,
  Her virgin bosom swell;
Such thoughts to Lucy I will give
While she and I together live
  Here in this happy dell.'

Thus Nature spake—The work was done—
How soon my Lucy's race was run!
  She died, and left to me
This heath, this calm and quiet scene;
The memory of what has been,
  And never more will be.

                          W. WORDSWORTH

180

A SLUMBER did my spirit seal;
  I had no human fears:
She seem'd a thing that could not feel
  The touch of earthly years.

181

No motion has she now, no force;
  She neither hears nor sees;
Roll'd round in earth's diurnal course
  With rocks, and stones, and trees!

W. WORDSWORTH

181

LORD ULLIN'S DAUGHTER

A CHIEFTAIN to the Highlands bound
Cries 'Boatman, do not tarry!
And I'll give thee a silver pound
To row us o'er the ferry!'

'Now who be ye, would cross Lochgyle
This dark and stormy water?'
'O I'm the chief of Ulva's isle,
And this, Lord Ullin's daughter.

'And fast before her father's men
Three days we've fled together,
For should he find us in the glen,
My blood would stain the heather.

'His horsemen hard behind us ride—
Should they our steps discover,
Then who will cheer my bonny bride
When they have slain her lover?'

Out spoke the hardy Highland wight,
'I'll go, my chief, I'm ready:
It is not for your silver bright,
But for your winsome lady:—

'And by my word! the bonny bird
In danger shall not tarry;
So though the waves are raging white
I'll row you o'er the ferry.'

By this the storm grew loud apace,
The water-wraith was shrieking;
And in the scowl of heaven each face
Grew dark as they were speaking.

But still as wilder blew the wind
And as the night grew drearer,
Adown the glen rode arméd men,
Their trampling sounded nearer.

'O haste thee, haste!' the lady cries,
'Though tempests round us gather;
I'll meet the raging of the skies,
But not an angry father.'

The boat has left a stormy land,
A stormy sea before her,—
When, O! too strong for human hand
The tempest gather'd o'er her.

And still they row'd amidst the roar
Of waters fast prevailing:
Lord Ullin reach'd that fatal shore,—
His wrath was changed to wailing.

For, sore dismay'd, through storm and shade
His child he did discover:—
One lovely hand she stretch'd for aid,
And one was round her lover.

'Come back! come back!' he cried in grief
'Across this stormy water:
And I'll forgive your Highland chief,
My daughter!—O my daughter!'

'Twas vain: the loud waves lash'd the shore,
Return or aid preventing:
The waters wild went o'er his child,
And he was left lamenting.

T. CAMPBELL

182

JOCK O' HAZELDEAN

'Why weep ye by the tide, ladie?
  Why weep ye by the tide?
I'll wed ye to my youngest son,
  And ye sall be his bride:

And ye sall be his bride, ladie,
  Sae comely to be seen'—
But ay she loot the tears down fa'
  For Jock of Hazeldean.

'Now let this wilfu' grief be done,
  And dry that cheek so pale;
Young Frank is chief of Errington
  And lord of Langley-dale;
His step is first in peaceful ha',
  His sword in battle keen'—
But ay she loot the tears down fa'
  For Jock of Hazeldean.

'A chain of gold ye sall not lack,
  Nor braid to bind your hair,
Nor mettled hound, nor managed hawk,
  Nor palfrey fresh and fair;
And you the foremost o' them a'
  Shall ride our forest-queen'—
But ay she loot the tears down fa'
  For Jock of Hazeldean.

The kirk was deck'd at morning tide,
  The tapers glimmer'd fair;
The priest and bridegroom wait the bride,
  And dame and knight are there:
They sought her baith by bower and ha':
  The ladie was not seen!
She's o'er the Border, and awa'
  Wi' Jock of Hazeldean.

SIR W. SCOTT

183

FREEDOM AND LOVE

How delicious is the winning
Of a kiss at love's beginning,
When two mutual hearts are sighing
For the knot there's no untying!

Yet remember, 'midst our wooing,
Love has bliss, but Love has ruing;
Other smiles may make you fickle,
Tears for other charms may trickle.

Love he comes, and Love he tarries,
Just as fate or fancy carries;
Longest stays, when sorest chidden;
Laughs and flies, when press'd and bidden.

Bind the sea to slumber stilly,
Bind its odour to the lily,
Bind the aspen ne'er to quiver,
Then bind Love to last for ever.

Love's a fire that needs renewal
Of fresh beauty for its fuel:
Love's wing moults when caged and captured,
Only free, he soars enraptured.

Can you keep the bee from ranging
Or the ringdove's neck from changing?
No! nor fetter'd Love from dying
In the knot there's no untying.

<small>T. CAMPBELL</small>

184

LOVE'S PHILOSOPHY

THE fountains mingle with the river
And the rivers with the ocean,
The winds of heaven mix for ever
With a sweet emotion;
Nothing in the world is single,
All things by a law divine
In one another's being mingle—
Why not I with thine?

See the mountains kiss high heaven
And the waves clasp one another;
No sister-flower would be forgiven
If it disdain'd its brother:

And the sunlight clasps the earth,
And the moonbeams kiss the sea—
What are all these kissings worth,
If thou kiss not me?

P. B. SHELLEY

185

ECHOES

How sweet the answer Echo makes
To Music at night
When, roused by lute or horn, she wakes,
And far away o'er lawns and lakes
Goes answering light!

Yet Love hath echoes truer far
And far more sweet
Than e'er, beneath the moonlight's star,
Of horn or lute or soft guitar
The songs repeat.

'Tis when the sigh,—in youth sincere
And only then,
The sigh that's breathed for one to hear—
Is by that one, that only Dear
Breathed back again.

T. MOORE

186

A SERENADE

AH! County Guy, the hour is nigh,
  The sun has left the lea,
The orange-flower perfumes the bower,
  The breeze is on the sea.
The lark, his lay who trill'd all day,
  Sits hush'd his partner nigh;
Breeze, bird, and flower confess the hour,
  But where is County Guy?

The village maid steals through the shade
   Her shepherd's suit to hear;
To Beauty shy, by lattice high,
   Sings high-born Cavalier.
The star of Love, all stars above,
   Now reigns o'er earth and sky,
And high and low the influence know—
   But where is County Guy?

SIR W. SCOTT

187

TO THE EVENING STAR

GEM of the crimson-colour'd Even,
Companion of retiring day,
Why at the closing gates of heaven,
Beloved Star, dost thou delay?

So fair thy pensile beauty burns
When soft the tear of twilight flows;
So due thy plighted love returns
To chambers brighter than the rose;

To Peace, to Pleasure, and to Love
So kind a star thou seem'st to be,
Sure some enamour'd orb above
Descends and burns to meet with thee!

Thine is the breathing, blushing hour
When all unheavenly passions fly,
Chased by the soul-subduing power
Of Love's delicious witchery.

O! sacred to the fall of day
Queen of propitious stars, appear,
And early rise, and long delay,
When Caroline herself is here!

Shine on her chosen green resort
Whose trees the sunward summit crown,
And wanton flowers, that well may court
An angel's feet to tread them down:—

Shine on her sweetly scented road
Thou star of evening's purple dome,
That lead'st the nightingale abroad,
And guid'st the pilgrim to his home.

Shine where my charmer's sweeter breath
Embalms the soft exhaling dew,
Where dying winds a sigh bequeath
To kiss the cheek of rosy hue:—

Where, winnow'd by the gentle air,
Her silken tresses darkly flow
And fall upon her brow so fair,
Like shadows on the mountain snow.

Thus, ever thus, at day's decline
In converse sweet to wander far—
O bring with thee my Caroline,
And thou shalt be my Ruling Star!

T. CAMPBELL

188

TO THE NIGHT

Swiftly walk over the western wave,
    Spirit of Night!
Out of the misty eastern cave
Where, all the long and lone daylight,
Thou wovest dreams of joy and fear
Which make thee terrible and dear,—
    Swift be thy flight!

Wrap thy form in a mantle grey
    Star-inwrought!
Blind with thine hair the eyes of day,
Kiss her until she be wearied out,
Then wander o'er city, and sea, and land,
Touching all with thine opiate wand—
    Come, long-sought!

When I arose and saw the dawn,
   I sigh'd for thee;
When light rode high, and the dew was gone,
And noon lay heavy on flower and tree,
And the weary Day turn'd to his rest
Lingering like an unloved guest,
   I sigh'd for thee.

Thy brother Death came, and cried
   Wouldst thou me?
Thy sweet child Sleep, the filmy-eyed,
Murmur'd like a noontide bee
Shall I nestle near thy side?
Wouldst thou me?—And I replied
   No, not thee!

Death will come when thou art dead,
   Soon, too soon—
Sleep will come when thou art fled;
Of neither would I ask the boon
I ask of thee, belovéd Night—
Swift be thine approaching flight,
   Come soon, soon!

       P. B. SHELLEY

189

TO A DISTANT FRIEND

Why art thou silent! Is thy love a plant
Of such weak fibre that the treacherous air
Of absence withers what was once so fair?
Is there no debt to pay, no boon to grant?

Yet have my thoughts for thee been vigilant,
Bound to thy service with unceasing care—
The mind's least generous wish a mendicant
For nought but what thy happiness could spare.

Speak!—though this soft warm heart, once free to hold
A thousand tender pleasures, thine and mine,
Be left more desolate, more dreary cold

Than a forsaken bird's-nest fill'd with snow
'Mid its own bush of leafless eglantine—
Speak, that my torturing doubts their end may know!
W. WORDSWORTH

190

WHEN we two parted
In silence and tears,
Half broken-hearted,
To sever for years,
Pale grew thy cheek and cold,
Colder thy kiss;
Truly that hour foretold
Sorrow to this!

The dew of the morning
Sunk chill on my brow;
It felt like the warning
Of what I feel now.
Thy vows are all broken,
And light is thy fame:
I hear thy name spoken
And share in its shame.

They name thee before me,
A knell to mine ear;
A shudder comes o'er me—
Why wert thou so dear?
They know not I knew thee
Who knew thee too well:
Long, long shall I rue thee
Too deeply to tell.

In secret we met:
In silence I grieve
That thy heart could forget,
Thy spirit deceive.
If I should meet thee
After long years,
How should I greet thee?—
With silence and tears.
LORD BYRON

191

HAPPY INSENSIBILITY

In a drear-nighted December,
  Too happy, happy Tree,
Thy branches ne'er remember
  Their green felicity:
The north cannot undo them
With a sleety whistle through them,
Nor frozen thawings glue them
  From budding at the prime.

In a drear-nighted December,
  Too happy, happy Brook,
Thy bubblings ne'er remember
  Apollo's summer look;
But with a sweet forgetting
They stay their crystal fretting,
Never, never petting
  About the frozen time.

Ah would 'twere so with many
  A gentle girl and boy!
But were there ever any
  Writhed not at passéd joy?
To know the change and feel it,
When there is none to heal it
Nor numbéd sense to steal it—
  Was never said in rhyme.

J. KEATS

192

Where shall the lover rest
  Whom the fates sever
From his true maiden's breast,
  Parted for ever?
Where through groves deep and high
  Sounds the far billow,

Where early violets die
　　Under the willow.
　　　Eleu loro!
Soft shall be his pillow.

There, through the summer day
　　Cool streams are laving:
There, while the tempests sway,
　　Scarce are boughs waving;
There thy rest shalt thou take,
　　Parted for ever,
Never again to wake,
　　Never, O never!
　　　Eleu loro!
　　Never, O never!

Where shall the traitor rest,
　　He, the deceiver,
Who could win maiden's breast,
　　Ruin, and leave her?
In the lost battle,
　　Borne down by the flying,
Where mingles war's rattle
　　With groans of the dying;
　　　Eleu loro!
　　There shall he be lying.

Her wing shall the eagle flap
　　O'er the falsehearted;
His warm blood the wolf shall lap
　　Ere life be parted:
Shame and dishonour sit
　　By his grave ever;
Blessing shall hallow it
　　Never, O never!
　　　Eleu loro!
　　Never, O never!

SIR W. SCOTT

LA BELLE DAME SANS MERCI

'O what can ail thee, knight-at-arms,
  Alone and palely loitering?
The sedge has wither'd from the lake,
  And no birds sing.

'O what can ail thee, knight-at-arms!
  So haggard and so woebegone?
The squirrel's granary is full,
  And the harvest's done.

'I see a lily on thy brow
  With anguish moist and fever-dew,
And on thy cheeks a fading rose
  Fast withereth too.'

'I met a lady in the meads,
  Full beautiful—a fairy's child,
Her hair was long, her foot was light,
  And her eyes were wild.

'I made a garland for her head,
  And bracelets too, and fragrant zone;
She look'd at me as she did love,
  And made sweet moan.

'I set her on my pacing steed
  And nothing else saw all day long,
For sidelong would she bend, and sing
  A fairy's song.

'She found me roots of relish sweet,
  And honey wild and manna-dew,
And sure in language strange she said
  "I love thee true."

'She took me to her elfin grot,
  And there she wept, and sigh'd full sore,
And there I shut her wild wild eyes
  With kisses four.

'And there she lulléd me asleep,
  And there I dream'd—Ah! woe betide!
The latest dream I ever dream'd
  On the cold hill's side.

'I saw pale kings and princes too,
  Pale warriors, death-pale were they all;
They cried—"La belle Dame sans Merci
  Hath thee in thrall!"

'I saw their starved lips in the gloam
  With horrid warning gapéd wide,
And I awoke and found me here
  On the cold hill's side.

'And this is why I sojourn here
  Alone and palely loitering,
Though the sedge is wither'd from the lake
  And no birds sing.'

J. KEATS

194

THE ROVER

'A WEARY lot is thine, fair maid,
  A weary lot is thine!
To pull the thorn thy brow to braid,
  And press the rue for wine.
A lightsome eye, a soldier's mien,
  A feather of the blue,
A doublet of the Lincoln green—
  No more of me you knew

          My Love!
No more of me you knew.

'This morn is merry June, I trow,
  The rose is budding fain;
But she shall bloom in winter snow
  Ere we two meet again.'
He turn'd his charger as he spake
  Upon the river shore,

194

He gave the bridle-reins a shake,
Said 'Adieu for evermore
My Love!
And adieu for evermore.'

SIR W. SCOTT

195

THE FLIGHT OF LOVE

WHEN the lamp is shatter'd
The light in the dust lies dead—
When the cloud is scatter'd,
The rainbow's glory is shed.
When the lute is broken,
Sweet tones are remember'd not;
When the lips have spoken,
Loved accents are soon forgot.

As music and splendour
Survive not the lamp and the lute,
The heart's echoes render
No song when the spirit is mute—
No song but sad dirges,
Like the wind through a ruin'd cell,
Or the mournful surges
That ring the dead seaman's knell.

When hearts have once mingled,
Love first leaves the well-built nest;
The weak one is singled
To endure what it once possess'd.
O Love! who bewailest
The frailty of all things here,
Why choose you the frailest
For your cradle, your home, and your bier?

Its passions will rock thee
As the storms rock the ravens on high;
Bright reason will mock thee
Like the sun from a wintry sky.

From thy nest every rafter
Will rot, and thine eagle home
Leave thee naked to laughter,
When leaves fall and cold winds come.

P. B. SHELLEY

196

THE MAID OF NEIDPATH

O LOVERS' eyes are sharp to see,
  And lovers' ears in hearing;
And love, in life's extremity,
  Can lend an hour of cheering.
Disease had been in Mary's bower
  And slow decay from mourning,
Though now she sits on Neidpath's tower
  To watch her Love's returning.

All sunk and dim her eyes so bright,
  Her form decay'd by pining,
Till through her wasted hand, at night,
  You saw the taper shining.
By fits a sultry hectic hue
  Across her cheek was flying;
By fits so ashy pale she grew
  Her maidens thought her dying.

Yet keenest powers to see and hear
  Seem'd in her frame residing;
Before the watch-dog prick'd his ear
  She heard her lover's riding;
Ere scarce a distant form was kenn'd
  She knew and waved to greet him,
And o'er the battlement did bend
  As on the wing to meet him.

He came—he pass'd—an heedless gaze
  As o'er some stranger glancing;
Her welcome, spoke in faltering phrase,
  Lost in his courser's prancing—

The castle-arch, whose hollow tone
    Returns each whisper spoken,
Could scarcely catch the feeble moan
    Which told her heart was broken.

SIR W. SCOTT

197

THE MAID OF NEIDPATH

EARL March look'd on his dying child,
    And, smit with grief to view her—
The youth, he cried, whom I exiled
    Shall be restored to woo her.

She's at the window many an hour
    His coming to discover:
And he look'd up to Ellen's bower
    And she look'd on her lover—

But ah! so pale, he knew her not,
    Though her smile on him was dwelling—
And am I then forgot—forgot?
    It broke the heart of Ellen.

In vain he weeps, in vain he sighs,
    Her cheek is cold as ashes;
Nor love's own kiss shall wake those eyes
    To lift their silken lashes.

T. CAMPBELL

198

BRIGHT Star! would I were steadfast as thou art—
Not in lone splendour hung aloft the night,
And watching, with eternal lids apart,
Like nature's patient sleepless Eremite,

The moving waters at their priestlike task
Of pure ablution round earth's human shores,
Or gazing on the new soft fallen mask
Of snow upon the mountains and the moors:—

No—yet still steadfast, still unchangeable,
Pillow'd upon my fair Love's ripening breast
To feel for ever its soft fall and swell,
Awake for ever in a sweet unrest;

Still, still to hear her tender-taken breath,
And so live ever,—or else swoon to death.

J. KEATS

199

THE TERROR OF DEATH

WHEN I have fears that I may cease to be
Before my pen has glean'd my teeming brain,
Before high-pilèd books, in charact'ry
Hold like rich garners the full-ripen'd grain;

When I behold, upon the night's starr'd face,
Huge cloudy symbols of a high romance,
And think that I may never live to trace
Their shadows, with the magic hand of chance;

And when I feel, fair Creature of an hour!
That I shall never look upon thee more,
Never have relish in the fairy power
Of unreflecting love—then on the shore

Of the wide world I stand alone, and think
Till Love and Fame to nothingness do sink.

J. KEATS

200

DESIDERIA

SURPRISED by joy—impatient as the wind—
I turn'd to share the transport—O with whom
But Thee—deep buried in the silent tomb,
That spot which no vicissitude can find?

Love, faithful love recall'd thee to my mind—
But how could I forget thee? Through what power

Even for the least division of an hour
Have I been so beguiled as to be blind

To my most grievous loss?—That thought's return
Was the worst pang that sorrow ever bore
Save one, one only, when I stood forlorn,

Knowing my heart's best treasure was no more;
That neither present time, nor years unborn
Could to my sight that heavenly face restore.

W. WORDSWORTH

201

AT the mid hour of night, when stars are weeping, I fly
To the lone vale we loved, when life shone warm in thine
    eye;
And I think oft, if spirits can steal from the regions of air
To revisit past scenes of delight, thou wilt come to me there
And tell me our love is remember'd, even in the sky!

Then I sing the wild song it once was rapture to hear
When our voices, commingling, breathed like one on the ear;
And as Echo far off through the vale my sad orison rolls,
I think, O my Love! 'tis thy voice, from the Kingdom of
    Souls
Faintly answering still the notes that once were so dear.

T. MOORE

202

ELEGY ON THYRZA

AND thou art dead, as young and fair
    As aught of mortal birth;
And forms so soft and charms so rare
    Too soon return'd to Earth!

199

Though Earth received them in her bed,
And o'er the spot the crowd may tread
   In carelessness or mirth,
There is an eye which could not brook
A moment on that grave to look.

I will not ask where thou liest low
   Nor gaze upon the spot;
There flowers or weeds at will may grow
   So I behold them not:
It is enough for me to prove
That what I loved and long must love
   Like common earth can rot;
To me there needs no stone to tell
'Tis Nothing that I loved so well.

Yet did I love thee to the last,
   As fervently as thou
Who didst not change through all the past
   And canst not alter now.
The love where Death has set his seal
Nor age can chill, nor rival steal,
   Nor falsehood disavow:
And, what were worse, thou canst not see
Or wrong, or change, or fault in me.

The better days of life were ours;
   The worst can be but mine:
The sun that cheers, the storm that lours,
   Shall never more be thine.
The silence of that dreamless sleep
I envy now too much to weep;
   Nor need I to repine
That all those charms have pass'd away
I might have watch'd through long decay.

The flower in ripen'd bloom unmatch'd
   Must fall the earliest prey;
Though by no hand untimely snatch'd,
   The leaves must drop away.
And yet it were a greater grief

To watch it withering, leaf by leaf,
   Than see it pluck'd today;
Since earthly eye but ill can bear
To trace the change to foul from fair.

I know not if I could have borne
   To see thy beauties fade;
The night that follow'd such a morn
   Had worn a deeper shade:
Thy day without a cloud hath past,
And thou wert lovely to the last,
   Extinguish'd, not decay'd;
As stars that shoot along the sky
Shine brightest as they fall from high.

As once I wept, if I could weep,
   My tears might well be shed
To think I was not near, to keep
   One vigil o'er thy bed:
To gaze, how fondly! on thy face,
To fold thee in a faint embrace,
   Uphold thy drooping head;
And show that love, however vain,
Nor thou nor I can feel again.

Yet how much less it were to gain,
   Though thou hast left me free,
The loveliest things that still remain
   Than thus remember thee!
The all of thine that cannot die
Through dark and dread Eternity
   Returns again to me,
And more thy buried love endears
Than aught except its living years.

LORD BYRON

203

ONE word is too often profaned
   For me to profane it,
One feeling too falsely disdain'd
   For thee to disdain it.

One hope is too like despair
   For prudence to smother,
And Pity from thee more dear
   Than that from another.

I can give not what men call love;
   But wilt thou accept not
The worship the heart lifts above
   And the Heavens reject not:
The desire of the moth for the star,
   Of the night for the morrow,
The devotion to something afar
   From the sphere of our sorrow?
P. B. SHELLEY

204

GATHERING SONG OF DONALD THE BLACK

PIBROCH of Donuil Dhu
   Pibroch of Donuil
Wake thy wild voice anew,
   Summon Clan Conuil.
Come away, come away,
   Hark to the summons!
Come in your war-array,
   Gentles and commons.

Come from deep glen, and
   From mountain so rocky;
The war-pipe and pennon
   Are at Inverlocky.
Come every hill-plaid, and
   True heart that wears one,
Come every steel blade, and
   Strong hand that bears one.

Leave untended the herd,
   The flock without shelter;
Leave the corpse uninterr'd,
   The bride at the altar;

Leave the deer, leave the steer,
  Leave nets and barges:
Come with your fighting gear,
  Broadswords and targes.

Come as the winds come, when
  Forests are rended,
Come as the waves come, when
  Navies are stranded:
Faster come, faster come,
  Faster and faster,
Chief, vassal, page and groom,
  Tenant and master.

Fast they come, fast they come;
  See how they gather!
Wide waves the eagle plume
  Blended with heather.
Cast your plaids, draw your blades,
  Forward each man set!
Pibroch of Donuil Dhu
  Knell for the onset!

SIR W. SCOTT

205

A WET sheet and a flowing sea,
  A wind that follows fast
And fills the white and rustling sail
  And bends the gallant mast;
And bends the gallant mast, my boys,
  While like the eagle free
Away the good ship flies and leaves
  Old England on the lee.

O for a soft and gentle wind!
  I heard a fair one cry;
But give to me the snoring breeze
  And white waves heaving high;

H

And white waves heaving high, my lads,
    The good ship tight and free—
The world of waters is our home,
    And merry men are we.

There's tempest in yon hornéd moon,
    And lightning in yon cloud;
But hark the music, mariners!
    The wind is piping loud;
The wind is piping loud, my boys,
    The lightning flashes free—
While the hollow oak our palace is,
    Our heritage the sea.

A. CUNNINGHAM

206

YE Mariners of England
That guard our native seas!
Whose flag has braved, a thousand years,
The battle and the breeze!
Your glorious standard launch again
To match another foe:
And sweep through the deep,
While the stormy winds do blow;
While the battle rages loud and long
And the stormy winds do blow.

The spirits of your fathers
Shall start from every wave—
For the deck it was their field of fame,
And Ocean was their grave:
Where Blake and mighty Nelson fell
Your manly hearts shall glow,
As ye sweep through the deep,
While the stormy winds do blow;
While the battle rages loud and long
And the stormy winds do blow.

Britannia needs no bulwarks,
No towers along the steep;

Her march is o'er the mountain-waves,
Her home is on the deep.
With thunders from her native oak
She quells the floods below—
As they roar on the shore,
When the stormy winds do blow;
When the battle rages loud and long,
And the stormy winds do blow.

The meteor flag of England
Shall yet terrific burn;
Till danger's troubled night depart
And the star of peace return.
Then, then, ye ocean-warriors!
Our song and feast shall flow
To the fame of your name,
When the storm has ceased to blow;
When the fiery fight is heard no more,
And the storm has ceased to blow.

T. CAMPBELL

207

BATTLE OF THE BALTIC

OF Nelson and the North
Sing the glorious day's renown,
When to battle fierce came forth
All the might of Denmark's crown,
And her arms along the deep proudly shone;
By each gun the lighted brand
In a bold determined hand,
And the Prince of all the land
Led them on.

Like leviathans afloat
Lay their bulwarks on the brine;
While the sign of battle flew
On the lofty British line:
It was ten of April morn by the chime:
As they drifted on their path

There was silence deep as death;
And the boldest held his breath
For a time.

But the might of England flush'd
To anticipate the scene;
And her van the fleeter rush'd
O'er the deadly space between.
'Hearts of oak!' our captains cried, when each gun
From its adamantine lips
Spread a death-shade round the ships,
Like the hurricane eclipse
Of the sun.

Again! again! again!
And the havoc did not slack,
Till a feeble cheer the Dane
To our cheering sent us back;—
Their shots along the deep slowly boom:—
Then ceased—and all is wail,
As they strike the shatter'd sail;
Or in conflagration pale
Light the gloom.

Out spoke the victor then
As he hail'd them o'er the wave,
'Ye are brothers! ye are men!
And we conquer but to save:—
So peace instead of death let us bring:
But yield, proud foe, thy fleet
With the crews, at England's feet,
And make submission meet
To our King.'

Then Denmark blest our chief
That he gave her wounds repose;
And the sounds of joy and grief
From her people wildly rose,
As death withdrew his shades from the day:
While the sun look'd smiling bright
O'er a wide and woful sight,
Where the fires of funeral light
Died away.

Now joy, old England, raise!
For the tidings of thy might,
By the festal cities' blaze,
Whilst the wine-cup shines in light;
And yet amidst that joy and uproar,
Let us think of them that sleep
Full many a fathom deep
By thy wild and stormy steep,
Elsinore!

Brave hearts! to Britain's pride
Once so faithful and so true,
On the deck of fame they died
With the gallant good Riou:
Soft sigh the winds of Heaven o'er their grave!
While the billow mournful rolls
And the mermaid's song condoles
Singing glory to the souls
Of the brave!

T. CAMPBELL

208

ODE TO DUTY

Stern Daughter of the Voice of God!
O Duty! if that name you love
Who art a light to guide, a rod
To check the erring, and reprove;
Thou who art victory and law
When empty terrors overawe;
From vain temptations dost set free,
And calm'st the weary strife of frail humanity!

There are who ask not if thine eye
Be on them; who, in love and truth
Where no misgiving is, rely
Upon the genial sense of youth:
Glad hearts! without reproach or blot,
Who do thy work, and know it not:
O! if through confidence misplaced
They fail, thy saving arms, dread Power! around them cast.

Serene will be our days and bright
And happy will our nature be
When love is an unerring light,
And joy its own security.
And they a blissful course may hold
Ev'n now who, not unwisely bold,
Live in the spirit of this creed;
Yet seek thy firm support, according to their need.

I, loving freedom, and untried,
No sport of every random gust,
Yet being to myself a guide,
Too blindly have reposed my trust:
And oft, when in my heart was heard
Thy timely mandate, I deferr'd
The task, in smoother walks to stray;
But thee I now would serve more strictly, if I may.

Through no disturbance of my soul
Or strong compunction in me wrought,
I supplicate for thy control,
But in the quietness of thought:
Me this uncharter'd freedom tires;
I feel the weight of chance desires:
My hopes no more must change their name;
I long for a repose that ever is the same.

Stern Lawgiver! yet thou dost wear
The Godhead's most benignant grace;
Nor know we anything so fair
As is the smile upon thy face:
Flowers laugh before thee on their beds,
And fragrance in thy footing treads;
Thou dost preserve the Stars from wrong;
And the most ancient Heavens, through Thee, are fresh and
    strong.

To humbler functions, awful Power!
I call thee: I myself commend
Unto thy guidance from this hour;
O let my weakness have an end!

Give unto me, made lowly wise,
The spirit of self-sacrifice;
The confidence of reason give;
And in the light of truth thy Bondman let me live.

W. WORDSWORTH

209

ON THE CASTLE OF CHILLON

ETERNAL Spirit of the chainless Mind!
Brightest in dungeons, Liberty, thou art—
For there thy habitation is the heart—
The heart which love of Thee alone can bind;

And when thy sons to fetters are consign'd,
To fetters, and the damp vault's dayless gloom,
Their country conquers with their martyrdom,
And Freedom's fame finds wings on every wind.

Chillon! thy prison is a holy place
And thy sad floor an altar, for 'twas trod,
Until his very steps have left a trace

Worn as if thy cold pavement were a sod,
By Bonnivard! May none those marks efface!
For they appeal from tyranny to God.

LORD BYRON

210

ENGLAND AND SWITZERLAND
1802

Two Voices are there, one is of the Sea,
One of the Mountains, each a mighty voice:
In both from age to age thou didst rejoice,
They were thy chosen music, Liberty!

There came a tyrant, and with holy glee
Thou fought'st against him,—but hast vainly striven:
Thou from thy Alpine holds at length art driven
Where not a torrent murmurs heard by thee.

—Of one deep bliss thine ear hath been bereft;
Then cleave, O cleave to that which still is left—
For, high-soul'd Maid, what sorrow would it be

That Mountain floods should thunder as before,
And Ocean bellow from his rocky shore,
And neither awful Voice be heard by Thee!

W. WORDSWORTH

211

ON THE EXTINCTION OF THE VENETIAN REPUBLIC

ONCE did She hold the gorgeous East in fee
And was the safeguard of the West; the worth
Of Venice did not fall below her birth,
Venice, the eldest child of liberty.

She was a maiden city, bright and free;
No guile seduced, no force could violate;
And when she took unto herself a mate,
She must espouse the everlasting Sea.

And what if she had seen those glories fade,
Those titles vanish, and that strength decay,—
Yet shall some tribute of regret be paid

When her long life hath reach'd its final day:
Men are we, and must grieve when even the shade
Of that which once was great has pass'd away.

W. WORDSWORTH

212

LONDON, MDCCCII

O FRIEND! I know not which way I must look
For comfort, being, as I am, opprest
To think that now our life is only drest
For show; mean handiwork of craftsman, cook,

Or groom!—We must run glittering like a brook
In the open sunshine, or we are unblest;
The wealthiest man among us is the best:
No grandeur now in Nature or in book

Delights us. Rapine, avarice, expense,
This is idolatry; and these we adore:
Plain living and high thinking are no more:

The homely beauty of the good old cause
Is gone; our peace, our fearful innocence,
And pure religion breathing household laws.

W. WORDSWORTH

213

THE SAME

MILTON! thou shouldst be living at this hour:
England hath need of thee: she is a fen
Of stagnant waters: altar, sword, and pen,
Fireside, the heroic wealth of hall and bower,

Have forfeited their ancient English dower
Of inward happiness. We are selfish men:
O! raise us up, return to us again;
And give us manners, virtue, freedom, power.

Thy soul was like a Star, and dwelt apart:
Thou hadst a voice whose sound was like the sea,
Pure as the naked heavens, majestic, free;

So didst thou travel on life's common way
In cheerful godliness; and yet thy heart
The lowliest duties on herself did lay.

W. WORDSWORTH

214

WHEN I have borne in memory what has tamed
Great nations; how ennobling thoughts depart
When men change swords for ledgers, and desert
The student's bower for gold,—some fears unnamed

I had, my Country!—am I to be blamed?
Now, when I think of thee, and what thou art,
Verily, in the bottom of my heart,
Of those unfilial fears I am ashamed.

For dearly must we prize thee; we who find
In thee a bulwark for the cause of men;
And I by my affection was beguiled:

What wonder if a Poet now and then,
Among the many movements of his mind,
Felt for thee as a lover or a child!

W. WORDSWORTH

215

HOHENLINDEN

On Linden, when the sun was low,
All bloodless lay the untrodden snow;
And dark as winter was the flow
    Of Iser, rolling rapidly.

But Linden saw another sight,
When the drum beat at dead of night
Commanding fires of death to light
    The darkness of her scenery.

By torch and trumpet fast array'd,
Each horseman drew his battle-blade,
And furious every charger neigh'd
    To join the dreadful revelry.

Then shook the hills with thunder riven;
Then rush'd the steed, to battle driven;
And louder than the bolts of Heaven
    Far flash'd the red artillery.

But redder yet that light shall glow
On Linden's hills of stainéd snow;
And bloodier yet the torrent flow
    Of Iser, rolling rapidly.

'Tis morn; but scarce yon level sun
Can pierce the war-clouds, rolling dun,
Where furious Frank and fiery Hun
　　Shout in their sulphurous canopy.

The combat deepens. On, ye Brave
Who rush to glory, or the grave!
Wave, Munich, all thy banners wave,
　　And charge with all thy chivalry!

Few, few shall part, where many meet!
The snow shall be their winding-sheet,
And every turf beneath their feet
　　Shall be a soldier's sepulchre.
　　　　　　　　　　　　T. CAMPBELL

216

AFTER BLENHEIM

It was a summer evening,
　Old Kaspar's work was done,
And he before his cottage door
　Was sitting in the sun;
And by him sported on the green
His little grandchild Wilhelmine.

She saw her brother Peterkin
　Roll something large and round
Which he beside the rivulet
　In playing there had found;
He came to ask what he had found
That was so large and smooth and round.

Old Kaspar took it from the boy
　Who stood expectant by;
And then the old man shook his head,
　And with a natural sigh
'Tis some poor fellow's skull,' said he,
'Who fell in the great victory.'

213

'I find them in the garden,
    For there's many here about;
And often when I go to plough
    The ploughshare turns them out.
For many thousand men,' said he,
'Were slain in that great victory.'

'Now tell us what 'twas all about,'
    Young Peterkin he cries;
And little Wilhelmine looks up
    With wonder-waiting eyes;
'Now tell us all about the war,
And what they fought each other for.'

'It was the English,' Kaspar cried,
    'Who put the French to rout;
But what they fought each other for
    I could not well make out.
But everybody said,' quoth he,
'That 'twas a famous victory.'

'My father lived at Blenheim then,
    Yon little stream hard by;
They burnt his dwelling to the ground,
    And he was forced to fly:
So with his wife and child he fled,
Nor had he where to rest his head.

'With fire and sword the country round
    Was wasted far and wide,
And many a childing mother then
    And newborn baby died:
But things like that, you know, must be
At every famous victory.

'They say it was a shocking sight
    After the field was won;
For many thousand bodies here
    Lay rotting in the sun:
But things like that, you know, must be
After a famous victory.

'Great praise the Duke of Marlbro' won
 And our good Prince Eugene;'
'Why, 'twas a very wicked thing!'
 Said little Wilhelmine;
'Nay . . nay . . my little girl,' quoth he,
'It was a famous victory.

'And everybody praised the Duke
 Who this great fight did win.'
'But what good came of it at last?'
 Quoth little Peterkin:—
'Why that I cannot tell,' said he,
'But 'twas a famous victory.'

R. SOUTHEY

217

PRO PATRIA MORI

WHEN he who adores thee has left but the name
 Of his fault and his sorrows behind,
O! say wilt thou weep, when they darken the fame
 Of a life that for thee was resign'd!
Yes, weep, and however my foes may condemn,
 Thy tears shall efface their decree;
For, Heaven can witness, though guilty to them,
 I have been but too faithful to thee.

With thee were the dreams of my earliest love;
 Every thought of my reason was thine:
In my last humble prayer to the Spirit above
 Thy name shall be mingled with mine!
O! blest are the lovers and friends who shall live
 The days of thy glory to see;
But the next dearest blessing that Heaven can give
 Is the pride of thus dying for thee.

T. MOORE

218

THE BURIAL OF SIR JOHN MOORE
AT CORUNNA

Not a drum was heard, not a funeral note,
  As his corpse to the rampart we hurried;
Not a soldier discharged his farewell shot
  O'er the grave where our hero we buried.

We buried him darkly at dead of night,
  The sods with our bayonets turning;
By the struggling moonbeam's misty light
  And the lantern dimly burning.

No useless coffin enclosed his breast,
  Not in sheet nor in shroud we wound him;
But he lay like a warrior taking his rest
  With his martial cloak around him.

Few and short were the prayers we said,
  And we spoke not a word of sorrow;
But we steadfastly gazed on the face that was dead,
  And we bitterly thought of the morrow.

We thought, as we hollow'd his narrow bed
  And smoothed down his lonely pillow,
That the foe and the stranger would tread o'er his head,
  And we far away on the billow!

Lightly they'll talk of the spirit that's gone
  And o'er his cold ashes upbraid him,—
But little he'll reck, if they let him sleep on
  In the grave where a Briton has laid him.

But half of our heavy task was done
  When the clock struck the hour for retiring:
And we heard the distant and random gun
  That the foe was sullenly firing.

Slowly and sadly we laid him down,
　　From the field of his fame fresh and gory;
We carved not a line, and we raised not a stone—
　　But we left him alone with his glory.

C. WOLFE

219

SIMON LEE THE OLD HUNTSMAN

IN the sweet shire of Cardigan,
Not far from pleasant Ivor Hall,
An old man dwells, a little man,—
'Tis said he once was tall.
Full five-and-thirty years he lived
A running huntsman merry;
And still the centre of his cheek
Is red as a ripe cherry.

No man like him the horn could sound,
And hill and valley rang with glee
When Echo bandied, round and round,
The halloo of Simon Lee.
In those proud days, he little cared
For husbandry or tillage;
To blither tasks did Simon rouse
The sleepers of the village.

He all the country could outrun,
Could leave both man and horse behind;
And often, ere the chase was done,
He reeled, and was stone-blind.
And still there's something in the world
At which his heart rejoices;
For when the chiming hounds are out,
He dearly loves their voices!

But O the heavy change!—bereft
Of health, strength, friends, and kindred, see!
Old Simon to the world is left
In liveried poverty:

His master's dead, and no one now
Dwells in the Hall of Ivor;
Men, dogs, and horses, all are dead;
He is the sole survivor.

And he is lean and he is sick;
His body, dwindled and awry,
Rests upon ankles swoln and thick;
His legs are thin and dry.
One prop he has, and only one,
His wife, an aged woman,
Lives with him, near the waterfall,
Upon the village common.

Beside their moss-grown hut of clay,
Not twenty paces from the door,
A scrap of land they have, but they
Are poorest of the poor.
This scrap of land he from the heath
Enclosed when he was stronger;
But what to them avails the land
Which he can till no longer?

Oft, working by her husband's side,
Ruth does what Simon cannot do;
For she, with scanty cause for pride,
Is stouter of the two.
And, though you with your utmost skill
From labour could not wean them,
'Tis little, very little, all
That they can do between them.

Few months of life has he in store
As he to you will tell,
For still, the more he works, the more
Do his weak ankles swell.
My gentle reader, I perceive
How patiently you've waited,
And now I feel that you expect
Some tale will be related.

WORDSWORTH

O reader! had you in your mind
Such stores as silent thought can bring,
O gentle reader! you would find
A tale in every thing.
What more I have to say is short,
And you must kindly take it:
It is no tale; but, should you think,
Perhaps a tale you'll make it.

One summer-day I chanced to see
This old man doing all he could
To unearth the root of an old tree,
A stump of rotten wood.
The mattock totter'd in his hand;
So vain was his endeavour
That at the root of the old tree
He might have work'd for ever.

'You're overtask'd, good Simon Lee,
Give me your tool,' to him I said;
And at the word right gladly he
Received my proffer'd aid.
I struck, and with a single blow
The tangled root I sever'd,
At which the poor old man so long
And vainly had endeavour'd.

The tears into his eyes were brought,
And thanks and praises seem'd to run
So fast out of his heart, I thought
They never would have done.
—I've heard of hearts unkind, kind deeds
With coldness still returning;
Alas! the gratitude of men
Hath oftener left me mourning.

W. WORDSWORTH

220

THE OLD FAMILIAR FACES

I HAVE had playmates, I have had companions
In my days of childhood, in my joyful school-days;
All, all are gone, the old familiar faces.

I have been laughing, I have been carousing,
Drinking late, sitting late, with my bosom cronies;
All, all are gone, the old familiar faces.

I loved a Love once, fairest among women:
Closed are her doors on me, I must not see her—
All, all are gone, the old familiar faces.

I have a friend, a kinder friend has no man:
Like an ingrate, I left my friend abruptly;
Left him, to muse on the old familiar faces,

Ghost-like I paced round the haunts of my childhood,
Earth seem'd a desert I was bound to traverse,
Seeking to find the old familiar faces.

Friend of my bosom, thou more than a brother,
Why wert not thou born in my father's dwelling?
So might we talk of the old familiar faces,

How some they have died, and some they have left me,
And some are taken from me; all are departed;
All, all are gone, the old familiar faces.

C. LAMB

221

THE JOURNEY ONWARDS

As slow our ship her foamy track
    Against the wind was cleaving,
Her trembling pennant still look'd back
    To that dear isle 'twas leaving.
So loath we part from all we love,
    From all the links that bind us;
So turn our hearts, as on we rove,
    To those we've left behind us!

When, round the bowl, of vanish'd years
    We talk with joyous seeming—
With smiles that might as well be tears,
    So faint, so sad their beaming;
While memory brings us back again
    Each early tie that twined us,
O, sweet's the cup that circles then
    To those we've left behind us!

And when in other climes, we meet
    Some isle or vale enchanting,
Where all looks flowery, wild, and sweet,
    And nought but love is wanting;
We think how great had been our bliss
    If Heaven had but assign'd us
To live and die in scenes like this,
    With some we've left behind us!

As travellers oft look back at eve
    When eastward darkly going,
To gaze upon that light they leave
    Still faint behind them glowing,—
So, when the close of pleasure's day
    To gloom hath near consign'd us,
We turn to catch one fading ray
    Of joy that's left behind us.

                T. MOORE

222

YOUTH AND AGE ·

THERE's not a joy the world can give like that it takes away
When the glow of early thought declines in feeling's dull
    decay;
'Tis not on youth's smooth cheek the blush alone which
    fades so fast,
But the tender bloom of heart is gone, ere youth itself be
    past.

Then the few whose spirits float above the wreck of
    happiness
Are driven o'er the shoals of guilt, or ocean of excess:
The magnet of their course is gone, or only points in vain
The shore to which their shiver'd sail shall never stretch
    again.

Then the mortal coldness of the soul like death itself comes
    down;
It cannot feel for others' woes, it dare not dream its own;
That heavy chill has frozen o'er the fountain of our tears,
And though the eye may sparkle still, 'tis where the ice
    appears.

Though wit may flash from fluent lips, and mirth distract
    the breast,
Through midnight hours that yield no more their former
    hope of rest;
'Tis but as ivy-leaves around the ruin'd turret wreathe,
All green and wildly fresh without, but worn and grey
    beneath.

Or could I feel as I have felt, or be what I have been,
Or weep as I could once have wept o'er many a vanish'd
    scene,—
As springs in deserts found seem sweet, all brackish though
    they be,
So midst the wither'd waste of life, those tears would flow
    to me!

LORD BYRON

223

A LESSON

THERE is a flower, the Lesser Celandine,
That shrinks like many more from cold and rain,
And the first moment that the sun may shine,
Bright as the sun himself, 'tis out again!

When hailstones have been falling, swarm on swarm,
Or blasts the green field and the trees distrest,
Oft have I seen it muffled up from harm
In close self-shelter, like a thing at rest.

But lately, one rough day, this flower I past,
And recognized it, though an alter'd form,
Now standing forth an offering to the blast,
And buffeted at will by rain and storm.

I stopp'd and said, with inly-mutter'd voice,
'It doth not love the shower, nor seek the cold;
This neither is its courage nor its choice,
But its necessity in being old.

'The sunshine may not cheer it, nor the dew;
It cannot help itself in its decay;
Stiff in its members, wither'd, changed of hue,'
And, in my spleen, I smiled that it was grey.

To be a prodigal's favourite—then, worse truth,
A miser's pensioner—behold our lot!
O Man! that from thy fair and shining youth
Age might but take the things Youth needed not!

W. WORDSWORTH

224

PAST AND PRESENT

I REMEMBER, I remember
The house where I was born,
The little window where the sun
Came peeping in at morn;
He never came a wink too soon
Nor brought too long a day;
But now, I often wish the night
Had borne my breath away.

I remember, I remember
The roses, red and white,
The violets, and the lily-cups—
Those flowers made of light!

The lilacs where the robin built,
And where my brother set
The laburnum on his birthday,—
The tree is living yet!

I remember, I remember
Where I was used to swing,
And thought the air must rush as fresh
To swallows on the wing;
My spirit flew in feathers then
That is so heavy now,
And summer pools could hardly cool
The fever on my brow.

I remember, I remember
The fir trees dark and high;
I used to think their slender tops
Were close against the sky:
It was a childish ignorance,
But now 'tis little joy
To know I'm farther off from Heaven
Than when I was a boy.

T. HOOD

225

THE LIGHT OF OTHER DAYS

OFT in the stilly night
    Ere slumber's chain has bound me,
Fond Memory brings the light
    Of other days around me:
        The smiles, the tears
        Of boyhood's years,
    The words of love then spoken;
        The eyes that shone,
        Now dimm'd and gone,
    The cheerful hearts now broken!
Thus in the stilly night
    Ere slumber's chain has bound me,
Sad Memory brings the light
    Of other days around me.

MOORE

When I remember all
   The friends so link'd together
I've seen around me fall
   Like leaves in wintry weather,
     I feel like one
     Who treads alone
   Some banquet-hall deserted,
     Whose lights are fled
     Whose garlands dead,
   And all but he departed!
Thus in the stilly night
   Ere slumber's chain has bound me,
Sad Memory brings the light
   Of other days around me.

T. MOORE

226

INVOCATION

RARELY, rarely, comest thou,
   Spirit of Delight!
Wherefore hast thou left me now
   Many a day and night?
Many a weary night and day
'Tis since thou art fled away.

How shall ever one like me
   Win thee back again?
With the joyous and the free
   Thou wilt scoff at pain.
Spirit false! thou hast forgot
All but those who need thee not.

As a lizard with the shade
   Of a trembling leaf,
Thou with sorrow art dismay'd;
   Even the sighs of grief
Reproach thee, that thou art not near,
And reproach thou wilt not hear.

SHELLEY

Let me set my mournful ditty
  To a merry measure;—
Thou wilt never come for pity,
  Thou wilt come for pleasure;—
Pity then will cut away
Those cruel wings, and thou wilt stay.

I love all that thou lovest,
  Spirit of Delight!
The fresh Earth in new leaves drest
  And the starry night;
Autumn evening, and the morn
When the golden mists are born.

I love snow and all the forms
  Of the radiant frost;
I love waves, and winds, and storms,
  Everything almost
Which is Nature's, and may be
Untainted by man's misery.

I love tranquil solitude,
  And such society
As is quiet, wise, and good.
  Between thee and me
What diff'rence? but thou dost possess
The things I seek, not love them less.

I love Love—though he has wings,
  And like light can flee,
But above all other things,
  Spirit, I love thee—
Thou art love and life! O come!
Make once more my heart thy home!

P. B. SHELLEY

227

STANZAS WRITTEN IN DEJECTION NEAR NAPLES

THE sun is warm, the sky is clear,
The waves are dancing fast and bright,
Blue isles and snowy mountains wear
The purple noon's transparent light:
The breath of the moist air is light
Around its unexpanded buds;
Like many a voice of one delight—
The winds', the birds', the ocean-floods'—
The City's voice itself is soft like Solitude's.

I see the Deep's untrampled floor
With green and purple sea-weeds strown;
I see the waves upon the shore
Like light dissolved in star-showers thrown:
I sit upon the sands alone;
The lightning of the noon-tide ocean
Is flashing round me, and a tone
Arises from its measured motion—
How sweet! did any heart now share in my emotion.

Alas! I have nor hope nor health,
Nor peace within nor calm around,
Nor that Content, surpassing wealth,
The sage in meditation found,
And walk'd with inward glory crown'd—
Nor fame, nor power, nor love, nor leisure;
Others I see whom these surround—
Smiling they live, and call life pleasure;
To me that cup has been dealt in another measure.

Yet now despair itself is mild
Even as the winds and waters are;
I could lie down like a tired child,
And weep away the life of care

Which I have borne, and yet must bear,
Till death like sleep might steal on me,
And I might feel in the warm air
My cheek grow cold, and hear the sea
Breathe o'er my dying brain its last monotony.

P. B. SHELLEY

228

THE SCHOLAR

MY days among the Dead are passed;
Around me I behold,
Where'er these casual eyes are cast,
The mighty minds of old:
My never-failing friends are they,
With whom I converse day by day.

With them I take delight in weal
And seek relief in woe;
And while I understand and feel
How much to them I owe,
My cheeks have often been bedew'd
With tears of thoughtful gratitude.

My thoughts are with the Dead; with them
I live in long-past years,
Their virtues love, their faults condemn,
Partake their hopes and fears,
And from their lessons seek and find
Instruction with an humble mind.

My hopes are with the Dead; anon
My place with them will be,
And I with them shall travel on
Through all Futurity;
Yet leaving here a name, I trust,
That will not perish in the dust.

R. SOUTHEY

229

THE MERMAID TAVERN

Souls of Poets dead and gone,
What Elysium have ye known,
Happy field or mossy cavern,
Choicer than the Mermaid Tavern?
Have ye tippled drink more fine
Than mine host's Canary wine?
Or are fruits of Paradise
Sweeter than those dainty pies
Of Venison? O generous food!
Drest as though bold Robin Hood
Would, with his Maid Marian,
Sup and bowse from horn and can.

I have heard that on a day
Mine host's signboard flew away
Nobody knew whither, till
An astrologer's old quill
To a sheepskin gave the story—
Said he saw you in your glory
Underneath a new-old Sign
Sipping beverage divine,
And pledging with contented smack
The Mermaid in the Zodiac!

Souls of Poets dead and gone
What Elysium have ye known—
Happy field or mossy cavern—
Choicer than the Mermaid Tavern?

J. KEATS

230

THE PRIDE OF YOUTH

Proud Maisie is in the wood,
 Walking so early;
Sweet Robin sits on the bush,
 Singing so rarely.

'Tell me, thou bonny bird,
   When shall I marry me?'
—'When six braw gentlemen
   Kirkward shall carry ye.'

'Who makes the bridal bed,
   Birdie, say truly?'
—'The grey-headed sexton
   That delves the grave duly.

'The glowworm o'er grave and stone
   Shall light thee steady;
The owl from the steeple sing
   Welcome, proud lady.'

SIR W. SCOTT

231

THE BRIDGE OF SIGHS

ONE more Unfortunate
Weary of breath,
Rashly importunate,
Gone to her death!

Take her up tenderly,
Lift her with care;
Fashion'd so slenderly,
Young, and so fair!

Look at her garments
Clinging like cerements;
Whilst the wave constantly
Drips from her clothing;
Take her up instantly,
Loving, not loathing.

Touch her not scornfully;
Think of her mournfully,
Gently and humanly;
Not of the stains of her—
All that remains of her
Now is pure womanly.

HOOD

Make no deep scrutiny
Into her mutiny
Rash and undutiful:
Past all dishonour,
Death has left on her
Only the beautiful.

Still, for all slips of hers,
One of Eve's family—
Wipe those poor lips of hers
Oozing so clammily.

Loop up her tresses
Escaped from the comb,
Her fair auburn tresses;
Whilst wonderment guesses
Where was her home?

Who was her father?
Who was her mother?
Had she a sister?
Had she a brother?
Or was there a dearer one
Still, and a nearer one
Yet, than all other?

Alas! for the rarity
Of Christian charity
Under the sun!
O! it was pitiful!
Near a whole city full,
Home she had none.

Sisterly, brotherly,
Fatherly, motherly
Feelings had changed:
Love, by harsh evidence,
Thrown from its eminence;
Even God's providence
Seeming estranged.

Where the lamps quiver
So far in the river,
With many a light
From window and casement,
From garret to basement,
She stood, with amazement,
Houseless by night.

The bleak wind of March
Made her tremble and shiver;
But not the dark arch,
Or the black flowing river:
Mad from life's history,
Glad to death's mystery
Swift to be hurl'd—
Anywhere, anywhere
Out of the world!

In she plunged boldly,
No matter how coldly
The rough river ran,
Over the brink of it,—
Picture it, think of it,
Dissolute Man!
Lave in it, drink of it,
Then, if you can!

Take her up tenderly,
Lift her with care;
Fashion'd so slenderly,
Young, and so fair!

Ere her limbs frigidly
Stiffen too rigidly,
Decently, kindly,
Smooth and compose them;
And her eyes, close them,
Staring so blindly!

Dreadfully staring
Thro' muddy impurity,
As when with the daring

Last look of despairing
Fix'd on futurity.

Perishing gloomily,
Spurr'd by contumely,
Cold inhumanity,
Burning insanity,
Into her rest.
—Cross her hands humbly
As if praying dumbly,
Over her breast!

Owning her weakness,
Her evil behaviour,
And leaving, with meekness,
Her sins to her Saviour!

T. HOOD

232

ELEGY

O SNATCH'D away in beauty's bloom!
On thee shall press no ponderous tomb;
But on thy turf shall roses rear
Their leaves, the earliest of the year,
And the wild cypress wave in tender gloom:

And oft by yon blue gushing stream
Shall Sorrow lean her drooping head,
And feed deep thought with many a dream,
And lingering pause and lightly tread;
Fond wretch! as if her step disturb'd the dead!

Away! we know that tears are vain,
That Death nor heeds nor hears distress:
Will this unteach us to complain?
Or make one mourner weep the less?
And thou, who tell'st me to forget,
Thy looks are wan, thine eyes are wet.

LORD BYRON

HESTER

WHEN maidens such as Hester die,
Their place ye may not well supply,
Though ye among a thousand try
        With vain endeavour.
A month or more hath she been dead,
Yet cannot I by force be led
To think upon the wormy bed
        And her together.

A springy motion in her gait,
A rising step, did indicate
Of pride and joy no common rate
        That flush'd her spirit:
I know not by what name beside
I shall it call: if 'twas not pride,
It was a joy to that allied
        She did inherit.

Her parents held the Quaker rule,
Which doth the human feeling cool,
But she was train'd in Nature's school,
        Nature had blest her.
A waking eye, a prying mind,
A heart that stirs, is hard to bind;
A hawk's keen sight ye cannot blind,
        Ye could not Hester.

My sprightly neighbour! gone before
To that unknown and silent shore,
Shall we not meet, as heretofore
        Some summer morning—
When from thy cheerful eyes a ray
Hath struck a bliss upon the day,
A bliss that would not go away,
        A sweet fore-warning?

                                C. LAMB

234

CORONACH

HE is gone on the mountain,
　He is lost to the forest,
Like a summer-dried fountain,
　When our need was the sorest.
The font reappearing
　From the raindrops shall borrow,
But to us comes no cheering,
　To Duncan no morrow!

The hand of the reaper
　Takes the ears that are hoary,
But the voice of the weeper
　Wails manhood in glory.
The autumn winds rushing
　Waft the leaves that are serest,
But our flower was in flushing
　When blighting was nearest.

Fleet foot on the correi,
　Sage counsel in cumber,
Red hand in the foray,
　How sound is thy slumber!
Like the dew on the mountain,
　Like the foam on the river,
Like the bubble on the fountain,
　Thou art gone, and for ever!

SIR W. SCOTT

235

THE DEATH BED

WE watch'd her breathing thro' the night,
　Her breathing soft and low,
As in her breast the wave of life
　Kept heaving to and fro.

I

But when the morn came dim and sad
  And chill with early showers,
Her quiet eyelids closed—she had
  Another morn than ours.

T. HOOD

236

ROSABELLE

O LISTEN, listen, ladies gay!
  No haughty feat of arms I tell;
Soft is the note, and sad the lay
  That mourns the lovely Rosabelle.

'Moor, moor the barge, ye gallant crew!
  And, gentle lady, deign to stay!
Rest thee in Castle Ravensheuch,
  Nor tempt the stormy firth today.

'The blackening wave is edged with white;
  To inch and rock the sea-mews fly;
The fishers have heard the Water-Sprite,
  Whose screams forebode that wreck is nigh.

'Last night the gifted Seer did view
  A wet shroud swathed round lady gay;
Then stay thee, Fair, in Ravensheuch;
  Why cross the gloomy firth today?'

''Tis not because Lord Lindesay's heir
  Tonight at Roslin leads the ball,
But that my lady-mother there
  Sits lonely in her castle-hall.

''Tis not because the ring they ride,
  And Lindesay at the ring rides well,
But that my sire the wine will chide
  If 'tis not fill'd by Rosabelle.'

—O'er Roslin all that dreary night
  A wondrous blaze was seen to gleam;
'Twas broader than the watch-fire's light,
  And redder than the bright moonbeam.

It glared on Roslin's castled rock,
　　It ruddied all the copse-wood glen;
'Twas seen from Dryden's groves of oak,
　　And seen from cavern'd Hawthornden.

Seem'd all on fire that chapel proud
　　Where Roslin's chiefs uncoffin'd lie,
Each Baron, for a sable shroud,
　　Sheath'd in his iron panoply.

Seem'd all on fire within, around,
　　Deep sacristy and altar's pale;
Shone every pillar foliage-bound,
　　And glimmer'd all the dead men's mail.

Blazed battlement and pinnet high,
　　Blazed every rose-carved buttress fair—
So still they blaze, when fate is nigh
　　The lordly line of high Saint Clair.

There are twenty of Roslin's barons bold
　　Lie buried within that proud chapelle;
Each one that holy vault doth hold,
　　But the sea holds lovely Rosabelle!

And each Saint Clair was buried there
　　With candle, with book, and with knell;
But the sea-caves rung, and the wild winds sung
　　The dirge of lovely Rosabelle.

SIR W. SCOTT

237

ON AN INFANT DYING AS SOON
AS BORN

I saw where in the shroud did lurk
A curious frame of Nature's work;
A flow'ret crushéd in the bud,
A nameless piece of Babyhood,
Was in her cradle-coffin lying;
Extinct, with scarce the sense of dying:
So soon to exchange the imprisoning womb
For darker closets of the tomb!

She did but ope an eye, and put
A clear beam forth, then straight up shut
For the long dark: ne'er more to see
Through glasses of mortality.
Riddle of destiny, who can show
What thy short visit meant, or know
What thy errand here below?
Shall we say, that Nature blind
Check'd her hand, and changed her mind
Just when she had exactly wrought
A finish'd pattern without fault?
Could she flag, or could she tire,
Or lack'd she the Promethean fire
(With her nine moons' long workings sicken'd)
That should thy little limbs have quicken'd?
Limbs so firm, they seem'd to assure
Life of health, and days mature;
Woman's self in miniature!
Limbs so fair, they might supply
(Themselves now but cold imagery)
The sculptor to make Beauty by.
Or did the stern-eyed Fate descry
That babe or mother, one must die;
So in mercy left the stock
And cut the branch; to save the shock
Of young years widow'd, and the pain
When Single State comes back again
To the lone man who, reft of wife,
Thenceforward drags a maiméd life?
The economy of Heaven is dark,
And wisest clerks have miss'd the mark
Why human buds, like this, should fall
More brief than fly ephemeral
That has his day; while shrivell'd crones
Stiffen with age to stocks and stones;
And crabbéd use the conscience sears
In sinners of an hundred years.
—Mother's prattle, mother's kiss,
Baby fond, thou ne'er wilt miss:
Rites, which custom does impose,

Silver bells, and baby clothes;
Coral redder than those lips
Which pale death did late eclipse;
Music framed for infants' glee,
Whistle never tuned for thee;
Though thou want'st not, thou shalt have them,
Loving hearts were they which gave them.
Let not one be missing; nurse,
See them laid upon the hearse
Of infant slain by doom perverse.
Why should kings and nobles have
Pictured trophies to their grave,
And we, churls, to thee deny
Thy pretty toys with thee to lie—
A more harmless vanity?

C. LAMB

238

THE AFFLICTION OF MARGARET

WHERE art thou, my beloved Son,
Where art thou, worse to me than dead!
O find me, prosperous or undone!
Or if the grave be now thy bed,
Why am I ignorant of the same
That I may rest; and neither blame
Nor sorrow may attend thy name?

Seven years, alas! to have received
No tidings of an only child—
To have despair'd, have hoped, believed,
And been for evermore beguiled,—
Sometimes with thoughts of very bliss!
I catch at them, and then I miss;
Was ever darkness like to this?

He was among the prime in worth,
An object beauteous to behold;
Well born, well bred; I sent him forth
Ingenuous, innocent, and bold:

If things ensued that wanted grace
As hath been said, they were not base;
And never blush was on my face.

Ah! little doth the young one dream
When full of play and childish cares,
What power is in his wildest scream
Heard by his mother unawares!
He knows it not, he cannot guess;
Years to a mother bring distress;
But do not make her love the less.

Neglect me! no, I suffer'd long
From that ill thought; and being blind
Said 'Pride shall help me in my wrong:
Kind mother have I been, as kind
As ever breathed:' and that is true;
I've wet my path with tears like dew,
Weeping for him when no one knew.

My Son, if thou be humbled, poor,
Hopeless of honour and of gain,
O! do not dread thy mother's door;
Think not of me with grief and pain:
I now can see with better eyes;
And worldly grandeur I despise
And fortune with her gifts and lies.

Alas! the fowls of heaven have wings,
And blasts of heaven will aid their flight;
They mount—how short a voyage brings
The wanderers back to their delight!
Chains tie us down by land and sea;
And wishes, vain as mine, may be
All that is left to comfort thee.

Perhaps some dungeon hears thee groan
Maim'd, mangled by inhuman men;
Or thou upon a desert thrown
Inheritest the lion's den;
Or hast been summon'd to the deep,
Thou, thou, and all thy mates to keep
An incommunicable sleep.

I look for ghosts: but none will force
Their way to me; 'tis falsely said
That there was ever intercourse
Between the living and the dead;
For surely then I should have sight
Of him I wait for day and night
With love and longings infinite.

My apprehensions come in crowds;
I dread the rustling of the grass;
The very shadows of the clouds
Have power to shake me as they pass;
I question things, and do not find
One that will answer to my mind;
And all the world appears unkind.

Beyond participation lie
My troubles, and beyond relief:
If any chance to heave a sigh
They pity me, and not my grief.
Then come to me, my Son, or send
Some tidings that my woes may end!
I have no other earthly friend.

W. WORDSWORTH

239

HUNTING SONG

WAKEN, lords and ladies gay,
On the mountain dawns the day;
All the jolly chase is here
With hawk and horse and hunting-spear;
Hounds are in their couples yelling,
Hawks are whistling, horns are knelling,
Merrily, merrily mingle they,
'Waken, lords and ladies gay.'

Waken, lords and ladies gay,
The mist has left the mountain grey,
Springlets in the dawn are steaming,
Diamonds on the brake are gleaming,

And foresters have busy been
To track the buck in thicket green;
Now we come to chant our lay,
'Waken, lords and ladies gay.'

Waken, lords and ladies gay,
To the greenwood haste away;
We can show you where he lies,
Fleet of foot and tall of size;
We can show the marks he made
When 'gainst the oak his antlers fray'd;
You shall see him brought to bay;
'Waken, lords and ladies gay.'

Louder, louder, chant the lay,
Waken, lords and ladies gay!
Tell them youth and mirth and glee
Run a course as well as we;
Time, stern huntsman! who can balk,
Stanch as hound and fleet as hawk;
Think of this, and rise with day,
Gentle lords and ladies gay!

SIR W. SCOTT

240

TO THE SKYLARK

ETHEREAL minstrel! pilgrim of the sky!
Dost thou despise the earth where cares abound?
Or while the wings aspire, are heart and eye
Both with thy nest upon the dewy ground?
Thy nest which thou canst drop into at will,
Those quivering wings composed, that music still!

To the last point of vision, and beyond
Mount, daring warbler!—that love-prompted strain
—'Twixt thee and thine a never-failing bond—
Thrills not the less the bosom of the plain:
Yet might'st thou seem, proud privilege! to sing
All independent of the leafy Spring.

Leave to the nightingale her shady wood;
A privacy of glorious light is thine,
Whence thou dost pour upon the world a flood
Of harmony, with instinct more divine;
Type of the wise, who soar, but never roam—
True to the kindred points of Heaven and Home!

W. WORDSWORTH

241

TO A SKYLARK

HAIL to thee, blithe Spirit!
    Bird thou never wert,
  That from heaven, or near it
    Pourest thy full heart
In profuse strains of unpremeditated art.

  Higher still and higher
    From the earth thou springest
  Like a cloud of fire;
    The blue deep thou wingest,
And singing still dost soar, and soaring ever singest.

  In the golden lightning
    Of the sunken sun
  O'er which clouds are brightening,
    Thou dost float and run,
Like an unbodied joy whose race is just begun.

  The pale purple even
    Melts around thy flight;
  Like a star of heaven
    In the broad daylight
Thou art unseen, but yet I hear thy shrill delight:

  Keen as are the arrows
    Of that silver sphere,
  Whose intense lamp narrows
    In the white dawn clear
Until we hardly see, we feel that it is there.

All the earth and air
　　With thy voice is loud,
As, when night is bare,
　　From one lonely cloud
The moon rains out her beams, and heaven is overflow'd.

What thou art we know not;
　　What is most like thee?
From rainbow clouds there flow not
　　Drops so bright to see
As from thy presence showers a rain of melody.

Like a poet hidden
　　In the light of thought,
Singing hymns unbidden,
　　Till the world is wrought
To sympathy with hopes and fears it heeded not:

Like a high-born maiden
　　In a palace tower,
Soothing her love-laden
　　Soul in secret hour
With music sweet as love, which overflows her bower:

Like a glow-worm golden
　　In a dell of dew,
Scattering unbeholden
　　Its aerial hue
Among the flowers and grass, which screen it from the view:

Like a rose embower'd
　　In its own green leaves,
By warm winds deflower'd,
　　Till the scent it gives
Makes faint with too much sweet these heavy-wingéd
　　　　thieves.

Sound of vernal showers
　　On the twinkling grass,
Rain-awaken'd flowers,
　　All that ever was
Joyous, and clear, and fresh, thy music doth surpass.

Teach us, sprite or bird,
    What sweet thoughts are thine:
I have never heard
    Praise of love or wine
That panted forth a flood of rapture so divine.

Chorus hymeneal
    Or triumphal chaunt
Match'd with thine, would be all
    But an empty vaunt—
A thing wherein we feel there is some hidden want.

What objects are the fountains
    Of thy happy strain?
What fields, or waves, or mountains?
    What shapes of sky or plain?
What love of thine own kind? what ignorance of pain?

With thy clear keen joyance
    Languor cannot be:
Shadow of annoyance
    Never came near thee:
Thou lovest; but ne'er knew love's sad satiety.

Waking or asleep
    Thou of death must deem
Things more true and deep
    Than we mortals dream,
Or how could thy notes flow in such a crystal stream?

We look before and after,
    And pine for what is not:
Our sincerest laughter
    With some pain is fraught;
Our sweetest songs are those that tell of saddest thought.

Yet if we could scorn
    Hate, and pride, and fear;
If we were things born
    Not to shed a tear,
I know not how thy joy we ever should come near.

Better than all measures
Of delightful sound,
Better than all treasures
That in books are found,
Thy skill to poet were, thou scorner of the ground!

Teach me half the gladness
That thy brain must know,
Such harmonious madness
From my lips would flow
The world should listen then, as I am listening now!

P. B. SHELLEY

242

THE GREEN LINNET

BENEATH these fruit-tree boughs that shed
Their snow-white blossoms on my head,
With brightest sunshine round me spread
Of Spring's unclouded weather,
In this sequester'd nook how sweet
To sit upon my orchard-seat!
And flowers and birds once more to greet,
My last year's friends together.

One have I mark'd, the happiest guest
In all this covert of the blest:
Hail to Thee, far above the rest
In joy of voice and pinion!
Thou, Linnet! in thy green array
Presiding Spirit here today
Dost lead the revels of the May,
And this is thy dominion.

While birds, and butterflies, and flowers,
Make all one band of paramours,
Thou, ranging up and down the bowers,
Art sole in thy employment;
A Life, a Presence like the air,
Scattering thy gladness without care,
Too blest with any one to pair,
Thyself thy own enjoyment.

Amid yon tuft of hazel trees
That twinkle to the gusty breeze,
Behold him perch'd in ecstasies
Yet seeming still to hover;
There, where the flutter of his wings
Upon his back and body flings
Shadows and sunny glimmerings,
That cover him all over.

My dazzled sight he oft deceives—
A brother of the dancing leaves;
Then flits, and from the cottage-eaves
Pours forth his song in gushes,
As if by that exulting strain
He mock'd and treated with disdain
The voiceless Form he chose to feign,
While fluttering in the bushes.

W. WORDSWORTH

243

TO THE CUCKOO

O BLITHE new-comer! I have heard,
I hear thee and rejoice:
O Cuckoo! shall I call thee bird,
Or but a wandering Voice?

While I am lying on the grass
Thy twofold shout I hear;
From hill to hill it seems to pass,
At once far off and near.

Though babbling only to the vale
Of sunshine and of flowers,
Thou bringest unto me a tale
Of visionary hours.

Thrice welcome, darling of the Spring!
Even yet thou art to me
No bird, but an invisible thing,
A voice, a mystery;

The same whom in my schoolboy days
I listen'd to; that Cry
Which made me look a thousand ways
In bush, and tree, and sky.

To seek thee did I often rove
Through woods and on the green;
And thou wert still a hope, a love;
Still long'd for, never seen!

And I can listen to thee yet;
Can lie upon the plain
And listen, till I do beget
That golden time again.

O blessèd birth! the earth we pace
Again appears to be
An unsubstantial, fairy place,
That is fit home for Thee!

W. WORDSWORTH

244

ODE TO A NIGHTINGALE

My heart aches, and a drowsy numbness pains
  My sense, as though of hemlock I had drunk,
Or emptied some dull opiate to the drains
  One minute past, and Lethe-wards had sunk:
'Tis not through envy of thy happy lot,
  But being too happy in thy happiness,—
    That thou, light-wingèd Dryad of the trees,
      In some melodious plot
Of beechen green, and shadows numberless,
  Singest of summer in full-throated ease.

O for a draught of vintage! that hath been
  Cool'd a long age in the deep-delvèd earth,
Tasting of Flora and the country-green,
  Dance, and Provençal song, and sunburnt mirth.
O for a beaker full of the warm South,
  Full of the true, the blushful Hippocrene,

KEATS

With beaded bubbles winking at the brim
  And purple-stainéd mouth;
That I might drink, and leave the world unseen,
  And with thee fade away into the forest dim.

Fade far away, dissolve, and quite forget
  What thou among the leaves hast never known,
The weariness, the fever, and the fret
  Here, where men sit and hear each other groan;
Where palsy shakes a few, sad, last grey hairs,
  Where youth grows pale, and spectre-thin, and dies;
    Where but to think is to be full of sorrow
      And leaden-eyed despairs;
  Where Beauty cannot keep her lustrous eyes,
    Or new Love pine at them beyond tomorrow.

Away! away! for I will fly to thee,
  Not charioted by Bacchus and his pards,
But on the viewless wings of Poesy,
  Though the dull brain perplexes and retards:
Already with thee! tender is the night,
  And haply the Queen-Moon is on her throne,
    Cluster'd around by all her starry Fays;
      But here there is no light
  Save what from heaven is with the breezes blown
    Through verdurous glooms and winding mossy ways.

I cannot see what flowers are at my feet,
  Nor what soft incense hangs upon the boughs,
But, in embalméd darkness, guess each sweet
  Wherewith the seasonable month endows
The grass, the thicket, and the fruit-tree wild;
  White hawthorn, and the pastoral eglantine;
    Fast-fading violets cover'd up in leaves;
      And mid-May's eldest child
  The coming musk-rose, full of dewy wine,
    The murmurous haunt of flies on summer eves.

Darkling I listen; and for many a time
  I have been half in love with easeful Death,
Call'd him soft names in many a muséd rhyme,
  To take into the air my quiet breath;

Now more than ever seems it rich to die,
　　To cease upon the midnight with no pain,
　　　　While thou art pouring forth thy soul abroad
　　　　　　In such an ecstasy!
　　Still wouldst thou sing, and I have ears in vain—
　　　　To thy high requiem become a sod.

Thou wast not born for death, immortal Bird!
　　No hungry generations tread thee down;
The voice I hear this passing night was heard
　　In ancient days by emperor and clown:
Perhaps the selfsame song that found a path
　　Through the sad heart of Ruth, when, sick for home,
　　　　She stood in tears amid the alien corn;
　　　　　　The same that oft-times hath
　　Charm'd magic casements, opening on the foam
　　Of perilous seas, in faery lands forlorn.

Forlorn! the very word is like a bell
　　To toll me back from thee to my sole self!
Adieu! the fancy cannot cheat so well
　　As she is famed to do, deceiving elf.
Adieu! adieu! thy plaintive anthem fades
　　Past the near meadows, over the still stream,
　　　　Up the hill-side; and now 'tis buried deep
　　　　　　In the next valley-glades:
　　Was it a vision, or a waking dream?
　　　　Fled is that music:—do I wake or sleep?

　　　　　　　　　　　　　　　　　　　　　　J. KEATS

245

UPON WESTMINSTER BRIDGE
Sept. 3, 1802

EARTH has not anything to show more fair:
Dull would he be of soul who could pass by
A sight so touching in its majesty:
This City now doth like a garment wear

The beauty of the morning: silent, bare,
Ships, towers, domes, theatres, and temples lie
Open unto the fields, and to the sky,
All bright and glittering in the smokeless air.

Never did sun more beautifully steep
In his first splendour valley, rock, or hill;
Ne'er saw I, never felt, a calm so deep!

The river glideth at his own sweet will:
Dear God! the very houses seem asleep;
And all that mighty heart is lying still!

W. WORDSWORTH

246

OZYMANDIAS OF EGYPT

I MET a traveller from an antique land
Who said: Two vast and trunkless legs of stone
Stand in the desert. Near them on the sand,
Half sunk, a shatter'd visage lies, whose frown
And wrinkled lip and sneer of cold command
Tell that its sculptor well those passions read
Which yet survive, stamp'd on these lifeless things,
The hand that mock'd them and the heart that fed;
And on the pedestal these words appear:
'My name is Ozymandias, king of kings:
Look on my works, ye Mighty, and despair!'
Nothing beside remains. Round the decay
Of that colossal wreck, boundless and bare,
The lone and level sands stretch far away.

P. B. SHELLEY

247

COMPOSED AT NEIDPATH CASTLE, THE PROPERTY OF LORD QUEENSBERRY, 1803

DEGENERATE Douglas! O the unworthy lord!
Whom mere despite of heart could so far please
And love of havoc (for with such disease
Fame taxes him) that he could send forth word

To level with the dust a noble horde,
A brotherhood of venerable trees,
Leaving an ancient dome, and towers like these
Beggar'd and outraged!—Many hearts deplored

The fate of those old trees; and oft with pain
The traveller at this day will stop and gaze
On wrongs, which Nature scarcely seems to heed:

For shelter'd places, bosoms, nooks, and bays,
And the pure mountains, and the gentle Tweed,
And the green silent pastures, yet remain.

W. WORDSWORTH

248

ADMONITION TO A TRAVELLER

YES, there is holy pleasure in thine eye!
—The lovely cottage in the guardian nook
Hath stirr'd thee deeply; with its own dear brook,
Its own small pasture, almost its own sky!

But covet not the abode—O do not sigh
As many do, repining while they look;
Intruders who would tear from Nature's book
This precious leaf with harsh impiety:

—Think what the home would be if it were thine,
Even thine, though few thy wants!—Roof, window, door,
The very flowers are sacred to the Poor,

The roses to the porch which they entwine:
Yea, all that now enchants thee, from the day
On which it should be touch'd would melt away!

W. WORDSWORTH

249

TO THE HIGHLAND GIRL OF INVERSNEYDE

Sweet Highland Girl, a very shower
Of beauty is thy earthly dower!
Twice seven consenting years have shed
Their utmost bounty on thy head:
And these grey rocks; that household lawn;
Those trees—a veil just half withdrawn,
This fall of water that doth make
A murmur near the silent lake,
This little bay, a quiet road
That holds in shelter thy abode;
In truth together ye do seem
Like something fashion'd in a dream;
Such forms as from their covert peep
When earthly cares are laid asleep!
But O fair Creature! in the light
Of common day, so heavenly bright,
I bless Thee, Vision as thou art,
I bless thee with a human heart:
God shield thee to thy latest years!
Thee, neither know I, nor thy peers;
And yet my eyes are fill'd with tears.

With earnest feeling I shall pray
For thee when I am far away;
For never saw I mien or face
In which more plainly I could trace
Benignity and home-bred sense
Ripening in perfect innocence.
Here scatter'd like a random seed,
Remote from men, Thou dost not need
The embarrass'd look of shy distress,
And maidenly shamefacedness:

Thou wear'st upon thy forehead clear
The freedom of a mountaineer:
A face with gladness overspread!
Soft smiles, by human kindness bred;
And seemliness complete, that sways
Thy courtesies, about thee plays;
With no restraint, but such as springs
From quick and eager visitings
Of thoughts that lie beyond the reach
Of thy few words of English speech:
A bondage sweetly brook'd, a strife
That gives thy gestures grace and life!
So have I, not unmoved in mind,
Seen birds of tempest-loving kind—
Thus beating up against the wind.

What hand but would a garland cull
For thee who art so beautiful?
O happy pleasure! here to dwell
Beside thee in some heathy dell;
Adopt your homely ways, and dress,
A shepherd, thou a shepherdess!
But I could frame a wish for thee
More like a grave reality:
Thou art to me but as a wave
Of the wild sea; and I would have
Some claim upon thee, if I could,
Though but of common neighbourhood.
What joy to hear thee, and to see!
Thy elder brother I would be,
Thy father—anything to thee!

Now thanks to Heaven! that of its grace
Hath led me to this lonely place.
Joy have I had; and going hence
I bear away my recompense.
In spots like these it is we prize
Our memory, feel that she hath eyes:
Then why should I be loath to stir?
I feel this place was made for her;

To give new pleasure like the past,
Continued long as life shall last.
Nor am I loath, though pleased at heart,
Sweet Highland Girl! from thee to part;
For I, methinks, till I grow old
As fair before me shall behold
As I do now, the cabin small,
The lake, the bay, the waterfall;
And Thee, the spirit of them all!

W. WORDSWORTH

250

THE REAPER

BEHOLD her, single in the field,
Yon solitary Highland Lass!
Reaping and singing by herself;
Stop here, or gently pass!
Alone she cuts and binds the grain,
And sings a melancholy strain;
O listen! for the vale profound
Is overflowing with the sound.

No nightingale did ever chaunt
More welcome notes to weary bands
Of travellers in some shady haunt,
Among Arabian sands:
A voice so thrilling ne'er was heard
In spring-time from the cuckoo-bird
Breaking the silence of the seas
Among the farthest Hebrides.

Will no one tell me what she sings?
Perhaps the plaintive numbers flow
For old, unhappy, far-off things,
And battles long ago:
Or is it some more humble lay,
Familiar matter of today?
Some natural sorrow, loss, or pain,
That has been, and may be again!

Whate'er the theme, the maiden sang
As if her song could have no ending;
I saw her singing at her work,
And o'er the sickle bending;
I listen'd, motionless and still;
And, as I mounted up the hill,
The music in my heart I bore,
Long after it was heard no more.

W. WORDSWORTH

251

THE REVERIE OF POOR SUSAN

At the corner of Wood Street, when daylight appears,
Hangs a Thrush that sings loud, it has sung for three years:
Poor Susan has pass'd by the spot, and has heard
In the silence of morning the song of the bird.

'Tis a note of enchantment; what ails her? She sees
A mountain ascending, a vision of trees;
Bright volumes of vapour through Lothbury glide,
And a river flows on through the vale of Cheapside.

Green pastures she views in the midst of the dale
Down which she so often has tripp'd with her pail;
And a single small cottage, a nest like a dove's,
The one only dwelling on earth that she loves.

She looks, and her heart is in heaven: but they fade,
The mist and the river, the hill and the shade;
The stream will not flow, and the hill will not rise,
And the colours have all pass'd away from her eyes!

W. WORDSWORTH

252

TO A LADY, WITH A GUITAR

ARIEL to Miranda:—Take
This slave of music, for the sake
Of him, who is the slave of thee;
And teach it all the harmony
In which thou canst, and only thou,
Make the delighted spirit glow,
Till joy denies itself again
And, too intense, is turn'd to pain.
For by permission and command
Of thine own Prince Ferdinand,
Poor Ariel sends this silent token
Of more than ever can be spoken;
Your guardian spirit, Ariel, who
From life to life must still pursue
Your happiness, for thus alone
Can Ariel ever find his own.
From Prospero's enchanted cell,
As the mighty verses tell,
To the throne of Naples he
Lit you o'er the trackless sea,
Flitting on, your prow before,
Like a living meteor.
When you die, the silent Moon
In her interlunar swoon
Is not sadder in her cell
Than deserted Ariel.
When you live again on earth.
Like an unseen Star of birth
Ariel guides you o'er the sea
Of life from your nativity.
Many changes have been run
Since Ferdinand and you begun
Your course of love, and Ariel still
Has track'd your steps and served your will.
Now in humbler, happier lot,
This is all remember'd not;

And now, alas! the poor sprite is
Imprison'd for some fault of his
In a body like a grave—
From you he only dares to crave,
For his service and his sorrow
A smile to-day, a song to-morrow.

The artist who this idol wrought
To echo all harmonious thought,
Fell'd a tree, while on the steep
The woods were in their winter sleep,
Rock'd in that repose divine
On the wind-swept Apennine;
And dreaming, some of Autumn past,
And some of Spring approaching fast,
And some of April buds and showers,
And some of songs in July bowers,
And all of love; and so this tree,—
O that such our death may be!—
Died in sleep, and felt no pain,
To live in happier form again:
From which, beneath Heaven's fairest star,
The artist wrought this loved Guitar;
And taught it justly to reply
To all who question skilfully
In language gentle as thine own;
Whispering in enamour'd tone
Sweet oracles of woods and dells,
And summer winds in sylvan cells;
—For it had learnt all harmonies
Of the plains and of the skies,
Of the forests and the mountains,
And the many-voicéd fountains;
The clearest echoes of the hills,
The softest notes of falling rills,
The melodies of birds and bees,
The murmuring of summer seas,
And pattering rain, and breathing dew,
And airs of evening; and it knew

That seldom-heard mysterious sound
Which, driven on its diurnal round,
As it floats through boundless day,
Our world enkindles on its way:
—All this it knows, but will not tell
To those who cannot question well
The Spirit that inhabits it;
It talks according to the wit
Of its companions; and no more
Is heard than has been felt before
By those who tempt it to betray
These secrets of an elder day.
But, sweetly as its answers will
Flatter hands of perfect skill,
It keeps its highest holiest tone
For one beloved Friend alone.

P. B. SHELLEY

253

THE DAFFODILS

I WANDER'D lonely as a cloud
That floats on high o'er vales and hills,
When all at once I saw a crowd,
A host of golden daffodils,
Beside the lake, beneath the trees
Fluttering and dancing in the breeze.

Continuous as the stars that shine
And twinkle on the milky way,
They stretch'd in never-ending line
Along the margin of a bay:
Ten thousand saw I at a glance
Tossing their heads in sprightly dance.

The waves beside them danced, but they
Out-did the sparkling waves in glee:—
A Poet could not but be gay
In such a jocund company!
I gazed—and gazed—but little thought
What wealth the show to me had brought.

For oft, when on my couch I lie
In vacant or in pensive mood,
They flash upon that inward eye
Which is the bliss of solitude;
And then my heart with pleasure fills
And dances with the daffodils.

W. WORDSWORTH

254

TO THE DAISY

WITH little here to do or see
Of things that in the great world be,
Sweet Daisy! oft I talk to thee
  For thou art worthy,
Thou unassuming Commonplace
Of Nature, with that homely face,
And yet with something of a grace
  Which love makes for thee!

Oft on the dappled turf at ease
I sit and play with similes
Loose types of things through all degrees,
  Thoughts of thy raising;
And many a fond and idle name
I give to thee, for praise or blame
As is the humour of the game,
  While I am gazing.

A nun demure, of lowly port;
Or sprightly maiden, of Love's court,
In thy simplicity the sport
  Of all temptations;
A queen in crown of rubies drest;
A starveling in a scanty vest;
Are all, as seems to suit thee best,
  Thy appellations.

A little Cyclops, with one eye
Staring to threaten and defy,
That thought comes next—and instantly
  The freak is over.

The shape will vanish, and behold!
A silver shield with boss of gold
That spreads itself, some fairy bold
    In fight to cover.

I see thee glittering from afar—
And then thou art a pretty star,
Not quite so fair as many are
    In heaven above thee!
Yet like a star, with glittering crest,
Self-poised in air thou seem'st to rest;—
May peace come never to his nest
    Who shall reprove thee!

Sweet Flower! for by that name at last
When all my reveries are past
I call thee, and to that cleave fast,
    Sweet silent Creature!
That breath'st with me in sun and air,
Do thou, as thou art wont, repair
My heart with gladness, and a share
    Of thy meek nature!

              W. WORDSWORTH

255

ODE TO AUTUMN

SEASON of mists and mellow fruitfulness!
Close bosom-friend of the maturing sun;
Conspiring with him how to load and bless
With fruit the vines that round the thatch-eaves **run**;
To bend with apples the moss'd cottage-trees,
And fill all fruit with ripeness to the core;
To swell the gourd, and plump the hazel shells
With a sweet kernel; to set budding more
And still more, later flowers for the bees,
Until they think warm days will never cease;
For Summer has o'erbrimm'd their clammy cells.

Who hath not seen Thee oft amid thy store?
Sometimes whoever seeks abroad may find
Thee sitting careless on a granary floor,
Thy hair soft-lifted by the winnowing wind;
Or on a half-reap'd furrow sound asleep,
Drowsed with the fume of poppies, while thy hook
Spares the next swath and all its twinéd flowers;
And sometimes like a gleaner thou dost keep
Steady thy laden head across a brook;
Or by a cider-press, with patient look,
Thou watchest the last oozings, hours by hours.

Where are the songs of Spring? Aye, where are they?
Think not of them,—thou hast thy music too,
While barréd clouds bloom the soft-dying day
And touch the stubble-plains with rosy hue;
Then in a wailful choir the small gnats mourn
Among the river-sallows, borne aloft
Or sinking as the light wind lives or dies;
And full-grown lambs loud bleat from hilly bourn;
Hedge-crickets sing, and now with treble soft
The redbreast whistles from a garden-croft,
And gathering swallows twitter in the skies.

J. KEATS

256

ODE TO WINTER

Germany, December, 1800

When first the fiery-mantled Sun
His heavenly race began to run,
Round the earth and ocean blue
His children four the Seasons flew:—
    First, in green apparel dancing,
The young Spring smiled with angel-grace;
    Rosy Summer, next advancing,
Rush'd into her sire's embrace—
Her bright-hair'd sire, who bade her keep
    For ever nearest to his smiles,

On Calpe's olive-shaded steep
   Or India's citron-cover'd isles.
More remote, and buxom-brown,
   The Queen of vintage bow'd before his throne;
A rich pomegranate gemm'd her crown,
   A ripe sheaf bound her zone.

But howling Winter fled afar
To hills that prop the polar star;
And loves on deer-borne car to ride
With barren darkness at his side,
Round the shore where loud Lofoden
   Whirls to death the roaring whale,
Round the hall where Runic Odin
   Howls his war-song to the gale—
Save when adown the ravaged globe
He travels on his native storm,
Deflowering Nature's grassy robe
   And trampling on her faded form;
Till light's returning Lord assume
   The shaft that drives him to his northern field,
Of power to pierce his raven plume
   And crystal-cover'd shield.

O sire of storms! whose savage ear
The Lapland drum delights to hear,
When Frenzy with her bloodshot eye
Implores thy dreadful deity—
Archangel! Power of desolation!
   Fast descending as thou art,
Say, hath mortal invocation
   Spells to touch thy stony heart:
Then, sullen Winter! hear my prayer,
   And gently rule the ruin'd year;
Nor chill the wanderer's bosom bare
   Nor freeze the wretch's falling tear:
To shuddering Want's unmantled bed
   Thy horror-breathing agues cease to lend,
And gently on the orphan head
   Of Innocence descend,

But chiefly spare, O king of clouds!
The sailor on his airy shrouds,
When wrecks and beacons strew the steep
And spectres walk along the deep.
Milder yet thy snowy breezes
   Pour on yonder tented shores,
Where the Rhine's broad billow freezes,
   Or the dark-brown Danube roars.
O winds of Winter! list ye there
   To many a deep and dying groan?
Or start, ye demons of the midnight air,
   At shrieks and thunders louder than your own?
Alas! e'en your unhallow'd breath
   May spare the victim fallen low;
But Man will ask no truce to death,
   No bounds to human woe.

                  T. CAMPBELL

257

YARROW UNVISITED
1803

From Stirling Castle we had seen
The mazy Forth unravell'd,
Had trod the banks of Clyde and Tay,
And with the Tweed had travell'd;
And when we came to Clovenford,
Then said my 'winsome Marrow,'
'Whate'er betide, we'll turn aside,
And see the Braes of Yarrow.'

'Let Yarrow folk, frae Selkirk town,
Who have been buying, selling,
Go back to Yarrow, 'tis their own,
Each maiden to her dwelling!
On Yarrow's banks let herons feed,
Hares couch, and rabbits burrow,
But we will downward with the Tweed,
Nor turn aside to Yarrow.

WORDSWORTH

'There's Galla Water, Leader Haughs,
Both lying right before us;
And Dryburgh, where with chiming Tweed
The lintwhites sing in chorus;
There's pleasant Tiviot-dale, a land
Made blithe with plough and harrow:
Why throw away a needful day
To go in search of Yarrow?

'What's Yarrow but a river bare
That glides the dark hills under?
There are a thousand such elsewhere
As worthy of your wonder.'
—Strange words they seem'd of slight and scorn;
My true-love sigh'd for sorrow,
And look'd me in the face, to think
I thus could speak of Yarrow!

'O green,' said I, 'are Yarrow's holms,
And sweet is Yarrow flowing!
Fair hangs the apple frae the rock,
But we will leave it growing.
O'er hilly path and open strath
We'll wander Scotland thorough;
But, though so near, we will not turn
Into the dale of Yarrow.

'Let beeves and home-bred kine partake
The sweets of Burn-mill meadow;
The swan on still Saint Mary's Lake
Float double, swan and shadow!
We will not see them; will not go
To-day, nor yet to-morrow;
Enough if in our hearts we know
There's such a place as Yarrow.

'Be Yarrow stream unseen, unknown;
It must, or we shall rue it:
We have a vision of our own,
Ah! why should we undo it?

The treasur'd dreams of times long past,
We'll keep them, winsome Marrow!
For when we'er there, although 'tis fair,
'Twill be another Yarrow!

'If Care with freezing years should come
And wandering seem but folly,—
Should we be loath to stir from home,
And yet be melancholy;
Should life be dull, and spirits low,
'Twill soothe us in our sorrow
That earth has something yet to show,
The bonny holms of Yarrow!'

W. WORDSWORTH

258

YARROW VISITED

September, 1814

AND is this—Yarrow?—This the Stream
Of which my fancy cherish'd
So faithfully, a waking dream,
An image that hath perish'd?
O that some minstrel's harp were near
To utter notes of gladness
And chase this silence from the air,
That fills my heart with sadness!

Yet why?—a silvery current flows
With uncontroll'd meanderings;
Nor have these eyes by greener hills
Been soothed, in all my wanderings.
And, through her depths, Saint Mary's Lake
Is visibly delighted;
For not a feature of those hills
Is in the mirror slighted.

A blue sky bends o'er Yarrow Vale,
Save where that pearly whiteness
Is round the rising sun diffused,
A tender hazy brightness;

Mild dawn of promise! that excludes
All profitless dejection;
Though not unwilling here to admit
A pensive recollection.

Where was it that the famous Flower
Of Yarrow Vale lay bleeding?
His bed perchance was yon smooth mound
On which the herd is feeding:
And haply from this crystal pool,
Now peaceful as the morning,
The Water-wraith ascended thrice,
And gave his doleful warning.

Delicious is the Lay that sings
The haunts of happy lovers,
The path that leads them to the grove,
The leafy grove that covers:
And pity sanctifies the verse
That paints, by strength of sorrow,
The unconquerable strength of love;
Bear witness, rueful Yarrow!

But thou that didst appear so fair
To fond imagination,
Dost rival in the light of day
Her delicate creation:
Meek loveliness is round thee spread,
A softness still and holy:
The grace of forest charms decay'd,
And pastoral melancholy.

That region left, the vale unfolds
Rich groves of lofty stature,
With Yarrow winding through the pomp
Of cultivated nature;
And rising from those lofty groves
Behold a ruin hoary,
The shatter'd front of Newark's Towers,
Renown'd in Border story.

WORDSWORTH

Fair scenes for childhood's opening bloom,
For sportive youth to stray in,
For manhood to enjoy his strength,
And age to wear away in!
Yon cottage seems a bower of bliss,
A covert for protection
Of tender thoughts, that nestle there—
The brood of chaste affection.

How sweet on this autumnal day
The wild-wood fruits to gather,
And on my true-love's forehead plant
A crest of blooming heather!
And what if I enwreathed my own?
'Twere no offence to reason;
The sober hills thus deck their brows
To meet the wintry season.

I see—but not by sight alone,
Loved Yarrow, have I won thee;
A ray of Fancy still survives—
Her sunshine plays upon thee!
Thy ever-youthful waters keep
A course of lively pleasure;
And gladsome notes my lips can breathe
Accordant to the measure.

The vapours linger round the heights,
They melt, and soon must vanish;
One hour is theirs, nor more is mine—
Sad thought! which I would banish,
But that I know, where'er I go,
Thy genuine image, Yarrow!
Will dwell with me—to heighten joy,
And cheer my mind in sorrow.

W. WORDSWORTH

259

THE INVITATION

BEST and brightest, come away,
Fairer far than this fair day,
Which, like thee, to those in sorrow
Comes to bid a sweet good-morrow
To the rough year just awake
In its cradle on the brake.
The brightest hour of unborn Spring
Through the Winter wandering,
Found, it seems, the halcyon morn
To hoar February born;
Bending from Heaven, in azure mirth,
It kiss'd the forehead of the earth,
And smiled upon the silent sea,
And bade the frozen streams be free,
And waked to music all their fountains,
And breathed upon the frozen mountains,
And like a prophetess of May
Strew'd flowers upon the barren way,
Making the wintry world appear
Like one on whom thou smilest, dear.

Away, away, from men and towns,
To the wild wood and the downs—
To the silent wilderness
Where the soul need not repress
Its music, lest it should not find
An echo in another's mind,
While the touch of Nature's art
Harmonizes heart to heart.

Radiant Sister of the Day
Awake! arise! and come away!
To the wild woods and the plains,
To the pools where winter rains
Image all their roof of leaves,
Where the pine its garland weaves

Of sapless green, and ivy dun,
Round stems that never kiss the sun,
Where the lawns and pastures be
And the sandhills of the sea,
Where the melting hoar-frost wets
The daisy-star that never sets,
And wind-flowers and violets
Which yet join not scent to hue
Crown the pale year weak and new;
When the night is left behind
In the deep east, dim and blind,
And the blue noon is over us,
And the multitudinous
Billows murmur at our feet,
Where the earth and ocean meet,
And all things seem only one
In the universal Sun.

P. B. SHELLEY

260

THE RECOLLECTION

Now the last day of many days
All beautiful and bright as thou,
The loveliest and the last, is dead,
Rise, Memory, and write its praise!
Up,—to thy wonted work! come, trace
The epitaph of glory fled,
For now the Earth has changed its face
A frown is on the Heaven's brow.

We wander'd to the Pine Forest
   That skirts the Ocean's foam;
The lightest wind was in its nest,
   The tempest in its home.
The whispering waves were half asleep,
   The clouds were gone to play,
And on the bosom of the deep
   The smile of Heaven lay;

It seem'd as if the hour were one
    Sent from beyond the skies
Which scatter'd from above the sun
    A light of Paradise!

We paused amid the pines that stood
    The giants of the waste,
Tortured by storms to shapes as rude
    As serpents interlaced,—
And soothed by every azure breath
    That under heaven is blown
To harmonies and hues beneath,
    As tender as its own:
Now all the tree-tops lay asleep
    Like green waves on the sea,
As still as in the silent deep
    The ocean-woods may be.

How calm it was!—the silence there
    By such a chain was bound,
That even the busy woodpecker
    Made stiller by her sound
The inviolable quietness;
    The breath of peace we drew
With its soft motion made not less
    The calm that round us grew.
There seem'd from the remotest seat
    Of the white mountain waste
To the soft flower beneath our feet,
    A magic circle traced,—
A spirit interfused around,
    A thrilling silent life;
To momentary peace it bound
    Our mortal nature's strife;—
And still I felt the centre of
    The magic circle there
Was one fair form that fill'd with love
    The lifeless atmosphere.

We paused beside the pools that lie
    Under the forest bough;

Each seem'd as 'twere a little sky
  Gulf'd in a world below;
A firmament of purple light
  Which in the dark earth lay,
More boundless than the depth of night
  And purer than the day—
In which the lovely forests grew
  As in the upper air,
More perfect both in shape and hue
  Than any spreading there.
There lay the glade and neighbouring lawn,
  And through the dark green wood
The white sun twinkling like the dawn
  Out of a speckled cloud.
Sweet views which in our world above
  Can never well be seen
Were imaged by the water's love
  Of that fair forest green:
And all was interfused beneath
  With an Elysian glow,
An atmosphere without a breath,
  A softer day below.
Like one beloved, the scene had lent
  To the dark water's breast
Its every leaf and lineament
  With more than truth exprest;
Until an envious wind crept by,
  Like an unwelcome thought
Which from the mind's too faithful eye
  Blots one dear image out.
—Though thou art ever fair and kind,
  The forests ever green,
Less oft is peace in Shelley's mind
  Than calm in waters seen.

P. B. SHELLEY

261

BY THE SEA

It is a beauteous evening, calm and free;
The holy time is quiet as a Nun
Breathless with adoration; the broad sun
Is sinking down in its tranquillity;

The gentleness of heaven is on the Sea:
Listen! the mighty Being is awake,
And doth with his eternal motion make
A sound like thunder—everlastingly.

Dear child! dear girl! that walkest with me here,
If thou appear untouch'd by solemn thought
Thy nature is not therefore less divine:

Thou liest in Abraham's bosom all the year,
And worship'st at the Temple's inner shrine,
God being with thee when we know it not.

W. WORDSWORTH

262

TO THE EVENING STAR

Star that bringest home the bee,
And sett'st the weary labourer free!
If any star shed peace, 'tis Thou
    That send'st it from above,
Appearing when Heaven's breath and brow
    Are sweet as hers we love.

Come to the luxuriant skies,
Whilst the landscape's odours rise,
Whilst far-off lowing herds are heard
    And songs when toil is done,
From cottages whose smoke unstirr'd
    Curls yellow in the sun.

Star of love's soft interviews,
Parted lovers on thee muse;
Their remembrancer in Heaven
    Of thrilling vows thou art,
Too delicious to be riven
    By absence from the heart.

T. CAMPBELL

263

DATUR HORA QUIETI

THE sun upon the lake is low,
    The wild birds hush their song,
The hills have evening's deepest glow,
    Yet Leonard tarries long.
Now all whom varied toil and care
    From home and love divide,
In the calm sunset may repair
    Each to the loved one's side.

The noble dame on turret high,
    Who waits her gallant knight,
Looks to the western beam to spy
    The flash of armour bright.
The village maid, with hand on brow
    The level ray to shade,
Upon the footpath watches now
    For Colin's darkening plaid.

Now to their mates the wild swans row,
    By day they swam apart,
And to the thicket wanders slow
    The hind beside the hart.
The woodlark at his partner's side
    Twitters his closing song—
All meet whom day and care divide,
    But Leonard tarries long!

SIR W. SCOTT

264

TO THE MOON

ART thou pale for weariness
Of climbing heaven, and gazing on the earth,
   Wandering companionless
Among the stars that have a different birth,—
And ever-changing, like a joyless eye
That finds no object worth its constancy?

P. B. SHELLEY

265

A WIDOW bird sate mourning for her Love
   Upon a wintry bough;
The frozen wind crept on above,
   The freezing stream below.

There was no leaf upon the forest bare,
   No flower upon the ground,
And little motion in the air
   Except the mill-wheel's sound.

P. B. SHELLEY

266

TO SLEEP

A FLOCK of sheep that leisurely pass by
One after one; the sound of rain, and bees
Murmuring; the fall of rivers, winds and seas,
Smooth fields, white sheets of water, and pure sky;

I've thought of all by turns, and still I lie
Sleeplesss; and soon the small birds' melodies
Must hear, first utter'd from my orchard trees,
And the first cuckoo's melancholy cry.

Even thus last night, and two nights more I lay,
    And could not win thee, Sleep! by any stealth:
So do not let me wear to-night away:

Without Thee what is all the morning's wealth?
    Come, blessèd barrier between day and day,
Dear mother of fresh thoughts and joyous health!
                                        W. WORDSWORTH

267

THE SOLDIER'S DREAM

Our bugles sang truce, for the night-cloud had lower'd,
    And the sentinel stars set their watch in the sky;
And thousands had sunk on the ground overpower'd,
    The weary to sleep, and the wounded to die.

When reposing that night on my pallet of straw
    By the wolf-scaring faggot that guarded the slain,
At the dead of the night a sweet Vision I saw;
    And thrice ere the morning I dreamt it again.

Methought from the battle-field's dreadful array
    Far, far, I had roam'd on a desolate track:
'Twas Autumn,—and sunshine arose on the way
    To the home of my fathers, that welcomed me back.

I flew to the pleasant fields traversed so oft
    In life's morning march, when my bosom was young;
I heard my own mountain-goats bleating aloft,
    And knew the sweet strain that the corn-reapers sung.

Then pledged me the wine-cup, and fondly I swore
    From my home and my weeping friends never to part;
My little ones kiss'd me a thousand times o'er,
    And my wife sobb'd aloud in her fullness of heart.

'Stay—stay with us!—rest!—thou art weary and worn!'—
    And fain was their war-broken soldier to stay;—
But sorrow return'd with the dawning of morn,
    And the voice in my dreaming ear melted away.
                                        T. CAMPBELL

268

A DREAM OF THE UNKNOWN

I DREAM'D that as I wander'd by the way
 Bare Winter suddenly was changed to Spring,
And gentle odours led my steps astray,
 Mix'd with a sound of waters murmuring
Along a shelving bank of turf, which lay
 Under a copse, and hardly dared to fling
Its green arms round the bosom of the stream,
But kiss'd it and then fled, as Thou mightest in dream.

There grew pied wind-flowers and violets,
 Daisies, those pearl'd Arcturi of the earth,
The constellated flower that never sets;
 Faint oxlips; tender bluebells at whose birth
The sod scarce heaved; and that tall flower that wets
 Its mother's face with heaven-collected tears,
When the low wind, its playmate's voice, it hears.

And in the warm hedge grew lush eglantine,
 Green cow-bind and the moonlight-colour'd May,
And cherry-blossoms, and white cups, whose wine
 Was the bright dew yet drain'd not by the day;
And wild roses, and ivy serpentine
 With its dark buds and leaves, wandering astray;
And flowers azure, black, and streak'd with gold,
Fairer than any waken'd eyes behold.

And nearer to the river's trembling edge
 There grew broad flag-flowers, purple prank'd with
  white,
And starry river-buds among the sedge,
 And floating water-lilies, broad and bright,
Which lit the oak that overhung the hedge
 With moonlight beams of their own watery light;
And bulrushes, and reeds of such deep green
As soothed the dazzled eye with sober sheen.

Methought that of these visionary flowers
   I made a nosegay, bound in such a way
That the same hues, which in their natural bowers
   Were mingled or opposed, the like array
Kept these imprison'd children of the Hours
   Within my hand,—and then, elate and gay,
I hasten'd to the spot whence I had come
That I might there present it—O! to Whom?

P. B. SHELLEY

269

THE INNER VISION

MOST sweet it is with unuplifted eyes
To pace the ground, if path be there or none,
While a fair region round the traveller lies
Which he forbears again to look upon;

Pleased rather with some soft ideal scene,
The work of Fancy, or some happy tone
Of meditation, slipping in between
The beauty coming and the beauty gone.

—If Thought and Love desert us, from that day
Let us break off all commerce with the Muse:
With Thought and Love companions of our way—

Whate'er the senses take or may refuse,—
The Mind's internal heaven shall shed her dews
Of inspiration on the humblest lay.

W. WORDSWORTH

270

THE REALM OF FANCY

EVER let the Fancy roam!
Pleasure never is at home:
At a touch sweet Pleasure melteth,
Like to bubbles when rain pelteth;

Then let wingéd Fancy wander
Through the thought still spread beyond her:
Open wide the mind's cage-door,
She'll dart forth, and cloudward soar.
O sweet Fancy! let her loose;
Summer's joys are spoilt by use,
And the enjoying of the Spring
Fades as does its blossoming:
Autumn's red-lipp'd fruitage too,
Blushing through the mist and dew,
Cloys with tasting: What do then?
Sit thee by the ingle, when
The sear faggot blazes bright,
Spirit of a winter's night;
When the soundless earth is muffled,
And the cakéd snow is shuffled
From the ploughboy's heavy shoon;
When the Night doth meet the Noon
In a dark conspiracy
To banish Even from her sky.
—Sit thee there, and send abroad,
With a mind self-overawed,
Fancy, high-commission'd:—send her!
She has vassals to attend her;
She will bring, in spite of frost,
Beauties that the earth hath lost;
She will bring thee, all together,
All delights of summer weather;
All the buds and bells of May
From dewy sward or thorny spray;
All the heapéd Autumn's wealth,
With a still, mysterious stealth;
She will mix these pleasures up
Like three fit wines in a cup,
And thou shalt quaff it;—thou shalt hear
Distant harvest-carols clear;
Rustle of the reapéd corn;
Sweet birds antheming the morn:
And in the same moment—hark!
'Tis the early April lark,

Or the rooks, with busy caw,
Foraging for sticks and straw.
Thou shalt, at one glance, behold
The daisy and the marigold;
White-plumed lilies, and the first
Hedge-grown primrose that hath burst;
Shaded hyacinth, alway
Sapphire queen of the mid-May;
And every leaf, and every flower
Pearlèd with the selfsame shower.
Thou shalt see the field-mouse peep
Meagre from its cellèd sleep;
And the snake all winter-thin
Cast on sunny bank its skin;
Freckled nest eggs thou shalt see
Hatching in the hawthorn-tree,
When the hen-bird's wing doth rest
Quiet on her mossy nest;
Then the hurry and alarm
When the bee-hive casts its swarm;
Acorns ripe down-pattering
While the autumn breezes sing.

O sweet Fancy! let her loose;
Everything is spoilt by use:
Where's the cheek that doth not fade,
Too much gazed at? Where's the maid
Whose lip mature is ever new?
Where's the eye, however blue,
Doth not weary? Where's the face
One would meet in every place?
Where's the voice, however soft,
One would hear so very oft?
At a touch sweet Pleasure melteth
Like to bubbles when rain pelteth.
Let them wingèd Fancy find
Thee a mistress to thy mind:
Dulcet-eyed as Ceres' daughter,
Ere the God of Torment taught her

How to frown and how to chide;
  With a waist and with a side
White as Hebe's, when her zone
Slipt its golden clasp, and down
Fell her kirtle to her feet
While she held the goblet sweet,
And Jove grew languid.—Break the mesh
  Of the Fancy's silken leash;
Quickly break her prison-string,
And such joys as these she'll bring:
  —Let the wingéd Fancy roam!
Pleasure never is at home.

J. KEATS

271

HYMN TO THE SPIRIT OF NATURE

LIFE of Life! Thy lips enkindle
  With their love the breath between them;
And thy smiles before they dwindle
  Make the cold air fire; then screen them
In those locks, where whoso gazes
Faints, entangled in their mazes.

Child of Light! Thy limbs are burning
  Through the veil which seems to hide them,
As the radiant lines of morning
  Through thin clouds, ere they divide them;
And this atmosphere divinest
Shrouds thee wheresoe'er thou shinest.

Fair are others: none beholds Thee;
  But thy voice sounds low and tender
Like the fairest, for it folds thee
  From the sight, that liquid splendour;
And all feel, yet see them never,—
As I feel now, lost for ever!

Lamp of Earth! where'er thou movest
  Its dim shapes are clad with brightness,

And the souls of whom thou lovest
   Walk upon the winds with lightness
Till they fail, as I am failing,
Dizzy, lost, yet unbewailing!

P. B. SHELLEY

272

WRITTEN IN EARLY SPRING

I HEARD a thousand blended notes
While in a grove I sat reclined,
In that sweet mood when pleasant thoughts
Bring sad thoughts to the mind.

To her fair works did Nature link
The human soul that through me ran;
And much it grieved my heart to think
What Man has made of Man.

Through primrose tufts, in that sweet bower,
The periwinkle trail'd its wreaths;
And 'tis my faith that every flower
Enjoys the air it breathes.

The birds around me hopp'd and play'd,
Their thoughts I cannot measure—
But the least motion which they made
It seem'd a thrill of pleasure.

The budding twigs spread out their fan
To catch the breezy air;
And I must think, do all I can,
That there was pleasure there.

If this belief from heaven be sent,
If such be Nature's holy plan,
Have I not reason to lament
What Man has made of Man?

W. WORDSWORTH

273

RUTH: OR THE INFLUENCES OF NATURE

WHEN Ruth was left half desolate
Her father took another mate;
And Ruth, not seven years old,
A slighted child, at her own will
Went wandering over dale and hill,
In thoughtless freedom, bold.

And she had made a pipe of straw,
And music from that pipe could draw
Like sounds of winds and floods;
Had built a bower upon the green,
As if she from her birth had been
An infant of the woods.

Beneath her father's roof, alone
She seem'd to live; her thoughts her own;
Herself her own delight:
Pleased with herself, nor sad nor gay.
And, passing thus the live-long day,
She grew to woman's height.

There came a youth from Georgia's shore—
A military casque he wore
With splendid feathers drest;
He brought them from the Cherokees;
The feathers nodded in the breeze
And made a gallant crest.

From Indian blood you deem him sprung:
But no! he spake the English tongue
And bore a soldier's name;
And, when America was free
From battle and from jeopardy,
He 'cross the ocean came.

With hues of genius on his cheek,
In finest tones the youth could speak:

—While he was yet a boy
The moon, the glory of the sun,
And streams that murmur as they run
Had been his dearest joy.

He was a lovely youth! I guess
The panther in the wilderness
Was not so fair as he;
And when he chose to sport and play,
No dolphin ever was so gay
Upon the tropic sea.

Among the Indians he had fought;
And with him many tales he brought
Of pleasure and of fear;
Such tales as, told to any maid
By such a youth, in the green shade,
Were perilous to hear.

He told of girls, a happy rout!
Who quit their fold with dance and shout,
Their pleasant Indian town,
To gather strawberries all day long;
Returning with a choral song
When daylight is gone down.

He spake of plants that hourly change
Their blossoms, through a boundless range
Of intermingling hues;
With budding, fading, faded flowers,
They stand the wonder of the bowers
From morn to evening dews.

He told of the Magnolia, spread
High as a cloud, high over head!
The cypress and her spire;
—Of flowers that with one scarlet gleam
Cover a hundred leagues, and seem
To set the hills on fire.

The youth of green savannahs spake,
And many an endless, endless lake

With all its fairy crowds
Of islands, that together lie
As quietly as spots of sky
Among the evening clouds.

'How pleasant,' then he said, 'it were
A fisher or a hunter there,
In sunshine or in shade
To wander with an easy mind,
And build a household fire, and find
A home in every glade!

'What days and what bright years! Ah me!
Our life were life indeed, with thee
So pass'd in quiet bliss;
And all the while,' said he, 'to know
That we were in a world of woe,
On such an earth as this!'

And then he sometimes interwove
Fond thoughts about a father's love,
'For there,' said he, 'are spun
Around the heart such tender ties,
That our own children to our eyes
Are dearer than the sun.

'Sweet Ruth! and could you go with me
My helpmate in the woods to be,
Our shed at night to rear;
Or run, my own adopted bride,
A sylvan huntress at my side,
And drive the flying deer!

'Beloved Ruth!'—No more he said.
The wakeful Ruth at midnight shed
A solitary tear:
She thought again—and did agree
With him to sail across the sea,
And drive the flying deer.

'And now, as fitting is and right,
We in the church our faith will plight,

A husband and a wife.'
Even so they did; and I may say
That to sweet Ruth that happy day
Was more than human life.

Through dream and vision did she sink,
Delighted all the while to think
That, on those lonesome floods
And green savannahs, she should share
His board with lawful joy, and bear
His name in the wild woods.

But, as you have before been told,
This Stripling, sportive, gay, and bold,
And with his dancing crest
So beautiful, through savage lands
Had roam'd about, with vagrant bands
Of Indians in the West.

The wind, the tempest roaring high,
The tumult of a tropic sky
Might well be dangerous food
For him, a youth to whom was given
So much of earth—so much of heaven,
And such impetuous blood.

Whatever in those climes he found
Irregular in sight or sound
Did to his mind impart
A kindred impulse, seem'd allied
To his own powers, and justified
The workings of his heart.

Nor less, to feed voluptuous thought,
The beauteous forms of Nature wrought,—
Fair trees and gorgeous flowers;
The breezes their own languor lent;
The stars had feelings, which they sent
Into those favour'd bowers.

Yet, in his worst pursuits, I ween
That sometimes there did intervene

Pure hopes of high intent:
For passions link'd to forms so fair
And stately, needs must have their share
Of noble sentiment.

But ill he lived, much evil saw,
With men to whom no better law
Nor better life was known;
Deliberately and undeceived
Those wild men's vices he received,
And gave them back his own.

His genius and his moral frame
Were thus impair'd, and he became
The slave of low desires:
A man who without self-control
Would seek what the degraded soul
Unworthily admires.

And yet he with no feign'd delight
Had woo'd the maiden, day and night
Had loved her, night and morn:
What could he less than love a maid
Whose heart with so much nature play'd—
So kind and so forlorn?

Sometimes most earnestly he said,
'O Ruth! I have been worse than dead;
False thoughts, thoughts bold and vain
Encompass'd me on every side
When I, in confidence and pride,
Had cross'd the Atlantic main.

'Before me shone a glorious world
Fresh as a banner bright, unfurl'd
To music suddenly:
I look'd upon those hills and plains,
And seem'd as if let loose from chains
To live at liberty!

'No more of this—for now, by thee,
Dear Ruth! more happily set free,

With nobler zeal I burn;
My soul from darkness is released
Like the whole sky when to the east
The morning doth return.'

Full soon that better mind was gone;
No hope, no wish remain'd, but one,—
They stirr'd him now no more;
New objects did new pleasure give,
And once again he wish'd to live
As lawless as before.

Meanwhile, as thus with him it fared,
They for the voyage were prepared,
And went to the seashore:
But, when they thither came, the youth
Deserted his poor bride, and Ruth
Could never find him more.

God help thee, Ruth!—Such pains she had,
That she in half a year was mad,
And in a prison housed;
And there, with many a doleful song
Made of wild words, her cup of wrong
She fearfully caroused.

Yet sometimes milder hours she knew,
Nor wanted sun, nor rain, nor dew,
Nor pastimes of the May,
—They all were with her in her cell;
And a clear brook with cheerful knell
Did o'er the pebbles play.

When Ruth three seasons thus had lain,
There came a respite to her pain;
She from her prison fled;
But of the Vagrant none took thought;
And where it liked her best she sought
Her shelter and her bread.

Among the fields she breathed again:
The master-current of her brain

Ran permanent and free;
And, coming to the banks of Tone,
There did she rest; and dwell alone
Under the greenwood tree.

The engines of her pain, the tools
That shaped her sorrow, rocks and pools,
And airs that gently stir
The vernal leaves—she loved them still,
Nor ever tax'd them with the ill
Which had been done to her.

A barn her Winter bed supplies;
But, till the warmth of Summer skies
And Summer days is gone,
(And all do in this tale agree)
She sleeps beneath the greenwood tree,
And other home hath none.

An innocent life, yet far astray!
And Ruth will, long before her day,
Be broken down and old.
Sore aches she needs must have! but less
Of mind, than body's wretchedness,
From damp, and rain, and cold.

If she is prest by want of food
She from her dwelling in the wood
Repairs to a roadside;
And there she begs at one steep place,
Where up and down with easy pace
The horsemen-travellers ride.

That oaten pipe of hers is mute
Or thrown away: but with a flute
Her loneliness she cheers;
This flute, made of a hemlock stalk,
At evening in his homeward walk
The Quantock woodman hears.

I, too, have pass'd her on the hills
Setting her little water-mills

By spouts and fountains wild—
Such small machinery as she turn'd
Ere she had wept, ere she had mourn'd,
A young and happy child!

Farewell! and when thy days are told,
Ill-fated Ruth! in hallow'd mould
Thy corpse shall buried be;
For thee a funeral bell shall ring,
And all the congregation sing
A Christian psalm for thee.

W. WORDSWORTH

274

WRITTEN IN THE EUGANEAN HILLS, NORTH ITALY

MANY a green isle needs must be
In the deep wide sea of Misery,
Or the mariner, worn and wan,
Never thus could voyage on
Day and night, and night and day,
Drifting on his dreary way,
With the solid darkness black
Closing round his vessel's track;
Whilst above, the sunless sky
Big with clouds, hangs heavily,
And behind the tempest fleet
Hurries on with lightning feet,
Riving sail, and cord, and plank,
Till the ship has almost drank
Death from the o'er-brimming deep;
And sinks down, down, like that sleep
When the dreamer seems to be
Weltering through eternity;
And the dim low line before
Of a dark and distant shore
Still recedes, as ever still
Longing with divided will,

But no power to seek or shun,
He is ever drifted on
O'er the unreposing wave,
To the haven of the grave.

Aye, many flowering islands lie
In the waters of wide agony:
To such a one this morn was led
My bark, by soft winds piloted.
—'Mid the mountains Euganean
I stood listening to the paean
With which the legion'd rooks did hail
The Sun's uprise majestical:
Gathering round with wings all hoar,
Through the dewy mist they soar
Like grey shades, till the eastern heaven
Bursts, and then,—as clouds of even
Fleck'd with fire and azure, lie
In the unfathomable sky,—
So their plumes of purple grain
Starr'd with drops of golden rain
Gleam above the sunlight woods,
As in silent multitudes
On the morning's fitful gale
Through the broken mist they sail;
And the vapours cloven and gleaming
Follow down the dark steep streaming,
Till all is bright, and clear, and still
Round the solitary hill.

Beneath is spread like a green sea
The waveless plain of Lombardy,
Bounded by the vaporous air,
Islanded by cities fair;
Underneath Day's azure eyes,
Ocean's nursling, Venice lies,—
A peopled labyrinth of walls,
Amphitrite's destined halls,
Which her hoary sire now paves
With his blue and beaming waves.

Lo! the sun upsprings behind,
Broad, red, radiant, half-reclined
On the level quivering line
Of the waters crystalline;
And before that chasm of light,
As within a furnace bright,
Column, tower, and dome, and spire,
Shine like obelisks of fire,
Pointing with inconstant motion
From the altar of dark ocean
To the sapphire-tinted skies;
As the flames of sacrifice
From the marble shrines did rise
As to pierce the dome of gold
Where Apollo spoke of old.

Sun-girt City! thou hast been
Ocean's child, and then his queen;
Now is come a darker day,
And thou soon must be his prey,
If the power that raised thee here
Hallow so thy watery bier.
A less drear ruin then than now,
With thy conquest-branded brow
Stooping to the slave of slaves
From thy throne, among the waves
Wilt thou be,—when the sea-mew
Flies, as once before it flew,
O'er thine isles depopulate,
And all is in its ancient state,
Save where many a palace-gate
With green sea-flowers overgrown
Like a rock of ocean's own,
Topples o'er the abandon'd sea
As the tides change sullenly.
The fisher on his watery way
Wandering at the close of day,
Will spread his sail and seize his oar
Till he pass the gloomy shore,

Lest thy dead should, from their sleep
Bursting o'er the starlight deep,
Lead a rapid masque of death
O'er the waters of his path.

Noon descends around me now:
'Tis the noon of autumn's glow,
When a soft and purple mist
Like a vaporous amethyst,
Or an air-dissolvéd star
Mingling light and fragrance, far
From the curved horizon's bound
To the point of heaven's profound,
Fills the overflowing sky;
And the plains that silent lie
Underneath; the leaves unsodden
Where the infant Frost has trodden
With his morning-wingéd feet
Whose bright print is gleaming yet;
And the red and golden vines
Piercing with their trellised lines
The rough, dark-skirted wilderness;
The dun and bladed grass no less,
Pointing from this hoary tower
In the windless air; the flower
Glimmering at my feet; the line
Of the olive-sandall'd Apennine
In the south dimly islanded;
And the Alps, whose snows are spread
High between the clouds and sun;
And of living things each one;
And my spirit, which so long
Darken'd this swift stream of song,—
Interpenetrated lie
By the glory of the sky;
Be it love, light, harmony,
Odour, or the soul of all
Which from heaven like dew doth fall,
Or the mind which feeds this verse
Peopling the lone universe.

Noon descends, and after noon
Autumn's evening meets me soon,
Leading the infantine moon
And that one star, which to her
Almost seems to minister
Half the crimson light she brings
From the sunset's radiant springs:
And the soft dreams of the morn
(Which like wingéd winds had borne
To that silent isle, which lies
'Mid remember'd agonies,
The frail bark of this lone being),
Pass, to other sufferers fleeing,
And its ancient pilot, Pain,
Sits beside the helm again.

Other flowering isles must be
In the sea of Life and Agony:
Other spirits float and flee
O'er that gulf: even now, perhaps,
On some rock the wild wave wraps,
With folding wings they waiting sit
For my bark, to pilot it
To some calm and blooming cove,
Where for me, and those I love,
May a windless bower be built,
Far from passion, pain, and guilt,
In a dell 'mid lawny hills
Which the wild sea-murmur fills,
And soft sunshine, and the sound
Of old forests echoing round,
And the light and smell divine
Of all flowers that breathe and shine.
—We may live so happy there,
That the Spirits of the Air
Envying us, may even entice
To our healing paradise
The polluting multitude;
But their rage would be subdued

By that clime divine and calm,
And the winds whose wings rain balm
On the uplifted soul, and leaves
Under which the bright sea heaves;
While each breathless interval
In their whisperings musical
The inspired soul supplies
With its own deep melodies;
And the Love which heals all strife
Circling, like the breath of life,
All things in that sweet abode
With its own mild brotherhood.
They, not it, would change; and soon
Every sprite beneath the moon
Would repent its envy vain,
And the Earth grow young again.

P. B. SHELLEY

275

ODE TO THE WEST WIND

O WILD West Wind, thou breath of Autumn's being,
Thou, from whose unseen presence the leaves dead
Are driven, like ghosts from an enchanter fleeing,
Yellow, and black, and pale, and hectic red,
Pestilence-stricken multitudes: O thou
Who chariotest to their dark wintry bed
The wingéd seeds, where they lie cold and low,
Each like a corpse within its grave, until
Thine azure sister of the Spring shall blow
Her clarion o'er the dreaming earth, and fill
(Driving sweet buds like flocks to feed in air)
With living hues and odours plain and hill:
Wild Spirit, which art moving everywhere;
Destroyer and Preserver; Hear, oh hear!

Thou on whose stream, 'mid the steep sky's commotion,
Loose clouds like earth's decaying leaves are shed,
Shook from the tangled boughs of Heaven and Ocean,
Angels of rain and lightning; there are spread

On the blue surface of thine airy surge,
Like the bright hair uplifted from the head
Of some fierce Maenad, ev'n from the dim verge
Of the horizon to the zenith's height—
The locks of the approaching storm. Thou dirge
Of the dying year, to which this closing night
Will be the dome of a vast sepulchre,
Vaulted with all thy congregated might
Of vapours, from whose solid atmosphere
Black rain, and fire, and hail, will burst: oh, hear!

Thou who didst waken from his summer-dreams,
The blue Mediterranean, where he lay,
Lull'd by the coil of his crystalline streams,
Beside a pumice isle in Baiae's bay,
And saw in sleep old palaces and towers
Quivering within the wave's intenser day,
All overgrown with azure moss and flowers
So sweet, the sense faints picturing them! Thou
For whose path the Atlantic's level powers
Cleave themselves into chasms, while far below
The sea-blooms and the oozy woods which wear
The sapless foliage of the ocean, know
Thy voice, and suddenly grow grey with fear
And tremble and despoil themselves: oh, hear!

If I were a dead leaf thou mightest bear;
If I were a swift cloud to fly with thee;
A wave to pant beneath thy power, and share
The impulse of thy strength, only less free
Than Thou, O uncontrollable! If even
I were as in my boyhood, and could be
The comrade of thy wanderings over heaven,
As then, when to outstrip the skyey speed
Scarce seem'd a vision, I would ne'er have striven
As thus with thee in prayer in my sore need.
Oh, lift me as a wave, a leaf, a cloud!
I fall upon the thorns of life! I bleed!
A heavy weight of hours has chain'd and bow'd
One too like thee: tameless, and swift, and proud.

Make me thy lyre, ev'n as the forest is:
What if my leaves are falling like its own!
The tumult of thy mighty harmonies
Will take from both a deep autumnal tone,
Sweet though in sadness. Be thou, Spirit fierce,
My spirit! be thou me, impetuous one!
Drive my dead thoughts over the universe
Like wither'd leaves to quicken a new birth;
And, by the incantation of this verse,
Scatter, as from an unextinguish'd hearth
Ashes and sparks, my words among mankind!
Be through my lips to unawaken'd earth
The trumpet of a prophecy! O Wind,
If Winter comes, can Spring be far behind?

P. B. SHELLEY

276

NATURE AND THE POET

*Suggested by a Picture of Peele Castle in a Storm,
painted by Sir George Beaumont*

I WAS thy neighbour once, thou rugged Pile!
Four summer weeks I dwelt in sight of thee:
I saw thee every day; and all the while
Thy Form was sleeping on a glassy sea.

So pure the sky, so quiet was the air!
So like, so very like, was day to day!
Whene'er I look'd, thy image still was there;
It trembled, but it never pass'd away.

How perfect was the calm! It seem'd no sleep,
No mood, which season takes away, or brings:
I could have fancied that the mighty Deep
Was even the gentlest of all gentle things.

Ah! then if mine had been the painter's hand
To express what then I saw; and add the gleam,
The light that never was on sea or land,
The consecration, and the Poet's dream,—

I would have planted thee, thou hoary pile,
Amid a world how different from this!
Beside a sea that could not cease to smile;
On tranquil land, beneath a sky of bliss.

A picture had it been of lasting ease,
Elysian quiet, without toil or strife;
No motion but the moving tide, a breeze,
Or merely silent Nature's breathing life.

Such, in the fond illusion of my heart,
Such picture would I at that time have made;
And seen the soul of truth in every part,
A steadfast peace that might not be betray'd.

So once it would have been,—'tis so no more;
I have submitted to a new control:
A power is gone, which nothing can restore;
A deep distress hath humanized my soul.

Not for a moment could I now behold
A smiling sea, and be what I have been:
The feeling of my loss will ne'er be old;
This, which I know, I speak with mind serene.

Then, Beaumont, Friend! who would have been the friend
If he had lived, of him whom I deplore,
This work of thine I blame not, but commend;
This sea in anger, and that dismal shore.

O 'tis a passionate work!—yet wise and well,
Well chosen is the spirit that is here;
That hulk which labours in the deadly swell,
This rueful sky, this pageantry of fear!

And this huge Castle, standing here sublime,
I love to see the look with which it braves,
—Cased in the unfeeling armour of old time—
The lightning, the fierce wind, and trampling waves.

Farewell, farewell the heart that lives alone,
Housed in a dream, at distance from the Kind!
Such happiness, wherever it be known,
Is to be pitied, for 'tis surely blind.

But welcome fortitude, and patient cheer,
And frequent sights of what is to be borne!
Such sights, or worse, as are before me here:—
Not without hope we suffer and we mourn.

W. WORDSWORTH

277

THE POET'S DREAM

On a Poet's lips I slept
Dreaming like a love-adept
In the sound his breathing kept;
Nor seeks nor finds he mortal blisses,
But feeds on the aerial kisses
Of shapes that haunt Thought's wildernesses.
He will watch from dawn to gloom
The lake-reflected sun illume
The yellow bees in the ivy-bloom,
   Nor heed nor see what things they be—
But from these create he can
Forms more real than living Man,
   Nurslings of Immortality!

P. B. SHELLEY

278

The World is too much with us; late and soon,
Getting and spending, we lay waste our powers;
Little we see in Nature that is ours;
We have given our hearts away, a sordid boon!

This Sea that bares her bosom to the moon,
The winds that will be howling at all hours
And are up-gather'd now like sleeping flowers,
For this, for everything, we are out of tune;

It moves us not.—Great God! I'd rather be
A Pagan suckled in a creed outworn,—
So might I, standing on this pleasant lea,

299

L

Have glimpses that would make me less forlorn;
Have sight of Proteus rising from the sea;
Or hear old Triton blow his wreathéd horn.

W. WORDSWORTH

279

WITHIN KING'S COLLEGE CHAPEL, CAMBRIDGE

TAX not the royal Saint with vain expense,
With ill-match'd aims the Architect who plann'd
(Albeit labouring for a scanty band
Of white-robed Scholars only) this immense

And glorious work of fine intelligence!
—Give all thou canst; high Heaven rejects the lore
Of nicely-calculated less or more:—
So deem'd the man who fashion'd for the sense

These lofty pillars, spread that branching roof
Self-poised, and scoop'd into ten thousand cells
Where light and shade repose, where music dwells

Lingering—and wandering on as loath to die;
Like thoughts whose very sweetness yieldeth proof
That they were born for immortality.

W. WORDSWORTH

280

YOUTH AND AGE

VERSE, a breeze 'mid blossoms straying,
Where Hope clung feeding, like a bee—
Both were mine! Life went a-maying
    With Nature, Hope, and Poesy,
      When I was young!
When I was young?—Ah, woeful when!
Ah! for the change 'twixt Now and Then!

This breathing house not built with hands,
This body that does me grievous wrong,
O'er aery cliffs and glittering sands
How lightly then it flash'd along:
Like those trim skiffs, unknown of yore,
On winding lakes and rivers wide,
That ask no aid of sail or oar,
That fear no spite of wind or tide!
Nought cared this body for wind or weather
When Youth and I lived in't together.

Flowers are lovely; Love is flower-like;
Friendship is a sheltering tree;
O! the joys, that came down shower-like,
Of Friendship, Love, and Liberty,
                    Ere I was old!
Ere I was old? Ah woeful Ere,
Which tells me, Youth's no longer here!
O Youth! for years so many and sweet
'Tis known that Thou and I were one,
I'll think it but a fond conceit—
It cannot be, that Thou art gone!
Thy vesper-bell hath not yet toll'd:—
And thou wert ay a masker bold!
What strange disguise hast now put on
To make believe that thou art gone?
I see these locks in silvery slips,
This drooping gait, this alter'd size:
But Springtide blossoms on thy lips,
And tears take sunshine from thine eyes
Life is but Thought: so think I will
That Youth and I are housemates still.

Dew-drops are the gems of morning,
But the tears of mournful eve!
Where no hope is, life's a warning
That only serves to make us grieve
                    When we are old:
—That only serves to make us grieve
With oft and tedious taking-leave,

Like some poor nigh-related guest
That may not rudely be dismist,
Yet hath out-stay'd his welcome while,
And tells the jest without the smile.

S. T. COLERIDGE

281

THE TWO APRIL MORNINGS

We walk'd along, while bright and red
Uprose the morning sun;
And Matthew stopp'd, he look'd, and said
'The will of God be done!'

A village schoolmaster was he,
With hair of glittering grey;
As blithe a man as you could see
On a spring holiday.

And on that morning, through the grass
And by the steaming rills
We travell'd merrily, to pass
A day among the hills.

'Our work,' said I, 'was well begun;
Then, from thy breast what thought,
Beneath so beautiful a sun,
So sad a sigh has brought?'

A second time did Matthew stop;
And fixing still his eye
Upon the eastern mountain-top,
To me he made reply:

'Yon cloud with that long purple cleft
Brings fresh into my mind
A day like this, which I have left
Full thirty years behind.

'And just above yon slope of corn
Such colours, and no other,
Were in the sky, that April morn,
Of this the very brother.

'With rod and line I sued the sport
Which that sweet season gave,
And, to the churchyard come, stopp'd short
Beside my daughter's grave.

'Nine summers had she scarcely seen,
The pride of all the vale;
And then she sang:—she would have been
A very nightingale.

'Six feet in earth my Emma lay;
And yet I loved her more—
For so it seem'd,—than till that day
I e'er had loved before.

'And turning from her grave, I met
Beside the churchyard yew
A blooming Girl, whose hair was wet
With points of morning dew.

'A basket on her head she bare;
Her brow was smooth and white:
To see a child so very fair,
It was a pure delight!

'No fountain from its rocky cave
E'er tripp'd with foot so free;
She seem'd as happy as a wave
That dances on the sea.

'There came from me a sigh of pain
Which I could ill confine;
I look'd at her, and look'd again:
And did not wish her mine!'

—Matthew is in his grave, yet now
Methinks I see him stand
As at that moment, with a bough
Of wilding in his hand.

W. WORDSWORTH

282

THE FOUNTAIN

A Conversation

We talk'd with open heart, and tongue
Affectionate and true,
A pair of friends, though I was young,
And Matthew seventy-two.

We lay beneath a spreading oak,
Beside a mossy seat;
And from the turf a fountain broke
And gurgled at our feet.

'Now, Matthew!' said I, 'let us match
This water's pleasant tune
With some old border-song, or catch
That suits a summer's noon;

'Or of the church-clock and the chimes
Sing here beneath the shade
That half-mad thing of witty rhymes
Which you last April made!'

In silence Matthew lay, and eyed
The spring beneath the tree;
And thus the dear old man replied,
The grey-hair'd man of glee:

'No check, no stay, this Streamlet fears,
How merrily it goes!
'Twill murmur on a thousand years
And flow as now it flows.

'And here, on this delightful day,
I cannot choose but think
How oft, a vigorous man, I lay
Beside this fountain's brink.

'My eyes are dim with childish tears,
My heart is idly stirr'd,
For the same sound is in my ears
Which in those days I heard.

 Thus fares it still in our decay:
And yet the wiser mind
Mourns less for what Age takes away,
Than what it leaves behind.

'The blackbird amid leafy trees,
The lark above the hill,
Let loose their carols when they please,
Are quiet when they will.

'With Nature never do they wage
A foolish strife; they see
A happy youth, and their old age
Is beautiful and free:

'But we are press'd by heavy laws;
And often, glad no more,
We wear a face of joy, because
We have been glad of yore.

'If there be one who need bemoan
His kindred laid in earth,
The household hearts that were his own,—
It is the man of mirth.

'My days, my friend, are almost gone,
My life has been approved,
And many love me; but by none
Am I enough beloved.'

'Now both himself and me he wrongs,
The man who thus complains!
I live and sing my idle songs
Upon these happy plains:

'And Matthew, for thy children dead
I'll be a son to thee!'
At this he grasp'd my hand and said,
'Alas! that cannot be.'

We rose up from the fountain-side;
  And down the smooth descent
Of the green sheep-track did we glide;
  And through the wood we went;

And ere we came to Leonard's Rock
  He sang those witty rhymes
About the crazy old church-clock,
  And the bewilder'd chimes.

W. WORDSWORTH

283

THE RIVER OF LIFE

The more we live, more brief appear
  Our life's succeeding stages:
A day to childhood seems a year,
  And years like passing ages.

The gladsome current of our youth,
  Ere passion yet disorders,
Steals lingering like a river smooth
  Along its grassy borders.

But as the careworn cheek grows wan,
  And sorrow's shafts fly thicker,
Ye Stars, that measure life to man,
  Why seem your courses quicker?

When joys have lost their bloom and breath
  And life itself is vapid,
Why, as we reach the Falls of Death,
  Feel we its tide more rapid?

It may be strange—yet who would change
  Time's course to slower speeding,
When one by one our friends have gone
  And left our bosoms bleeding?

Heaven gives our years of fading strength
  Indemnifying fleetness;
And those of youth, a seeming length,
  Proportion'd to their sweetness.

T. CAMPBELL

284

THE HUMAN SEASONS

Four Seasons fill the measure of the year;
There are four seasons in the mind of Man:
He has his lusty Spring, when fancy clear
Takes in all beauty with an easy span:

He has his Summer, when luxuriously
Spring's honey'd cud of youthful thought he loves
To ruminate, and by such dreaming high
Is nearest unto heaven: quiet coves

His soul has in its Autumn, when his wings
He furleth close; contented so to look
On mists in idleness—to let fair things
Pass by unheeded as a threshold brook:—

He has his Winter too of pale misfeature,
Or else he would forgo his mortal nature.

J. KEATS

285

A LAMENT

O World! O Life! O Time!
On whose last steps I climb,
   Trembling at that where I had stood before;
When will return the glory of your prime?
     No more—Oh, never more!

Out of the day and night
A joy has taken flight:
   Fresh spring, and summer, and winter hoar
Move my faint heart with grief, but with delight
     No more—Oh, never more!

P. B. SHELLEY

286

M y heart leaps up when I behold
 A rainbow in the sky:
So was it when my life began,
So is it now I am a man,
So be it when I shall grow old
  Or let me die!
The Child is father of the Man:
And I could wish my days to be
Bound each to each by natural piety.
W. WORDSWORTH

287

ODE ON INTIMATIONS OF
IMMORTALITY FROM RECOLLECTIONS
OF EARLY CHILDHOOD

THERE was a time when meadow, grove, and stream,
The earth, and every common sight
   To me did seem
  Apparell'd in celestial light,
The glory and the freshness of a dream.
It is not now as it hath been of yore;—
  Turn wheresoe'er I may,
   By night or day,
The things which I have seen I now can see no more.

  The rainbow comes and goes,
  And lovely is the rose;
  The moon doth with delight
Look round her when the heavens are bare;
  Waters on a starry night
  Are beautiful and fair;
 The sunshine is a glorious birth;
 But yet I know, where'er I go,
That there hath past away a glory from the earth.

Now, while the birds thus sing a joyous song,
    And while the young lambs bound
        As to the tabor's sound,
To me alone there came a thought of grief:
A timely utterance gave that thought relief,
    And I again am strong.
The cataracts blow their trumpets from the steep,—
No more shall grief of mine the season wrong:
I hear the echoes through the mountains throng,
The winds come to me from the fields of sleep,
        And all the earth is gay;
           Land and sea
    Give themselves up to jollity,
        And with the heart of May
    Doth every beast keep holiday;—
          Thou child of joy   [Shepherd-boy!
Shout round me, let me hear thy shouts, thou happy

Ye blessèd Creatures, I have heard the call
    Ye to each other make; I see
The heavens laugh with you in your jubilee;
    My heart is at your festival,
    My head hath its coronal,
The fullness of your bliss, I feel—I feel it all.
    O evil day! if I were sullen
    While Earth herself is adorning
        This sweet May-morning;
    And the children are culling
        On every side
    In a thousand valleys far and wide
    Fresh flowers; while the sun shines warm,
And the babe leaps up on his mother's arm:—
    I hear, I hear, with joy I hear!
    —But there's a tree, of many, one,
A single field which I have look'd upon,
Both of them speak of something that is gone:
        The pansy at my feet
        Doth the same tale repeat:
Whither is fled the visionary gleam?
Where is it now, the glory and the dream?

Our birth is but a sleep and a forgetting;
The Soul that rises with us, our life's Star,
      Hath had elsewhere its setting
        And cometh from afar;
    Not in entire forgetfulness,
    And not in utter nakedness,
But trailing clouds of glory do we come
        From God, who is our home:
Heaven lies about us in our infancy!
Shades of the prison-house begin to close
        Upon the growing Boy,
But he beholds the light, and whence it flows,
      He see it in his joy;
The Youth, who daily farther from the east
    Must travel, still is Nature's priest,
      And by the vision splendid
      Is on his way attended;
At length the Man perceives it die away,
And fade into the light of common day.

Earth fills her lap with pleasures of her own;
Yearnings she hath in her own natural kind,
And, even with something of a mother's mind
      And no unworthy aim,
    The homely nurse doth all she can
To make her foster-child, her inmate, Man,
        Forget the glories he hath known,
And that imperial palace whence he came.

Behold the Child among his new-born blisses,
A six years' darling of a pigmy size!
See, where 'mid work of his own hand he lies,
Fretted by sallies of his mother's kisses,
With light upon him from his father's eyes!
See, at his feet, some little plan or chart,
Some fragment from his dream of human life,
Shaped by himself with newly-learnéd art;
    A wedding or a festival,
    A mourning or a funeral;
        And this hath now his heart,

And unto this he frames his song:
      Then will he fit his tongue
To dialogues of business, love, or strife;
      But it will not be long
      Ere this be thrown aside,
      And with new joy and pride
The little actor cons another part;
Filling from time to time his 'humorous stage'
With all the Persons, down to palsied Age,
That life brings with her in her equipage;
      As if his whole vocation
      Were endless imitation.

Thou, whose exterior semblance doth belie
      Thy soul's immensity;
Thou best philosopher, who yet dost keep
Thy heritage, thou eye among the blind,
That, deaf and silent, read'st the eternal deep,
Haunted for ever by the eternal Mind,—
      Mighty Prophet! Seer blest!
      On whom those truths do rest
Which we are toiling all our lives to find,
In darkness lost, the darkness of the grave;
Thou, over whom thy Immortality
Broods like a day, a master o'er a slave,
A Presence which is not to be put by;
Thou little child, yet glorious in the might
Of heaven-born freedom on thy being's height,
Why with such earnest pains dost thou provoke
The years to bring the inevitable yoke,
Thus blindly with thy blessedness at strife?
Full soon thy soul shall have her earthly freight,
And custom lies upon thee with a weight
Heavy as frost, and deep almost as life!

      O joy! that in our embers
      Is something that doth live,
      That Nature yet remembers
      What was so fugitive!
The thought of our past years in me doth breed
Perpetual benediction: not indeed

311

For that which is most worthy to be blest,
Delight and liberty, the simple creed
Of Childhood, whether busy or at rest,
With new-fledged hope still fluttering in his breast:—
    —Not for these I raise
    The song of thanks and praise;
    But for those obstinate questionings
    Of sense and outward things,
    Fallings from us, vanishings,
    Blank misgivings of a creature
Moving about in worlds not realized,
High instincts, before which our mortal nature
Did tremble like a guilty thing surprised:
    But for those first affections,
    Those shadowy recollections,
      Which, be they what they may,
Are yet the fountain-light of all our day,
Are yet a master-light of all our seeing;
    Uphold us—cherish—and have power to make
Our noisy years seem moments in the being
Of the eternal Silence: truths that wake,
      To perish never;
Which neither listlessness, nor mad endeavour,
      Nor man nor boy,
Nor all that is at enmity with joy,
Can utterly abolish or destroy!
    Hence, in a season of calm weather
      Though inland far we be,
Our souls have sight of that immortal sea
      Which brought us hither;
      Can in a moment travel thither—
And see the children sport upon the shore,
And hear the mighty waters rolling evermore.

Then, sing, ye birds, sing, sing a joyous song!
      And let the young lambs bound
      As to the tabor's sound!
    We, in thought, will join your throng
      Ye that pipe and ye that play,
      Ye that through your hearts to-day
      Feel the gladness of the May!

What though the radiance which was once so bright
Be now for ever taken from my sight,
 Though nothing can bring back the hour
Of splendour in the grass, of glory in the flower;
   We will grieve not, rather find
   Strength in what remains behind;
   In the primal sympathy
   Which having been must ever be;
   In the soothing thoughts that spring
   Out of human suffering;
   In the faith that looks through death,
In years that bring the philosophic mind.

And O, ye Fountains, Meadows, Hills, and Groves,
Forbode not any severing of our loves!
Yet in my heart of hearts I feel your might;
I only have relinquish'd one delight
To live beneath your more habitual sway;
I love the brooks which down their channels fret
Even more than when I tripp'd lightly as they;
The innocent brightness of a new-born day
   Is lovely yet;
The clouds that gather round the setting sun
Do take a sober colouring from an eye
That hath kept watch o'er man's mortality;
Another race hath been, and other palms are won.
Thanks to the human heart by which we live,
Thanks to its tenderness, its joys, and fears,
To me the meanest flower that blows can give
Thoughts that do often lie too deep for tears.

W. WORDSWORTH

288

  MUSIC, when soft voices die,
  Vibrates in the memory—
  Odours, when sweet violets sicken,
  Live within the sense they quicken.

Rose leaves, when the rose is dead,
Are heap'd for the beloved's bed;
And so thy thoughts, when thou art gone,
Love itself shall slumber on.

P. B. SHELLEY

BOOK FIVE

Selected by
JOHN PRESS

WALTER SAVAGE LANDOR

1775–1864

IRELAND

IRELAND never was contented . . .
Say you so? you are demented.
Ireland was contented when
All could use the sword and pen,
And when Tara rose so high
That her turrets split the sky,
And about her courts were seen
Liveried Angels robed in green,
Wearing, by Saint Patrick's bounty,
Emeralds big as half a county.

WILLIAM GIFFORD

CLAP, clap the double nightcap on!
    Gifford will read you his amours . . .
Lazy as Scheld and cold as Don . . .
    Kneel, and thank Heaven they are not yours.

—

ALAS! 'tis very sad to hear,
Your and your Muse's end draws near:
I only wish, if this be true,
To lie a little way from you.
The grave is cold enough for me
Without you and your poetry.

INTERLUDE

M Y guest! I have not led you thro'
    The old footpath of swamp and sedges;
But . . . mind your step . . . you're coming to
    Shingle and shells with sharpish edges.

Here a squash jelly-fish, and here
    An old shark's head with open jaw
We hap may hit on: never fear
    Scent rather rank and crooked saw.

Step forward: we shall pass them soon,
    And then before you will arise
A fertile scene; a placid moon
    Above, and star-besprinkled skies.

And we shall reach at last (where ends
    The field of thistles, sharp and light)
A dozen brave and honest friends,
    And there wish one and all good-night.

LATELY our poets loiter'd in green lanes,
Content to catch the ballads of the plains;
I fancied I had strength enough to climb
A loftier station at no distant time,
And might securely from intrusion doze
Upon the flowers thro' which Ilissus flows.
In those pale olive grounds all voices cease,
And from afar dust fills the paths of Greece.
My slumber broken and my doublet torn,
I find the laurel also bears a thorn.

DYING SPEECH OF AN OLD PHILOSOPHER

I STROVE with none, for none was worth my strife:
    Nature I loved, and, next to Nature, Art:
I warm'd both hands before the fire of Life;
    It sinks; and I am ready to depart.

JOHN CLARE

1793–1864

I AM

I am: yet what I am none cares or knows
   My friends forsake me like a memory lost,
I am the self-consumer of my woes—
   They rise and vanish in oblivious host,
Like shadows in love's frenzied, stifled throes:—
And yet I am, and live—like vapours tost

Into the nothingness of scorn and noise,
   Into the living sea of waking dreams,
Where there is neither sense of life or joys,
   But the vast shipwreck of my life's esteems;
Even the dearest, that I love the best,
Are strange—nay, rather stranger than the rest.

I long for scenes, where man hath never trod,
   A place where woman never smiled or wept—
There to abide with my Creator, God,
   And sleep as I in childhood sweetly slept,
Untroubling, and untroubled where I lie,
The grass below—above the vaulted sky.

DEATH

Flowers shall hang upon the palls,
Brighter than patterns upon shawls,
And blossoms shall be in the coffin lids,
Sadder than tears on grief's eyelids,
Garlands shall hide pale corpses' faces
When beauty shall rot in charnel places,
Spring flowers shall come in dews of sorrow
For the maiden goes down to her grave to-morrow.

Last week she went walking and stepping along,
Gay as first flowers of spring or the tune of a song;
Her eye was as bright as the sun in its calm,
Her lips they were rubies, her bosom was warm,

319

CLARE

And white as the snowdrop that lies on her breast;
Now death like a dream is her bedfellow guest,
And white as the sheets—ay and paler than they,
Now her face in its beauty has perished to clay.

Spring flowers they shall hang on her pall,
More bright than the pattern that bloomed on her
    shawl,
And blooms shall be strown where the corpse lies hid,
More sad than the tears upon grief's eyelid;
And ere the return of another sweet May
She'll be rotting to dust in the coffined clay,
And the grave whereon the bright snowdrops grow
Shall be the same soil as the beauty below.

February 11th, 1847

HESPERUS

HESPERUS! the day is gone,
Soft falls the silent dew,
A tear is now on many a flower
And heaven lives in you.

Hesperus! the evening mild
Falls round us soft and sweet.
'Tis like the breathings of a child
When day and evening meet.

Hesperus! the closing flower
Sleeps on the dewy ground,
While dews fall in a silent shower
And heaven breathes around.

Hesperus! thy twinkling ray
Beams in the blue of heaven,
And tells the traveller on his way
That Earth shall be forgiven!

A VISION

I LOST the love of heaven above,
　I spurned the lust of earth below,
I felt the sweets of fancied love,
　And hell itself my only foe.

I lost earth's joys, but felt the glow
　Of heaven's flame abound in me,
Till loveliness and I did grow
　The bard of immortality.

I loved but woman fell away,
　I hid me from her faded fame,
I snatch'd the sun's eternal ray
　And wrote till earth was but a name.

In every language upon earth,
　On every shore, o'er every sea,
I gave my name immortal birth
　And kept my spirit with the free.

August 2nd, 1844

WILLIAM BARNES

1801–1886

THE WIND AT THE DOOR

A s day did darken on the dewless grass
　There still wi' nwone a-come by me,
To staÿ a-while at hwome by me;
　Within the house, all dumb by me,
I zot me sad as the eventide did pass.

An' there a win'-blast shook the rattlèn door,
　An' seemed, as win' did mwone without,
As if my Jeäne, alwone without,
　A-stannèn on the stone without,
Wer there a-come wi' happiness oonce mwore.

BARNES

I went to door; an' out vrom trees above
My head, upon the blast by me,
Sweet blossoms wer a-cast by me,
As if my love, a-past by me,
Did fling em down—a token ov her love.

'Sweet blossoms o' the tree where I do murn,'
I thought, 'if you did blow vor her,
Vor apples that should grow vor her,
A-vallèn down below vor her,
O then how happy I should zee you kern.'

But no. Too soon I voun' my charm abroke.
Noo comely soul in white like her—
Noo soul a-steppèn light like her—
An' nwone o' comely height like her—
Went by; but all my grief ageän awoke.

1867

WHITE AN' BLUE

My love is o' comely height, an' straïght,
An' comely in all her waÿs and gaït;
In feäce she do show the rwose's hue,
An' her lids on her eyes be white on blue.

When Elemley clubmen walk'd in Maÿ,
An' vo'k come in clusters, ev'ry waÿ,
As soon as the zun dried up the dew,
An' clouds in the sky wer white on blue,

She come by the down, wi' trippèn talk,
By deäsies, an' sheenèn banks o' chalk,
An' brooks, where the crowvoot flow'rs did strew
The sky-tinted water, white on blue.

She nodded her head, as plaÿ'd the band;
She dapp'd wi' her voot, as she did stand;
She danced in a reel, a-weärèn new
A skirt wi' a jacket, white wi' blue.

I singled her out vrom thin an' stout,
Vrom slender an' stout I chose her out;
An' what, in the evenèn, could I do,
But gi'e her my breast-knot, white an' blue?

Written 31st October 1867

TROUBLES OF THE DAY

As there, along the elmy hedge, I go
  By banksides white with parsley—parsley-bloom—
Where smell of new-mown hay comes wafted by
  On wind of dewy evening, evening gloom,
And homeward take my shaded way between
The hedge's high-tipp'd wood, and barley green,
    I sing, or mean
'O troubles of the day, flee to the west,
Come not my homeward way. I seek my rest.'

The dairy cows, by meadow trees, lie free
  Of calls to milkers' pails—the milkmaids' calls;
The horses now have left their rolling wheels
  And reel'd in home to stable, to their stalls,
And down the grey-pool'd stream the fish awhile
Are free from all the prowling angler's guile,
    And o'er the stile
I sink, and sing or say, 'Flee to the west,
O troubles of the day. I seek my rest.'

My boy—whose little high-rigged boat, athwart
  The windy pool, by day, at afternoon,
Has fluttered, tippling like a bird
  That tries to fly unfledged, to fly too soon—
Now sleeps forgetful of the boat, and fond
Old dog that he has taught to swim the pond.
    So flee beyond
The edge of sinking day, towards the west,
Ye troubles, flee away. I seek my rest.

A star is o'er the tower on the hill
　　Whence rings no clanging knell, no evening peal;
The mill stands dark beside the flouncing foam,
　　But still is all its gear, its mossy wheel.
No rooks now sweep along the darkened sky,
And o'er the road few feet or wheels go by.
　　　　　So fly, O fly
Ye troubles, with the day, adown the west,
Come not along my way. I seek my rest.

1869

ELIZABETH BARRETT BROWNING

1806–1861

BIANCA AMONG THE NIGHTINGALES

I

THE cypress stood up like a church
　　That night we felt our love would hold,
And saintly moonlight seemed to search
　　And wash the whole world clean as gold;
The olives crystallized the vales'
　　Broad slopes until the hills grew strong:
The fireflies and the nightingales
　　Throbbed each to either, flame and song.
The nightingales, the nightingales.

II

Upon the angle of its shade
　　The cypress stood, self-balanced high;
Half up, half down, as double-made,
　　Along the ground, against the sky.
And *we*, too! from such soul-height went
　　Such leaps of blood, so blindly driven,
We scarce knew if our nature meant
　　Most passionate earth or intense heaven.
The nightingales, the nightingales.

III

We paled with love, we shook with love,
　　We kissed so close we could not vow;
Till Giulio whispered, 'Sweet, above
　　God's Ever guarantees this Now.'
And through his words the nightingales
　　Drove straight and full their long clear call,
Like arrows through heroic mails,
　　And love was awful in it all.
The nightingales, the nightingales.

IV

O cold white moonlight of the north,
　　Refresh these pulses, quench this hell!
O coverture of death drawn forth
　　Across this garden-chamber . . . well!
But what have nightingales to do
　　In gloomy England, called the free.
(Yes, free to die in! . . .) when we two
　　Are sundered, singing still to me?
And still they sing, the nightingales.

V

I think I hear him, how he cried
　　'My own soul's life' between their notes.
Each man has but one soul supplied,
　　And that's immortal. Though his throat's
On fire with passion now, to *her*
　　He can't say what to me he said!
And yet he moves her, they aver.
　　The nightingales sing through my head.
The nightingales, the nightingales.

VI

He says to *her* what moves her most.
　　He would not name his soul within
Her hearing,—rather pays her cost
　　With praises to her lips and chin.

Man has but one soul, 'tis ordained,
    And each soul but one love, I add;
Yet souls are damned and love's profaned.
    These nightingales will sing me mad!
The nightingales, the nightingales.

VII

I marvel how the birds can sing.
    There's little difference, in their view,
Betwixt our Tuscan trees that spring
    As vital flames into the blue,
And dull round blots of foliage meant
    Like saturated sponges here
To suck the fogs up. As content
    Is *he* too in this land, 'tis clear.
And still they sing, the nightingales.

VIII

My native Florence! dear, forgone!
    I see across the Alpine ridge
How the last feast-day of Saint John
    Shot rockets from Carraia bridge.
The luminous city, tall with fire,
    Trod deep down in that river of ours,
While many a boat with lamp and choir
    Skimmed birdlike over glittering towers.
I will not hear these nightingales.

IX

I seem to float, *we* seem to float
    Down Arno's stream in festive guise;
A boat strikes flame into our boat,
    And up that lady seems to rise
As then she rose. The shock had flashed
    A vision on us! What a head,
What leaping eyeballs!—beauty dashed
    To splendour by a sudden dread.
And still they sing, the nightingales.

X

Too bold to sin, too weak to die;
    Such women are so. As for me,
I would we had drowned there, he and I,
    That moment, loving perfectly.
He had not caught her with her loosed
    Gold ringlets . . . rarer in the south . . .
Nor heard the 'Grazie tanto' bruised
    To sweetness by her English mouth.
And still they sing, the nightingales.

XI

She had not reached him at my heart
    With her fine tongue, as snakes indeed
Kill flies; nor had I, for my part,
    Yearned after, in my desperate need,
And followed him as he did her
    To coasts left bitter by the tide,
Whose very nightingales, elsewhere
    Delighting, torture and deride!
For still they sing, the nightingales.

XII

A worthless woman! mere cold clay
    As all false things are! but so fair,
She takes the breath of men away
    Who gaze upon her unaware.
I would not play her larcenous tricks
    To have her looks! She lied and stole,
And spat into my love's pure pyx
    The rank saliva of her soul.
And still they sing, the nightingales.

XIII

I would not for her white and pink,
    Though such he likes—her grace of limb,
Though such he has praised—nor yet, I think,
    For life itself, though spent with him,

Commit such sacrilege, affront
    God's nature which is love, intrude
'Twixt two affianced souls, and hunt
    Like spiders, in the altar's wood.
I cannot bear these nightingales.

XIV

If she chose sin, some gentler guise
    She might have sinned in, so it seems:
She might have pricked out both my eyes,
    And I still seen him in my dreams!
—Or drugged me in my soup or wine,
    Nor left me angry afterward:
To die here with his hand in mine
    His breath upon me, were not hard.
(Our Lady hush these nightingales!)

XV

But set a springe for *him*, 'mio ben',
    My only good, my first last love!—
Though Christ knows well what sin is, when
    He sees some things done they must move
Himself to wonder. Let her pass.
    I think of her by night and day.
Must *I* too join her . . . out, alas! . . .
    With Giulio, in each word I say!
And evermore the nightingales!

XVI

Giulio, my Giulio!—sing they so,
    And you be silent? Do I speak,
And you not hear? An arm you throw
    Round some one, and I feel so weak?
—Oh, owl-like birds! They sing for spite,
    They sing for hate, they sing for doom!
They'll sing through death who sing through
        night,
    They'll sing and stun me in the tomb—
The nightingales, the nightingales!

EDWARD FITZGERALD

1809–1883

From the RUBÁIYÁT OF OMAR KHAYYÁM
OF NAISHÁPÚR

67

AH, with the Grape my fading Life provide,
And wash my Body whence the Life has died,
    And in a Winding-sheet of Vine-leaf wrapt,
So bury me by some sweet Garden-side.

68

That ev'n my buried Ashes such a Snare
Of Perfume shall fling up into the Air,
    As not a True Believer passing by
But shall be overtaken unaware.

69

Indeed the Idols I have loved so long
Have done my Credit in Men's Eye much wrong:
    Have drown'd my Honour in a shallow Cup,
And sold my Reputation for a Song.

70

Indeed, indeed, Repentance oft before
I swore—but was I sober when I swore?
    And then and then came Spring, and Rose-in-hand
My thread-bare Penitence apieces tore.

71

And much as Wine has play'd the Infidel,
And robb'd me of my Robe of Honour—well,
    I often wonder what the Vintners buy
One-half so precious as the Goods they sell.

72

Alas, that Spring should vanish with the Rose!
That Youth's sweet-scented Manuscript should close!
   The Nightingale that in the Branches sang,
Ah, whence, and whither flown again, who knows!

73

Ah, Love! could thou and I with Fate conspire
To grasp this sorry Scheme of Things entire,
   Would not we shatter it to bits—and then
Re-mould it nearer to the Heart's Desire!

74

Ah, Moon of my Delight who know'st no wane,
The Moon of Heav'n is rising once again:
   How oft hereafter rising shall she look
Through this same Garden after me—in vain!

75

And when Thyself with shining Foot shall pass
Among the Guests Star-scatter'd on the Grass,
   And in thy joyous Errand reach the Spot
Where I made one—turn down an empty Glass!

TAMAM SHUD

ALFRED, LORD TENNYSON

1809–1892

SONG

I

A SPIRIT haunts the year's last hours
Dwelling amid these yellowing bowers:
   To himself he talks;
For at eventide, listening earnestly,
At his work you may hear him sob and sigh
   In the walks;
   Earthward he boweth the heavy stalks

Of the mouldering flowers:
  Heavily hangs the broad sunflower
    Over its grave i' the earth so chilly;
  Heavily hangs the hollyhock,
    Heavily hangs the tiger-lily.

II

The air is damp, and hush'd, and close,
As a sick man's room when he taketh repose
    An hour before death;
My very heart faints and my whole soul grieves
At the moist rich smell of the rotting leaves,
    And the breath
    Of the fading edges of box beneath,
And the year's last rose.
  Heavily hangs the broad sunflower
    Over its grave i' the earth so chilly;
  Heavily hangs the hollyhock,
    Heavily hangs the tiger-lily.

THE EAGLE

FRAGMENT

He clasps the crag with crooked hands;
Close to the sun in lonely lands,
Ring'd with the azure world, he stands.

The wrinkled sea beneath him crawls;
He watches from his mountain walls,
And like a thunderbolt he falls.

Break, break, break,
  On thy cold gray stones, O Sea!
And I would that my tongue could utter
  The thoughts that arise in me.

O well for the fisherman's boy,
  That he shouts with his sister at play!
O well for the sailor lad,
  That he sings in his boat on the bay!

And the stately ships go on
    To their haven under the hill;
But O for the touch of a vanish'd hand,
    And the sound of a voice that is still!

Break, break, break,
    At the foot of thy crags, O sea!
But the tender grace of a day that is dead
    Will never come back to me.

From THE PRINCESS

THE splendour falls on castle walls
    And snowy summits old in story:
The long light shakes across the lakes,
    And the wild cataract leaps in glory.
Blow, bugle, blow, set the wild echoes flying,
Blow, bugle; answer, echoes, dying, dying, dying.

O hark, O hear! how thin and clear,
    And thinner, clearer, farther going!
O sweet and far from cliff and scar
    The horns of Elfland faintly blowing!
Blow, let us hear the purple glens replying:
Blow, bugle; answer, echoes, dying, dying, dying.

O love, they die in yon rich sky,
    They faint on hill or field or river:
Our echoes roll from soul to soul,
    And grow for ever and for ever.
Blow, bugle, blow, set the wild echoes flying,
And answer, echoes, answer, dying, dying, dying.

Tears, idle tears, I know not what they mean,
Tears from the depth of some divine despair
Rise in the heart, and gather to the eyes,
In looking on the happy Autumn-fields,
And thinking of the days that are no more.

Fresh as the first beam glittering on a sail,
That brings our friends up from the underworld,
Sad as the last which reddens over one
That sinks with all we love below the verge;
So sad, so fresh, the days that are no more.

Ah, sad and strange as in dark summer dawns
The earliest pipe of half-awaken'd birds
To dying ears, when unto dying eyes
The casement slowly grows a glimmering square;
So sad, so strange, the days that are no more.

Dear as remember'd kisses after death,
And sweet as those by hopeless fancy feign'd
On lips that are for others; deep as love,
Deep as first love, and wild with all regret;
O Death in Life, the days that are no more.

Now sleeps the crimson petal, now the white;
Nor waves the cypress in the palace walk;
Nor winks the gold fin in the porphyry font:
The firefly wakens: waken thou with me.

Now droops the milkwhite peacock like a ghost,
And like a ghost she glimmers on to me.

Now lies the Earth all Danaë to the stars,
And all thy heart lies open unto me.

Now slides the silent meteor on, and leaves
A shining furrow, as thy thoughts in me.

Now folds the lily all her sweetness up,
And slips into the bosom of the lake:
So fold thyself, my dearest, thou, and slip
Into my bosom and be lost in me.

Come down, O maid, from yonder mountain
        height:
What pleasure lives in height (the shepherd sang)
In height and cold, the splendour of the hills?

But cease to move so near the Heavens, and cease
To glide a sunbeam by the blasted Pine,
To sit a star upon the sparkling spire;
And come, for Love is of the valley, come,
For Love is of the valley, come thou down
And find him; by the happy threshold, he,
Or hand in hand with Plenty in the maize,
Or red with spirted purple of the vats,
Or foxlike in the vine; nor cares to walk
With Death and Morning on the silver horns,
Nor wilt thou snare him in the white ravine,
Nor find him dropt upon the firths of ice,
That huddling slant in furrow-cloven falls
To roll the torrent out of dusky doors:
But follow; let the torrent dance thee down
To find him in the valley; let the wild
Lean-headed Eagles yelp alone, and leave
The monstrous ledges there to slope, and spill
Their thousand wreaths of dangling watersmoke,
That like a broken purpose waste in air:
So waste not thou; but come; for all the vales
Await thee; azure pillars of the hearth
Arise to thee: the children call, and I
Thy shepherd pipe, and sweet is every sound,
Sweeter thy voice, but every sound is sweet;
Myriads of rivulets hurrying thro' the lawn,
The moan of doves in immemorial elms,
And murmuring of innumerable bees.

TO THE REV. F. D. MAURICE

COME, when no graver cares employ,
Godfather, come and see your boy:
    Your presence will be sun in winter,
Making the little one leap for joy.

For, being of that honest few,
Who give the Fiend himself his due,
    Should eighty-thousand college-councils
Thunder 'Anathema,' friend, at you;

Should all our churchmen foam in spite
At you, so careful of the right,
    Yet one lay-heath would give you welcome
(Take it and come) to the Isle of Wight;

Where, far from noise and smoke of town,
I watch the twilight falling brown
    All round a careless-order'd garden
Close to the ridge of a noble down.

You'll have no scandal while you dine,
But honest talk and wholesome wine,
    And only hear the magpie gossip
Garrulous under a roof of pine:

For groves of pine on either hand,
To break the blast of winter, stand;
    And further on, the hoary Channel
Tumbles a billow on chalk and sand;

Where, if below the milky steep
Some ship of battle slowly creep,
    And on thro' zones of light and shadow
Glimmer away to the lonely deep,

We might discuss the Northern sin
Which made a selfish war begin;
    Dispute the claims, arrange the chances;
Emperor, Ottoman, which shall win:

Or whether war's avenging rod
Shall lash all Europe into blood;
    Till you should turn to dearer matters,
Dear to the man that is dear to God;

How best to help the slender store,
How mend the dwellings, of the poor;
    How gain in life, as life advances,
Valour and charity more and more.

Come, Maurice, come: the lawn as yet
Is hoar with rime, or spongy-wet;
    But when the wreath of March has blossom'd,
Crocus, anemone, violet,

Or later, pay one visit here,
For those are few we hold as dear;
   Nor pay but one, but come for many,
Many and many a happy year.

January, 1854

From IN MEMORIAM A. H. H.

OBIIT MDCCCXXXIII

II

OLD Yew, which graspest at the stones
   That name the under-lying dead,
   Thy fibres net the dreamless head,
Thy roots are wrapt about the bones.

The seasons bring the flower again,
   And bring the firstling to the flock;
   And in the dusk of thee, the clock
Beats out the little lives of men.

O not for thee the glow, the bloom,
   Who changest not in any gale,
   Nor branding summer suns avail
To touch thy thousand years of gloom:

And gazing on thee, sullen tree,
   Sick for thy stubborn hardihood,
   I seem to fail from out my blood
And grow incorporate into thee.

VII

Dark house, by which once more I stand
   Here in the long unlovely street,
   Doors, where my heart was used to beat
So quickly, waiting for a hand,

A hand that can be clasp'd no more—
   Behold me, for I cannot sleep,
   And like a guilty thing I creep
At earliest morning to the door.

He is not here; but far away
   The noise of life begins again,
   And ghastly thro' the drizzling rain
On the bald street breaks the blank day.

XV

To-night the winds begin to rise
   And roar from yonder dropping day:
   The last red leaf is whirl'd away,
The rooks are blown about the skies;

The forest crack'd, the waters curl'd,
   The cattle huddled on the lea;
   And wildly dash'd on tower and tree
The sunbeam strikes along the world:

And but for fancies, which aver
   That all thy motions gently pass
   Athwart a plane of molten glass,
I scarce could brook the strain and stir

That makes the barren branches loud;
   And but for fear it is not so,
   The wild unrest that lives in woe
Would dote and pore on yonder cloud

That rises upward always higher,
   And onward drags a labouring breast,
   And topples round the dreary west,
A looming bastion fringed with fire.

XIX

The Danube to the Severn gave
   The darken'd heart that beat no more;
   They laid him by the pleasant shore,
And in the hearing of the wave.

There twice a day the Severn fills;
   The salt sea-water passes by,
   And hushes half the babbling Wye,
And makes a silence in the hills.

The Wye is hush'd nor moved along,
　　And hush'd my deepest grief of all,
　　When fill'd with tears that cannot fall,
I brim with sorrow drowning song.

The tide flows down, the wave again
　　Is vocal in its wooded walls;
　　My deeper anguish also falls,
And I can speak a little then.

XCV

.　　.　　.　　.　　.

Till now the doubtful dusk reveal'd
　　The knolls once more where, couch'd at ease,
　　The white kine glimmer'd, and the trees
Laid their dark arms about the field:

And suck'd from out the distant gloom
　　A breeze began to tremble o'er
　　The large leaves of the sycamore,
And fluctuate all the still perfume,

And gathering freshlier overhead,
　　Rock'd the full-foliaged elms, and swung
　　The heavy-folded rose, and flung
The lilies to and fro, and said

'The dawn, the dawn,' and died away;
　　And East and West, without a breath,
　　Mixt their dim lights, like life and death,
To broaden into boundless day.

CI

Unwatch'd, the garden bough shall sway,
　　The tender blossom flutter down,
　　Unloved, that beech will gather brown,
This maple burn itself away;

Unloved, the sun-flower, shining fair,
　　Ray round with flames her disk of seed,
　　And many a rose-carnation feed
With summer spice the humming air;

Unloved, by many a sandy bar,
    The brook shall babble down the plain,
    At noon or when the lesser wain
Is twisting round the polar star;

Uncared for, gird the windy grove,
    And flood the haunts of hern and crake;
    Or into silver arrows break
The sailing moon in creek and cove;

Till from the garden and the wild
    A fresh association blow,
    And year by year the landscape grow
Familiar to the stranger's child;

As year by year the labourer tills
    His wonted glebe, or lops the glades;
    And year by year our memory fades
From all the circle of the hills.

CXLV

Now fades the last long streak of snow,
    Now burgeons every maze of quick
    About the flowering squares, and thick
By ashen roots the violets blow.

Now rings the woodland loud and long,
    The distance takes a lovelier hue,
    And drown'd in yonder living blue
The lark becomes a sightless song.

Now dance the lights on lawn and lea,
    The flocks are whiter down the vale,
    And milkier every milky sail
On winding stream or distant sea;

Where now the seamew pipes, or dives
    In yonder greening gleam, and fly
    The happy birds, that change their sky
To build and brood; that live their lives

From land to land; and in my breast
 Spring wakens too; and my regret
 Becomes an April violet,
And buds and blossoms like the rest.

TO VIRGIL

WRITTEN AT THE REQUEST OF THE MANTUANS FOR THE NINETEENTH CENTENARY OF VIRGIL'S DEATH

I

ROMAN VIRGIL, thou that singest
 Ilion's lofty temples robed in fire,
Ilion falling, Rome arising,
 wars, and filial faith, and Dido's pyre;

II

Landscape-lover, lord of language
 more than he that sang the Works and Days,
All the chosen coin of fancy
 flashing out from many a golden phrase;

III

Thou that singest wheat and woodland,
 tilth and vineyard, hive and horse and herd;
All the charm of all the Muses
 often flowering in a lonely word;

IV

Poet of the happy Tityrus
 piping underneath his beechen bowers;
Poet of the poet-satyr
 whom the laughing shepherd bound with flowers;

V

Chanter of the Pollio, glorying
 in the blissful years again to be,
Summers of the snakeless meadow,
 unlaborious earth and oarless sea;

VI

Thou that seëst Universal
  Nature moved by Universal Mind;
Thou majestic in thy sadness
  at the doubtful doom of human kind;

VII

Light among the vanish'd ages;
  star that gildest yet this phantom shore;
Golden branch amid the shadows,
  kings and realms that pass to rise no more;

VIII

Now thy Forum roars no longer,
  fallen every purple Cæsar's dome—
Tho' thine ocean-roll of rhythm
  sound for ever of Imperial Rome—

IX

Now the Rome of slaves hath perish'd,
  and the Rome of freemen holds her place,
I, from out the Northern Island
  sunder'd once from all the human race,

X

I salute thee, Mantovano,
  I that loved thee since my day began,
Wielder of the stateliest measure
  ever moulded by the lips of man.

'FRATER AVE ATQUE VALE'

Row us out from Desenzano, to your Sirmione row!
So they row'd, and there we landed—'O venusta Sirmio!'
There to me thro' all the groves of olive in the summer glow,
There beneath the Roman ruin where the purple flowers
  grow,
Came that 'Ave atque Vale' of the Poet's hopeless woe,
Tenderest of Roman poets nineteen-hundred years ago,
'Frater Ave atque Vale'—as we wander'd to and fro
Gazing at the Lydian laughter of the Garda Lake below
Sweet Catullus's all-but-island, olive-silvery Sirmio!

ROBERT BROWNING

1812–1889

UP AT A VILLA—DOWN IN THE CITY

(AS DISTINGUISHED BY AN ITALIAN
PERSON OF QUALITY)

I

HAD I but plenty of money, money enough and to spare,
The house for me, no doubt, were a house in the city-square;
Ah, such a life, such a life, as one leads at the window there!

II

Something to see, by Bacchus, something to hear, at least!
There, the whole day long, one's life is a perfect feast;
While up at a villa one lives, I maintain it, no more than a
beast.

III

Well now, look at our villa! stuck like the horn of a bull
Just on a mountain-edge as bare as the creature's skull,
Save a mere shag of a bush with hardly a leaf to pull!
—I scratch my own, sometimes, to see if the hair's turned
wool.

IV

But the city, oh the city—the square with the houses! Why?
They are stone-faced, white as a curd, there's something to
take the eye!
Houses in four straight lines, not a single front awry;
You watch who crosses and gossips, who saunters, who
hurries by;
Green blinds, as a matter of course, to draw when the sun
gets high;
And the shops with fanciful signs which are painted pro-
perly.

V

What of a villa? Though winter be over in March by rights,
'Tis May perhaps ere the snow shall have withered well off
    the heights:
You've the brown ploughed land before, where the oxen
    steam and wheeze,
And the hills over-smoked behind by the faint grey olive-
    trees.

VI

Is it better in May, I ask you? You've summer all at once;
In a day he leaps complete with a few strong April suns.
'Mid the sharp short emerald wheat, scarce risen three
    fingers well,
The wild tulip, at end of its tube, blows out its great red bell
Like a thin clear bubble of blood, for the children to pick
    and sell.

VII

Is it ever hot in the square? There's a fountain to spout and
    splash!
In the shade it sings and springs; in the shine such foam-
    bows flash
On the horses with curling fish-tails, that prance and paddle
    and pash
Round the lady atop in her conch—fifty gazers do not abash,
Though all that she wears is some weeds round her waist in
    a sort of sash.

VIII

All the year long at the villa, nothing to see though you
    linger,
Except yon cypress that points like death's lean lifted fore-
    finger.
Some think fireflies pretty, when they mix i' the corn and
    mingle,
Or thrid the stinking hemp till the stalks of it seem a-tingle.
Late August or early September, the stunning cicala is shrill,

And the bees keep their tiresome whine round the resinous firs on the hill.
Enough of the seasons,—I spare you the months of the fever and chill.

IX

Ere you open your eyes in the city, the blessed church-bells begin:
No sooner the bells leave off than the diligence rattles in:
You get the pick of the news, and it costs you never a pin.
By-and-by there's the travelling doctor gives pills, lets blood, draws teeth;
Or the Pulcinello-trumpet breaks up the market beneath.
At the post-office such a scene-picture—the new play, piping hot!
And a notice how, only this morning, three liberal thieves were shot.
Above it, behold the Archbishop's most fatherly of rebukes,
And beneath, with his crown and his lion, some little new law of the Duke's!
Or a sonnet with flowery marge, to the Reverend Don So-and-so
Who is Dante, Boccaccio, Petrarca, Saint Jerome and Cicero,
'And moreover,' (the sonnet goes rhyming,) 'the skirts of Saint Paul has reached,
'Having preached us those six Lent-lectures more unctuous than ever he preached.'
Noon strikes,—here sweeps the procession! our Lady borne smiling and smart
With a pink gauze gown all spangles, and seven swords stuck in her heart!
Bang-whang-whang goes the drum, *tootle-te-tootle* the fife;
No keeping one's haunches still: it's the greatest pleasure in life.

X

But bless you, it's dear—it's dear! fowls, wine, at double the rate.
They have clapped a new tax upon salt, and what oil pays passing the gate

It's a horror to think of. And so, the villa for me, not the city!
Beggars can scarcely be choosers: but still—ah, the pity, the
　　pity!
Look, two and two go the priests, then the monks with cowls
　　and sandals,
And the penitents dressed in white shirts, a-holding the
　　yellow candles;
One, he carries a flag up straight, and another a cross with
　　handles,
And the Duke's guard brings up the rear, for the better pre-
　　vention of scandals:
Bang-whang-whang goes the drum, *tootle-te-tootle* the fife.
Oh, a day in the city-square, there is no such pleasure in life!

A TOCCATA OF GALUPPI'S

I

OH Galuppi, Baldassaro, this is very sad to find!
I can hardly misconceive you; it would prove me deaf and
　　blind;
But although I take your meaning, 'tis with such a heavy
　　mind!

II

Here you come with your old music, and here's all the good
　　it brings.
What, they lived once thus at Venice where the merchants
　　were the kings,
Where Saint Mark's is, where the Doges used to wed the sea
　　with rings?

III

Ay, because the sea's the street there; and 'tis arched by . . .
　　what you call
. . . Shylock's bridge with houses on it, where they kept the
　　carnival:
I was never out of England—it's as if I saw it all.

IV

Did young people take their pleasure when the sea was
    warm in May?
Balls and masks begun at midnight, burning ever to mid-
    day,
When they made up fresh adventures for the morrow, do
    you say?

V

Was a lady such a lady, cheeks so round and lips so red,—
On her neck the small face buoyant, like a bell-flower on its
    bed,
O'er the breast's superb abundance where a man might base
    his head?

VI

Well, and it was graceful of them—they'd break talk off and
    afford
—She, to bite her mask's black velvet—he, to finger on his
    sword,
While you sat and played Toccatas, stately at the clavi-
    chord?

VII

What? Those lesser thirds so plaintive, sixths diminished,
    sigh on sigh,
Told them something? Those suspensions, those solutions—
    'Must we die?'
Those commiserating sevenths—'Life might last! we can
    but try!'

VIII

'Were you happy?'—'Yes.'—'And are you still as happy?'—
    'Yes. And you?'
—'Then, more kisses!'—'Did I stop them, when a million
    seemed so few?'
Hark, the dominant's persistence till it must be answered to!

IX

So, an octave struck the answer. Oh, they praised you, I dare
say!
'Brave Galuppi! that was music! good alike at grave and
gay!
'I can always leave off talking when I hear a master play!'

X

Then they left you for their pleasure: till in due time, one
by one,
Some with lives that came to nothing, some with deeds as
well undone,
Death stepped tacitly and took them where they never see
the sun.

XI

But when I sit down to reason, think to take my stand nor
swerve,
While I triumph o'er a secret wrung from nature's close
reserve,
In you come with your cold music till I creep thro' every
nerve.

XII

Yes, you, like a ghostly cricket, creaking where a house was
burned:
'Dust and ashes, dead and done with, Venice spent what
Venice earned.
'The soul, doubtless, is immortal—where a soul can be
discerned.

XIII

'Yours for instance: you know physics, something of geology,
'Mathematics are your pastime; souls shall rise in their
degree;
'Butterflies may dread extinction,—you'll not die, it cannot
be!

XIV

'As for Venice and her people, merely born to bloom and
    drop,
'Here on earth they bore their fruitage, mirth and folly were
    the crop:
'What of soul was left, I wonder, when the kissing had to
    stop?

XV

'Dust and ashes!' So you creak it; and I want the heart to
    scold.
Dear dead women, with such hair, too—what's become of
    all the gold
Used to hang and brush their bosoms? I feel chilly and
    grown old.

TWO IN THE CAMPAGNA

I

I WONDER do you feel to-day
    As I have felt since, hand in hand,
We sat down on the grass, to stray
    In spirit better through the land,
This morn of Rome and May?

II

For me, I touched a thought, I know,
    Has tantalized me many times,
(Like turns of thread the spiders throw
    Mocking across our path) for rhymes
To catch at and let go.

III

Help me to hold it! First it left
    The yellowing fennel, run to seed
There, branching from the brickwork's cleft,
    Some old tomb's ruin: yonder weed
Took up the floating weft,

IV

Where one small orange cup amassed
    Five beetles,—blind and green they grope
Among the honey-meal: and last,
    Everywhere on the grassy slope
I traced it. Hold it fast!

V

The champaign with its endless fleece
    Of feathery grasses everywhere!
Silence and passion, joy and peace,
    An everlasting wash of air—
Rome's ghost since her decease.

VI

Such life here, through such lengths of hours,
    Such miracles performed in play,
Such primal naked forms of flowers,
    Such letting nature have her way
While heaven looks from its towers!

VII

How say you? Let us, O my dove,
    Let us be unashamed of soul,
As earth lies bare to heaven above!
    How is it under our control
To love or not to love?

VIII

I would that you were all to me,
    You that are just so much, no more.
Nor yours nor mine, nor slave nor free!
    Where does the fault lie? What the core
O' the wound, since wound must be?

IX

I would I could adopt your will,
    See with your eyes, and set my heart
Beating by yours, and drink my fill
    At your soul's springs,—your part my part
In life, for good and ill.

X

No. I yearn upward, touch you close,
　　Then stand away. I kiss your cheek,
Catch your soul's warmth,—I pluck the rose
　　And love it more than tongue can speak—
Then the good minute goes.

XI

Already how am I so far
　　Out of that minute? Must I go
Still like the thistle-ball, no bar,
　　Onward, whenever light winds blow,
Fixed by no friendly star?

XII

Just when I seemed about to learn!
　　Where is the thread now? Off again!
The old trick! Only I discern—
　　Infinite passion, and the pain
Of finite hearts that yearn.

MY LAST DUCHESS

FERRARA

THAT's my last Duchess painted on the wall,
Looking as if she were alive. I call
That piece a wonder, now: Frà Pandolf's hands
Worked busily a day, and there she stands.
Will't please you sit and look at her? I said
'Frà Pandolf' by design, for never read
Strangers like you that pictured countenance,
The depth and passion of its earnest glance,
But to myself they turned (since none puts by
The curtain I have drawn for you, but I)
And seemed as they would ask me, if they durst,
How such a glance came there; so, not the first
Are you to turn and ask thus. Sir, 'twas not
Her husband's presence only, called that spot
Of joy into the Duchess' cheek: perhaps
Frà Pandolf chanced to say 'Her mantle laps

'Over my lady's wrist too much,' or 'Paint
'Must never hope to reproduce the faint
'Half-flush that dies along her throat:' such stuff
Was courtesy, she thought, and cause enough
For calling up that spot of joy. She had
A heart—how shall I say?—too soon made glad,
Too easily impressed; she liked whate'er
She looked on, and her looks went everywhere.
Sir, 'twas all one! My favour at her breast,
The dropping of the daylight in the West,
The bough of cherries some officious fool
Broke in the orchard for her, the white mule
She rode with round the terrace—all and each
Would draw from her alike the approving speech,
Or blush, at least. She thanked men,—good! but thanked
Somehow—I know not how—as if she ranked
My gift of a nine-hundred-years-old name
With anybody's gift. Who'd stoop to blame
This sort of trifling? Even had you skill
In speech—(which I have not)—to make your will
Quite clear to such an one, and say, 'Just this
'Or that in you disgusts me; here you miss,
'Or there exceed the mark'—and if she let
Herself be lessoned so, nor plainly set
Her wits to yours, forsooth, and made excuse,
—E'en then would be some stooping; and I choose
Never to stoop. Oh sir, she smiled, no doubt,
Whene'er I passed her; but who passed without
Much the same smile? This grew; I gave commands;
Then all smiles stopped together. There she stands
As if alive. Will't please you rise? We'll meet
The company below, then. I repeat,
The Count your master's known munificence
Is ample warrant that no just pretence
Of mine for dowry will be disallowed;
Though his fair daughter's self, as I avowed
At starting, is my object. Nay, we'll go
Together down, sir. Notice Neptune, though,
Taming a sea-horse, thought a rarity,
Which Claus of Innsbruck cast in bronze for me!

ROBERT BROWNING

HOW IT STRIKES A CONTEMPORARY

I ONLY knew one poet in my life:
And this, or something like it, was his way.

You saw go up and down Valladolid,
A man of mark, to know next time you saw.
His very serviceable suit of black
Was courtly once and conscientious still,
And many might have worn it, though none did:
The cloak, that somewhat shone and showed the threads,
Had purpose, and the ruff, significance.
He walked and tapped the pavement with his cane,
Scenting the world, looking it full in face,
An old dog, bald and blindish, at his heels.
They turned up, now, the alley by the church,
That leads nowhither; now, they breathed themselves
On the main promenade just at the wrong time:
You'd come upon his scrutinizing hat,
Making a peaked shade blacker than itself
Against the single window spared some house
Intact yet with its mouldered Moorish work,—
Or else surprise the ferrel of his stick
Trying the mortar's temper 'tween the chinks
Of some new shop a-building, French and fine.
He stood and watched the cobbler at his trade,
The man who slices lemons into drink,
The coffee-roaster's brazier, and the boys
That volunteer to help him turn its winch.
He glanced o'er books on stalls with half an eye,
And fly-leaf ballads on the vendor's string,
And broad-edge bold-print posters by the wall.
He took such cognizance of men and things,
If any beat a horse, you felt he saw;
If any cursed a woman, he took note;
Yet stared at nobody,—you stared at him,
And found, less to your pleasure than surprise,
He seemed to know you and expect as much.
So, next time that a neighbour's tongue was loosed,
It marked the shameful and notorious fact,

We had among us, not so much a spy,
As a recording chief-inquisitor,
The town's true master if the town but knew!
We merely kept a governor for form,
While this man walked about and took account
Of all thought, said and acted, then went home,
And wrote it fully to our Lord the King
Who has an itch to know things, he knows why,
And reads them in his bedroom of a night.
Oh, you might smile! there wanted not a touch,
A tang of . . . well, it was not wholly ease
As back into your mind the man's look came.
Stricken in years a little,—such a brow
His eyes had to live under!—clear as flint
On either side the formidable nose
Curved, cut and coloured like an eagle's claw.
Had he to do with A.'s surprising fate?
When altogether old B. disappeared
And young C. got his mistress,—was't our friend,
His letter to the King, that did it all?
What paid the bloodless man for so much pains?
Our Lord the King has favourites manifold,
And shifts his ministry some once a month;
Our city gets new governors at whiles,—
But never word or sign, that I could hear,
Notified to this man about the streets
The King's approval of those letters conned
The last thing duly at the dead of night.
Did the man love his office? Frowned our Lord,
Exhorting when none heard—'Beseech me not!
'Too far above my people,—beneath me!
'I set the watch,—how should the people know?
'Forget them, keep me all the more in mind!'
Was some such understanding 'twixt the two?

    I found no truth in one report at least—
That if you tracked him to his home, down lanes
Beyond the Jewry, and as clean to pace,
You found he ate his supper in a room,
Blazing with lights, four Titians on the wall,

And twenty naked girls to change his plate!
Poor man, he lived another kind of life
In that new stuccoed third house by the bridge,
Fresh-painted, rather smart than otherwise!
The whole street might o'erlook him as he sat,
Leg crossing leg, one foot on the dog's back,
Playing a decent cribbage with his maid
(Jacynth, you're sure her name was) o'er the cheese
And fruit, three red halves of starved winter-pears,
Or treat of radishes in April. Nine,
Ten, struck the church clock, straight to bed went he.

My father, like the man of sense he was,
Would point him out to me a dozen times;
''St—'St,' he'd whisper, 'the Corregidor!'
I had been used to think that personage
Was one with lacquered breeches, lustrous belt,
And feathers like a forest in his hat,
Who blew a trumpet and proclaimed the news,
Announced the bull-fights, gave each church its turn,
And memorized the miracle was in vogue!
He had a great observance from us boys;
We were in error; that was not the man.

I'd like now, yet had haply been afraid,
To have just looked, when this man came to die,
And seen who lined the clean gay garret-sides
And stood about the neat low truckle-bed,
With the heavenly manner of relieving guard.
Here had been, mark, the general-in-chief,
Thro' a whole campaign of the world's life and death,
Doing the King's work all the dim day long,
In his old coat and up to knees in mud,
Smoked like a herring, dining on a crust,—
And, now the day was won, relieved at once!
No further show or need for that old coat,
You are sure, for one thing! Bless us, all the while
How sprucely we are dressed out, you and I!
A second, and the angels alter that.
Well, I could never write a verse,—could you?
Let's to the Prado and make the most of time.

CONFESSIONS

I

WHAT is he buzzing in my ears?
　'Now that I come to die,
'Do I view the world as a vale of tears?'
　Ah, reverend sir, not I!

II

What I viewed there once, what I view again
　Where the physic bottles stand
On the table's edge,—is a suburb lane,
　With a wall to my bedside hand.

III

That lane sloped, much as the bottles do,
　From a house you could descry
O'er the garden-wall: is the curtain blue
　Or green to a healthy eye?

IV

To mine, it serves for the old June weather
　Blue above lane and wall;
And that farthest bottle labelled 'Ether'
　Is the house o'ertopping all.

V

At a terrace, somewhere near the stopper,
　There watched for me, one June,
A girl: I know, sir, it's improper,
　My poor mind's out of tune.

VI

Only, there was a way . . . you crept
　Close by the side, to dodge
Eyes in the house, two eyes except:
　They styled their house 'The Lodge.'

VII

What right had a lounger up their lane?
  But, by creeping very close,
With the good wall's help,—their eyes might strain
  And stretch themselves to Oes,

VIII

Yet never catch her and me together,
  As she left the attic, there,
By the rim of the bottle labelled 'Ether,'
  And stole from stair to stair,

IX

And stood by the rose-wreathed gate. Alas,
  We loved, sir—used to meet:
How sad and bad and mad it was—
  But then, how it was sweet!

EDWARD LEAR

1812–1888

BY WAY OF PREFACE

How pleasant to know Mr. Lear!
  Who has written such volumes of stuff!
Some think him ill-tempered and queer,
  But a few think him pleasant enough.

His mind is concrete and fastidious,
  His nose is remarkably big;
His visage is more or less hideous,
  His beard it resembles a wig.

He has ears, and two eyes, and ten fingers,
  Leastways if you reckon two thumbs;
Long ago he was one of the singers,
  But now he is one of the dumbs.

LEAR

He sits in a beautiful parlour,
    With hundreds of books on the wall;
He drinks a great deal of Marsala,
    But never gets tipsy at all.

He has many friends, laymen and clerical,
    Old Foss is the name of his cat:
His body is perfectly spherical,
    He weareth a runcible hat.

When he walks in a waterproof white,
    The children run after him so!
Calling out, 'He's come out in his night-
    gown, that crazy old Englishman, oh!'

He weeps by the side of the ocean,
    He weeps on the top of the hill;
He purchases pancakes and lotion,
    And chocolate shrimps from the mill.

He reads but he cannot speak Spanish,
    He cannot abide ginger-beer:
Ere the days of his pilgrimage vanish,
    How pleasant to know Mr. Lear!

THE OWL AND THE PUSSY CAT

THE Owl and the Pussy-Cat went to sea
    In a beautiful pea-green boat.
They took some honey, and plenty of money
    Wrapped up in a five-pound note.
The Owl looked up to the stars above,
    And sang to a small guitar,
'O lovely Pussy! O Pussy, my love,
What a beautiful Pussy you are,
        You are,
        You are!
What a beautiful Pussy you are!'

LEAR

Pussy said to the Owl, 'You elegant fowl!
　　How charmingly sweet you sing!
O let us be married! too long we have tarried:
　　But what shall we do for a ring?'
They sailed away, for a year and a day,
　　To the land where the Bong-Tree grows,
And there in a wood a Piggy-wig stood,
With a ring at the end of his nose,
　　　　　His nose,
　　　　　His nose!
With a ring at the end of his nose.

'Dear Pig, are you willing to sell for one shilling
　　Your ring?' Said the Piggy, 'I will.'
So they took it away, and were married next day
　　By the Turkey who lives on the hill.
They dinèd on mince, and slices of quince,
　　Which they ate with a runcible spoon;
And hand in hand, on the edge of the sand
　　They danced by the light of the moon,
　　　　　The moon,
　　　　　The moon,
They danced by the light of the moon.

ARTHUR HUGH CLOUGH

1819–1861

THE LATEST DECALOGUE

THOU shalt have one God only; who
Would be at the expense of two?
No graven images may be
Worshipped, except the currency:
Swear not at all; for for thy curse
Thine enemy is none the worse:
At church on Sunday to attend
Will serve to keep the world thy friend:

Honour thy parents; that is, all
From whom advancement may befall:
Thou shalt not kill; but needst not strive
Officiously to keep alive:
Do not adultery commit;
Advantage rarely comes of it:
Thou shalt not steal; an empty feat,
When it's so lucrative to cheat:
Bear not false witness; let the lie
Have time on its own wings to fly:
Thou shalt not covet; but tradition
Approves all forms of competition.

The sum of all is, thou shalt love,
If any body, God above:
At any rate shall never labour
More than thyself to love thy neighbour.

—

Say not the struggle nought availeth,
   The labour and the wounds are vain,
The enemy faints not, nor faileth,
   And as things have been, things remain.

If hopes were dupes, fears may be liars;
   It may be, in yon smoke concealed,
Your comrades chase e'en now the fliers,
   And, but for you, possess the field.

For while the tired waves, vainly breaking,
   Seem here no painful inch to gain,
Far back through creeks and inlets making
   Came, silent, flooding in, the main,

And not by eastern windows only,
   When daylight comes, comes in the light,
In front the sun climbs slow, how slowly,
   But westward, look, the land is bright.

CLOUGH

From AMOURS DE VOYAGE

Canto II

XI. CLAUDE TO EUSTACE

THERE are two different kinds, I believe, of human attraction:
One which simply disturbs, unsettles, and makes you uneasy,
And another that poises, retains, and fixes and holds you.
I have no doubt, for myself, in giving my voice for the latter
I do not wish to be moved, but growing where I was growing,
There more truly to grow, to live where as yet I had languished.
I do not like being moved: for the will is excited; and action
Is a most dangerous thing; I tremble for something factitious
Some malpractice of heart and illegitimate process;
We are so prone to these things with our terrible notions of
duty.

Canto III

XI. CLAUDE TO EUSTACE

TIBUR is beautiful, too, and the orchard slopes, and the Anio
Falling, falling yet, to the ancient lyrical cadence;
Tibur and Anio's tide; and cool from Lucretilis ever,
With the Digentian stream, and with the Bandusian fountain
Folded in Sabine recesses, the valley and villa of Horace:—
So not seeing I sang; so seeing and listening say I,
Here as I sit by the stream, as I gaze at the cell of the Sibyl,
Here with Albunea's home and the grove of Tiburnus beside
me; [1]
Tivoli beautiful is, and musical, O Teverone,
Dashing from mountain to plain, thy parted impetuous
waters!
Tivoli's waters and rocks; and fair under Monte Gennaro

---

[1] —— domus Albuneæ resonantis,
Et præceps Anio, et Tiburni lucus, et uda
Mobilibus pomaria rivis.

360

CLOUGH

(Haunt even yet, I must think, as I wander and gaze, of the
    shadows,
Faded and pale, yet immortal, of Faunus, the Nymphs, and
    the Graces),
Fair in itself, and yet fairer with human completing creations,
Folded in Sabine recesses the valley and villa of Horace:—
So not seeing I sang; so now—Nor seeing, nor hearing,
Neither by waterfall lulled, nor folded in sylvan embraces,
Neither by cell of the Sibyl, nor stepping the Monte Gen-
    naro,
Seated on Anio's bank, nor sipping Bandusian waters,
But on Montorio's height, looking down on the tile-clad
    streets, the
Cupolas, crosses, and domes, the bushes and kitchen-gardens,
Which, by the grace of the Tiber, proclaim themselves Rome
    of the Romans,—
But on Montorio's height, looking forth to the vapoury
    mountains,
Cheating the prisoner Hope with illusions of vision and
    fancy,—
But on Montorio's height, with these weary soldiers by me,
Waiting till Oudinot enter, to reinstate Pope and Tourist.

SPECTATOR AB EXTRA

I

As I sat at the Café I said to myself,
    They may talk as they please about what they call pelf,
    They may sneer as they like about eating and drinking,
    But help it I cannot, I cannot help thinking
        How pleasant it is to have money, heigh-ho!
        How pleasant it is to have money.

I sit at my table *en grand seigneur*,
    And when I have done, throw a crust to the poor;
    Not only the pleasure itself of good living,
    But also the pleasure of now and then giving:
        So pleasant it is to have money, heigh-ho!
        So pleasant it is to have money.

CLOUGH

They may talk as they please about what they call pelf,
And how one ought never to think of one's self,
How pleasures of thought surpass eating and drinking,—
My pleasure of thought is the pleasure of thinking
    How pleasant it is to have money, heigh-ho!
    How pleasant it is to have money.

MATTHEW ARNOLD

1822–1888

A DREAM

Was it a dream? We sail'd, I thought we sail'd,
Martin and I, down a green Alpine stream,
Border'd, each bank, with pines; the morning sun,
On the wet umbrage of their glossy tops,
On the red pinings of their forest-floor,
Drew a warm scent abroad; behind the pines
The mountain-skirts, with all their sylvan change
Of bright-leaf'd chestnuts and moss'd walnut-trees
And the frail scarlet-berried ash, began.
Swiss chalets glitter'd on the dewy slopes,
And from some swarded shelf, high up, there came
Notes of wild pastoral music—over all
Ranged, diamond-bright, the eternal wall of snow.
Upon the mossy rocks at the stream's edge,
Back'd by the pines, a plank-built cottage stood,
Bright in the sun; the climbing gourd-plant's leaves
Muffled its walls, and on the stone-strewn roof
Lay the warm golden gourds; golden, within,
Under the eaves, peer'd rows of Indian corn.
We shot beneath the cottage with the stream.
On the brown, rude-carved balcony, two forms
Came forth—Olivia's, Marguerite! and thine.
Clad were they both in white, flowers in their breast;
Straw hats bedeck'd their heads, with ribbons blue,
Which danced, and on their shoulders, fluttering, play'd.
They saw us, they conferr'd; their bosoms heaved,
And more than mortal impulse fill'd their eyes.

362

Their lips moved; their white arms, waved eagerly,
Flash'd once, like falling streams; we rose, we gazed.
One moment, on the rapid's top, our boat
Hung poised—and then the darting river of Life
(Such now, methought, it was), the river of Life,
Loud thundering, bore us by; swift, swift it foam'd,
Black under cliffs it raced, round headlands shone.
Soon the plank'd cottage by the sun-warm'd pines
Faded—the moss—the rocks; us burning plains,
Bristled with cities, us the sea received.

From SOHRAB AND RUSTUM

So, on the bloody sand, Sohrab lay dead;
And the great Rustum drew his horseman's cloak
Down o'er his face, and sate by his dead son.
As those black granite pillars, once high-rear'd
By Jemshid in Persepolis, to bear
His house, now 'mid their broken flights of steps
Lie prone, enormous, down the mountain side—
So in the sand lay Rustum by his son.
    And night came down over the solemn waste,
And the two gazing hosts, and that sole pair,
And darken'd all; and a cold fog, with night,
Crept from the Oxus. Soon a hum arose,
As of a great assembly loosed, and fires
Began to twinkle through the fog; for now
Both armies moved to camp, and took their meal;
The Persians took it on the open sands
Southward, the Tartars by the river marge;
And Rustum and his son were left alone.
    But the majestic river floated on,
Out of the mist and hum of that low land,
Into the frosty starlight, and there moved,
Rejoicing, through the hush'd Chorasmian waste,
Under the solitary moon;—he flow'd
Right for the polar star, past Orgunjè,
Brimming, and bright, and large; then sands begin
To hem his watery march, and dam his streams,

And split his currents; that for many a league
The shorn and parcell'd Oxus strains along
Through beds of sand and matted rushy isles—
Oxus, forgetting the bright speed he had
In his high mountain-cradle in Pamere,
A foil'd circuitous wanderer—till at last
The long'd-for dash of waves is heard, and wide
His luminous home of waters opens, bright
And tranquil, from whose floor the new-bathed stars
Emerge, and shine upon the Aral Sea.

SWITZERLAND

TO MARGUERITE—CONTINUED

YES! in the sea of life enisled,
With echoing straits between us thrown,
Dotting the shoreless watery wild,
We mortal millions live *alone*.
The islands feel the enclasping flow,
And then their endless bounds they know.

But when the moon their hollows lights,
And they are swept by balms of spring,
And in their glens, on starry nights,
The nightingales divinely sing;
And lovely notes, from shore to shore,
Across the sounds and channels pour—

Oh! then a longing like despair
Is to their farthest caverns sent;
For surely once, they feel, we were
Parts of a single continent!
Now round us spreads the watery plain—
Oh might our marges meet again!

Who order'd, that their longing's fire
Should be, as soon as kindled, cool'd?
Who renders vain their deep desire?—
A God, a God their severance ruled!
And bade betwixt their shores to be
The unplumb'd, salt, estranging sea.

DOVER BEACH

THE sea is calm to-night.
The tide is full, the moon lies fair
Upon the straits;—on the French coast the light
Gleams and is gone; the cliffs of England stand,
Glimmering and vast, out in the tranquil bay.
Come to the window, sweet is the night-air!
Only, from the long line of spray
Where the sea meets the moon-blanch'd land,
Listen! you hear the grating roar
Of pebbles which the waves draw back, and fling,
At their return, up the high strand,
Begin, and cease, and then again begin,
With tremulous cadence slow, and bring
The eternal note of sadness in.

Sophocles long ago
Heard it on the Ægæan, and it brought
Into his mind the turbid ebb and flow
Of human misery; we
Find also in the sound a thought,
Hearing it by this distant northern sea.

The Sea of Faith
Was once, too, at the full, and round earth's shore
Lay like the folds of a bright girdle furl'd.
But now I only hear
Its melancholy, long, withdrawing roar,
Retreating, to the breath
Of the night-wind, down the vast edges drear
And naked shingles of the world.

Ah, love, let us be true
To one another! for the world, which seems
To lie before us like a land of dreams,
So various, so beautiful, so new,
Hath really neither joy, nor love, nor light,
Nor certitude, nor peace, nor help for pain;
And we are here as on a darkling plain
Swept with confused alarms of struggle and flight,
Where ignorant armies clash by night.

PALLADIUM

Set where the upper streams of Simois flow
Was the Palladium, high 'mid rock and wood;
And Hector was in Ilium, far below,
And fought, and saw it not—but there it stood!

It stood, and sun and moonshine rain'd their light
On the pure columns of its glen-built hall.
Backward and forward roll'd the waves of fight
Round Troy—but while this stood, Troy could not fall.

So, in its lovely moonlight, lives the soul.
Mountains surround it, and sweet virgin air;
Cold plashing, past it, crystal waters roll;
We visit it by moments, ah, too rare!

We shall renew the battle in the plain
To-morrow;—red with blood will Xanthus be;
Hector and Ajax will be there again,
Helen will come upon the wall to see.

Then we shall rust in shade, or shine in strife,
And fluctuate 'twixt blind hopes and blind despairs,
And fancy that we put forth all our life,
And never know how with the soul it fares.

Still doth the soul, from its lone fastness high,
Upon our life a ruling effluence send.
And when it fails, fight as we will, we die;
And while it lasts, we cannot wholly end.

From EMPEDOCLES ON ETNA

Far far from here,
The Adriatic breaks in a warm bay
Among the green Illyrian hills; and there
The sunshine in the happy glens is fair,
And by the sea, and in the brakes.
The grass is cool, the sea-side air
Buoyant and fresh, the mountain flowers
More virginal and sweet than ours.

And there, they say, two bright and aged snakes,
Who once were Cadmus and Harmonia,
Bask in the glens or on the warm sea-shore,
In breathless quiet, after all their ills;
Nor do they see their country, nor the place
Where the Sphinx lived among the frowning hills,
Nor the unhappy palace of their race,
Nor Thebes, nor the Ismenus, any more.

There those two live, far in the Illyrian brakes!
They had stay'd long enough to see,
In Thebes, the billow of calamity
Over their own dear children roll'd,
Curse upon curse, pang upon pang,
For years, they sitting helpless in their home,
A grey old man and woman; yet of old
The Gods had to their marriage come,
And at the banquet all the Muses sang.

Therefore they did not end their days
In sight of blood; but were rapt, far away,
To where the west-wind plays,
And murmurs of the Adriatic come
To those untrodden mountain-lawns; and there
Placed safely in changed forms, the pair
Wholly forget their first sad life, and home,
And all that Theban woe, and stray
For ever through the glens, placid and dumb.

COVENTRY PATMORE

1823–1896

From THE ANGEL IN THE HOUSE

Book I: Canto VIII (II)

THE REVELATION

An idle poet, here and there,
  Looks around him; but, for all the rest,
The world, unfathomably fair,
  Is duller than a witling's jest.

Love wakes men, once a lifetime each;
   They lift their heavy lids, and look;
And, lo, what one sweet page can teach,
   They read with joy, then shut the book.
And some gives thanks, and some blaspheme,
   And most forget; but, either way,
That and the Child's unheeded dream
   Is all the light of all their day.

Book II: Canto III (II)

THE RAINBOW

A stately rainbow came and stood,
   When I was young, in High-Hurst Park;
Its bright feet lit the hill and wood
   Beyond, and cloud and sward were dark;
And I, who thought the splendour ours
   Because the place was, t'wards it flew,
And there, amidst the glittering showers,
   Gazed vainly for the glorious view.
With whatsoever's lovely, know
   It is not ours; stand off to see,
Or beauty's apparition so
   Puts on invisibility.

From TO THE UNKNOWN EROS

Book I: XII MAGNA EST VERITAS

   Here, in this little Bay,
Full of tumultuous life and great repose,
Where, twice a day,
The purposeless, glad ocean comes and goes,
Under high cliffs, and far from the huge town,
I sit me down.
For want of me the world's course will not fail:
When all its work is done, the lie shall rot;
The truth is great, and shall prevail,
When none cares whether it prevail or not.

Book I: XVI A FAREWELL

   With all my will, but much against my heart,
We two now part.

My Very Dear,
Our solace is, the sad road lies so clear.
It needs no art,
With faint, averted feet
And many a tear,
In our opposed paths to persevere.
Go thou to East, I West.
We will not say
There's any hope, it is so far away.
But, O, my Best,
When the one darling of our widowhead,
The nursling Grief,
Is dead,
And no dews blur our eyes
To see the peach-bloom come in evening skies,
Perchance we may,
Where now this night is day,
And even through faith of still averted feet,
Making full circle of our banishment,
Amazed meet;
The bitter journey to the bourne so sweet
Seasoning the termless feast of our content
With tears of recognition never dry.

GEORGE MEREDITH

1828–1909

From MODERN LOVE

XLVII

WE saw the swallows gathering in the sky,
And in the osier-isle we heard them noise.
We had not to look back on summer joys,
Or forward to a summer of bright dye:
But in the largeness of the evening earth
Our spirits grew as we went side by side.
The hour became her husband and my bride.
Love, that had robbed us so, thus blessed our dearth!

The pilgrims of the year waxed very loud
In multitudinous chatterings, as the flood
Full brown came from the West, and like pale blood
Expanded to the upper crimson cloud.
Love, that had robbed us of immortal things,
This little moment mercifully gave,
Where I have seen across the twilight wave
The swan sail with her young beneath her wings.

L

Thus piteously Love closed what he begat:
The union of this ever-diverse pair!
These two were rapid falcons in a snare,
Condemned to do the flitting of the bat.
Lovers beneath the singing sky of May,
They wandered once; clear as the dew on flowers:
But they fed not on the advancing hours:
Their hearts held cravings for the buried day.
Then each applied to each that fatal knife,
Deep questioning, which probes to endless dole.
Ah, what a dusty answer gets the soul
When hot for certainties in this our life!—
In tragic hints here see what evermore
Moves dark as yonder midnight ocean's force,
Thundering like ramping hosts of warrior horse,
To throw that faint thin line upon the shore!

DANTE GABRIEL ROSSETTI

1828–1882

From THE HOUSE OF LIFE

SONNET III

LOVESIGHT

WHEN do I see thee most, beloved one?
  When in the light the spirits of mine eyes
  Before thy face, their altar, solemnize
The worship of that Love through thee made known?

Or when in the dusk hours, (we two alone,)
　　Close-kissed and eloquent of still replies
　　Thy twilight-hidden glimmering visage lies,
And my soul only sees thy soul its own?

O love, my love! if I no more should see
　　Thyself, nor on the earth the shadow of thee,
　　Nor image of thine eyes in any spring,—
How then should sound upon Life's darkening slope
The ground-whirl of the perished leaves of Hope,
　　The wind of Death's imperishable wing?

Sonnet XXXVII

THE CHOICE

Think thou and act; to-morrow thou shalt die.
　　Outstretched in the sun's warmth upon the shore,
　　Thou say'st: 'Man's measured path is all gone o'er:
Up all his years, steeply, with strain and sigh,
Man clomb until he touched the truth; and I,
　　Even I, am he whom it was destined for.'
　　How should this be? Art thou then so much more
Than they who sowed, that thou shouldst reap thereby?

Nay, come up hither. From this wave-washed mound
　　Unto the furthest flood-brim look with me;
Then reach on with thy thought till it be drown'd.
　　Miles and miles distant though the grey line be,
And though thy soul sail leagues and leagues beyond,—
　　Still, leagues beyond those leagues, there is more sea.

Sonnet XLVI

A SUPERSCRIPTION

Look in my face; my name is Might-have-been;
　　I am also called No-more, Too-late, Farewell;
　　Unto thine ear I hold the dead-sea shell
Cast up thy Life's foam-fretted feet between;

Unto thine eyes the glass where that is seen
   Which had Life's form and Love's, but by my spell
   Is now a shaken shadow intolerable,
Of ultimate things unuttered the frail screen.

Mark me, how still I am! But should there dart
   One moment through thy soul the soft surprise
   Of that winged Peace which lulls the breath of sighs,—
Then shalt thou see me smile, and turn apart
Thy visage to mine ambush at thy heart
   Sleepless with cold commemorative eyes.

Song VIII

THE WOODSPURGE

THE wind flapped loose, the wind was still,
Shaken out dead from tree and hill:
I had walked on at the wind's will,—
I sat now, for the wind was still.

Between my knees my forehead was,—
My lips, drawn in, said not Alas!
My hair was over in the grass,
My naked ears heard the day pass.

My eyes, wide open, had the run
Of some ten weeds to fix upon;
Among those few, out of the sun,
The woodspurge flowered, three cups in one.

From perfect grief there need not be
Wisdom or even memory:
One thing then learnt remains to me,—
The woodspurge has a cup of three.

CHRISTINA ROSSETTI

1830–1894

SPRING QUIET

GONE were but the Winter,
  Come were but the Spring,
I would go to a covert
  Where the birds sing;

Where in the whitethorn
  Singeth a thrush,
And a robin sings
  In the holly-bush.

Full of fresh scents
  Are the budding boughs
Arching high over
  A cool green house;

Full of sweet scents,
  And whispering air
Which sayeth softly:
  'We spread no snare;

'Here dwell in safety,
  Here dwell alone,
With a clear stream
  And a mossy stone.

'Here the sun shineth
  Most shadily;
Here is heard an echo
  Of the far sea,
  Though far off it be.'

Towards May 1847

SONG

OH roses for the flush of youth,
    And laurel for the perfect prime;
But pluck an ivy branch for me
    Grown old before my time.

Oh violets for the grave of youth,
    And bay for those dead in their prime;
Give me the withered leaves I chose
    Before in the old time.

6 February 1849

A SKETCH

THE blindest buzzard that I know
    Does not wear wings to spread and stir;
    Nor does my special mole wear fur,
And grub among the roots below:
He sports a tail indeed, but then
It's to a coat: he's man with men:
    His quill is cut to a pen.

In other points our friend's a mole,
    A buzzard, beyond scope of speech.
    He sees not what's within his reach,
Misreads the part, ignores the whole;
Misreads the part, so reads in vain,
Ignores the whole though patent plain,—
    Misreads both parts again.

My blindest buzzard that I know,
    My special mole, when will you see?
    Oh no, you must not look at me,
There's nothing hid for me to show.
I might show facts as plain as day:
But, since your eyes are blind, you'd say,
    'Where? What?' and turn away.

15 August 1864

EVE

'WHILE I sit at the door,
Sick to gaze within,
Mine eye weepeth sore
For sorrow and sin:
As a tree my sin stands
To darken all lands;
Death is the fruit it bore.

'How have Eden bowers grown
Without Adam to bend them?
How have Eden flowers blown,
Squandering their sweet breath,
Without me to tend them?
The Tree of Life was ours,
Tree twelvefold-fruited,
Most lofty tree that flowers,
Most deeply rooted:
I chose the Tree of Death.

'Hadst thou but said me nay,
Adam my brother,
I might have pined away—
I, but none other:
God might have let thee stay
Safe in our garden,
By putting me away
Beyond all pardon.

'I, Eve, sad mother
Of all who must live,
I, not another,
Plucked bitterest fruit to give
My friend, husband, lover.
O' wanton eyes, run over!
Who but I should grieve?
Cain hath slain his brother:
Of all who must die mother,
Miserable Eve!'

Thus she sat weeping,
Thus Eve our mother,
Where one lay sleeping
Slain by his brother.
Greatest and least
Each piteous beast
To hear her voice
Forgot his joys
And set aside his feast.

The mouse paused in his walk
And dropped his wheaten stalk;
Grave cattle wagged their heads
In rumination;
The eagle gave a cry
From his cloud station:
Larks on thyme beds
Forbore to mount or sing;
Bees drooped upon the wing;
The raven perched on high
Forgot his ration;
The conies in their rock,
A feeble nation,
Quaked sympathetical;
The mocking-bird left off to mock;
Huge camels knelt as if
In deprecation;
The kind hart's tears were falling;
Chattered the wistful stork;
Dove-voices with a dying fall
Cooed desolation,
Answering grief by grief.

Only the serpent in the dust,
Wriggling and crawling,
Grinned an evil grin and thrust
His tongue out with its fork.

30 January 1865

LEWIS CARROLL

1832–1898

HUMPTY DUMPTY'S SONG

In winter, when the fields are white,
I sing this song for your delight—

    o   o   o

In spring, when woods are getting green,
I'll try and tell you what I mean.

    o   o   o

In summer, when the days are long,
Perhaps you'll understand the song:

In autumn, when the leaves are brown,
Take pen and ink, and write it down.

    o   o   o

I sent a message to the fish:
I told them 'This is what I wish.'

The little fishes of the sea
They sent an answer back to me.

The little fishes' answer was
'We cannot do it, Sir, because——'

    o   o   o

I sent to them again to say
'It will be better to obey.'

The fishes answered with a grin
'Why, what a temper you are in!'

I told them once, I told them twice:
They would not listen to advice.

I took a kettle large and new,
Fit for the deed I had to do.

My heart went hop, my heart went thump;
I filled the kettle at the pump.

Then some one came to me and said
'The little fishes are in bed.'

I said to him, I said it plain,
'Then you must wake them up again.'

I said it very loud and clear;
I went and shouted in his ear.

    o   o   o

But he was very stiff and proud;
He said 'You needn't shout so loud!'

And he was very proud and stiff;
He said 'I'd go and wake them, if——'

I took a corkscrew from the shelf:
I went to wake them up myself.

And when I found the door was locked,
I pulled and pushed and kicked and knocked.

And when I found the door was shut
I tried to turn the handle, but——

EVIDENCE READ AT THE TRIAL OF
THE KNAVE OF HEARTS

THEY told me you had been to her,
    And mentioned me to him:
She gave me a good character,
    But said I could not swim.

He sent them word I had not gone,
    (We know it to be true:)
If she should push the matter on,
    What would become of you?

CARROLL

I gave her one, they gave him two,
    You gave us three or more;
They all returned from him to you,
    Though they were mine before.

If I or she should chance to be
    Involved in this affair,
He trusts to you to set them free,
    Exactly as we were.

My notion was that you had been
    (Before she had this fit)
An obstacle that came between
    Him, and ourselves, and it.

Don't let him know she liked them best,
    For this must ever be
A secret, kept from all the rest,
    Between yourself and me.

RICHARD WATSON DIXON

1833–1900

SONG

The feathers of the willow
Are half of them grown yellow
    Above the swelling stream;
And ragged are the bushes,
And rusty are the rushes,
    And wild the clouded gleam.

The thistle now is older,
His stalk begins to moulder,
    His head is white as snow;
The branches all are barer,
The linnet's song is rarer,
    The robin pipeth now.

WINTER WILL FOLLOW

THE heaving roses of the hedge are stirred
By the sweet breath of summer, and the bird
Makes from within his jocund voice be heard.

The winds that kiss the roses sweep the sea
Of uncut grass, whose billows rolling free
Half drown the hedges which part lea from lea.

But soon shall look the wondering roses down
Upon an empty field cut close and brown,
That lifts no more its height against their own.

And in a little while those roses bright,
Leaf after leaf, shall flutter from their height,
And on the reaped field lie pink and white.

And yet again the bird that sings so high
Shall ask the snow for alms with piteous cry,
Take fright in his bewildering bower, and die.

WILLIAM MORRIS

1834–1896

SHAMEFUL DEATH

THERE were four of us about that bed;
   The mass-priest knelt at the side,
I and his mother stood at the head,
   Over his feet lay the bride;
We were quite sure that he was dead,
   Though his eyes were open wide.

He did not die in the night,
   He did not die in the day,
But in the morning twilight
   His spirit pass'd away,
When neither sun nor moon was bright,
   And the trees were merely grey.

He was not slain with the sword,
   Knight's axe, or the knightly spear,
Yet spoke he never a word
   After he came in here;
I cut away the cord
   From the neck of my brother dear.

He did not strike one blow,
   For the recreants came behind,
In a place where the hornbeams grow,
   A path right hard to find
For the hornbeam boughs swing so,
   That the twilight makes it blind.

They lighted a great torch then,
   When his arms were pinion'd fast,
Sir John the knight of the Fen,
   Sir Guy of the Dolorous Blast,
With knights threescore and ten,
   Hung brave Lord Hugh at last.

I am threescore and ten,
   And my hair is all turn'd grey,
But I met Sir John of the Fen
   Long ago on a summer day,
And am glad to think of the moment when
   I took his life away.

I am threescore and ten,
   And my strength is mostly pass'd,
But long ago I and my men,
   When the sky was overcast,
And the smoke roll'd over the reeds of the fen,
   Slew Guy of the Dolorous Blast.

And now, knights all of you,
I pray you pray for Sir Hugh,
A good knight and a true,
And for Alice, his wife, pray too.

JAMES THOMSON

1834–1882

From THE CITY OF DREADFUL NIGHT

XVI

ANEAR the centre of that northern crest
  Stands out a level upland bleak and bare,
From which the city east and south and west
  Sinks gently in long waves; and thronèd there
An Image sits, stupendous, superhuman,
The bronze colossus of a wingèd Woman,
  Upon a graded granite base foursquare.

Low-seated she leans forward massively,
  With cheek on clenched left hand, the forearm's might
Erect, its elbow on her rounded knee;
  Across a clasped book in her lap the right
Upholds a pair of compasses; she gazes
With full set eyes, but wandering in thick mazes
  Of sombre thought beholds no outward sight.

Words cannot picture her; but all men know
  That solemn sketch the pure sad artist wrought
Three centuries and threescore years ago,
  With phantasies of his peculiar thought:
The instruments of carpentry and science
Scattered about her feet, in strange alliance
  With the keen wolf-hound sleeping undistraught;

Scales, hour-glass, bell, and magic-square above;
  The grave and solid infant perched beside,
With open winglets that might bear a dove,
  Intent upon its tablets, heavy-eyed;
Her folded wings as of a mighty eagle,
But all too impotent to lift the regal
  Robustness of her earth-born strength and pride;

And with those wings, and that light wreath which seems
    To mock her grand head and the knotted frown
Of forehead charged with baleful thoughts and dreams,
    The household bunch of keys, the housewife's gown
Voluminous, indented, and yet rigid
As if a shell of burnished metal frigid,
    The feet thick-shod to tread all weakness down;

The comet hanging o'er the waste dark seas,
    The massy rainbow curved in front of it
Beyond the village with the masts and trees;
    The snaky imp, dog-headed, from the Pit,
Bearing upon its batlike leathern pinions
Her name unfolded in the sun's dominions,
    The 'MELENCOLIA' that transcends all wit.

Thus has the artist copied her, and thus
    Surrounded to expound her form sublime,
Her fate heroic and calamitous;
    Fronting the dreadful mysteries of Time,
Unvanquished in defeat and desolation,
Undaunted in the hopeless conflagration
    Of the day setting on her baffled prime.

Baffled and beaten back she works on still,
    Weary and sick of soul she works the more,
Sustained by her indomitable will:
    The hands shall fashion and the brain shall pore,
And all her sorrow shall be turned to labour,
Till Death the friend-foe piercing with his sabre
    That mighty heart of hearts ends bitter war.

But as if blacker night could dawn on night,
    With tenfold gloom on moonless night unstarred,
A sense more tragic than defeat and blight,
    More desperate than strife with hope debarred,
More fatal than the adamantine Never
Encompassing her passionate endeavour,
    Dawns glooming in her tenebrous regard:

The sense that every struggle brings defeat
   Because Fate holds no prize to crown success;
That all the oracles are dumb or cheat
   Because they have no secret to express;
That none can pierce the vast black veil uncertain
Because there is no light beyond the curtain;
   That all is vanity and nothingness.

Titanic from her high throne in the north,
   That City's sombre Patroness and Queen,
In bronze sublimity she gazes forth
   Over her Capital of teen and threne,
Over the river with its isles and bridges,
The marsh and moorland, to the stern rock-ridges,
   Confronting them with a coëval mien.

The moving moon and stars from east to west
   Circle before her in the sea of air;
Shadows and gleams glide round her solemn rest.
   Her subjects often gaze up to her there:
The strong to drink new strength of iron endurance,
The weak new terrors; all, renewed assurance
   And confirmation of the old despair.

JOHN LEICESTER WARREN
LORD DE TABLEY

1835–1895

NUPTIAL SONG

Sigh, heart, and break not; rest, lark, and wake not!
   Day I hear coming to draw my Love away.
As mere-waves whisper, and clouds grow crisper,
   Ah, like a rose he will waken up with day!

In moon-light lonely, he is my Love only,
   I share with none when Luna rides in grey.
As dawn-beams quicken, my rivals thicken,
   The light and deed and turmoil of the day.

To watch my sleeper to me is sweeter,
    Than any waking words my Love can say;
In dream he finds me and closer winds me!
    Let him rest by me a little more and stay.

Ah, mine eyes, close not: and, tho' he knows not,
    My lips, on his be tender while you may;
Ere leaves are shaken, and ring-doves waken,
    And infant buds begin to scent new day.

Fair Darkness, measure thine hours, as treasure
    Shed each one slowly from thine urn, I pray;
Hoard in and cover each from my lover;
    I cannot lose him yet; dear night, delay!

Each moment dearer, true-love lie nearer,
    My hair shall blind thee lest thou see the ray;
My locks encumber thine ears in slumber,
    Lest any bird dare give thee note of day.

He rests so calmly; we lie so warmly;
    Hand within hand, as children after play;—
In shafted amber on roof and chamber
    Dawn enters; my Love wakens; here is day.

ALGERNON CHARLES SWINBURNE

1837–1909

A FORSAKEN GARDEN

In a coign of the cliff between lowland and highland,
    At the sea-down's edge between windward and lee,
Walled round with rocks as an inland island,
    The ghost of a garden fronts the sea.
A girdle of brushwood and thorn encloses
    The steep square slope of the blossomless bed
Where the weeds that grew green from the graves of its roses
        Now lie dead.

The fields fall southward, abrupt and broken,
    To the low last edge of the long lone land.
If a step should sound or a word be spoken,
    Would a ghost not rise at the strange guest's hand?
So long have the grey bare walks lain guestless,
    Through branches and briers if a man make way
He shall find no life but the sea-wind's, restless
        Night and day.

The dense hard passage is blind and stifled
    That crawls by a track none turn to climb
To the strait waste place that the years have rifled
    Of all but the thorns that are touched not of time.
The thorns he spares when the rose is taken;
    The rocks are left when he wastes the plain.
The wind that wanders, the weeds wind-shaken,
        These remain.

Not a flower to be pressed of the foot that falls not;
    As the heart of a dead man the seed-plots are dry;
From the thicket of thorns whence the nightingale calls not,
    Could she call, there were never a rose to reply.
Over the meadows that blossom and wither
    Rings but the note of a sea-bird's song;
Only the sun and the rain come hither
        All year long.

The sun burns sere and the rain dishevels
    One gaunt bleak blossom of scentless breath.
Only the wind here hovers and revels
    In a round where life seems barren as death.
Here there was laughing of old, there was weeping,
    Haply, of lovers none ever will know,
Whose eyes went seaward a hundred sleeping
        Years ago.

Heart handfast in heart as they stood, 'Look thither,'
    Did he whisper? 'look forth from the flowers to the sea;
For the foam-flowers endure when the rose-blossoms wither,
    And men that love lightly may die—but we?'

And the same wind sang and the same waves whitened,
   And or ever the garden's last petals were shed,
In the lips that had whispered, the eyes that had lightened,
      Love was dead.

Or they loved their life through, and then went whither?
   And were one to the end—but what end who knows?
Love deep as the sea as a rose must wither,
   As the rose-red seaweed that mocks the rose.
Shall the dead take thought for the dead to love them?
   What love was ever as deep as a grave?
They are loveless now as the grass above them,
      Or the wave.

All are at one now, roses and lovers,
   Not known of the cliffs and the fields and the sea.
Not a breath of the time that has been hovers
   In the air now soft with a summer to be.
Not a breath shall there sweeten the seasons hereafter
   Of the flowers or the lovers that laugh now or weep,
When as they that are free now of weeping and laughter
      We shall sleep.

Here death may deal not again for ever;
   Here change may come not till all change end.
From the graves they have made they shall rise up never,
   Who have left nought living to ravage and rend.
Earth, stones, and thorns of the wild ground growing,
   While the sun and the rain live, these shall be;
Till a last wind's breath upon all these blowing
      Roll the sea.

Till the slow sea rise and the sheer cliff crumble,
   Till terrace and meadows the deep gulfs drink,
Till the strength of the waves of the high tides humble
   The fields that lessen, the rocks that shrink;
Here now in his triumph where all things falter,
   Stretched out on the spoils that his own hand spread,
As a god self-slain on his own strange altar,
      Death lies dead.

SWINBURNE

CHORUS *from* ATALANTA IN CALYDON

When the hounds of spring are on winter's traces,
   The mother of months in meadow or plain
Fills the shadows and windy places
   With lisp of leaves and ripple of rain;
And the brown bright nightingale amorous
Is half assuaged for Itylus,
For the Thracian ships and the foreign faces,
   The tongueless vigil, and all the pain.

Come with bows bent and with emptying of quivers,
   Maiden most perfect, lady of light,
With a noise of winds and many rivers,
   With a clamour of waters, and with might;
Bind on thy sandals, O thou most fleet,
Over the splendour and speed of thy feet;
For the faint east quickens, the wan west shivers,
   Round the feet of the day and the feet of the night.

Where shall we find her, how shall we sing to her,
   Fold our hands round her knees, and cling?
O that man's heart were as fire and could spring to her,
   Fire, or the strength of the streams that spring!
For the stars and the winds are unto her
As raiment, as songs of the harp-player;
For the risen stars and the fallen cling to her,
   And the southwest-wind and the west-wind sing.

For winter's rains and ruins are over,
   And all the season of snows and sins;
The days dividing lover and lover,
   The light that loses, the night that wins;
And time remembered is grief forgotten,
And frosts are slain and flowers begotten,
And in green underwood and cover
   Blossom by blossom the spring begins.

The full streams feed on flower of rushes,
   Ripe grasses trammel a travelling foot,

The faint fresh flame of the young year flushes
　　From leaf to flower and flower to fruit;
And fruit and leaf are as gold and fire,
And the oat is heard above the lyre,
And the hoofèd heel of a satyr crushes
　　The chestnut-husk at the chestnut-root.

And Pan by noon and Bacchus by night,
　　Fleeter of foot than the fleet-foot kid,
Follows with dancing and fills with delight
　　The Mænad and the Bassarid;
And soft as lips that laugh and hide
The laughing leaves of the trees divide,
And screen from seeing and leave in sight
　　The god pursuing, the maiden hid.

The ivy falls with the Bacchanal's hair
　　Over her eyebrows hiding her eyes;
The wild vine slipping down leaves bare
　　Her bright breast shortening into sighs;
The wild vine slips with the weight of its leaves,
But the berried ivy catches and cleaves
To the limbs that glitter, the feet that scare
　　The wolf that follows, the fawn that flies.

GERARD MANLEY HOPKINS

1844–1889

THE STARLIGHT NIGHT

LOOK at the stars! look, look up at the skies!
　　O look at all the fire-folk sitting in the air!
　　The bright boroughs, the circle-citadels there!
Down in dim woods the diamond delves! the elves'-eyes!

The grey lawns cold where gold, where quickgold lies!
　　Wind-beat whitebeam! airy abeles set on a flare!
　　Flake-doves sent floating forth at a farmyard scare!—
Ah well! it is all a purchase, all is a prize.

Buy then! bid then!—What?—Prayer, patience, alms, vows.
Look, look: a May-mess, like on orchard boughs!
   Look! March-bloom, like on mealed-with-yellow sallows!
These are indeed the barn; withindoors house
The shocks. This piece-bright paling shuts the spouse
   Christ home, Christ and his mother and all his hallows.

THE WINDHOVER

TO CHRIST OUR LORD

I CAUGHT this morning morning's minion, king-
   dom of daylight's dauphin, dapple-dawn-drawn Falcon, in his riding
   Of the rolling level underneath him steady air, and striding
High there, how he rung upon the rein of a wimpling wing
In his ecstasy! then off, off forth on swing,
   As a skate's heel sweeps smooth on a bow-bend: the hurl and gliding
   Rebuffed the big wind. My heart in hiding
Stirred for a bird,—the achieve of, the mastery of the thing!

Brute beauty and valour and act, oh, air, pride, plume here
   Buckle! AND the fire that breaks from thee then, a billion
Times told lovelier, more dangerous, O my chevalier!

   No wonder of it: shéer plód makes plough down sillion
Shine, and blue-bleak embers, ah my dear,
   Fall, gall themselves, and gash gold-vermilion.

PIED BEAUTY

GLORY be to God for dappled things—
   For skies of couple-colour as a brinded cow;
      For rose-moles all in stipple upon trout that swim;
Fresh-firecoal chestnut-falls; finches' wings;
   Landscape plotted and pieced—fold, fallow, and plough;
      And áll trádes, their gear and tackle and trim.

All things counter, original, spare, strange;
  Whatever is fickle, freckled (who knows how?)
    With swift, slow; sweet, sour; adazzle, dim;
He fathers-forth whose beauty is past change:
                    Praise him.

DUNS SCOTUS'S OXFORD

TOWERY city and branchy between towers;
Cuckoo-echoing, bell-swarmèd, lark-charmèd, rook-racked,
        river-rounded;
The dapple-eared lily below thee; that country and town did
Once encounter in, here coped and poisèd powers;

Thou hast a base and brickish skirt there, sours
That neighbour-nature thy grey beauty is grounded
Best in; graceless growth, thou hast confounded
Rural rural keeping—folk, flocks, and flowers.

Yet ah! this air I gather and I release
He lived on; these weeds and waters, these walls are what
He haunted who of all men most sways my spirits to peace;

Of realty the rarest-veinèd unraveller; a not
Rivalled insight, be rival Italy or Greece;
Who fired France for Mary without spot.

PEACE

WHEN will you ever, Peace, wild wooddove, shy wings shut,
Your round me roaming end, and under be my boughs?
When, when, Peace, will you, Peace? I'll not play hypocrite
To own my heart: I yield you do come sometimes; but
That piecemeal peace is poor peace. What pure peace allows
Alarms of wars, the daunting wars, the death of it?

O surely, reaving Peace, my Lord should leave in lieu
Some good! And so he does leave Patience exquisite,
That plumes to Peace thereafter. And when Peace here does
        house
He comes with work to do, he does not come to coo,
        He comes to brood and sit.

FELIX RANDAL

FELIX RANDAL the farrier, O he is dead then? my duty
    all ended,
Who have watched his mould of man, big-boned and hardy-
    handsome
Pining, pining, till time when reason rambled in it and some
Fatal four disorders, fleshed there, all contended?

Sickness broke him. Impatient he cursed at first, but mended
Being anointed and all; though a heavenlier heart began
    some
Months earlier, since I had our sweet reprieve and ransom
Tendered to him. Ah well, God rest him all road ever he
    offended!

This seeing the sick endears them to us, us too it endears.
My tongue had taught thee comfort, touch had quenched
    thy tears,
Thy tears that touched my heart, child, Felix, poor Felix
    Randal;

How far from then forethought of, all thy more boisterous
    years,
When thou at the random grim forge, powerful amidst peers,
Didst fettle for the great grey drayhorse his bright and
    battering sandal!

SPRING AND FALL

TO A YOUNG CHILD

MÁRGARÉT, are you gríeving
Over Goldengrove unleaving?
Leáves, líke the things of man, you
With your fresh thoughts care for, can you?
Áh! ás the heart grows older
It will come to such sights colder

392

By and by, nor spare a sigh
Though worlds of wanwood leafmeal lie;
And yet you will weep and know why.
Now no matter, child, the name:
Sórrow's springs áre the same.
Nor mouth had, no nor mind, expressed
What heart heard of, ghost guessed:
It ís the blight man was born for,
It is Margaret you mourn for.

INVERSNAID

THIS darksome burn, horseback brown,
His rollrock highroad roaring down,
In coop and in comb the fleece of his foam
Flutes and low to the lake falls home.

A windpuff-bonnet of fáwn-fróth
Turns and twindles over the broth
Of a pool so pitchblack, féll-frówning,
It rounds and rounds Despair to drowning.

Degged with dew, dappled with dew
Are the groins of the braes that the brook treads through,
Wiry heathpacks, flitches of fern,
And the beadbonny ash that sits over the burn.

What would the world be, once bereft
Of wet and of wildness? Let them be left,
O let them be left, wildness and wet;
Long live the weeds and the wilderness yet.

THE LEADEN ECHO AND THE GOLDEN ECHO

(Maidens' song from St. Winefred's Well)

THE LEADEN ECHO

How to kéep—is there ány any, is there none such, nowhere
    known some, bow or brooch or braid or brace, láce,
    latch or catch or key to keep

Back beauty, keep it, beauty, beauty, beauty, . . . from
    vanishing away?
Ó is there no frowning of these wrinkles, rankèd wrinkles
    deep,
Dówn? no waving off of these most mournful messengers,
    still messengers, sad and stealing messengers of grey?
No there's none, there's none, O no there's none,
Nor can you long be, what you now are, called fair,
Do what you may do, what, do what you may,
And wisdom is early to despair:
Be beginning; since, no, nothing can be done
To keep at bay
Age and age's evils, hoar hair,
Ruck and wrinkle, drooping, dying, death's worst, winding
    sheets, tombs and worms and tumbling to decay;
So be beginning, be beginning to despair.
O there's none; no no no there's none:
Be beginning to despair, to despair,
Despair, despair, despair, despair.

THE GOLDEN ECHO

    Spare!
There ís one, yes I have one (Hush there!);
Only not within seeing of the sun,
Not within the singeing of the strong sun,
Tall sun's tingeing, or treacherous the tainting of the earth's
    air,
Somewhere elsewhere there is ah well where! one,
Óne. Yes I cán tell such a key, I dó know such a place,
Where whatever's prized and passes of us, everything that's
    fresh and fast flying of us, seems to us sweet of us and
    swiftly away with, done away with, undone,
Undone, done with, soon done with, and yet dearly and
    dangerously sweet
Of us, the wimpled-water-dimpled, not-by-morning-matchèd
    face,
The flower of beauty, fleece of beauty, too too apt to, ah! to
    fleet,
Never fleets móre, fastened with the tenderest truth

To its own best being and its loveliness of youth: it is an
    everlastingness of, O it is an all youth!
Come then, your ways and airs and looks, locks, maiden
    gear, gallantry and gaiety and grace,
Winning ways, airs innocent, maiden manners, sweet looks,
    loose locks, long locks, lovelocks, gaygear, going gallant,
    girlgrace—
Resign them, sign them, seal them, send them, motion them
    with breath,
And with sighs soaring, soaring síghs deliver
Them; beauty-in-the-ghost, deliver it, early now, long before
    death
Give beauty back, beauty, beauty, beauty, back to God,
    beauty's self and beauty's giver.
See; not a hair is, not an eyelash, not the least lash lost; every
    hair
Is, hair of the head, numbered.
Nay, what we had lighthanded left in surly the mere mould
Will have waked and have waxed and have walked with the
    wind what while we slept,
This side, that side hurling a heavyheaded hundredfold
What while we, while we slumbered.
O then, weary then whý should we tread? O why are we so
    haggard at the heart, so care-coiled, care-killed, so
    fagged, so fashed, so cogged, so cumbered,
When the thing we freely fórfeit is kept with fonder a care,
Fonder a care kept than we could have kept it, kept
Far with fonder a care (and we, we should have lost it) finer,
    fonder
A care kept.—Where kept? Do but tell us where kept,
    where.—
Yonder.—What high as that! We follow, now we follow.—
    Yonder, yes yonder, yonder,
Yonder.

———

No worst, there is none. Pitched past pitch of grief,
More pangs will, schooled at forepangs, wilder wring.
Comforter, where, where is your comforting?
Mary, mother of us, where is your relief?

My cries heave, herds-long; huddle in a main, a chief
Woe, world-sorrow; on an age-old anvil wince and sing—
Then lull, then leave off. Fury had shrieked 'No ling-
ering! Let me be fell: force I must be brief'.

O the mind, mind has mountains; cliffs of fall
Frightful, sheer, no-man-fathomed. Hold them cheap
May who ne'er hung there. Nor does long our small
Durance deal with that steep or deep. Here! creep,
Wretch, under a comfort serves in a whirlwind: all
Life death does end and each day dies with sleep.

———

I WAKE and feel the fell of dark, not day.
What hours, O what black hoürs we have spent
This night! what sights you, heart, saw; ways you went!
And more must, in yet longer light's delay.
   With witness I speak this. But where I say
Hours I mean years, mean life. And my lament
Is cries countless, cries like dead letters sent
To dearest him that lives alas! away.

   I am gall, I am heartburn. God's most deep decree
Bitter would have me taste: my taste was me;
Bones built in me, flesh filled, blood brimmed the curse.
   Selfyeast of spirit a dull dough sours. I see
The lost are like this, and their scourge to be
As I am mine, their sweating selves; but worse.

THAT NATURE IS A HERACLITEAN FIRE
AND OF THE COMFORT OF THE
RESURRECTION

CLOUD-PUFFBALL, torn tufts, tossed pillows ǀ flaunt forth,
   then chevy on an air-
built thoroughfare: heaven-roysterers, in gay-gangs ǀ they
   throng; they glitter in marches.

Down roughcast, down dazzling whitewash, | wherever an
    elm arches,
Shivelights and shadowtackle in long | lashes lace, lance,
    and pair.
Delightfully the bright wind boisterous | ropes, wrestles,
    beats earth bare
Of yestertempest's creases; | in pool and rut peel parches
Squandering ooze to squeezed | dough, crust, dust; stanches,
    starches
Squadroned masks and manmarks | treadmire toil there
Footfretted in it. Million-fuelèd, | nature's bonfire burns on.
But quench her bonniest, dearest | to her, her clearest-selvèd
    spark
Man, how fast his firedint, | his mark on mind, is gone!
Both are in an unfathomable, all is in an enormous dark
Drowned. O pity and indig|nation! Manshape, that shone
Sheer off, disseveral, a star, | death blots black out; nor mark
        Is any of him at all so stark
But vastness blurs and time | beats level. Enough! the Resur-
    rection,
A heart's-clarion! Away grief's gasping, | joyless days, dejec-
    tion.
            Across my foundering deck shone
A beacon, an eternal beam. | Flesh fade, and mortal trash
Fall to the residuary worm; | world's wildfire, leave but ash:
        In a flash, at a trumpet crash,
I am all at once what Christ is, | since he was what I am, and
This Jack, joke, poor potsherd, | patch, matchwood, immortal
    diamond,
        Is immortal diamond.

             —

*Justus quidem tu es, Domine, si disputem tecum: verumtamen
justa loquar ad te: Quare via impiorum prosperatur? &c.*

    Thou art indeed just, Lord, if I contend
    With thee; but, sir, so what I plead is just.
    Why do sinners' ways prosper? and why must
    Disappointment all I endeavour end?

Wert thou my enemy, O thou my friend,
How wouldst thou worse, I wonder, than thou dost
Defeat, thwart me? Oh, the sots and thralls of lust
Do in spare hours more thrive than I that spend,
Sir, life upon thy cause. See, banks and brakes
Now, leavèd how thick! lacèd they are again
With fretty chervil, look, and fresh wind shakes
Them; birds build—but not I build; no, but strain,
Time's eunuch, and not breed one work that wakes.
Mine, O thou lord of life, send my roots rain.

TO R. B.

THE fine delight that fathers thought; the strong
Spur, live and lancing like the blowpipe flame,
Breathes once and, quenchèd faster than it came,
Leaves yet the mind a mother of immortal song.
Nine months she then, nay years, nine years she long
Within her wears, bears, cares and combs the same:
The widow of an insight lost she lives, with aim
Now known and hand at work now never wrong.

Sweet fire the sire of muse, my soul needs this;
I want the one rapture of an inspiration.
O then if in my lagging lines you miss
The roll, the rise, the carol, the creation,
My winter world, that scarcely breathes that bliss
Now, yields you, with some sighs, our explanation.

FRANCIS THOMPSON

1859–1907

THE KINGDOM OF GOD

'In no Strange Land'

O WORLD invisible, we view thee,
O world intangible, we touch thee,
O world unknowable, we know thee,
Inapprehensible, we clutch thee!

Does the fish soar to find the ocean,
The eagle plunge to find the air—
That we ask of the stars in motion
If they have rumour of thee there?

Not where the wheeling systems darken,
And our benumbed conceiving soars!—
The drift of pinions, would we hearken,
Beats at our own clay-shuttered doors.

The angels keep their ancient places;—
Turn but a stone, and start a wing!
'Tis ye, 'tis your estrangèd faces,
That miss the many-splendoured thing.

But (when so sad thou canst not sadder)
Cry;—and upon thy so sore loss
Shall shine the traffic of Jacob's ladder
Pitched betwixt Heaven and Charing Cross.

Yea, in the night, my Soul, my daughter,
Cry,—clinging Heaven by the hems;
And lo, Christ walking on the water
Not of Gennesareth, but Thames!

From THE HEART

CORRELATED GREATNESS

O NOTHING, in this corporal earth of man,
  That to the imminent heaven of his high soul
Responds with colour and with shadow, can
  Lack correlated greatness. If the scroll
Where thoughts lie fast in spell of hieroglyph
  Be mighty through its mighty habitants;
If God be in His Name; grave potence if
  The sounds unbind of hieratic chants;
All's vast that vastness means. Nay, I affirm
  Nature is whole in her least things exprest,
Nor know we with what scope God builds the worm.
  Our towns are copied fragments from our breast;
      And all man's Babylons strive but to impart
      The grandeurs of his Babylonian heart.

ERNEST DOWSON

1867–1900

NON SUM QUALIS ERAM BONAE SUB REGNO CYNARAE

LAST night, ah, yesternight, betwixt her lips and min
There fell thy shadow, Cynara! thy breath was shed
Upon my soul between the kisses and the wine;
And I was desolate and sick of an old passion,
    Yea, I was desolate and bowed my head:
I have been faithful to thee, Cynara! in my fashion.

All night upon mine heart I felt her warm heart beat,
Night-long within mine arms in love and sleep she lay
Surely the kisses of her bought red mouth were sweet
But I was desolate and sick of an old passion,
    When I awoke and found the dawn was gray:
I have been faithful to thee, Cynara! in my fashion.

I have forgot much, Cynara! gone with the wind,
Flung roses, roses riotously with the throng,
Dancing, to put thy pale, lost lilies out of mind;
But I was desolate and sick of an old passion,
    Yea, all the time, because the dance was long:
I have been faithful to thee, Cynara! in my fashion.

I cried for madder music and for stronger wine,
But when the feast is finished and the lamps expire,
Then falls thy shadow, Cynara! the night is thine;
And I am desolate and sick of an old passion,
    Yea hungry for the lips of my desire:
I have been faithful to thee, Cynara! in my fashion.

LIONEL JOHNSON

1867–1902

THE DARK ANGEL

DARK Angel, with thine aching lust
To rid the world of penitence:
Malicious Angel, who still dost
My soul such subtile violence!

Because of thee, no thought, no thing
Abides for me undesecrate:
Dark Angel, ever on the wing,
Who never reachest me too late!

When music sounds, then changest thou
Its silvery to a sultry fire:
Nor will thine envious heart allow
Delight untortured by desire.

Through thee, the gracious Muses turn
To Furies, O mine Enemy!
And all the things of beauty burn
With flames of evil ecstasy.

Because of thee, the land of dreams
Becomes a gathering-place of fears:
Until tormented slumber seems
One vehemence of useless tears.

When sunlight glows upon the flowers,
Or ripples down the dancing sea:
Thou, with thy troop of passionate powers,
Beleaguerest, bewilderest me.

Within the breath of autumn woods,
Within the winter silences:
Thy venomous spirit stirs and broods,
O Master of impieties!

The ardour of red flame is thine,
And thine the steely soul of ice:
Thou poisonest the fair design
Of nature, with unfair device.

Apples of ashes, golden bright;
Waters of bitterness, how sweet!
O banquet of a foul delight,
Prepared by thee, dark Paraclete.

Thou art the whisper in the gloom,
The hinting tone, the haunting laugh:
Thou art the adorner of my tomb,
The minstrel of mine epitaph.

I fight thee, in the Holy Name!
Yet, what thou dost, is what God saith:
Tempter! should I escape thy flame,
Thou wilt have helped my soul from Death:

The second Death, that never dies,
That cannot die, when time is dead:
Live Death, wherein the lost soul cries,
Eternally uncomforted.

Dark Angel, with thine aching lust!
Of two defeats, of two despairs:
Less dread, a change to drifting dust,
Than thine eternity of cares.

Do what thou wilt, thou shalt not so,
Dark Angel! triumph over me:
Lonely, unto the Lone I go;
Divine, to the Divinity.

THOMAS HARDY

1840–1928

FRIENDS BEYOND

William Dewy, Tranter Reuben, Farmer Ledlow late at plough,
  Robert's kin, and John's, and Ned's,
And the Squire, and Lady Susan, lie in Mellstock churchyard now!

'Gone,' I call them, gone for good, that group of local hearts and heads;
  Yet at mothy curfew-tide,
And at midnight when the noon-heat breathes it back from walls and leads,

They've a way of whispering to me—fellow-wight who yet abide—
  In the muted, measured note
Of a ripple under archways, or a lone cave's stillicide:

'We have triumphed: this achievement turns the bane to antidote,
  Unsuccesses to success,
Many thought-worn eves and morrows to a morrow free of thought.

'No more need we corn and clothing, feel of old terrestrial stress;
  Chill detraction stirs no sigh;
Fear of death has even bygone us: death gave all that we possess.'

W. D.—'Ye mid burn the old bass-viol that I set such value by.'
Squire.—'You may hold the manse in fee,
  You may wed my spouse, may let my children's memory of me die.'

403

Lady S.—'You may have my rich brocades, my laces; take each household key;
    Ransack coffer, desk, bureau;
Quiz the few poor treasures hid there, con the letters kept by me.'

Far.—'Ye mid zell my favourite heifer, ye mid let the charlock grow,
    Foul the grinterns, give up thrift.'

Far. Wife.—'If ye break my best blue china, children, I shan't care or ho.'

All.—'We've no wish to hear the tidings, how the people's fortunes shift;
    What your daily doings are;
Who are wedded, born, divided; if your lives beat slow or swift.

'Curious not the least are we if our intents you make or mar,
    If you quire to our old tune,
If the City stage still passes, if the weirs still roar afar.'

—Thus, with very gods' composure, freed those crosses late and soon
    Which, in life, the Trine allow
(Why, none witteth), and ignoring all that haps beneath the moon,

William Dewy, Tranter Reuben, Farmer Ledlow late at plough,
    Robert's kin, and John's, and Ned's,
And the Squire, and Lady Susan, murmur mildly to me now.

DRUMMER HODGE

I

    THEY throw in Drummer Hodge, to rest
       Uncoffined—just as found:
    His landmark is a kopje-crest
       That breaks the veldt around:
    And foreign constellations west
       Each night above his mound.

II

Young Hodge the Drummer never knew—
    Fresh from his Wessex home—
The meaning of the broad Karoo,
    The Bush, the dusty loam,
And why uprose to nightly view
    Strange stars amid the gloam.

III

Yet portion of that unknown plain
    Will Hodge for ever be;
His homely Northern breast and brain
    Grow to some Southern tree,
And strange-eyed constellations reign
    His stars eternally.

TO AN UNBORN PAUPER CHILD

I

BREATHE not, hid Heart: cease silently,
And though thy birth-hour beckons thee,
    Sleep the long sleep:
    The Doomsters heap
Travails and teens around us here,
And Time-wraiths turn our songsingings to fear.

II

Hark, how the peoples surge and sigh,
And laughters fail, and greetings die:
    Hopes dwindle; yea,
    Faiths waste away,
Affections and enthusiasms numb;
Thou canst not mend these things if thou dost come.

III

Had I the ear of wombèd souls
Ere their terrestrial chart unrolls,
    And thou wert free
    To cease, or be,
Then would I tell thee all I know,
And put it to thee: Wilt thou take Life so?

IV

Vain vow! No hint of mine may hence
To theeward fly: to thy locked sense
    Explain none can
    Life's pending plan:
Thou wilt thy ignorant entry make
Though skies spout fire and blood and nations quake.

V

Fain would I, dear, find some shut plot
Of earth's wide wold for thee, where not
    One tear, one qualm,
    Should break the calm.
But I am weak as thou and bare;
No man can change the common lot to rare.

VI

Must come and bide. And such are we—
Unreasoning, sanguine, visionary—
    That I can hope
    Health, love, friends, scope
In full for thee; can dream thou wilt find
Joys seldom yet attained by humankind!

THE VOICE

Woman much missed, how you call to me, call to me,
Saying that now you are not as you were
When you had changed from the one who was all to me,
But as at first, when our day was fair.

Can it be you that I hear? Let me view you, then,
Standing as when I drew near to the town
Where you would wait for me: yes, as I knew you then,
Even to the original air-blue gown!

Or is it only the breeze, in its listlessness
Travelling across the wet mead to me here,
You being ever dissolved to existlessness,
Heard no more again far or near?

Thus I; faltering forward,
  Leaves around me falling,
Wind oozing thin through the thorn from norward,
  And the woman calling.

December 1912

AFTER A JOURNEY

HERETO I come to view a voiceless ghost;
  Whither, O whither will its whim now draw me?
Up the cliff, down, till I'm lonely, lost,
  And the unseen waters' ejaculations awe me.
Where you will next be there's no knowing,
  Facing round about me everywhere,
    With your nut-coloured hair,
And gray eyes, and rose-flush coming and going.

Yes: I have re-entered your olden haunts at last;
  Through the years, through the dead scenes I have
      tracked you;
What have you now found to say of our past—
  Scanned across the dark space wherein I have lacked you?
Summer gave us sweets, but autumn wrought division?
  Things were not lastly as firstly well
    With us twain, you tell?
But all's closed now, despite Time's derision.

I see what you are doing: you are leading me on
  To the spots we knew when we haunted here together,
The waterfall, above which the mist-bow shone
  At the then fair hour in the then fair weather,
And the cave just under, with a voice still so hollow
  That it seems to call out to me from forty years ago,
    When you were all aglow,
And not the thin ghost that I now frailly follow!

Ignorant of what there is flitting here to see,
  The waked birds preen and the seals flop lazily,
Soon you will have, Dear, to vanish from me,
  For the stars close their shutters and the dawn whitens
      hazily.

Trust me, I mind not, though Life lours,
   The bringing me here; nay, bring me here again!
      I am just the same as when
Our days were a joy, and our paths through flowers.

Pentargan Bay

AT CASTLE BOTEREL

As I drive to the junction of lane and highway,
   And the drizzle bedrenches the waggonette,
I look behind at the fading byway,
   And see on its slope, now glistening wet,
      Distinctly yet

Myself and a girlish form benighted
   In dry March weather. We climb the road
Beside a chaise. We have just alighted
   To ease the sturdy pony's load
      When he sighed and slowed.

What we did as we climbed, and what we talked of
   Matters not much, nor to what it led,—
Something that life will not be balked of
   Without rude reason till hope is dead,
      And feeling fled.

It filled but a minute. But was there ever
   A time of such quality, since or before,
In that hill's story? To one mind never,
   Though it has been climbed, foot-swift, foot-sore,
      By thousands more.

Primaeval rocks form the road's steep border,
   And much have they faced there, first and last,
Of the transitory in Earth's long order;
   But what they record in colour and cast
      Is—that we two passed.

And to me, though Time's unflinching rigour,
　In mindless rote, has ruled from sight
The substance now, one phantom figure
　　Remains on the slope, as when that night
　　　Saw us alight.

I look and see it there, shrinking, shrinking,
　I look back at it amid the rain
For the very last time; for my sand is sinking,
　　And I shall traverse old love's domain
　　　Never again.

March 1913

GREAT THINGS

SWEET cyder is a great thing,
　A great thing to me,
Spinning down to Weymouth town
　By Ridgway thirstily,
And maid and mistress summoning
　Who tend the hostelry:
O cyder is a great thing,
　A great thing to me!

The dance it is a great thing,
　A great thing to me,
With candles lit and partners fit
　For night-long revelry;
And going home when day-dawning
　Peeps pale upon the lea:
O dancing is a great thing,
　A great thing to me!

Love is, yea, a great thing,
　A great thing to me,
When, having drawn across the lawn
　In darkness silently,
A figure flits like one a-wing
　Out from the nearest tree:
O love is, yes, a great thing,
　Aye, greatest thing to me!

Will these be always great things,
  Greatest things to me? . . .
Let it befall that One will call,
  'Soul, I have need of thee':
What then? Joy-jaunts, impassioned flings,
  Love, and its ecstasy,
Will always have been great things,
  Greatest things to me!

THE FIVE STUDENTS

The sparrow dips in his wheel-rut bath,
  The sun grows passionate-eyed,
And boils the dew to smoke by the paddock-path;
  As strenuously we stride,—
Five of us; dark He, fair He, dark She, fair She, I,
  All beating by.

The air is shaken, the high-road hot,
  Shadowless swoons the day,
The greens are sobered and cattle at rest; but not
  We on our urgent way,—
Four of us; fair She, dark She, fair He, I, are there,
  But one—elsewhere.

Autumn moulds the hard fruit mellow,
  And forward still we press
Through moors, briar-meshed plantations, clay-pits yellow,
  As in the spring hours—yes,
Three of us; fair He, fair She, I, as heretofore,
  But—fallen one more.

The leaf drops: earthworms draw it in
  At night-time noiselessly,
The fingers of birch and beech are skeleton-thin,
  And yet on the beat are we,—
Two of us; fair She, I. But no more left to go
  The track we know.

Icicles tag the church-aisle leads,
    The flag-rope gibbers hoarse,
The home-bound foot-folk wrap their snow-flaked heads,
    Yet I still stalk the course—
One of us. . . . Dark and fair He, dark and fair She, gone:
    The rest—anon.

DURING WIND AND RAIN

THEY sing their dearest songs—
He, she, all of them—yea,
Treble and tenor and bass,
    And one to play;
With the candles mooning each face. . . .
    Ah, no; the years O!
How the sick leaves reel down in throngs!

They clear the creeping moss—
Elders and juniors—aye,
Making the pathways neat
    And the garden gay;
And they build a shady seat. . . .
    Ah, no; the years, the years;
See, the webbed white storm-birds wing across.

They are blithely breakfasting all—
Men and maidens—yea,
Under the summer tree,
    With a glimpse of the bay,
While pet fowl come to the knee. . . .
    Ah, no; the years O!
And the rotten rose is ript from the wall.

They change to a high new house,
He, she, all of them—aye,
Clocks and carpets and chairs
    On the lawn all day,
And brightest things that are theirs. . . .
    Ah, no; the years, the years;
Down their chiselled names the rain-drop ploughs.

411

AFTERWARDS

WHEN the Present has latched its postern behind my
    tremulous stay,
  And the May month flaps its glad green leaves like wings,
Delicate-filmed as new-spun silk, will the neighbours say
  'He was a man who used to notice such things'?

If it be in the dusk when, like an eyelid's soundless blink,
  The dewfall-hawk comes crossing the shades to alight
Upon the wind-warped upland thorn, a gazer may think,
  'To him this must have been a familiar sight.'

If I pass during some nocturnal blackness, mothy and warm,
  When the hedgehog travels furtively over the lawn,
One may say, 'He strove that such innocent creatures should
    come to no harm,
  But he could do little for them; and now he is gone.'

If, when hearing that I have been stilled at last, they stand
    at the door,
  Watching the full-starred heavens that winter sees,
Will this thought rise on those who will meet my face no
    more,
  'He was one who had an eye for such mysteries'?

And will any say when my bell of quittance is heard in the
    gloom,
  And a crossing breeze cuts a pause in its outrollings,
Till they rise again, as they were a new bell's boom,
  'He hears it not now, but used to notice such things'?

AN ANCIENT TO ANCIENTS

WHERE once we danced, where once we sang,
        Gentlemen,
The floors are sunken, cobwebs hang,
And cracks creep; worms have fed upon
The doors. Yea, sprightlier times were then
Than now, with harps and tabrets gone,
        Gentlemen!

Where once we rowed, where once we sailed,
      Gentlemen,
And damsels took the tiller, veiled
Against too strong a stare (God wot
Their fancy, then or anywhen!)
Upon that shore we are clean forgot,
      Gentlemen!

We have lost somewhat, afar and near,
      Gentlemen,
The thinning of our ranks each year
Affords a hint we are nigh undone,
That we shall not be ever again
The marked of many, loved of one,
      Gentlemen.

In dance the polka hit our wish,
      Gentlemen,
The paced quadrille, the spry schottische,
'Sir Roger'.—And in opera spheres
The 'Girl' (the famed 'Bohemian'),
And 'Trovatore', held the ears,
      ' Gentlemen.

This season's paintings do not please,
      Gentlemen,
Like Etty, Mulready, Maclise;
Throbbing romance has waned and wanned;
No wizard wields the witching pen
Of Bulwer, Scott, Dumas, and Sand,
      Gentlemen.

The bower we shrined to Tennyson,
      Gentlemen,
Is roof-wrecked; damps there drip upon
Sagged seats, the creeper-nails are rust,
The spider is sole denizen;
Even she who voiced those rhymes is dust,
      Gentlemen!

We who met sunrise sanguine-souled,
     Gentlemen,
Are wearing weary. We are old;
These younger press; we feel our rout
Is imminent to Aïdes' den,—
That evening shades are stretching out,
     Gentlemen!

And yet, though ours be failing frames,
     Gentlemen,
So were some others' history names,
Who trode their track light-limbed and fast
As these youth, and not alien
From enterprise, to their long last,
     Gentlemen.

Sophocles, Plato, Socrates,
     Gentlemen,
Pythagoras, Thucydides,
Herodotus, and Homer,—yea,
Clement, Augustin, Origen,
Burnt brightlier towards their setting-day,
     Gentlemen.

And ye, red-lipped and smooth-browed; list,
     Gentlemen;
Much is there waits you we have missed;
Much lore we leave you worth the knowing,
Much, much has lain outside our ken:
Nay, rush not: time serves: we are going,
     Gentlemen.

ROBERT BRIDGES

1844–1930

LONDON SNOW

WHEN men were all asleep the snow came flying,
In large white flakes falling on the city brown,
Stealthily and perpetually settling and loosely lying,
    Hushing the latest traffic of the drowsy town;

Deadening, muffling, stifling its murmurs failing;
Lazily and incessantly floating down and down:
    Silently sifting and veiling road, roof and railing;
Hiding difference, making unevenness even,
Into angles and crevices softly drifting and sailing.
    All night it fell, and when full inches seven
It lay in the depth of its uncompacted lightness,
The clouds blew off from a high and frosty heaven;
    And all woke earlier for the unaccustomed brightness
Of the winter dawning, the strange unheavenly glare:
The eye marvelled—marvelled at the dazzling whiteness;
    The ear hearkened to the stillness of the solemn air;
No sound of wheel rumbling nor of foot falling,
And the busy morning cries came thin and spare.
    Then boys I heard, as they went to school, calling,
They gathered up the crystal manna to freeze
Their tongues with tasting, their hands with snowballing;
    Or rioted in a drift, plunging up to the knees;
Or peering up from under the white-mossed wonder,
'O look at the trees!' they cried, 'O look at the trees!'
    With lessened load a few carts creak and blunder,
Following along the white deserted way,
A country company long dispersed asunder:
    When now already the sun, in pale display
Standing by Paul's high dome, spread forth below
His sparkling beams, and awoke the stir of the day.
    For now doors open, and war is waged with the snow;
And trains of sombre men, past tale of number,
Tread long brown paths, as toward their toil they go:
    But even for them awhile no cares encumber
Their minds diverted; the daily word is unspoken,
The daily thoughts of labour and sorrow slumber
At the sight of the beauty that greets them, for the charm
        they have broken.

～

    AWAKE, my heart, to be loved, awake, awake!
    The darkness silvers away, the morn doth break,
    It leaps in the sky: unrisen lustres slake
    The o'ertaken moon. Awake, O heart, awake!

She too that loveth awaketh and hopes for thee;
Her eyes already have sped the shades that flee,
Already they watch the path thy feet shall take:
Awake, O heart, to be loved, awake, awake!

And if thou tarry from her,—if this could be,—
She cometh herself, O heart, to be loved, to thee;
For thee would unashamèd herself forsake:
Awake to be loved, my heart, awake, awake!

Awake, the land is scattered with light, and see,
Uncanopied sleep is flying from field and tree:
And blossoming boughs of April in laughter shake;
Awake, O heart, to be loved, awake, awake!

Lo all things wake and tarry and look for thee:
She looketh and saith, 'O sun, now bring him to me.
Come more adored, O adored, for his coming's sake,
And awake my heart to be loved: awake, awake!'

The storm is over, the land hushes to rest:
The tyrannous wind, its strength fordone,
Is fallen back in the west
To couch with the sinking sun.
The last clouds fare
With fainting speed, and their thin streamers fly
In melting drifts of the sky.
Already the birds in the air
Appear again; the rooks return to their haunt,
And one by one,
Proclaiming aloud their care,
Renew their peaceful chant.

Torn and shattered the trees their branches again reset,
They trim afresh the fair
Few green and golden leaves withheld from the storm,
And awhile will be handsome yet.
To-morrow's sun shall caress
Their remnant of loveliness:

In quiet days for a time
Sad Autumn lingering warm
Shall humour their faded prime.

But ah! the leaves of summer that lie on the ground!
What havoc! The laughing timbrels of June,
That curtained the birds' cradles, and screened their song,
That sheltered the cooing doves at noon,
Of airy fans the delicate throng,—
Torn and scattered around:
Far out afield they lie,
In the watery furrows die,
In grassy pools of the flood they sink and drown,
Green-golden, orange, vermilion, golden and brown,
The high year's flaunting crown
Shattered and trampled down.

The day is done: the tired land looks for night:
She prays to the night to keep
In peace her nerves of delight:
While silver mist upstealeth silently,
And the broad cloud-driving moon in the clear sky
Lifts o'er the firs her shining shield,
And in her tranquil light
Sleep falls on forest and field.
Sée! sléep hath fallen: the trees are asleep:
The night is come. The land is wrapt in sleep.

A. E. HOUSMAN

1859–1936

From A SHROPSHIRE LAD

XXXI

On Wenlock Edge the wood's in trouble;
    His forest fleece the Wrekin heaves;
The gale, it plies the saplings double,
    And thick on Severn snow the leaves.

'Twould blow like this through holt and hanger
 When Uricon the city stood:
'Tis the old wind in the old anger,
 But then it threshed another wood.

Then, 'twas before my time, the Roman
 At yonder heaving hill would stare:
The blood that warms an English yeoman,
 The thoughts that hurt him, they were there.

There, like the wind through woods in riot,
 Through him the gale of life blew high;
The tree of man was never quiet:
 Then 'twas the Roman, now 'tis I.

The gale, it plies the saplings double,
 It blows so hard, 'twill soon be gone:
To-day the Roman and his trouble
 Are ashes under Uricon.

From LAST POEMS

XL

TELL me not here, it needs not saying,
 What tune the enchantress plays
In aftermaths of soft September
 Or under blanching mays,
For she and I were long acquainted
 And I knew all her ways.

On russet floors, by waters idle,
 The pine lets fall its cone;
The cuckoo shouts all day at nothing
 In leafy dells alone;
And traveller's joy beguiles in autumn
 Hearts that have lost their own.

418

On acres of the seeded grasses
  The changing burnish heaves;
Or marshalled under moons of harvest
  Stand still all night the sheaves;
Or beeches strip in storms for winter
  And stain the wind with leaves.

Possess, as I possessed a season,
  The countries I resign,
Where over elmy plains the highway
  Would mount the hills and shine,
And full of shade the pillared forest
  Would murmur and be mine.

For nature, heartless, witless nature,
  Will neither care nor know
What stranger's feet may find the meadow
  And trespass there and go,
Nor ask amid the dews of morning
  If they are mine or no.

From MORE POEMS

XXIII

CROSSING alone the nighted ferry
  With the one coin for fee,
Whom, on the wharf of Lethe waiting,
  Count you to find? Not me.

The brisk fond lackey to fetch and carry,
  The true, sick-hearted slave,
Expect him not in the just city
  And free land of the grave.

From ADDITIONAL POEMS

XVII

THE stars have not dealt me the worst they could do:
My pleasures are plenty, my troubles are two.
But oh, my two troubles they reave me of rest,
The brains in my head and the heart in my breast.

Oh grant me the ease that is granted so free,
The birthright of multitudes, give it to me,
That relish their victuals and rest on their bed
With flint in the bosom and guts in the head.

RUDYARD KIPLING

1865–1936

DANNY DEEVER

'WHAT are the bugles blowin' for?' said Files-on-Parade.
'To turn you out, to turn you out,' the Colour-Sergeant said.
'What makes you look so white, so white?' said Files-on-
Parade.
'I'm dreadin' what I've got to watch,' the Colour-Sergeant
said.
  For they're hangin' Danny Deever, you can hear the Dead
  March play,
  The Regiment's in 'ollow square—they're hangin' him
  today;
  They've taken of his buttons off an' cut his stripes away,
  An' they're hangin' Danny Deever in the mornin'.

'What makes the rear-rank breathe so 'ard?' said Files-on-
Parade.
'It's bitter cold, it's bitter cold,' the Colour-Sergeant said.
'What makes that front-rank man fall down?' said Files-on-
Parade.
'A touch o' sun, a touch o' sun,' the Colour-Sergeant said.
  They are hangin' Danny Deever, they are marchin' of 'im
  round,
  They 'ave 'alted Danny Deever by 'is coffin on the ground;
  An' 'e'll swing in 'arf a minute for a sneakin' shootin'
  hound—
  O they're hangin' Danny Deever in the mornin'!

''Is cot was right-'and cot to mine,' said Files-on-Parade.
''E's sleepin' out an' far tonight,' the Colour-Sergeant said.
'I've drunk 'is beer a score o' times,' said Files-on-Parade.
''E's drinkin' bitter beer alone,' the Colour-Sergeant said.

They are hangin' Danny Deever, you must mark 'im to 'is
    place,
For 'e shot a comrade sleepin'—you must look 'im in the
    face;
Nine 'undred of 'is county an' the Regiment's disgrace,
While they're hangin' Danny Deever in the mornin'.

'What's that so black agin the sun?' said Files-on-Parade.
'It's Danny fightin' 'ard for life,' the Colour-Sergeant said.
'What's that that whimpers over'ead?' said Files-on-Parade.
'It's Danny's soul that's passin' now,' the Colour-Sergeant
    said.
For they're done with Danny Deever, you can 'ear the
    quickstep play,
The Regiment's in column, an' they're marchin' us away;
Ho! the young recruits are shakin', an' they'll want their
    beer today,
After hangin' Danny Deever in the mornin'!

SONG OF THE GALLEY-SLAVES

WE pulled for you when the wind was against us and
the sails were low.

    Will you never let us go?

We ate bread and onions when you took towns, or ran
aboard quickly when you were beaten back by the foe,

The captains walked up and down the deck in fair
weather singing songs, but we were below.

We fainted with our chins on the oars and you did not
see that we were idle, for we still swung to and fro.

    Will you never let us go?

The salt made the oar-handles like shark-skin; our knees
were cut to the bone with salt-cracks; our hair was stuck to
our foreheads; and our lips were cut to our gums, and you
whipped us because we could not row.

    Will you never let us go?

But in a little time we shall run out of the portholes as the water runs along the oar-blade, and though you tell the others to row after us you will never catch us till you catch the oar-thresh and tie up the winds in the belly of the sail. Aho!

Will you never let us go?

W. B. YEATS

1865–1939

NO SECOND TROY

WHY should I blame her that she filled my days
With misery, or that she would of late
Have taught to ignorant men most violent ways,
Or hurled the little streets upon the great,
Had they but courage equal to desire?
What could have made her peaceful with a mind
That nobleness made simple as a fire,
With beauty like a tightened bow, a kind
That is not natural in an age like this,
Being high and solitary and most stern?
Why, what could she have done, being what she is?
Was there another Troy for her to burn?

SEPTEMBER 1913

WHAT need you, being come to sense,
But fumble in a greasy till
And add the halfpence to the pence
And prayer to shivering prayer, until
You have dried the marrow from the bone?
For men were born to pray and save:
Romantic Ireland's dead and gone,
It's with O'Leary in the grave.

Yet they were of a different kind,
The names that stilled your childish play,
They have gone about the world like wind,
But little time had they to pray
For whom the hangman's rope was spun,
And what, God help us, could they save?
Romantic Ireland's dead and gone,
It's with O'Leary in the grave.

Was it for this the wild geese spread
The grey wing upon every tide;
For this that all that blood was shed,
For this Edward Fitzgerald died,
And Robert Emmet and Wolfe Tone,
All that delirium of the brave?
Romantic Ireland's dead and gone,
It's with O'Leary in the grave.

Yet could we turn the years again,
And call those exiles as they were
In all their loneliness and pain,
You'd cry, 'Some woman's yellow hair
Has maddened every mother's son':
They weighed so lightly what they gave.
But let them be, they're dead and gone,
They're with O'Leary in the grave.

THE COLD HEAVEN

SUDDENLY I saw the cold and rook-delighting heaven
That seemed as though ice burned and was but the more ice,
And thereupon imagination and heart were driven
So wild that every casual thought of that and this
Vanished, and left but memories, that should be out of
season
With the hot blood of youth, of love crossed long ago;
And I took all the blame out of all sense and reason,
Until I cried and trembled and rocked to and fro,
Riddled with light. Ah! when the ghost begins to quicken,
Confusion of the death-bed over, is it sent
Out naked on the roads, as the books say, and stricken
By the injustice of the skies for punishment?

AN IRISH AIRMAN FORESEES HIS DEATH

I KNOW that I shall meet my fate
Somewhere among the clouds above;
Those that I fight I do not hate,
Those that I guard I do not love;
My country is Kiltartan Cross,
My countrymen Kiltartan's poor,
No likely end could bring them loss
Or leave them happier than before.
Nor law, nor duty bade me fight,
Nor public men, nor cheering crowds,
A lonely impulse of delight
Drove to this tumult in the clouds;
I balanced all, brought all to mind,
The years to come seemed waste of breath,
A waste of breath the years behind
In balance with this life, this death.

THE SECOND COMING

TURNING and turning in the widening gyre
The falcon cannot hear the falconer;
Things fall apart; the centre cannot hold;
Mere anarchy is loosed upon the world,
The blood-dimmed tide is loosed, and everywhere
The ceremony of innocence is drowned;
The best lack all conviction, while the worst
Are full of passionate intensity.

Surely some revelation is at hand;
Surely the Second Coming is at hand.
The Second Coming! Hardly are those words out
When a vast image out of *Spiritus Mundi*
Troubles my sight: somewhere in sands of the desert
A shape with lion body and the head of a man,
A gaze blank and pitiless as the sun,
Is moving its slow thighs, while all about it
Reel shadows of the indignant desert birds.

The darkness drops again; but now I know
That twenty centuries of stony sleep
Were vexed to nightmare by a rocking cradle,
And what rough beast, its hour come round at last,
Slouches towards Bethlehem to be born?

SAILING TO BYZANTIUM

I

THAT is no country for old men. The young
In one another's arms, birds in the trees
—Those dying generations—at their song,
The salmon-falls, the mackerel-crowded seas,
Fish, flesh, or fowl, commend all summer long
Whatever is begotten, born, and dies.
Caught in that sensual music all neglect
Monuments of unageing intellect.

II

An aged man is but a paltry thing,
A tattered coat upon a stick, unless
Soul clap its hands and sing, and louder sing
For every tatter in its mortal dress,
Nor is there singing school but studying
Monuments of its own magnificence;
And therefore I have sailed the seas and come
To the holy city of Byzantium.

III

O sages standing in God's holy fire
As in the gold mosaic of a wall,
Come from the holy fire, perne in a gyre,
And be the singing-masters of my soul.
Consume my heart away; sick with desire
And fastened to a dying animal
It knows not what it is; and gather me
Into the artifice of eternity.

IV

Once out of nature I shall never take
My bodily form from any natural thing,
But such a form as Grecian goldsmiths make
Of hammered gold and gold enamelling
To keep a drowsy Emperor awake;
Or set upon a golden bough to sing
To lords and ladies of Byzantium
Of what is past, or passing, or to come.

1927

From MEDITATIONS IN TIME OF CIVIL WAR

VI THE STARE'S NEST BY MY WINDOW

THE bees build in the crevices
Of loosening masonry, and there
The mother birds bring grubs and flies.
My wall is loosening; honey-bees,
Come build in the empty house of the stare.

We are closed in, and the key is turned
On our uncertainty; somewhere
A man is killed, or a house burned,
Yet no clear fact to be discerned:
Come build in the empty house of the stare.

A barricade of stone or of wood;
Some fourteen days of civil war;
Last night they trundled down the road
That dead young soldier in his blood:
Come build in the empty house of the stare.

We had fed the heart on fantasies,
The heart's grown brutal from the fare;
More substance in our enmities
Than in our love; O honey-bees,
Come build in the empty house of the stare.

THE WHEEL

THROUGH winter-time we call on spring,
And through the spring on summer call,
And when abounding hedges ring
Declare that winter's best of all;
And after that there's nothing good
Because the spring-time has not come—
Nor know that what disturbs our blood
Is but its longing for the tomb.

THE NEW FACES

IF you, that have grown old, were the first dead,
Neither catalpa tree nor scented lime
Should hear my living feet, nor would I tread
Where we wrought that shall break the teeth of Time.
Let the new faces play what tricks they will
In the old rooms; night can outbalance day,
Our shadows rove the garden gravel still,
The living seem more shadowy than they.

LEDA AND THE SWAN

A SUDDEN blow: the great wings beating still
Above the staggering girl, her thighs caressed
By the dark webs, her nape caught in his bill,
He holds her helpless breast upon his breast.

How can those terrified vague fingers push
The feathered glory from her loosening thighs?
And how can body, laid in that white rush,
But feel the strange heart beating where it lies?

A shudder in the loins engenders there
The broken wall, the burning roof and tower
And Agamemnon dead.
           Being so caught up,
So mastered by the brute blood of the air,
Did she put on his knowledge with his power
Before the indifferent beak could let her drop?

1923

AMONG SCHOOL CHILDREN

I

I WALK through the long schoolroom questioning;
A kind old nun in a white hood replies;
The children learn to cipher and to sing,
To study reading-books and histories,
To cut and sew, be neat in everything
In the best modern way—the children's eyes
In momentary wonder stare upon
A sixty-year-old smiling public man.

II

I dream of a Ledaean body, bent
Above a sinking fire, a tale that she
Told of a harsh reproof, or trivial event
That changed some childish day to tragedy—
Told, and it seemed that our two natures blent
Into a sphere from youthful sympathy,
Or else, to alter Plato's parable,
Into the yolk and white of the one shell.

III

And thinking of that fit of grief or rage
I look upon one child or t'other there
And wonder if she stood so at that age—
For even daughters of the swan can share
Something of every paddler's heritage—
And had that colour upon cheek or hair,
And thereupon my heart is driven wild:
She stands before me as a living child.

IV

Her present image floats into the mind—
Did Quattrocento finger fashion it
Hollow of cheek as though it drank the wind
And took a mess of shadows for its meat?
And I though never of Ledaean kind
Had pretty plumage once—enough of that,
Better to smile on all that smile, and show
There is a comfortable kind of old scarecrow.

v

What youthful mother, a shape upon her lap
Honey of generation had betrayed,
And that must sleep, shriek, struggle to escape
As recollection or the drug decide,
Would think her son, did she but see that shape
With sixty or more winters on its head,
A compensation for the pang of his birth,
Or the uncertainty of his setting forth?

vi

Plato thought nature but a spume that plays
Upon a ghostly paradigm of things;
Solider Aristotle played the taws
Upon the bottom of a king of kings;
World-famous golden-thighed Pythagoras
Fingered upon a fiddle-stick or strings
What a star sang and careless Muses heard:
Old clothes upon old sticks to scare a bird.

vii

Both nuns and mothers worship images,
But those the candles light are not as those
That animate a mother's reveries,
But keep a marble or a bronze repose.
And yet they too break hearts—O Presences
That passion, piety or affection knows,
And that all heavenly glory symbolise—
O self-born mockers of man's enterprise;

viii

Labour is blossoming or dancing where
The body is not bruised to pleasure soul,
Nor beauty born out of its own despair,
Nor blear-eyed wisdom out of midnight oil.
O chestnut-tree, great-rooted blossomer,
Are you the leaf, the blossom or the bole?
O body swayed to music, O brightening glance,
How can we know the dancer from the dance?

COOLE PARK AND BALLYLEE, 1931

Under my window-ledge the waters race,
Otters below and moor-hens on the top,
Run for a mile undimmed in Heaven's face
Then darkening through 'dark' Raftery's 'cellar' drop,
Run underground, rise in a rocky place
In Coole demesne, and there to finish up
Spread to a lake and drop into a hole.
What's water but the generated soul?

Upon the border of that lake's a wood
Now all dry sticks under a wintry sun,
And in a copse of beeches there I stood,
For Nature's pulled her tragic buskin on
And all the rant's a mirror of my mood:
At sudden thunder of the mounting swan
I turned about and looked where branches break
The glittering reaches of the flooded lake.

Another emblem there! That stormy white
But seems a concentration of the sky;
And, like the soul, it sails into the sight
And in the morning's gone, no man knows why;
And is so lovely that it sets to right
What knowledge or its lack had set awry,
So arrogantly pure, a child might think
It can be murdered with a spot of ink.

Sound of a stick upon the floor, a sound
From somebody that toils from chair to chair;
Beloved books that famous hands have bound,
Old marble heads, old pictures everywhere;
Great rooms where travelled men and children found
Content or joy; a last inheritor
Where none has reigned that lacked a name and fame
Or out of folly into folly came.

A spot whereon the founders lived and died
Seemed once more dear than life; ancestral trees,
Or gardens rich in memory glorified
Marriages, alliances and families,
And every bride's ambition satisfied.
Where fashion or mere fantasy decrees
We shift about—all that great glory spent—
Like some poor Arab tribesman and his tent.

We were the last romantics—chose for theme
Traditional sanctity and loveliness;
Whatever's written in what poets name
The book of the people; whatever most can bless
The mind of man or elevate a rhyme;
But all is changed, that high horse riderless,
Though mounted in that saddle Homer rode
Where the swan drifts upon a darkening flood.

BEFORE THE WORLD WAS MADE

If I make the lashes dark
And the eyes more bright
And the lips more scarlet,
Or ask if all be right
From mirror after mirror,
No vanity's displayed:
I'm looking for the face I had
Before the world was made.

What if I look upon a man
As though on my beloved,
And my blood be cold the while
And my heart unmoved?
Why should he think me cruel
Or that he is betrayed?
I'd have him love the thing that was
Before the world was made.

THE GYRES

THE GYRES! the gyres! Old Rocky Face, look forth;
Things thought too long can be no longer thought,
For beauty dies of beauty, worth of worth,
And ancient lineaments are blotted out.
Irrational streams of blood are staining earth;
Empedocles has thrown all things about;
Hector is dead and there's a light in Troy;
We that look on but laugh in tragic joy.

What matter though numb nightmare ride on top,
And blood and mire the sensitive body stain?
What matter? Heave no sigh, let no tear drop,
A greater, a more gracious time has gone;
For painted forms or boxes of make-up
In ancient tombs I sighed, but not again;
What matter? Out of cavern comes a voice,
And all it knows is that one word 'Rejoice!'

Conduct and work grow coarse, and coarse the soul,
What matter? Those that Rocky Face holds dear,
Lovers of horses and of women, shall,
From marble of a broken sepulchre,
Or dark betwixt the polecat and the owl,
Or any rich, dark nothing disinter
The workman, noble and saint, and all things run
On that unfashionable gyre again.

THE MUNICIPAL GALLERY REVISITED

I

AROUND me the images of thirty years:
An ambush; pilgrims at the water-side;
Casement upon trial, half hidden by the bars,
Guarded; Griffith staring in hysterical pride;
Kevin O'Higgins' countenance that wears
A gentle questioning look that cannot hide
A soul incapable of remorse or rest;
A revolutionary soldier kneeling to be blessed;

II

An Abbot or Archbishop with an upraised hand
Blessing the Tricolour. 'This is not,' I say,
'The dead Ireland of my youth, but an Ireland
The poets have imagined, terrible and gay.'
Before a woman's portrait suddenly I stand,
Beautiful and gentle in her Venetian way.
I met her all but fifty years ago
For twenty minutes in some studio.

III

Heart-smitten with emotion I sink down,
My heart recovering with covered eyes;
Wherever I had looked I had looked upon
My permanent or impermanent images:
Augusta Gregory's son; her sister's son,
Hugh Lane, 'onlie begetter' of all these;
Hazel Lavery living and dying, that tale
As though some ballad-singer had sung it all;

IV

Mancini's portrait of Augusta Gregory,
'Greatest since Rembrandt,' according to John Synge;
A great ebullient portrait certainly;
But where is the brush that could show anything
Of all that pride and that humility?
And I am in despair that time may bring
Approved patterns of women or of men
But not that selfsame excellence again.

V

My mediaeval knees lack health until they bend,
But in that woman, in that household where
Honour had lived so long, all lacking found.
Childless I thought, 'My children may find here
Deep-rooted things,' but never foresaw its end,
And now that end has come I have not wept;
No fox can foul the lair the badger swept—

VI

(An image out of Spenser and the common tongue).
John Synge, I and Augusta Gregory, thought
All that we did, all that we said or sang
Must come from contact with the soil, from that
Contact everything Antaeus-like grew strong.
We three alone in modern times had brought
Everything down to that sole test again,
Dream of the noble and the beggar-man.

VII

And here's John Synge himself, that rooted man,
'Forgetting human words,' a grave deep face.
You that would judge me, do not judge alone
This book or that, come to this hallowed place
Where my friends' portraits hang and look thereon;
Ireland's history in their lineaments trace;
Think where man's glory most begins and ends,
And say my glory was I had such friends.

LAURENCE BINYON

1869–1943

From THE BURNING OF THE LEAVES

I

Now is the time for the burning of the leaves.
They go to the fire; the nostril pricks with smoke
Wandering slowly into a weeping mist.
Brittle and blotched, ragged and rotten sheaves!
A flame seizes the smouldering ruin and bites
On stubborn stalks that crackle as they resist.

The last hollyhock's fallen tower is dust;
All the spices of June are a bitter reek,
All the extravagant riches spent and mean.
All burns! The reddest rose is a ghost;
Sparks whirl up, to expire in the mist: the wild
Fingers of fire are making corruption clean.

BINYON

Now is the time for stripping the spirit bare,
Time for the burning of days ended and done,
Idle solace of things that have gone before:
Rootless hope and fruitless desire are there;
Let them go to the fire, with never a look behind.
The world that was ours is a world that is ours no more.

They will come again, the leaf and the flower, to arise
From squalor of rottenness into the old splendour,
And magical scents to a wondering memory bring;
The same glory, to shine upon different eyes.
Earth cares for her own ruins, naught for ours.
Nothing is certain, only the certain spring.

W. H. DAVIES

1871–1940

THE INQUEST

I TOOK my oath I would inquire,
    Without affection, hate, or wrath,
Into the death of Ada Wright—
    So help me God! I took that oath.

When I went out to see the corpse,
    The four months' babe that died so young,
I judged it was seven pounds in weight,
    And little more than one foot long.

One eye, that had a yellow lid,
    Was shut—so was the mouth, that smiled;
The left eye open, shining bright—
    It seemed a knowing little child.

For as I looked at that one eye,
    It seemed to laugh, and say with glee:
'What caused my death you'll never know—
    Perhaps my mother murdered me.'

When I went into court again,
    To hear the mother's evidence—
It was a love-child, she explained.
    And smiled, for our intelligence.

'Now, Gentlemen of the Jury,' said
    The coroner—'this woman's child
By misadventure met its death.'
    'Aye, aye,' said we. The mother smiled.

And I could see that child's one eye
    Which seemed to laugh, and say with glee:
'What caused my death you'll never know—
    Perhaps my mother murdered me.'

RALPH HODGSON
1871–1962

TIME

SPIRALWISE it spins
And twirls about the Sun,
Both with and withershins
At once, a dual run
Anomalously one;
Its speed is such it gains
Upon itself: outsped,
Outdistanced, it remains
At every point ahead,
No less at all points led,
At none with either strains
Or lapses in the rush
Of its almighty vanes
To mar the poise or hush;
Comparing it for speed:
Lightning is a snail
That pauses on its trail
From bank to underbrush,
Mindful of its need,
With dawn astir, to feed
Before the morning thrush;

Comparing it for poise:
The tops we spun to sleep,
Seemingly so deep
Stockstill, when we were boys,
No more than stumbled round,
Boxwoods though they were,
The best we ever wound
Or whipped of all such toys;
Comparing it for sound:
The wisp of gossamer
Caught in a squirrel's fur,
Groans like a ship aground;
Shadow makes more noise.

WALTER DE LA MARE

1873–1956

RESERVED

. . . 'I was thinking, Mother, of that poor old horse
   They killed the other day;
Nannie *says* it was only a bag of bones,
   But I hated it taken away.'
'Of course, sweet; but now the baker's man
Will soon have a nice new motor van.'

'Yes, Mother. But when on our walk a squirrel
   Crept up to my thumb to be fed,
She shoo'd it away with her gloves—like this!
   They ought to be shot, she said.'
'She may have been reading, darling, that
Squirrels are only a kind of *rat*.'

'Goldfinches, Mother, owls and mice,
   Tom-tits and bunnies and jays—
Everything in my picture-books
   Will soon be gone, she says.'
'You see, my precious, so many creatures,
   Though exquisitely made,
Steal, or are dirty and dangerous,
   Or else they are bad for Trade.'

'I wonder, Mother, if when poor Noah
    Was alone in the rain and dark,
He can ever have thought what wicked things
    Were round him in the Ark. . . .
And are all children—like the rest—
Like me, as Nannie says, a pest?

'I woke last night from a dreadful dream
    Of a place—it was all of stone;
And dark. And the walls went up, and up—
    And oh, I was lost: alone!
I was *terrified*, Mother, and tried to call;
    But a gabble, like echoes, came back.
It will soon, I suppose, be bedtime again?
    And I hate lying there awake.'

'You mustn't, angel.' She glanced at the window—
    Smiled at the questioning mite.
'There's nothing to fear.' A wild bird scritched.
    The sun's last beam of light
Gilded the Globe, reserved for Man,
    Preparing for the Night.

AT EASE

MOST wounds can Time repair;
    But some are mortal—these:
For a broken heart there is no balm,
    No cure for a heart at ease—

At ease, but cold as stone,
    Though the intellect spin on,
And the feat and practised face may show
    Nought of the life that is gone;

But smiles, as by habit taught;
    And sighs, as by custom led;
And the soul within is safe from damnation,
    Since it is dead.

THE OLD SUMMERHOUSE

This blue-washed, old, thatched summerhouse—
Paint scaling, and fading from its walls—
How often from its hingeless door
I have watched—dead leaf, like the ghost of a mouse,
Rasping the worn brick floor—
The snows of the weir descending below,
And their thunderous waterfall.

Fall—fall: dark, garrulous rumour,
Until I could listen no more.
Could listen no more—for beauty with sorrow
Is a burden hard to be borne:
The evening light on the foam, and the swans, there;
That music, remote, forlorn.

FARE WELL

When I lie where shades of darkness
Shall no more assail mine eyes,
Nor the rain make lamentation
    When the wind sighs;
How will fare the world whose wonder
Was the very proof of me?
Memory fades, must the remembered
    Perishing be?

Oh, when this my dust surrenders
Hand, foot, lip, to dust again,
May these loved and loving faces
    Please other men!
May the rusting harvest hedgerow
Still the Traveller's Joy entwine,
And as happy children gather
    Posies once mine.

Look thy last on all things lovely,
Every hour. Let no night
Seal thy sense in deathly slumber
    Till to delight
Thou have paid thy utmost blessing;
Since that all things thou wouldst praise
Beauty took from those who loved them
    In other days.

JOHN MASEFIELD

1878–1967

THE DEAD KNIGHT

The cleanly rush of the mountain air,
And the mumbling, grumbling humble-bees,
Are the only things that wander there,
The pitiful bones are laid at ease,
The grass has grown in his tangled hair,
And a rambling bramble binds his knees.

To shrieve his soul from the pangs of hell,
The only requiem-bells that rang
Were the hare-bell and the heather-bell.
Hushed he is with the holy spell
In the gentle hymn the wind sang,
And he lies quiet, and sleeps well.

He is bleached and blanched with the summer sun;
The misty rain and cold dew
Have altered him from the kingly one
(That his lady loved, and his men knew)
And dwindled him to a skeleton.

The vetches have twined about his bones,
The straggling ivy twists and creeps
In his eye-sockets; the nettle keeps
Vigil about him while he sleeps.
Over his body the wind moans

With a dreary tune throughout the day,
In a chorus wistful, eerie, thin
As the gull's cry—as the cry in the bay,
The mournful word the seas say
When tides are wandering out or in.

EDWARD THOMAS

1878–1917

TEARS

IT seems I have no tears left. They should have fallen—
Their ghosts, if tears have ghosts, did fall—that day
When twenty hounds streamed by me, not yet combed out
But still all equals in their rage of gladness
Upon the scent, made one, like a great dragon
In Blooming Meadow that bends towards the sun
And once bore hops: and on that other day
When I stepped out from the double-shadowed Tower
Into an April morning, stirring and sweet
And warm. Strange solitude was there and silence.
A mightier charm than any in the Tower
Possessed the courtyard. They were changing guard,
Soldiers in line, young English countrymen,
Fair-haired and ruddy, in white tunics. Drums
And fifes were playing 'The British Grenadiers'.
The men, the music piercing that solitude
And silence, told me truths I had not dreamed,
And have forgotten since their beauty passed.

THE OWL

DOWNHILL I came, hungry, and yet not starved;
Cold, yet had heat within me that was proof
Against the North wind; tired, yet so that rest
Had seemed the sweetest thing under a roof.

441

Then at the inn I had food, fire, and rest,
Knowing how hungry, cold, and tired was I.
All of the night was quite barred out except
An owl's cry, a most melancholy cry

Shaken out long and clear upon the hill,
No merry note, nor cause of merriment,
But one telling me plain what I escaped
And others could not, that night, as in I went.

And salted was my food, and my repose,
Salted and sobered, too, by the bird's voice
Speaking for all who lay under the stars,
Soldiers and poor, unable to rejoice.

AS THE TEAM'S HEAD-BRASS

As the team's head-brass flashed out on the turn
The lovers disappeared into the wood.
I sat among the boughs of the fallen elm
That strewed the angle of the fallow, and
Watched the plough narrowing a yellow square
Of charlock. Every time the horses turned
Instead of treading me down, the ploughman leaned
Upon the handles to say or ask a word,
About the weather, next about the war.
Scraping the share he faced towards the wood,
And screwed along the furrow till the brass flashed
Once more.
    The blizzard felled the elm whose crest
I sat in, by a woodpecker's round hole,
The ploughman said. 'When will they take it away?'
'When the war's over.' So the talk began—
One minute and an interval of ten,
A minute more and the same interval.
'Have you been out?' 'No.' 'And don't want to, perhaps?'
'If I could only come back again, I should.

I could spare an arm. I shouldn't want to lose
A leg. If I should lose my head, why, so,
I should want nothing more. . . . Have many gone
From here?' 'Yes.' 'Many lost?' 'Yes, a good few.
Only two teams work on the farm this year.
One of my mates is dead. The second day
In France they killed him. It was back in March,
The very night of the blizzard, too. Now if
He had stayed here we should have moved the tree.'
'And I should not have sat here. Everything
Would have been different. For it would have been
Another world.' 'Ay, and a better, though
If we could see all all might seem good.' Then
The lovers came out of the wood again:
The horses started and for the last time
I watched the clods crumble and topple over
After the ploughshare and the stumbling team.

THAW

OVER the land freckled with snow half-thawed
The speculating rooks at their nests cawed
And saw from elm-tops, delicate as flower of grass,
What we below could not see, Winter pass.

THE COMBE

THE Combe was ever dark, ancient and dark.
Its mouth is stopped with bramble, thorn, and briar;
And no one scrambles over the sliding chalk
By beech and yew and perishing juniper
Down the half precipices of its sides, with roots
And rabbit holes for steps. The sun of Winter,
The moon of Summer, and all the singing birds
Except the missel-thrush that loves juniper,
Are quite shut out. But far more ancient and dark
The Combe looks since they killed the badger there,
Dug him out and gave him to the hounds,
That most ancient Briton of English beasts.

IN MEMORIAM (EASTER, 1915)

THE flowers left thick at nightfall in the wood
This Eastertide call into mind the men,
Now far from home, who, with their sweethearts, should
Have gathered them and will do never again.

COCK-CROW

OUT of the wood of thoughts that grows by night
To be cut down by the sharp axe of light,—
Out of the night, two cocks together crow,
Cleaving the darkness with a silver blow:
And bright before my eyes twin trumpeters stand,
Heralds of splendour, one at either hand,
Each facing each as in a coat of arms:
The milkers lace their boots up at the farms.

A PRIVATE

THIS ploughman dead in battle slept out of doors
Many a frozen night, and merrily
Answered staid drinkers, good bedmen, and all bores:
'At Mrs. Greenland's Hawthorn Bush', said he,
'I slept.' None knew which bush. Above the town,
Beyond 'The Drover', a hundred spot the down
In Wiltshire. And where now at last he sleeps
More sound in France—that, too, he secret keeps.

OUT IN THE DARK

OUT in the dark over the snow
The fallow fawns invisible go
With the fallow doe;
And the winds blow
Fast as the stars are slow.

Stealthily the dark haunts round
And, when the lamp goes, without sound
At a swifter bound
Than the swiftest hound,
Arrives, and all else is drowned;

And star and I and wind and deer,
Are in the dark together,—near,
Yet far,—and fear
Drums on my ear
In that sage company drear.

How weak and little is the light,
All the universe of sight,
Love and delight,
Before the might,
If you love it not, of night.

T. E. HULME

1883–1917

ABOVE THE DOCK

ABOVE the quiet dock in midnight,
Tangled in the tall mast's corded height,
Hangs the moon. What seemed so far away
Is but a child's balloon, forgotten after play.

THE EMBANKMENT

(The fantasia of a fallen gentleman on a cold, bitter night)

ONCE, in finesse of fiddles found I ecstasy,
In a flash of gold heels on the hard pavement.
Now see I
That warmth's the very stuff of poesy.
Oh, God, make small
The old star-eaten blanket of the sky,
That I may fold it round me and in comfort lie.

445

ISAAC ROSENBERG

1890–1918

BREAK OF DAY IN THE TRENCHES

THE darkness crumbles away—
It is the same old druid Time as ever.
Only a live thing leaps my hand—
A queer sardonic rat—
As I pull the parapet's poppy
To stick behind my ear.
Droll rat, they would shoot you if they knew
Your cosmopolitan sympathies
(And God knows what antipathies).
Now you have touched this English hand
You will do the same to a German—
Soon, no doubt, if it be your pleasure
To cross the sleeping green between.
It seems you inwardly grin as you pass
Strong eyes, fine limbs, haughty athletes
Less chanced than you for life,
Bonds to the whims of murder,
Sprawled in the bowels of the earth,
The torn fields of France.
What do you see in our eyes
At the shrieking iron and flame
Hurled through still heavens?
What quaver—what heart aghast?
Poppies whose roots are in man's veins
Drop, and are ever dropping;
But mine in my ear is safe,
Just a little white with the dust.

DEAD MAN'S DUMP

THE plunging limbers over the shattered track
Racketed with their rusty freight,
Stuck out like many crowns of thorns,

ROSENBERG

And the rusty stakes like sceptres old
To stay the flood of brutish men
Upon our brothers dear.

The wheels lurched over sprawled dead
But pained them not, though their bones crunched;
Their shut mouths made no moan.
They lie there huddled, friend and foeman,
Man born of man, and born of woman;
And shells go crying over them
From night till night and now.

Earth has waited for them,
All the time of their growth
Fretting for their decay:
Now she has them at last!
In the strength of their strength
Suspended—stopped and held.

What fierce imaginings their dark souls lit?
Earth! Have they gone into you?
Somewhere they must have gone,
And flung on your hard back
Is their souls' sack,
Emptied of God-ancestralled essences.
Who hurled them out? Who hurled?

None saw their spirits' shadow shake the grass,
Or stood aside for the half used life to pass
Out of those doomed nostrils and the doomed mouth,
When the swift iron burning bee
Drained the wild honey of their youth.

What of us who, flung on the shrieking pyre,
Walk, our usual thoughts untouched,
Our lucky limbs as on ichor fed,
Immortal seeming ever?
Perhaps when the flames beat loud on us,
A fear may choke in our veins
And the startled blood may stop.

The air is loud with death,
The dark air spurts with fire,
The explosions ceaseless are.
Timelessly now, some minutes past,
These dead strode time with vigorous life,
Till the shrapnel called 'An end!'
But not to all. In bleeding pangs
Some borne on stretchers dreamed of home,
Dear things, war-blotted from their hearts.

A man's brains splattered on
A stretcher-bearer's face;
His shook shoulders slipped their load,
But when they bent to look again
The drowning soul was sunk too deep
For human tenderness.

They left this dead with the older dead,
Stretched at the cross roads.

Burnt black by strange decay
Their sinister faces lie,
The lid over each eye;
The grass and coloured clay
More motion have than they,
Joined to the great sunk silences.

Here is one not long dead.
His dark hearing caught our far wheels,
And the choked soul stretched weak hands
To reach the living word the far wheels said;
The blood-dazed intelligence beating for light,
Crying through the suspense of the far torturing wheels
Swift for the end to break
Or the wheels to break,
Cried as the tide of the world broke over his sight,
'Will they come? Will they ever come?'
Even as the mixed hoofs of the mules,
The quivering-bellied mules,
And the rushing wheels all mixed
With his tortured upturned sight.

So we crashed round the bend,
We heard his weak scream,
We heard his very last sound,
And our wheels grazed his dead face.

WILFRED OWEN

1893–1918

GREATER LOVE

RED lips are not so red
   As the stained stones kissed by the English dead.
Kindness of wooed and wooer
Seems shame to their love pure.
O Love, your eyes lose lure
   When I behold eyes blinded in my stead!

Your slender attitude
   Trembles not exquisite like limbs knife-skewed,
Rolling and rolling there
Where God seems not to care;
Till the fierce Love they bear
   Cramps them in death's extreme decrepitude.

Your voice sings not so soft,—
   Though even as wind murmuring through raftered loft,—
Your dear voice is not dear,
Gentle, and evening clear,
As theirs whom none now hear,
   Now earth has stopped their piteous mouths that coughed.

Heart, you were never hot,
   Nor large, nor full like hearts made great with shot;
And though your hand be pale,
Paler are all which trail
Your cross through flame and hail:
   Weep, you may weep, for you may touch them not.

FUTILITY

MOVE him into the sun—
Gently its touch awoke him once,
At home, whispering of fields unsown.
Always it woke him, even in France,
Until this morning and this snow.
If anything might rouse him now
The kind old sun will know.

Think how it wakes the seeds,—
Woke, once, the clays of a cold star.
Are limbs, so dear-achieved, are sides,
Full-nerved—still warm—too hard to stir?
Was it for this the clay grew tall?
—O what made fatuous sunbeams toil
To break earth's sleep at all?

ANTHEM FOR DOOMED YOUTH

WHAT passing-bells for these who die as cattle?
    Only the monstrous anger of the guns.
    Only the stuttering rifles' rapid rattle
Can patter out their hasty orisons.
No mockeries now for them; no prayers nor bells,
    Nor any voice of mourning save the choirs,—
The shrill, demented choirs of wailing shells;
    And bugles calling for them from sad shires.

What candles may be held to speed them all?
    Not in the hands of boys, but in their eyes
Shall shine the holy glimmers of good-byes.
    The pallor of girls' brows shall be their pall;
Their flowers the tenderness of patient minds,
And each slow dusk a drawing-down of blinds.

SPRING OFFENSIVE

HALTED against the shade of a last hill,
They fed, and, lying easy, were at ease
And, finding comfortable chests and knees,
Carelessly slept. But many there stood still
To face the stark, blank sky beyond the ridge,
Knowing their feet had come to the end of the world.

Marvelling they stood, and watched the long grass swirled
By the May breeze, murmurous with wasp and midge,
For though the summer oozed into their veins
Like an injected drug for their bodies' pains,
Sharp on their souls hung the imminent line of grass,
Fearfully flashed the sky's mysterious glass.

Hour after hour they ponder the warm field—
And the far valley behind, where the buttercup
Had blessed with gold their slow boots coming up,
Where even the little brambles would not yield,
But clutched and clung to them like sorrowing hands;
They breathe like trees unstirred.

Till like a cold gust thrills the little word
At which each body and its soul begird
And tighten them for battle. No alarms
Of bugles, no high flags, no clamorous haste—
Only a lift and flare of eyes that faced
The sun, like a friend with whom their love is done.
O larger shone that smile against the sun,—
Mightier than his whose bounty these have spurned.

So, soon they topped the hill, and raced together
Over an open stretch of herb and heather
Exposed. And instantly the whole sky burned
With fury against them; earth set sudden cups
In thousands for their blood; and the green slope
Chasmed and steepened sheer to infinite space.

· · · · · ·

OWEN

Of them who running on that last high place
Leapt to swift unseen bullets, or went up
On the hot blast and fury of hell's upsurge,
Or plunged and fell away past this world's verge,
Some say God caught them even before they fell.

But what say such as from existence' brink
Ventured but drave too swift to sink,
The few who rushed in the body to enter hell,
And there out-fiending all its fiends and flames
With superhuman inhumanities,
Long-famous glories, immemorial shames—
And crawling slowly back, have by degrees
Regained cool peaceful air in wonder—
Why speak not they of comrades that went under?

STRANGE MEETING

It seemed that out of battle I escaped
Down some profound dull tunnel, long since scooped
Through granites which titanic wars had groined.
Yet also there encumbered sleepers groaned,
Too fast in thought or death to be bestirred.
Then, as I probed them, one sprang up, and stared
With piteous recognition in fixed eyes,
Lifting distressful hands as if to bless.
And by his smile, I knew that sullen hall,
By his dead smile I knew we stood in Hell.
With a thousand pains that vision's face was grained;
Yet no blood reached there from the upper ground,
And no guns thumped, or down the flues made moan.
'Strange friend,' I said, 'here is no cause to mourn.'
'None,' said that other, 'save the undone years,
The hopelessness. Whatever hope is yours,
Was my life also; I went hunting wild
After the wildest beauty in the world,
Which lies not calm in eyes, or braided hair,
But mocks the steady running of the hour,
And if it grieves, grieves richlier than here.
For by my glee might many men have laughed,

And of my weeping something had been left,
Which must die now. I mean the truth untold,
The pity of war, the pity war distilled.
Now men will go content with what we spoiled.
Or, discontent, boil bloody, and be spilled.
They will be swift with swiftness of the tigress,
None will break ranks, though nations trek from progress.
Courage was mine, and I had mystery,
Wisdom was mine, and I had mastery;
To miss the march of this retreating world
Into vain citadels that are not walled.
Then, when much blood had clogged their chariot-wheels
I would go up and wash them from sweet wells,
Even with truths that lie too deep for taint.
I would have poured my spirit without stint
But not through wounds; not on the cess of war.
Foreheads of men have bled where no wounds were.
I am the enemy you killed, my friend.
I knew you in this dark; for so you frowned
Yesterday through me as you jabbed and killed.
I parried; but my hands were loath and cold.
Let us sleep now. . . .'

SIEGFRIED SASSOON
1886–1967

EVERYONE SANG

EVERYONE suddenly burst out singing;
And I was filled with such delight
As prisoned birds must find in freedom
Winging wildly across the white
Orchards and dark-green fields; on; on; and out of sight.

Everyone's voice was suddenly lifted,
And beauty came like the setting sun.
My heart was shaken with tears; and horror
Drifted away . . . O but every one
Was a bird; and the song was wordless; the singing will
never be done.

AT THE GRAVE OF HENRY VAUGHAN

ABOVE the voiceful windings of a river
An old green slab of simply graven stone
Shuns notice, overshadowed by a yew.
Here Vaughan lies dead, whose name flows on for ever
Through pastures of the spirit washed with dew
And starlit with eternities unknown.

Here sleeps the Silurist; the loved physician;
The face that left no portraiture behind;
The skull that housed white angels and had vision
Of daybreak through the gateways of the mind.
  Here faith and mercy, wisdom and humility
  (Whose influence shall prevail for evermore)
  Shine. And this lowly grave tells Heaven's tranquillity.
  And here stand I, a suppliant at the door.

ROBERT NICHOLS

1893–1944

THE SPRIG OF LIME

HE lay, and those who watched him were amazed
To see unheralded beneath the lids
Twin tears, new-gathered at the price of pain,
Start and at once run crookedly athwart
Cheeks channelled long by pain, never by tears.
So desolate, too, the sigh next uttered
They had wept also, but his great lips moved,
And bending down one heard 'A sprig of lime;
Bring me a sprig of lime.' Whereat she stole
With dumb sign forth to pluck the thing he craved.

So lay he till a lime-twig had been snapped
From some still branch that swept the outer grass
Far from the silver pillar of the bole,
Which, mounting past the house's crusted roof,
Split into massy limbs, crossed boughs, a maze

454

Of close-compacted intercontorted staffs
Bowered in foliage, wherethrough the sun
Shot sudden showers of light or crystal spars
Or wavered in a green and vitreous flood.

And all the while in faint and fainter tones,
Scarce audible on deepened evening's hush,
He framed his curious and last request
For 'lime, a sprig of lime.' Her trembling hand
Closed his loose fingers on the awkward stem,
Covered above with gentle heart-shaped leaves
And under dangling, pale as honey-wax,
Square clusters of sweet-scented starry flowers.
She laid his bent arm back upon his breast,
Then watched above white knuckles clenched in prayer.
He never moved. Only at last his eyes
Opened, then brightened in such avid gaze
She feared the coma mastered him again . . .
But no; strange sobs rose chuckling in his throat,
A stranger ecstasy suffused the flesh
Of that just mask so sun-dried, gouged and old,
Which few—too few!—had loved, too many feared.
'Father!' she cried; 'Father!'

He did not hear.

She knelt, and, kneeling, drank the scent of limes,
Blown round the slow blind by a vesperal gust,
Till the room swam. So the lime-incense blew
Into her life as once it had in his,
Though how and when and with what ageless charge
Of sorrow and deep joy how could she know?

Sweet lime so hushèdly at the height of noon
Diffusing dizzy fragrance from your boughs,
Tasselled with blossoms more innumerable
Than the black bees, the uproar of whose toil
Fills your green vaults, winning such metheglin
As clouds their sappy cells, distil, as once
Ye used, your sunniest emanations
Towards the window where a woman kneels—
She who within that room in childish hours

455

Lay through the lasting murmur of blanch'd noon
Behind the sultry blind, now full, now flat,
Drinking anew of every odorous breath,
Supremely happy in her ignorance
Of Time that hastens hourly and of Death
Who need not haste. Scatter your fumes, O lime,
Loose from each hispid star of citron bloom,
Tangled beneath the labyrinthine boughs,
Cloud on such stinging cloud of exhalation
As reeks of youth, fierce life, and summer's prime,
Though hardly now shall he in that dusk room
Savour your sweetness, since the very sprig,
Profuse of blossom and of essences,
He smells not, who in a paltering hand
Clasps it laid close his peaked and gleaming face
Propped in the pillow. Breathe silent, lofty lime,
Your curfew secrets out in fervid scent
To the attendant shadows! Tinge the air
Of the midsummer night that now begins,
At an owl's oaring flight from dusk to dusk,
And downward caper of the giddy bat
Hawking against the lustre of bare skies,
With something of th' unfathomable bliss
He, who lies dying there, knew once of old
In the serene trance of a summer night,
When with th' abundance of his young bride's hair
Loosed on his breast he lay and dared not sleep,
Listening for the scarce motion of your boughs,
Which sighed with bliss as she with blissful sleep,
And, drinking desperately each honied wave
Of perfume wafted past the ghostly blind,
First knew th' implacable and bitter sense
Of Time that hastes and Death who need not haste.
Shed your last sweetness, limes!

> But now no more
She, fruit of that night's love, she heeds you not,
Who bent, compassionate, to the dim floor,
Takes up the sprig of lime and presses it
In pain against the stumbling of her heart,
Knowing, untold, he cannot need it now.

D. H. LAWRENCE

1885–1930

SORROW

WHY does the thin grey strand
Floating up from the forgotten
Cigarette between my fingers,
Why does it trouble me?

Ah, you will understand;
When I carried my mother downstairs,
A few times only, at the beginning
Of her soft-foot malady,

I should find, for a reprimand
To my gaiety, a few long grey hairs
On the breast of my coat; and one by one
I watched them float up the dark chimney.

PIANO

SOFTLY, in the dusk, a woman is singing to me;
Taking me back down the vista of years, till I see
A child sitting under the piano, in the boom of the tingling
    strings
And pressing the small, poised feet of a mother who smiles
    as she sings.

In spite of myself, the insidious mastery of song
Betrays me back, till the heart of me weeps to belong
To the old Sunday evenings at home, with winter outside
And hymns in the cosy parlour, the tinkling piano our guide.

So now it is vain for the singer to burst into clamour
With the great black piano appassionato. The glamour
Of childish days is upon me, my manhood is cast
Down in the flood of remembrance, I weep like a child for
    the past.

457

LAWRENCE

SONG OF A MAN WHO HAS COME
THROUGH

NOT I, not I, but the wind that blows through me!
A fine wind is blowing the new direction of Time.
If only I let it bear me, carry me, if only it carry me!
If only I am sensitive, subtle, oh, delicate, a winged gift!
If only, most lovely of all, I yield myself and am borrowed
By the fine, fine wind that takes its course through the chaos
    of the world
Like a fine, an exquisite chisel, a wedge-blade inserted;
If only I am keen and hard like the sheer tip of a wedge
Driven by invisible blows,
The rock will split, we shall come at the wonder, we shall
    find the Hesperides.

Oh, for the wonder that bubbles into my soul,
I would be a good fountain, a good well-head,
Would blur no whisper, spoil no expression.

What is the knocking?
What is the knocking at the door in the night?
It is somebody wants to do us harm.

No, no, it is the three strange angels.
Admit them, admit them.

BAT

AT evening, sitting on this terrace,
When the sun from the west, beyond Pisa, beyond the
    mountains of Carrara
Departs, and the world is taken by surprise . . .

When the tired flower of Florence is in gloom beneath the
    glowing
Brown hills surrounding . . .

When under the arches of the Ponte Vecchio
A green light enters against stream, flush from the west,
Against the current of obscure Arno . . .

458

Look up, and you see things flying
Between the day and the night;
Swallows with spools of dark thread sewing the shadows
    together.

A circle swoop, and a quick parabola under the bridge arches
Where light pushes through;
A sudden turning upon itself of a thing in the air.
A dip to the water.

And you think:
'The swallows are flying so late!'

Swallows?

Dark air-life looping
Yet missing the pure loop . . .
A twitch, a twitter, an elastic shudder in flight
And serrated wings against the sky,
Like a glove, a black glove thrown up at the light,
And falling back.

Never swallows!
Bats!
The swallows are gone.

At a wavering instant the swallows give way to bats
By the Ponte Vecchio . . .
Changing guard.

Bats, and an uneasy creeping in one's scalp
As the bats swoop overhead!
Flying madly.

Pipistrello!
Black piper on an infinitesimal pipe.
Little lumps that fly in air and have voices indefinite, wildly
    vindictive;

Wings like bits of umbrella.

Bats!

Creatures that hang themselves up like an old rag, to sleep;
And disgustingly upside down.
Hanging upside down like rows of disgusting old rags
And grinning in their sleep.
Bats!

In China the bat is symbol of happiness.

Not for me!

RED GERANIUM AND GODLY
MIGNONETTE

IMAGINE that any mind ever *thought* a red geranium!
As if the redness of a red geranium could be anything but
 a sensual experience,
and as if sensual experience could take place before there
 were any senses.
We know that even God could not imagine the redness of a
 red geranium
nor the smell of mignonette
when geraniums were not, and mignonette neither.
And even when they were, even God would have to have a
 nose
to smell at the mignonette.
You can't imagine the Holy Ghost sniffing at cherry-pie
 heliotrope.
Or the Most High, during the coal age, cudgelling his mighty
 brains
even if he had any brains: straining his mighty mind
to think, among the moss and mud of lizards and mastodons
to think out, in the abstract, when all was twilit green and
 muddy:
'Now there shall be tum-tiddly-um, and tum-tiddly-um,
hey-presto! scarlet geranium!'

We know it couldn't be done.
But imagine, among the mud and the mastodons

god sighing and yearning with tremendous creative yearn-
    ing, in that dark green mess
oh, for some other beauty, some other beauty
that blossomed at last, red geranium, and mignonette.

BAVARIAN GENTIANS

NOT every man has gentians in his house
in Soft September, at slow, Sad Michaelmas.

Bavarian gentians, big and dark, only dark
darkening the day-time torch-like with the smoking blueness
    of Pluto's gloom,
ribbed and torch-like, with their blaze of darkness spread
    blue
down flattening into points, flattened under the sweep of
    white day
torch-flower of the blue-smoking darkness, Pluto's dark-blue
    daze,
black lamps from the halls of Dis, burning dark blue,
giving off darkness, blue darkness, as Demeter's pale lamps
    give off light,
lead me then, lead me the way.

Reach me a gentian, give me a torch
let me guide myself with the blue, forked torch of this flower
down the darker and darker stairs, where blue is darkened
    on blueness,
even where Persephone goes, just now, from the frosted
    September
to the sightless realm where darkness is awake upon the dark
and Persephone herself is but a voice
or a darkness invisible enfolded in the deeper dark
of the arms Plutonic, and pierced with the passion of dense
    gloom,
among the splendour of torches of darkness, shedding dark-
    ness on the lost bride and her groom.

LAWRENCE

THE SHIP OF DEATH

I

Now it is autumn and the falling fruit
and the long journey towards oblivion.

The apples falling like great drops of dew
to bruise themselves an exit from themselves.

And it is time to go, to bid farewell
to one's own self, and find an exit
from the fallen self.

II

Have you built your ship of death, O have you?
O build your ship of death, for you will need it.

The grim frost is at hand, when the apples will fall
thick, almost thundrous, on the hardened earth.

And death is on the air like a smell of ashes!
Ah! can't you smell it?
And in the bruised body, the frightened soul
finds itself shrinking, wincing from the cold
that blows upon it through the orifices.

III

And can a man his own quietus make
with a bare bodkin?

With daggers, bodkins, bullets, man can make
a bruise or break of exit for his life;
but is that a quietus, O tell me, is it quietus?

Surely not so! for how could murder, even self-murder
ever a quietus make?

IV

O let us talk of quiet that we know,
that we can know, the deep and lovely quiet
of a strong heart at peace!

How can we this, our own quietus, make?

V

Build then the ship of death, for you must take
the longest journey, to oblivion.

And die the death, the long and painful death
that lies between the old self and the new.

Already our bodies are fallen, bruised, badly bruised,
already our souls are oozing through the exit
of the cruel bruise.

Already the dark and endless ocean of the end
is washing in through the breaches of our wounds,
already the flood is upon us.

Oh build your ship of death, your little ark
and furnish it with food, with little cakes, and wine
for the dark flight down oblivion.

VI

Piecemeal the body dies, and the timid soul
has her footing washed away, as the dark flood rises.

We are dying, we are dying, we are all of us dying
and nothing will stay the death-flood rising within us
and soon it will rise on the world, on the outside world.

We are dying, we are dying, piecemeal our bodies are dying
and our strength leaves us,
and our soul cowers naked in the dark rain over the flood,
cowering in the last branches of the tree of our life.

VII

We are dying, we are dying, so all we can do
is now to be willing to die, and to build the ship
of death to carry the soul on the longest journey.
A little ship, with oars and food
and little dishes, and all accoutrements
fitting and ready for the departing soul.

Now launch the small ship, now as the body dies
and life departs, launch out, the fragile soul
in the fragile ship of courage, the ark of faith
with its store of food and little cooking pans
and change of clothes,
upon the flood's black waste
upon the waters of the end
upon the sea of death, where still we sail
darkly, for we cannot steer, and have no port.

There is no port, there is nowhere to go
only the deepening blackness darkening still
blacker upon the soundless, ungurgling flood
darkness at one with darkness, up and down
and sideways utterly dark, so there is no direction any more
and the little ship is there; yet she is gone.
She is not seen, for there is nothing to see her by.
She is gone! gone! and yet
somewhere she is there.
Nowhere!

VIII

And everything is gone, the body is gone
completely under, gone, entirely gone.
The upper darkness is heavy as the lower,
between them the little ship
is gone

It is the end, it is oblivion.

IX

And yet out of eternity, a thread
separates itself on the blackness,
a horizontal thread
that fumes a little with pallor upon the dark.

Is it illusion? or does the pallor fume
a little higher?
Ah wait, wait, for there's the dawn,
the cruel dawn of coming back to life
out of oblivion.

Wait, wait, the little ship
drifting, beneath the deathly ashy grey
of a flood-dawn.

Wait, wait! even so, a flush of yellow
and strangely, O chilled wan soul, a flush of rose.

A flush of rose, and the whole thing starts again.

x

The flood subsides, and the body, like a worn sea-shell
emerges strange and lovely.
And the little ship wings home, faltering and lapsing
on the pink flood,
and the frail soul steps out, into the house again
filling the heart with peace.

Swings the heart renewed with peace
even of oblivion.

Oh build your ship of death. Oh build it!
for you will need it.
For the voyage of oblivion awaits you.

ANDREW YOUNG

1885–1971

WILTSHIRE DOWNS

THE cuckoo's double note
Loosened like bubbles from a drowning throat
Floats through the air
In mockery of pipit, lark and stare.

The stable-boys thud by
Their horses slinging divots at the sky
And with bright hooves
Printing the sodden turf with lucky grooves.

YOUNG

As still as a windhover
A shepherd in his flapping coat leans over
His tall sheep-crook
And shearlings, tegs and yoes cons like a book.

And one tree-crowned long barrow
Stretched like a sow that has brought forth her farrow
Hides a king's bones
Lying like broken sticks among the stones.

A DEAD MOLE

STRONG-shouldered mole,
That so much lived below the ground,
Dug, fought and loved, hunted and fed,
For you to raise a mound
Was as for us to make a hole;
What wonder now that being dead
Your body lies here stout and square
Buried within the blue vault of the air?

CULBIN SANDS

HERE lay a fair fat land;
    But now its townships, kirks, graveyards
Beneath bald hills of sand
    Lie buried deep as Babylonian shards.

But gales may blow again;
    And like a sand-glass turned about
The hills in a dry rain
    Will flow away and the old land look out;

And where now hedgehog delves
    And conies hollow their long caves
Houses will build themselves
    And tombstones rewrite names on dead men's graves.

YOUNG

FIELD-GLASSES

THOUGH buds still speak in hints
And frozen ground has set the flints
As fast as precious stones
And birds perch on the boughs, silent as cones,

Suddenly waked from sloth
Young trees put on a ten year's growth
And stones double their size,
Drawn nearer through field-glasses' greater eyes.

Why I borrow their sight
Is not to give small birds a fright
Creeping up close by inches;
I make the trees come, bringing tits and finches.

I lift a field itself
As lightly as I might a shelf,
And the rooks do not rage
Caught for a moment in my crystal cage.

And while I stand and look,
Their private lives an open book,
I feel so privileged
My shoulders prick, as though they were half-fledged.

EDWIN MUIR

1887–1959

THE FACE

SEE me with all the terrors on my roads,
The crusted shipwrecks rotting in my seas,
And the untroubled oval of my face
That alters idly with the moonlike modes
And is unfathomably framed to please
And deck the angular bone with passing grace.

467

I should have worn a terror-mask, should be
A sight to frighten hope and faith away,
Half charnel field, half battle and rutting ground.
Instead I am a smiling summer sea
That sleeps while underneath from bound to bound
The sun- and star-shaped killers gorge and play.

THE CHILD DYING

UNFRIENDLY friendly universe,
I pack your stars into my purse,
And bid you, bid you so farewell.
That I can leave you, quite go out,
Go out, go out beyond all doubt,
My father says, is the miracle.

You are so great, and I so small:
I am nothing, you are all:
Being nothing, I can take this way.
Oh I need neither rise nor fall,
For when I do not move at all
I shall be out of all your day.

It's said some memory will remain
In the other place, grass in the rain,
Light on the land, sun on the sea,
A flitting grace, a phantom face,
But the world is out. There is no place
Where it and its ghost can ever be.

Father, father, I dread this air
Blown from the far side of despair,
The cold cold corner. What house, what hold,
What hand is there? I look and see
Nothing-filled eternity,
And the great round world grows weak and old.

Hold my hand, oh hold it fast—
I am changing!—until at last
My hand in yours no more will change,
Though yours change on. You here, I there,
So hand in hand, twin-leafed despair—
I did not know death was so strange.

FOR ANN SCOTT-MONCRIEFF

(1914–1943)

DEAR Ann, wherever you are
Since you lately learnt to die,
You are this unsetting star
That shines unchanged in my eye;
So near, inaccessible,
Absent and present so much
Since out of the world you fell,
Fell from hearing and touch—
So near. But your mortal tongue
Used for immortal use,
The grace of a woman young,
The air of an early muse,
The wealth of the chambered brow
And soaring flight of your eyes:
These are no longer now.
Death has a princely prize.

You who were Ann much more
Than others are that or this,
Extravagant over the score
To be what only is,
Would you not still say now
What you once used to say
Of the great Why and How,
On that or the other day?
For though of your heritage
The minority here began,
Now you have come of age
And are entirely Ann.

Under the years' assaults,
In the storm of good and bad,
You too had the faults
That Emily Brontë had,
Ills of body and soul,
Of sinner and saint and all
Who strive to make themselves whole,
Smashed to bits by the Fall.
Yet 'the world is a pleasant place'
I can hear your voice repeat,
While the sun shone in your face
Last summer in Princes Street.

ONE FOOT IN EDEN

ONE foot in Eden still, I stand
And look across the other land.
The world's great day is growing late,
Yet strange these fields that we have planted
So long with crops of love and hate.
Time's handiworks by time are haunted,
And nothing now can separate
The corn and tares compactly grown.
The armorial weed in stillness bound
About the stalk; these are our own.
Evil and good stand thick around
In the fields of charity and sin
Where we shall lead our harvest in.

Yet still from Eden springs the root
As clean as on the starting day.
Time takes the foliage and the fruit
And burns the archetypal leaf
To shapes of terror and of grief
Scattered along the winter way.
But famished field and blackened tree
Bear flowers in Eden never known.
Blossoms of grief and charity
Bloom in these darkened fields alone.

What had Eden ever to say
Of hope and faith and pity and love
Until was buried all its day
And memory found its treasure trove?
Strange blessings never in Paradise
Fall from these beclouded skies.

THE BROTHERS

LAST night I watched my brothers play,
The gentle and the reckless one,
In a field two yards away.
For half a century they were gone
Beyond the other side of care
To be among the peaceful dead.
Even in a dream how could I dare
Interrogate that happiness
So wildly spent yet never less?
For still they raced about the green
And were like two revolving suns;
A brightness poured from head to head,
So strong I could not see their eyes
Or look into their paradise.
What were they doing, the happy ones?
Yet where I was they once had been.

I thought, How could I be so dull,
Twenty thousand days ago,
Not to see they were beautiful?
I asked them, Were you really so
As you are now, that other day?
And the dream was soon away.

For then we played for victory
And not to make each other glad.
A darkness covered every head,
Frowns twisted the original face,
And through that mask we could not see
The beauty and the buried grace.

I have observed in foolish awe
The dateless mid-days of the law
And seen indifferent justice done
By everyone on everyone.
And in a vision I have seen
My brothers playing on the green.

EDITH SITWELL

1887–1964

HORNPIPE

SAILORS come
To the drum
Out of Babylon;
Hobby-horses
Foam, the dumb
Sky rhinoceros-glum

Watched the courses of the breakers' rocking-horses and
with Glaucis,
Lady Venus on the settee of the horsehair sea!
Where Lord Tennyson in laurels wrote a gloria free,
In a borealic iceberg came Victoria; she
Knew Prince Albert's tall memorial took the colours of the
floreal
And the borealic iceberg; floating on they see
New-arisen Madam Venus for whose sake from far
Came the fat and zebra'd emperor from Zanzibar
Where like golden bouquets lay far Asia, Africa, Cathay,
All laid before that shady lady by the fibroid Shah.
Captain Fracasse stout as any water-butt came, stood
With Sir Bacchus both a-drinking the black tarr'd grapes'
blood
Plucked among the tartan leafage
By the furry wind whose grief age
Could not wither—like a squirrel with a gold star-nut.

472

Queen Victoria sitting shocked upon the rocking-horse
Of a wave said to the Laureate, 'This minx of course
Is as sharp as any lynx and blacker-deeper than the drinks
    and quite as
Hot as any hottentot, without remorse!
          For the minx,'
               Said she,
                  'And the drinks,
                     You can see
Are hot as any hottentot and not the goods for me!'

MOST LOVELY SHADE

FOR ALICE BOUVERIE

MOST lovely Dark, my Æthiopia born
Of the shade's richest splendour, leave not me
Where in the pomp and splendour of the shade
The dark air's leafy plumes no more a lulling music made.

Dark is your fleece, and dark the airs that grew
Amid those weeping leaves.
Plantations of the East drop precious dew
That, ripened by the light, rich leaves perspire.
Such are the drops that from the dark airs' feathers flew.

Most lovely Shade . . . Syrinx and Dryope
And that smooth nymph that changed into a tree
Are dead . . . the shade, that Æthiopia, sees
Their beauty make more bright its treasuries—
Their amber blood in porphyry veins still grows
Deep in the dark secret of the rose
And the smooth stem of many a weeping tree,
And in your beauty grows.

Come then, my pomp and splendour of the shade,
Most lovely cloud that the hot sun made black
As dark-leaved airs,—
               Come then, O precious cloud,
Lean to my heart: no shade of a rich tree
Shall pour such splendour as your heart to me.

T. S. ELIOT

1888–1965

GERONTION

> *Thou hast nor youth nor age*
> *But as it were an after dinner sleep*
> *Dreaming of both.*

HERE I am, an old man in a dry month,
Being read to by a boy, waiting for rain.
I was neither at the hot gates
Nor fought in the warm rain
Nor knee deep in the salt marsh, heaving a cutlass,
Bitten by flies, fought.
My house is a decayed house,
And the jew squats on the window sill, the owner,
Spawned in some estaminet of Antwerp,
Blistered in Brussels, patched and peeled in London.
The goat coughs at night in the field overhead;
Rocks, moss, stonecrop, iron, merds.
The woman keeps the kitchen, makes tea,
Sneezes at evening, poking the peevish gutter.
                              I an old man,
A dull head among windy spaces.

Signs are taken for wonders. 'We would see a sign!'
The word within a word, unable to speak a word,
Swaddled with darkness. In the juvescence of the year
Came Christ the tiger

In depraved May, dogwood and chestnut, flowering judas,
To be eaten, to be divided, to be drunk
Among whispers; by Mr. Silvero
With caressing hands, at Limoges
Who walked all night in the next room;
By Hakagawa, bowing among the Titians;
By Madame de Tornquist, in the dark room
Shifting the candles; Fräulein von Kulp
Who turned in the hall, one hand on the door. Vacant
    shuttles

Weave the wind. I have no ghosts,
An old man in a draughty house
Under a windy knob.

After such knowledge, what forgiveness? Think now
History has many cunning passages, contrived corridors
And issues, deceives with whispering ambitions,
Guides us by vanities. Think now
She gives when our attention is distracted
And what she gives, gives with such supple confusions
That the giving famishes the craving. Gives too late
What's not believed in, or if still believed,
In memory only, reconsidered passion. Gives too soon
Into weak hands, what's thought can be dispensed with
Till the refusal propagates a fear. Think
Neither fear nor courage saves us. Unnatural vices
Are fathered by our heroism. Virtues
Are forced upon us by our impudent crimes.
These tears are shaken from the wrath-bearing tree.

The tiger springs in the new year. Us he devours. Think at
        last
We have not reached conclusion, when I
Stiffen in a rented house. Think at last
I have not made this show purposelessly
And it is not by any concitation
Of the backward devils.

I would meet you upon this honestly..
I that was near your heart was removed therefrom
To lose beauty in terror, terror in inquisition.
I have lost my passion: why should I need to keep it
Since what is kept must be adulterated?
I have lost my sight, smell, hearing, taste and touch:
How should I use them for your closer contact?

These with a thousand small deliberations
Protract the profit of their chilled delirium,
Excite the membrane, when the sense has cooled,
With pungent sauces, multiply variety

In a wilderness of mirrors. What will the spider do,
Suspend its operations, will the weevil
Delay? De Bailhache, Fresca, Mrs. Cammel, whirled
Beyond the circuit of the shuddering Bear
In fractured atoms. Gull against the wind, in the windy
    straits
Of Belle Isle, or running on the Horn,
White feathers in the snow, the Gulf claims,
And an old man driven by the Trades
To a sleepy corner.

                     Tenants of the house,
Thoughts of a dry brain in a dry season.

MARINA

Quis hic locus, quae
regio, quae mundi plaga?

WHAT seas what shores what grey rocks and what islands
What water lapping the bow
And scent of pine and the woodthrush singing through the fog
What images return
O my daughter.

Those who sharpen the tooth of the dog, meaning
Death
Those who glitter with the glory of the hummingbird,
    meaning
Death
Those who sit in the stye of contentment, meaning
Death
Those who suffer the ecstasy of the animals, meaning
Death

Are become unsubstantial, reduced by a wind,
A breath of pine, and the woodsong fog
By this grace dissolved in place

What is this face, less clear and clearer
The pulse in the arm, less strong and stronger—
Given or lent? more distant than stars and nearer than the eye

Whispers and small laughter between leaves and hurrying feet
Under sleep, where all the waters meet.
Bowsprit cracked with ice and paint cracked with heat.
I made this, I have forgotten
And remember.
The rigging weak and the canvas rotten
Between one June and another September.
Made this unknowing, half conscious, unknown, my own.
The garboard strake leaks, the seams need caulking.
This form, this face, this life
Living to live in a world of time beyond me; let me
Resign my life for this life, my speech for that unspoken,
The awakened, lips parted, the hope, the new ships.

What seas what shores what granite islands towards my
        timbers
And woodthrush calling through the fog
My daughter.

LANDSCAPES

I. NEW HAMPSHIRE

CHILDREN's voices in the orchard
Between the blossom- and the fruit-time:
Golden head, crimson head,
Between the green tip and the root.
Black wing, brown wing, hover over;
Twenty years and the spring is over;
To-day grieves, to-morrow grieves,
Cover me over, light-in-leaves;
Golden head, black wing,
Cling, swing,
Spring, sing,
Swing up into the apple-tree.

LITTLE GIDDING

I

MIDWINTER spring is its own season
Sempiternal though sodden towards sundown,
Suspended in time, between pole and tropic.
When the short day is brightest, with frost and fire,
The brief sun flames the ice, on pond and ditches,
In windless cold that is the heart's heat,
Reflecting in a watery mirror
A glare that is blindness in the early afternoon.
And glow more intense than blaze of branch, or brazier,
Stirs the dumb spirit: no wind, but pentecostal fire
In the dark time of the year. Between melting and freezing
The soul's sap quivers. There is no earth smell
Or smell of living thing. This is the spring time
But not in time's covenant. Now the hedgerow
Is blanched for an hour with transitory blossom
Of snow, a bloom more sudden
Than that of summer, neither budding nor fading,
Not in the scheme of generation.
Where is the summer, the unimaginable
Zero summer?

         If you came this way,
Taking the route you would be likely to take
From the place you would be likely to come from,
If you came this way in may time, you would find the hedges
White again, in May, with voluptuary sweetness.
It would be the same at the end of the journey,
If you came at night like a broken king,
If you came by day not knowing what you came for,
It would be the same, when you leave the rough road
And turn behind the pig-sty to the dull façade
And the tombstone. And what you thought you came for
Is only a shell, a husk of meaning
From which the purpose breaks only when it is fulfilled
If at all. Either you had no purpose
Or the purpose is beyond the end you figured
And is altered in fulfilment. There are other places

Which also are the world's end, some at the sea jaws,
Or over a dark lake, in a desert or a city—
But this is the nearest, in place and time,
Now and in England.

If you came this way,

Taking any route, starting from anywhere,
At any time or at any season,
It would always be the same: you would have to put off
Sense and notion. You are not here to verify,
Instruct yourself, or inform curiosity
Or carry report. You are here to kneel
Where prayer has been valid. And prayer is more
Than an order of words, the conscious occupation
Of the praying mind, or the sound of the voice praying.
And what the dead had no speech for, when living,
They can tell you, being dead: the communication
Of the dead is tongued with fire beyond the language of the
    living.
Here, the intersection of the timeless moment
Is England and nowhere. Never and always.

II

Ash on an old man's sleeve
Is all the ash the burnt roses leave.
Dust in the air suspended
Marks the place where a story ended.
Dust inbreathed was a house—
The wall, the wainscot and the mouse.
The death of hope and despair,
    This is the death of air.

There are flood and drouth
Over the eyes and in the mouth,
Dead water and dead sand
Contending for the upper hand.
The parched eviscerate soil
Gapes at the vanity of toil,
Laughs without mirth.
    This is the death of earth.

479

Water and fire succeed
The town, the pasture and the weed.
Water and fire deride
The sacrifice that we denied.
Water and fire shall rot
The marred foundations we forgot,
Of sanctuary and choir.
This is the death of water and fire.

In the uncertain hour before the morning
   Near the ending of interminable night
   At the recurrent end of the unending
After the dark dove with the flickering tongue
   Had passed below the horizon of his homing
   While the dead leaves still rattled on like tin
Over the asphalt where no other sound was
   Between three districts whence the smoke arose
   I met one walking, loitering and hurried
As if blown towards me like the metal leaves
   Before the urban dawn wind unresisting.
   And as I fixed upon the down-turned face
That pointed scrutiny with which we challenge
   The first-met stranger in the waning dusk
   I caught the sudden look of some dead master
Whom I had known, forgotten, half recalled
   Both one and many; in the brown baked features
   The eyes of a familiar compound ghost
Both intimate and unidentifiable.
   So I assumed a double part, and cried
   And heard another's voice cry: 'What! are *you* here?'
Although we were not. I was still the same,
   Knowing myself yet being someone other—
   And he a face still forming; yet the words sufficed
To compel the recognition they preceded.
   And so, compliant to the common wind,
   Too strange to each other for misunderstanding,
In concord at this intersection time
   Of meeting nowhere, no before and after,
   We trod the pavement in a dead patrol.

I said: 'The wonder that I feel is easy,
  Yet ease is cause of wonder. Therefore speak:
  I may not comprehend, may not remember.'
And he: 'I am not eager to rehearse
  My thought and theory which you have forgotten.
  These things have served their purpose: let them be.
So with your own, and pray they be forgiven
  By others, as I pray you to forgive
  Both bad and good. Last season's fruit is eaten
And the fullfed beast shall kick the empty pail.
  For last year's words belong to last year's language
  And next year's words await another voice.
But, as the passage now presents no hindrance
  To the spirit unappeased and peregrine
  Between two worlds become much like each other,
So I find words I never thought to speak
  In streets I never thought I should revisit
  When I left my body on a distant shore.
Since our concern was speech, and speech impelled us
  To purify the dialect of the tribe
  And urge the mind to aftersight and foresight,
Let me disclose the gifts reserved for age
  To set a crown upon your lifetime's effort.
  First, the cold friction of expiring sense
Without enchantment, offering no promise
  But bitter tastelessness of shadow fruit
  As body and soul begin to fall asunder.
Second, the conscious impotence of rage
  At human folly, and the laceration
  Of laughter at what ceases to amuse.
And last, the rending pain of re-enactment
  Of all that you have done, and been; the shame
  Of motives late revealed, and the awareness
Of things ill done and done to others' harm
  Which once you took for exercise of virtue.
  Then fools' approval stings, and honour stains.
From wrong to wrong the exasperated spirit
  Proceeds, unless restored by that refining fire
  Where you must move in measure, like a dancer.'

The day was breaking. In the disfigured street
   He left me, with a kind of valediction,
    And faded on the blowing of the horn.

III

There are three conditions which often look alike
Yet differ completely, flourish in the same hedgerow:
Attachment to self and to things and to persons, detachment
From self and from things and from persons; and, growing
     between them, indifference
Which resembles the others as death resembles life,
Being between two lives—unflowering, between
The live and the dead nettle. This is the use of memory:
For liberation—not less of love but expanding
Of love beyond desire, and so liberation
From the future as well as the past. Thus, love of a country
Begins as attachment to our own field of action
And comes to find that action of little importance
Though never indifferent. History may be servitude,
History may be freedom. See, now they vanish,
The faces and places, with the self which, as it could, loved
    them,
To become renowned, transfigured, in another pattern.

Sin is Behovely, but
All shall be well, and
All manner of thing shall be well.
If I think, again, of this place,
And of people, not wholly commendable,
Of no immediate kin or kindness,
But some of peculiar genius,
All touched by a common genius,
United in the strife which divided them;
If I think of a king at nightfall,
Of three men, and more, on the scaffold
And a few who died forgotten
In other places, here and abroad,
And of one who died blind and quiet,

Why should we celebrate
These dead men more than the dying?
It is not to ring the bell backward
Nor is it an incantation
To summon the spectre of a Rose.
We cannot revive old factions
We cannot restore old policies
Or follow an antique drum.
These men, and those who opposed them
And those whom they opposed
Accept the constitution of silence
And are folded in a single party.
Whatever we inherit from the fortunate
We have taken from the defeated
What they had to leave us—a symbol:
A symbol perfected in death.
And all shall be well and
All manner of thing shall be well
By the purification of the motive
In the ground of our beseeching.

IV

The dove descending breaks the air
With flame of incandescent terror
Of which the tongues declare
The one discharge from sin and error.
The only hope, or else despair
   Lies in the choice of pyre or pyre—
   To be redeemed from fire by fire.

Who then devised the torment? Love.
Love is the unfamiliar Name
Behind the hands that wove
The intolerable shirt of flame
Which human power cannot remove.
   We only live, only suspire
   Consumed by either fire or fire.

v

What we call the beginning is often the end
And to make an end is to make a beginning.
The end is where we start from. And every phrase
And sentence that is right (where every word is at home,
Taking its place to support the others,
The word neither diffident nor ostentatious,
An easy commerce of the old and the new,
The common word exact without vulgarity,
The formal word precise but not pedantic,
The complete consort dancing together)
Every phrase and every sentence is an end and a beginning,
Every poem an epitaph. And any action
Is a step to the block, to the fire, down the sea's throat
Or to an illegible stone: and that is where we start.
We die with the dying:
See, they depart, and we go with them.
We are born with the dead:
See, they return, and bring us with them.
The moment of the rose and the moment of the yew-tree
Are of equal duration. A people without history
Is not redeemed from time, for history is a pattern
Of timeless moments. So, while the light fails
On a winter's afternoon, in a secluded chapel
History is now and England.

 With the drawing of this Love and the voice of this
  Calling

 We shall not cease from exploration
And the end of all our exploring
Will be to arrive where we started
And know the place for the first time.
Through the unknown, remembered gate
When the last of earth left to discover
Is that which was the beginning;
At the source of the longest river
The voice of the hidden waterfall
And the children in the apple-tree

Not known, because not looked for
But heard, half-heard, in the stillness
Between two waves of the sea.
Quick now, here, now, always—
A condition of complete simplicity
(Costing not less than everything)
And all shall be well and
All manner of thing shall be well
When the tongues of flame are in-folded
Into the crowned knot of fire
And the fire and the rose are one.

HUGH MacDIARMID

b. 1892

O WHA'S THE BRIDE?

O WHA's the bride that cairries the bunch
O' thistles blinterin' white?
Her cuckold bridegroom little dreids
What he sall ken this nicht.

For closer than gudeman can come
And closer to'r than hersel',
Wha didna need her maidenheid
Has wrocht his purpose fell.

O wha's been here afore me, lass,
And hoo did he get in?
—*A man that deed or was I born
This evil thing has din.*

And left, as it were on a corpse,
Your maidenheid to me?
—*Nae lass, gudeman, sin' Time began
'S hed ony mair to gi'e.*

But I can gi'e ye kindness, lad,
And a pair o' willin' hands,
And you sall ha'e my breists like stars,
My limbs like willow wands.

And on my lips ye'll heed nae mair,
And in my hair forget,
The seed o' a' the men that in
My virgin womb ha'e met. . . .

AT MY FATHER'S GRAVE

THE sunlicht still on me, you row'd in clood,
We look upon each ither noo like hills
Across a valley. I'm nae mair your son.
It is my mind, nae son o' yours, that looks,
And the great darkness o' your death comes up
And equals it across the way.
A livin' man upon a deid man thinks
And ony sma'er thocht's impossible.

ROBERT GRAVES

b. 1895

LOVE WITHOUT HOPE

LOVE without hope, as when the young bird-catcher
Swept off his tall hat to the Squire's own daughter,
So let the imprisoned larks escape and fly
Singing about her head as she rode by.

THE COOL WEB

CHILDREN are dumb to say how hot the day is,
How hot the scent is of the summer rose,
How dreadful the black wastes of evening sky,
How dreadful the tall soldiers drumming by.

GRAVES

But we have speech, to chill the angry day,
And speech, to dull the rose's cruel scent.
We spell away the overhanging night,
We spell away the soldiers and the fright.

There's a cool web of language winds us in,
Retreat from too much joy or too much fear:
We grow sea-green at last and coldly die
In brininess and volubility.

But if we let our tongues lose self-possession,
Throwing off language and its watery clasp
Before our death, instead of when death comes,
Facing the wide glare of the children's day,
Facing the rose, the dark sky and the drums
We shall go mad no doubt and die that way.

VANITY

BE assured, the Dragon is not dead
But once more from the pools of peace
Shall rear his fabulous green head.

The flowers of innocence shall cease
And like a harp the wind shall roar
And the clouds shake an angry fleece.

'Here, here is certitude,' you swore,
'Below this lightning-blasted tree.
Where once it strikes, it strikes no more.

'Two lovers in one house agree.
The roof is tight, the walls unshaken.
As now, so must it always be.'

Such prophecies of joy awaken
The toad who dreams away the past
Under your hearth-stone, light forsaken,

Who knows that certitude at last
Must melt away in vanity—
No gate is fast, no door is fast—

That thunder bursts from the blue sky,
That gardens of the mind fall waste,
That fountains of the heart run dry.

PURE DEATH

WE looked, we loved, and therewith instantly
Death became terrible to you and me.
By love we disenthralled our natural terror
From every comfortable philosopher
Or tall, grey doctor of divinity:
Death stood at last in his true rank and order.

It happened soon, so wild of heart were we,
Exchange of gifts grew to a malady:
Their worth rose always higher on each side
Till there seemed nothing but ungivable pride
That yet remained ungiven, and this degree
Called a conclusion not to be denied.

Then we at last bethought ourselves, made shift
And simultaneously this final gift
Gave: each with shaking hands unlocks
The sinister, long, brass-bound coffin-box,
Unwraps pure death, with such bewilderment
As greeted our love's first acknowledgement.

SICK LOVE

O LOVE, be fed with apples while you may,
And feel the sun and go in royal array,
A smiling innocent on the heavenly causeway,

Though in what listening horror for the cry
That soars in outer blackness dismally,
The dumb blind beast, the paranoiac fury:

GRAVES

Be warm, enjoy the season, lift your head,
Exquisite in the pulse of tainted blood,
That shivering glory not to be despised.

Take your delight in momentariness,
Walk between dark and dark—a shining space
With the grave's narrowness, though not its peace.

CERTAIN MERCIES

Now must all satisfaction
Appear mere mitigation
Of an accepted curse?

Must we henceforth be grateful
That the guards, though spiteful,
Are slow of foot and wit?

That by night we may spread
Over the plank bed
A thin coverlet?

That the rusty water
In the unclean pitcher
Our thirst quenches?

That the rotten, detestable
Food is yet eatable
By us ravenous?

That the prison censor
Permits a weekly letter?
(We may write: 'we are well.')

That, with patience and deference,
We do not experience
The punishment cell?

That each new indignity
Defeats only the body,
Pampering the spirit
With obscure, proud merit?

THE THIEVES

LOVERS in the act dispense
With such meum-teum sense
As might warningly reveal
What they must not pick or steal,
And their nostrum is to say:
'I and you are both away.'

After, when they disentwine
You from me and yours from mine,
Neither can be certain who
Was that I whose mine was you.
To the act again they go
More completely not to know.

Theft is theft and raid is raid
Though reciprocally made.
Lovers, the conclusion is
Doubled sighs and jealousies
In a single heart that grieves
For lost honour among thieves.

COUNTING THE BEATS

You, love, and I,
(He whispers) you and I,
And if no more than only you and I
What care you or I?

Counting the beats,
Counting the slow heart beats,
The bleeding to death of time in slow heart beats,
Wakeful they lie.

Cloudless day,
Night, and a cloudless day,
Yet the huge storm will burst upon their heads one day
From a bitter sky.

GRAVES

Where shall we be,
(She whispers) where shall we be,
When death strikes home, O where then shall we be
Who were you and I?

Not there but here,
(He whispers) only here,
As we are, here, together, now and here,
Always you and I.

Counting the beats,
Counting the slow heart beats,
The bleeding to death of time in slow heart beats,
Wakeful they lie.

A PLEA TO BOYS AND GIRLS

You learned Lear's *Nonsense Rhymes* by heart, not rote;
   You learned Pope's *Iliad* by rote, not heart;
These terms should be distinguished if you quote
   My verses, children—keep them poles apart—
And call the man a liar who says I wrote
   All that I wrote in love, for love of art.

EDMUND BLUNDEN

1896–1974

THE MIDNIGHT SKATERS

THE hop-poles stand in cones,
   The icy pond lurks under,
The pole-tops steeple to the thrones
   Of stars, sound gulfs of wonder;
But not the tallest there, 'tis said,
Could fathom to this pond's black bed.

Then is not death at watch
   Within those secret waters?
What wants he but to catch
   Earth's heedless sons and daughters?
With but a crystal parapet
Between, he has his engines set.

Then on, blood shouts, on, on,
   Twirl, wheel and whip above him,
Dance on this ball-floor thin and wan,
   Use him as though you love him;
Court him, elude him, reel and pass,
And let him hate you through the glass.

REPORT ON EXPERIENCE

I HAVE been young, and now am not too old;
And I have seen the righteous forsaken,
His health, his honour and his quality taken.
   This is not what we were formerly told.

I have seen a green country, useful to the race,
Knocked silly with guns and mines, its villages vanished,
Even the last rat and last kestrel banished—
   God bless us all, this was peculiar grace.

I knew Seraphina; Nature gave her hue,
Glance, sympathy, note, like one from Eden.
I saw her smile warp, heard her lyric deaden;
   She turned to harlotry;—this I took to be new.

Say what you will, our God sees how they run.
These disillusions are His curious proving
That He loves humanity and will go on loving;
   Over there are faith, life, virtue in the sun.

AT THE GREAT WALL OF CHINA

PERCHED in a tower of this ancestral Wall,
Of man's huge warlike works the hugest still,
We scan its highway lashing hill to hill,
We dream its form as though we saw it all;

Where these few miles to thousands grow, and yet
Ever the one command and genius haunt
Each stairway, sally-port, loop, parapet,
In mute last answer to the invader's vaunt.

But I half know at this bleak turret here,
In snow-dimmed moonlight where sure answers quail,
This new-set sentry of a long dead year,
This boy almost, trembling lest he may fail
To espy the rueful raiders, and his mind
Torn with sharp love of the home left far behind.

AUSTIN CLARKE

1896–1974

PENAL LAW

Burn Ovid with the rest. Lovers will find
A hedge-school for themselves and learn by heart
All that the clergy banish from the mind,
When hands are joined and head bows in the dark.

MARRIAGE

Parents are sinful now, for they must whisper
Too much in the dark. Aye, there's the rub! What grace
Can snatch the small hours from that costly kiss?
Those who slip off the ring, try to be chaste
And when they cannot help it, steal the crumbs
From their own wedding breakfast, spare expense
And keep in warmth the children they have nourished.
But shall the sweet promise of the sacrament
Gladden the heart, if mortals calculate
Their pleasures by the calendar? Night-school
Of love where all, who learn to cheat, grow pale
With guilty hope at every change of moon!

ROY CAMPBELL

1902–1957

THE SERF

His naked skin clothed in the torrid mist
That puffs in smoke around the patient hooves,
The ploughman drives, a slow somnambulist,
And through the green his crimson furrow grooves.
His heart, more deeply than he wounds the plain,
Long by the rasping share of insult torn,
Red clod, to which the war-cry once was rain
And tribal spears the fatal sheaves of corn,
Lies fallow now. But as the turf divides
I see in the slow progress of his strides
Over the toppled clods and falling flowers,
The timeless, surly patience of the serf
That moves the nearest to the naked earth
And ploughs down palaces, and thrones, and towers.

HORSES ON THE CAMARGUE

TO A. F. TSCHIFFELY

In the grey wastes of dread,
The haunt of shattered gulls where nothing moves
But in a shroud of silence like the dead,
I heard a sudden harmony of hooves,
And, turning, saw afar
A hundred snowy horses unconfined,
The silver runaways of Neptune's car
Racing, spray-curled, like waves before the wind.
Sons of the Mistral, fleet
As him with whose strong gusts they love to flee,
Who shod the flying thunders on their feet
And plumed them with the snortings of the sea;
Theirs is no earthly breed
Who only haunt the verges of the earth
And only on the sea's salt herbage feed—
Surely the great white breakers gave them birth.

For when for years a slave,
A horse of the Camargue,[1] in alien lands,
Should catch some far-off fragrance of the wave
Carried far inland from his native sands,
Many have told the tale
Of how in fury, foaming at the rein,
He hurls his rider; and with lifted tail,
With coal-red eyes and cataracting mane,
Heading his course for home,
Though sixty foreign leagues before him sweep,
Will never rest until he breathes the foam
And hears the native thunder of the deep.
But when the great gusts rise
And lash their anger on these arid coasts,
When the scared gulls career with mournful cries
And whirl across the waste like driven ghosts:
When hail and fire converge,
The only souls to which they strike no pain
Are the white-crested fillies of the surge
And the white horses of the windy plain.
Then in their strength and pride
The stallions of the wilderness rejoice;
They feel their Master's trident[2] in their side,
And high and shrill they answer to his voice.
With white tails smoking free,
Long streaming manes, and arching necks, they show
Their kinship to their sisters of the sea—
And forward hurl their thunderbolts of snow.
Still out of hardship bred,
Spirits of power and beauty and delight
Have ever on such frugal pastures fed
And loved to course with tempests through the night.

---

[1] *Camargue*: pampa at the mouth of the Rhône which together
with the Sauvage and the desert Crau form a vast grazing ground
for thousands of wild cattle and horses. The Camarguais horses
are a distinct race.

[2] *Trident*: dual allusion to the trident of Neptune and that
carried by the guardians or cowboys of the Camargue.

AUTUMN

I LOVE to see, when leaves depart,
The clear anatomy arrive,
Winter, the paragon of art,
That kills all forms of life and feeling
Save what is pure and will survive.

Already now the clanging chains
Of geese are harnessed to the moon:
Stripped are the great sun-clouding planes:
And the dark pines, their own revealing,
Let in the needles of the noon.

Strained by the gale the olives whiten
Like hoary wrestlers bent with toil
And, with the vines, their branches lighten
To brim our vats where summer lingers
In the red froth and sun-gold oil.

Soon on our hearth's reviving pyre
Their rotted stems will crumble up:
And like a ruby, panting, fire,
The grape will redden on your fingers
Through the lit crystal of the cup.

ON PROFESSOR DRENNAN'S VERSE

WHO forced the Muse to this alliance?
A Man of more degrees than parts—
The jilted Bachelor of Science
And Widower of Arts.

ON SOME SOUTH AFRICAN NOVELISTS

YOU praise the firm restraint with which they write—
I'm with you there, of course:
They use the snaffle and the curb all right,
But where's the bloody horse?

C. DAY LEWIS

1904–1972

From O DREAMS, O DESTINATIONS

9

To travel like a bird, lightly to view
Deserts where stone gods founder in the sand,
Ocean embraced in a white sleep with land;
To escape time, always to start anew.
To settle like a bird, make one devoted
Gesture of permanence upon the spray
Of shaken stars and autumns; in a bay
Beyond the crestfallen surges to have floated.
Each is our wish. Alas, the bird flies blind,
Hooded by a dark sense of destination:
Her weight on the glass calm leaves no impression,
Her home is soon a basketful of wind.
Travellers, we're fabric of the road we go;
We settle, but like feathers on time's flow.

EMILY BRONTË

ALL is the same still. Earth and heaven locked in
A wrestling dream the seasons cannot break:
Shrill the wind tormenting my obdurate thorn trees,
Moss-rose and stone-chat silent in its wake.
Time has not altered here the rhythms I was rocked in,
Creation's throb and ache.

All is yet the same, for mine was a country
Stoic, unregenerate, beyond the power
Of man to mollify or God to disburden—
An ingrown landscape none might long endure
But one who could meet with a passion wilder-wintry
The scalding breath of the moor.

497

All is yet the same as when I roved the heather
Chained to a demon through the shrieking night,
Took him by the throat while he flailed my sibylline
Assenting breast, and won him to delight.
O truth and pain immortally bound together!
O lamp the storm made bright!

Still on those heights prophetic winds are raving,
Heath and harebell intone a plainsong grief:
'Shrink, soul of man, shrink into your valleys—
Too sharp that agony, that spring too brief!
Love, though your love is but the forged engraving
Of hope on a stricken leaf!'

Is there one whom blizzards warm and rains enkindle
And the bitterest furnace could no more refine?
Anywhere one too proud for consolation,
Burning for pure freedom so that he will pine,
Yes, to the grave without her? Let him mingle
His barren dust with mine.

But is there one who faithfully has planted
His seed of light in the heart's deepest scar?
When the night is darkest, when the wind is keenest,
He, he shall find upclimbing from afar
Over his pain my chaste, my disenchanted
And death-rebuking star.

NORMAN CAMERON

1905–1953

THE THESPIANS AT THERMOPYLAE

THE honours that the people give always
Pass to those use-besotted gentlemen
Whose numskull courage is a kind of fear,
A fear of thought and of the oafish mothers
('Or with your shield or on it') in their rear.
Spartans cannot retreat. Why, then, their praise
For going forward should be less than others'.

CAMERON

But we, actors and critics of one play,
Of sober-witted judgment, who could see
So many roads, and chose the Spartan way,
What has the popular report to say
Of us, the Thespians at Thermopylae?

THE COMPASSIONATE FOOL

My enemy had bidden me as guest.
His table all set out with wine and cake,
His ordered chairs, he to beguile me dressed
So neatly, moved my pity for his sake.

I knew it was an ambush, but could not
Leave him to eat his cake up by himself
And put his unused glasses on the shelf.
I made pretence of falling in his plot,

And trembled when in his anxiety
He bared it too absurdly to my view.
And even as he stabbed me through and through
I pitied him for his small strategy.

FORGIVE ME, SIRE

Forgive me, Sire, for cheating your intent,
That I, who should command a regiment,
Do amble amiably here, O God,
One of the neat ones in your awkward squad.

THREE LOVE POEMS

FROM A WOMAN TO A GREEDY LOVER

What is this recompense you'd have from me?
Melville asked no compassion of the sea.
Roll to and fro, forgotten in my wrack,
Love as you please—I owe you nothing back.

IN THE QUEEN'S ROOM

IN smoky outhouses of the court of love
I chattered, a recalcitrant underling
Living on scraps. 'Below stairs or above,
All's one,' I said. 'We valets have our fling.'

Now I am come, by a chance beyond reach,
Into your room, my body smoky and soiled
And on my tongue the taint of chattering speech,
Tell me, Queen, am I irredeemably spoiled?

SHEPHERDESS

ALL day my sheep have mingled with yours. They strayed
Into your valley seeking a change of ground.
Held and bemused with what they and I had found,
Pastures and wonders, heedlessly I delayed.

Now it is late. The tracks leading home are steep,
The stars and landmarks in your country are strange.
How can I take my sheep back over the range?
Shepherdess, show me now where I may sleep.

JOHN BETJEMAN

b. 1906

IRELAND WITH EMILY

BELLS are booming down the bohreens,
    White the mist along the grass.
Now the Julias, Maeves and Maureens
    Move between the fields to Mass.
Twisted trees of small green apple
Guard the decent whitewashed chapel,
Gilded gates and doorway grained
Pointed windows richly stained
    With many-coloured Munich glass.

See the black-shawled congregations
    On the broidered vestment gaze
Murmur past the painted stations
    As Thy Sacred Heart displays
Lush Kildare of scented meadows,
Roscommon, thin in ash-tree shadows,
And Westmeath the lake-reflected,
Spreading Leix the hill-protected,
    Kneeling all in silver haze?

In yews and woodbine, walls and guelder,
    Nettle-deep the faithful rest,
Winding leagues of flowering elder,
    Sycamore with ivy dressed,
Ruins in demesnes deserted,
Bog-surrounded bramble-skirted—
Townlands rich or townlands mean as
These, oh, counties of them screen us
    In the Kingdom of the West.

Stony seaboard, far and foreign,
    Stony hills poured over space,
Stony outcrop of the Burren,
    Stones in every fertile place,
Little fields with boulders dotted,
Grey-stone shoulders saffron-spotted,
Stone-walled cabins thatched with reeds,
Where a Stone Age people breeds
    The last of Europe's stone age race.

Has it held, the warm June weather?
    Draining shallow sea-pools dry,
When we bicycled together
    Down the bohreens fuchsia-high.
Till there rose, abrupt and lonely,
A ruined abbey, chancel only,
Lichen-crusted, time-befriended,
Soared the arches, splayed and splendid,
    Romanesque against the sky.

There in pinnacled protection,
  One extinguished family waits
A Church of Ireland resurrection
  By the broken, rusty gates.
Sheepswool, straw and droppings cover,
Graves of spinster, rake and lover,
Whose fantastic mausoleum
Sings its own seablown Te Deum,
  In and out the slipping slates.

THE COTTAGE HOSPITAL

At the end of a long-walled garden
  in a red provincial town,
A brick path led to a mulberry—
  scanty grass at its feet.
I lay under blackening branches
  where the mulberry leaves hung down
Sheltering ruby fruit globes
  from a Sunday-tea-time heat.
Apple and plum espaliers
  basked upon bricks of brown;
The air was swimming with insects,
  and children played in the street.

Out of this bright intentness
  into the mulberry shade
Musca domestica (housefly)
  swung from the August light
Slap into slithery rigging
  by the waiting spider made
Which spun the lithe elastic
  till the fly was shrouded tight.
Down came the hairy talons
  and horrible poison blade
And none of the garden noticed
  that fizzing, hopeless fight.

Say in what Cottage Hospital
    whose pale green walls resound
With the tap upon polished parquet
    of inflexible nurses' feet
Shall I myself be lying
    when they range the screen around?
And say shall I groan in dying,
    as I twist the sweaty sheet?
Or gasp for breath uncrying,
    as I feel my senses drown'd
While the air is swimming with insects
    and children play in the street?

RONALD BOTTRALL

b. 1906

ICARUS

In his father's face flying
He soared until the cities of the Aegean
Opened like bloodvessels lying
Under a microscope. End on
He saw below the trunks of trees
While space-time flowered in his sunward eyes.
His feathered arms, extension
Of nimble thoughts, pride of invention,
Were lifting him high above man.
'And if I fly,'
He said, 'to the source of mortal energy
I shall capture the receipt
To administer light and heat.'
But sunlight to all eyes is not bearable
Or sunheat to all blood.
His motion turned to earth, unable
To sustain its presumptuous mood.
Falling he saw the cantilevered birds,
Their great humerus muscles bearing
Them in their spacious veering

Over shores and sherds
Over swords and words.
Like a detached leaf, feeble
In the wind, he fell,
A multitude of molecules
Organized in equal and parallel
Velocities (according to the rules
Of motion) to seek the ground.
And on the slope above the sea
The hard-handed peasants go their round
Turning the soil, blind to the body
Ambitious and viable, whose pride
Will leave no trace in the quenching tide.

WILLIAM EMPSON

b. 1906

TO AN OLD LADY

RIPENESS is all; her in her cooling planet
Revere; do not presume to think her wasted.
Project her no projectile, plan nor man it;
Gods cool in turn, by the sun long outlasted.

Our earth alone given no name of god
Gives, too, no hold for such a leap to aid her;
Landing, you break some palace and séem odd;
Bees sting their need, the keeper's queen invader.

No, to your telescope; spy out the land;
Watch while her ritual is still to see,
Still stand her temples emptying in the sand
Whose waves o'erthrew their crumbled tracery;

Still stand uncalled-on her soul's appanage;
Much social detail whose successor fades,
Wit used to run a house and to play Bridge,
And tragic fervour, to dismiss her maids.

Years her precession do not throw from gear.
She reads a compass certain of her pole;
Confident, finds no confines on her sphere,
Whose failing crops are in her sole control.

Stars how much further from me fill my night.
Strange that she too should be inaccessible,
Who shares my sun. He curtains her from sight,
And but in darkness is she visible.

THIS LAST PAIN

THIS last pain for the damned the Fathers found:
'They knew the bliss with which they were not crowned.'
    Such, but on earth, let me foretell,
    Is all, of heaven or of hell.

Man, as the prying housemaid of the soul,
May know her happiness by eye to hole:
    He's safe; the key is lost; he knows
    Door will not open, nor hole close.

'What is conceivable can happen too,'
Said Wittgenstein, who had not dreamt of you;
    But wisely; if we worked it long
    We should forget where it was wrong.

Those thorns are crowns which, woven into knots,
Crackle under and soon boil fools' pots;
    And no man's watching, wise and long,
    Would ever stare them into song.

Thorns burn to a consistent ash, like man;
A splendid cleanser for the frying-pan:
    And those who leap from pan to fire
    Should this brave opposite admire.

All those large dreams by which men long live well
Are magic-lanterned on the smoke of hell;
    This then is real, I have implied,
    A painted, small, transparent slide.

These the inventive can hand-paint at leisure,
Or most emporia would stock our measure;
    And feasting in their dappled shade
    We should forget how they were made.

Feign then what's by a decent tact believed
And act that state is only so conceived,
    And build an edifice of form
    For house where phantoms may keep warm.

Imagine, then, by miracle, with me,
(Ambiguous gifts, as what gods give must be)
    What could not possibly be there,
    And learn a style from a despair.

VERNON WATKINS

1906–1967

THE HERON

THE cloud-backed heron will not move:
He stares into the stream.
He stands unfaltering while the gulls
And oyster-catchers scream.
He does not hear, he cannot see
The great white horses of the sea,
But fixes eyes on stillness
Below their flying team.

How long will he remain, how long
Have the grey woods been green?
The sky and the reflected sky,
Their glass he has not seen,
But silent as a speck of sand
Interpreting the sea and land,
His fall pulls down the fabric
Of all that windy scene.

Sailing with clouds and woods behind,
Pausing in leisured flight,
He stepped, alighting on a stone,
Dropped from the stars of night.
He stood there unconcerned with day,
Deaf to the tumult of the bay,
Watching a stone in water,
A fish's hidden light.

Sharp rocks drive back the breaking waves,
Confusing sea with air.
Bundles of spray blown mountain-high
Have left the shingle bare.
A shipwrecked anchor wedged by rocks,
Loosed by the thundering equinox,
Divides the herded waters,
The stallion and his mare.

Yet no distraction breaks the watch
Of that time-killing bird.
He stands unmoving on the stone;
Since dawn he has not stirred.
Calamity about him cries,
But he has fixed his golden eyes
On water's crooked tablet,
On light's reflected word.

PEACE IN THE WELSH HILLS

CALM is the landscape when the storm has passed.
Brighter the fields, and fresh with fallen rain.
Where gales beat out new colour from the hills
Rivers fly faster, and upon their banks
Birds preen their wings, and irises revive.
Not so the cities burnt alive with fire
Of man's destruction: when their smoke is spent,
No phoenix rises from the ruined walls.

I ponder now the grief of many rooms.
Was it a dream, that age, when fingers found
A satisfaction sleeping in dumb stone,
When walls were built responding to the touch

WATKINS

In whose high gables, in the lengthening days,
Martins would nest? Though crops, though lives, would fail,
Though friends dispersed, unchanged the walls would stay,
And still those wings return to build in Spring.

Here, where the earth is green, where heaven is true
Opening the windows, touched with earliest dawn,
In the first frost of cool September days,
Chrysanthemum weather, presaging great birth,
Who in his heart could murmur or complain:
'The light we look for is not in this land'?
That light is present, and that distant time
Is always here, continually redeemed.

There is a city we must build with joy
Exactly where the fallen city sleeps.
There is one road through village, town and field,
On whose robust foundations Chaucer dreamed
A ride could wed the opposites in man.
There proud walls may endure, and low walls feed
The imagination if they have a vine
Or shadowy barn made rich with gathered corn.

Great mansions fear from their surrounding trees
The invasion of a wintry desolation
Filling their room with leaves. And cottages
Bring the sky down as flickering candles do,
Leaning on their own shadows. I have seen
Vases and polished brass reflect black windows
And draw the ceiling down to their vibrations.
Thick, deep, and white-washed, like a bank of snow.

To live entwined in pastoral loveliness
May rest the eyes, throw pictures on the mind,
But most we need a metaphor of stone
Such as those painters had whose mountain-cities
Cast long low shadows on the Umbrian hills.
There, in some courtyard on the cobbled stone,
A fountain plays, and through a cherub's mouth
Ages are linked by water in the sunlight.

All of good faith that fountain may recall,
Woman, musician, boy, or else a scholar
Reading a Latin book. They seem distinct,
And yet are one, because tranquillity
Affirms the Judgement. So, in these Welsh hills,
I marvel, waking from a dream of stone,
That such a peace surrounds me, while the city
For which all long has never yet been built.

W. H. AUDEN

1907–1973

CHORUS

Doom is dark and deeper than any sea-dingle.
Upon what man it fall
In spring, day-wishing flowers appearing,
Avalanche sliding, white snow from rock-face,
That he should leave his house,
No cloud-soft hand can hold him, restraint by women;
But ever that man goes
Through place-keepers, through forest trees,
A stranger to strangers over undried sea,
Houses for fishes, suffocating water,
Or lonely on fell as chat,
By pot-holed becks
A bird stone-haunting, an unquiet bird.

There head falls forward, fatigued at evening,
And dreams of home,
Waving from window, spread of welcome,
Kissing of wife under single sheet;
But waking sees
Bird-flocks nameless to him, through doorway voices
Of new men making another love.

Save him from hostile capture,
From sudden tiger's spring at corner;
Protect his house,
His anxious house where days are counted

509

From thunderbolt protect,
From gradual ruin spreading like a stain;
Converting number from vague to certain,
Bring joy, bring day of his returning,
Lucky with day approaching, with leaning dawn.

SEASCAPE

LOOK, stranger, on this island now
The leaping light for your delight discovers,
Stand stable here
And silent be,
That through the channels of the ear
May wander like a river
The swaying sound of the sea.

Here at a small field's ending pause
When the chalk wall falls to the foam and its tall ledges
Oppose the pluck
And knock of the tide,
And the shingle scrambles after the suck-
-ing surf,
And a gull lodges
A moment on its sheer side.

Far off like floating seeds the ships
Diverge on urgent voluntary errands,
And this full view
Indeed may enter
And move in memory as now these clouds do,
That pass the harbour mirror
And all the summer through the water saunter.

MUSÉE DES BEAUX ARTS

ABOUT suffering they were never wrong,
The Old Masters: how well they understood
Its human position; how it takes place
While someone else is eating or opening a window or just
     walking dully along;

How, when the aged are reverently, passionately waiting
For the miraculous birth, there always must be
Children who did not specially want it to happen, skating
On a pond at the edge of the wood:
     They never forgot
That even the dreadful martyrdom must run its course
Anyhow in a corner, some untidy spot
Where the dogs go on with their doggy life and the torturer's
          horse
Scratches its innocent behind on a tree.

In Brueghel's *Icarus*, for instance: how everything turns
          away
Quite leisurely from the disaster; the ploughman may
Have heard the splash, the forsaken cry,
But for him it was not an important failure; the sun shone
As it had to on the white legs disappearing into the green
Water; and the expensive delicate ship that must have seen
Something amazing, a boy falling out of the sky,
Had somewhere to get to and sailed calmly on.

SONG

Deftly, admiral, cast your fly
     Into the slow deep hover,
Till the wise old trout mistake and die;
     Salt are the deeps that cover
     The glittering fleets you led,
          White is your head.

Read on, ambassador, engrossed
     In your favourite Stendhal;
The Outer Provinces are lost,
     Unshaven horsemen swill
     The great wines of the Châteaux
          Where you danced long ago.

Do not turn, do not lift, your eyes
Toward the still pair standing
On the bridge between your properties,
Indifferent to your minding:
In its glory, in its power,
This is their hour.

Nothing your strength, your skill, could do
Can alter their embrace
Or dispersuade the Furies who
At the appointed place
With claw and dreadful brow
Wait for them now.

THE SHIELD OF ACHILLES

SHE looked over his shoulder
For vines and olive trees,
Marble well-governed cities
And ships upon untamed seas,
But there on the shining metal
His hands had put instead
An artificial wilderness
And a sky like lead.

A plain without a feature, bare and brown,
No blade of grass, no sign of neighbourhood,
Nothing to eat and nowhere to sit down,
Yet, congregated on its blankness, stood
An unintelligible multitude.
A million eyes, a million boots in line,
Without expression, waiting for a sign.

Out of the air a voice without a face
Proved by statistics that some cause was just
In tones as dry and level as the place:
No one was cheered and nothing was discussed;
Column by column in a cloud of dust
They marched away enduring a belief
Whose logic brought them, somewhere else, to grief.

She looked over his shoulder
    For ritual pieties,
White flower-garlanded heifers,
    Libation and sacrifice,
But there on the shining metal
    Where the altar should have been,
She saw by his flickering forge-light
    Quite another scene.

Barbed wire enclosed an arbitrary spot
    Where bored officials lounged (one cracked a joke)
And sentries sweated for the day was hot:
    A crowd of ordinary decent folk
    Watched from without and neither moved nor spoke
As three pale figures were led forth and bound
To three posts driven upright in the ground.

The mass and majesty of this world, all
    That carries weight and always weighs the same
Lay in the hands of others; they were small
    And could not hope for help and no help came:
    What their foes liked to do was done, their shame
Was all the worst could wish; they lost their pride
And died as men before their bodies died.

She looked over his shoulder
    For athletes at their games,
Men and women in a dance
    Moving their sweet limbs
Quick, quick, to music,
    But there on the shining shield
His hands had set no dancing-floor
    But a weed-choked field.

A ragged urchin, aimless and alone,
    Loitered about that vacancy, a bird
Flew up to safety from his well-aimed stone:
    That girls are raped, that two boys knife a third,
    Were axioms to him, who'd never heard
Of any world where promises were kept,
Or one could weep because another wept.

The thin-lipped armourer,
　　Hephaestos hobbled away,
Thetis of the shining breasts
　　Cried out in dismay
At what the god had wrought
　　To please her son, the strong
Iron-hearted man-slaying Achilles
　　Who would not live long.

PATRICK KAVANAGH

1907–1967

OCTOBER

O LEAFY yellowness you create for me
A world that was and now is poised above time,
I do not need to puzzle out Eternity
As I walk this arboreal street on the edge of a town.
The breeze too, even the temperature
And pattern of movement is precisely the same
As broke my heart for youth passing. Now I am sure
Of something. Something will be mine wherever I am.
I want to throw myself on the public street without caring
For anything but the prayering that the earth offers.
It is October over all my life and the light is staring
As it caught me once in a plantation by the fox coverts.
A man is ploughing ground for winter wheat
And my nineteen years weigh heavily on my feet.

TO THE MAN AFTER THE HARROW

Now leave the check-reins slack,
　The seed is flying far today—
The seed like stars against the black
　Eternity of April clay.

This seed is potent as the seed
　Of knowledge in the Hebrew Book,
So drive your horses in the creed
　Of God the Father as a stook.

KAVANAGH

Forget the men on Brady's hill.
Forget what Brady's boy may say.
For destiny will not fulfil
Unless you let the harrow play.

Forget the worm's opinion, too,
Of hooves and pointed harrow-pins,
For you are driving your horses through
The mist where Genesis begins.

LOUIS MacNEICE

1907–1963

THE SUNLIGHT ON THE GARDEN

The sunlight on the garden
Hardens and grows cold,
We cannot cage the minute
Within its nets of gold,
When all is told
We cannot beg for pardon.

Our freedom as free lances
Advances towards its end;
The earth compels, upon it
Sonnets and birds descend;
And soon, my friend,
We shall have no time for dances.

The sky was good for flying
Defying the church bells
And every evil iron
Siren and what it tells:
The earth compels,
We are dying, Egypt, dying

MacNEICE

And not expecting pardon,
Hardened in heart anew,
But glad to have sat under
Thunder and rain with you,
And grateful too
For sunlight on the garden.

BAGPIPE MUSIC

It's no go the merrygoround, it's no go the rickshaw,
All we want is a limousine and a ticket for the peepshow.
Their knickers are made of crêpe-de-chine, their shoes are
made of python,
Their halls are lined with tiger rugs and their walls with
heads of bison.

John MacDonald found a corpse, put it under the sofa,
Waited till it came to life and hit it with a poker,
Sold its eyes for souvenirs, sold its blood for whiskey,
Kept its bones for dumb-bells to use when he was fifty.

It's no go the Yogi-Man, it's no go Blavatsky,
All we want is a bank balance and a bit of skirt in a taxi.

Annie MacDougall went to milk, caught her foot in the
heather,
Woke to hear a dance record playing of Old Vienna.
It's no go your maidenheads, it's no go your culture,
All we want is a Dunlop tyre and the devil mend the
puncture.

The Laird o' Phelps spent Hogmanay declaring he was
sober,
Counted his feet to prove the fact and found he had one
foot over.
Mrs. Carmichael had her fifth, looked at the job with repul-
sion,
Said to the midwife 'Take it away; I'm through with over-
production'.

516

MacNEICE

It's no go the gossip column, it's no go the Ceilidh,
All we want is a mother's help and a sugar-stick for the baby.

Willie Murray cut his thumb, couldn't count the damage,
Took the hide of an Ayrshire cow and used it for a bandage.
His brother caught three hundred cran when the seas were
      lavish,
Threw the bleeders back in the sea and went upon the
      parish.

It's no go the Herring Board, it's no go the Bible,
All we want is a packet of fags when our hands are idle.

It's no go the picture palace, it's no go the stadium,
It's no go the country cot with a pot of pink geraniums,
It's no go the Government grants, it's no go the elections,
Sit on your arse for fifty years and hang your hat on a
      pension.

It's no go my honey love, it's no go my poppet;
Work your hands from day to day, the winds will blow the
      profit.
The glass is falling hour by hour, the glass will fall for ever,
But if you break the bloody glass you won't hold up the
      weather.

PRAYER BEFORE BIRTH

I am not yet born; O hear me.
Let not the bloodsucking bat or the rat or the stoat or the
      club-footed ghoul come near me.

I am not yet born, console me.
I fear that the human race may with tall walls wall me,
      with strong drugs dope me, with wise lies lure me,
         on black racks rack me, in blood-baths roll me.

I am not yet born; provide me
With water to dandle me, grass to grow for me, trees to talk
      to me, sky to sing to me, birds and a white light
         in the back of my mind to guide me.

517

I am not yet born; forgive me
For the sins that in me the world shall commit, my words
    when they speak me, my thoughts when they think me,
      my treason engendered by traitors beyond me,
        my life when they murder by means of my
          hands, my death when they live me.

I am not yet born; rehearse me
In the parts I must play and the cues I must take when
    old men lecture me, bureaucrats hector me, mountains
      frown at me, lovers laugh at me, the white
        waves call me to folly and the desert calls
          me to doom and the beggar refuses
            my gift and my children curse me.

I am not yet born; O hear me,
Let not the man who is beast or who thinks he is God
    come near me.

I am not yet born; O fill me
With strength against those who would freeze my
    humanity, would dragoon me into a lethal automaton,
      would make me a cog in a machine, a thing with
        one face, a thing, and against all those
          who would dissipate my entirety, would
            blow me like thistledown hither and
              thither or hither and thither
                like water held in the
                  hands would spill me.

Let them not make me a stone and let them not spill me.
Otherwise kill me.

BERNARD SPENCER

1909–1963

A SPRING WIND

Spring shakes the windows; doors whang to,
the sky moves half in dark and half
shining like knives: upon this table

SPENCER

Elytis' poems lie
uttering the tangle of sea, the 'breathing caves'
and the fling of Aegean waves.

I am caught here in this scattering, vagrant season
where telephones ring;
and all Greece goes through me
as the wind goes searching through the city streets.
Greece, I have so much loved you
out of all reason;
that this unquiet time
its budding and its pride
the news and the nostalgia of Spring
swing towards you their tide:

Towards the windmills on the islands;
Alefkandra loved by winds,
luminous with foam and morning, Athens,
her blinded marble heads,
her pepper-trees, the bare heels of her girls,
old songs that bubble up from where thought starts,
Greek music treading like the beat of hearts;
haunted Seferis, smiling, playing with beads.

And since especially at this time
statues and blossoms, birth and death require
we give account of manhood and of youth,
the wind that whirls through London also rings
with the bang and echo of the Easter gun,
as in days gone,
from where the pilgrims' torches climb
over a darkening town
to set that bony peak Lykahvetoss,
Athens, and all the opening year on fire.

THE RENDEZVOUS

I TAKE the twist-about, empty street
—balconies and drapes of shadow
—and glimpse chalk slogans on each wall,
(now governments have done their work)

519

that the fanatic or the duped,
even children are taught to scrawl:
the patriotic, 'Tyrants', 'Vengeance',
'Death to', etc.

                    Hooped
the barbed wire lies to left and right
since glass crashing, cars on fire,
since the mob howled loose that night,
gawky, rusty, useful wire
with little dirty fangs each way,
(what craftsman makes this fright?).
Black on that chemist's lighted window
steel helmets, rifle tops. I sense
the full moon wild upon my back
and count the weeks. Not long from this
the time we named comes round.

                    And true
to loves love never thought of, here
with bayonet and with tearing fence,
with cry of crowds and doors slammed to,
waits the once known and dear, once chosen
city of our rendezvous.

STEPHEN SPENDER

b. 1909

ICE

(TO M——)

SHE came in from the snowing air
Where icicle-hung architecture
Strung white fleece round the Baroque square.
I saw her face freeze in her fur,
Then my lips ran to her with fire
From the chimney corner of the room,
Where I had waited in my chair.

I kissed their heat against her skin
And watched the red make the white bloom,
While, at my care, her smiling eyes
Shone with brilliance of the ice
Outside, whose dazzling they brought in.
    That day, until this, I forgot.
How is it now I so remember
Who, when she came indoors, saw not
The passion of her white December?

MISSING MY DAUGHTER

THIS wall-paper has lines that rise
Upright like bars, and overhead,
The ceiling's patterned with red roses.
On the wall opposite the bed
The staring looking-glass encloses
Six roses in its white of eyes.

Here at my desk, with note-book open
Missing my daughter, makes those bars
Draw their lines upward through my mind.
This blank page stares at me like glass
Where stared-at roses wish to pass
Through petalling of my pen.

An hour ago, there came an image
Of a beast that pressed its muzzle
Between bars. Next, through tick and tock
Of the reiterating clock
A second glared with the white dazzle
Of deserts. The door, in a green mirage,

Opened. In my daughter came.
Her eyes were wide as those she has,
The round gaze of her childhood was
White as the distance in the glass
Or on a white page, a white poem.
The roses raced around her name.

NORMAN MacCAIG

b. 1910

TOO BRIGHT A DAY

I LIVE invisible (in my whole sky
That is the light of where you are)
Calling the night to welcome my
Sad and procrastinating star,
Which will not leave, as it must do,
Its short conjunction here with you.

Light so engrossing cannot show
More than itself. I fade in it
And have no shadow even to throw.
But when I leave you, I'll commit
Such darkness on myself you'll stare
At the great conflagration there.

EGO

STARE at the stars, the stars say. Look at me,
Whispers the water and protests the tree;
The rose is its own exclamation and
Frost touches with an insinuating hand.
Yet they prefigure to my human mind
Categories only of a human kind.

I see a rose, that strange thing, and what's there
But a seeming something coloured on the air
With the transparencies that make up me,
Thickened to existence by my notice. Tree
And star are ways of finding out what I
Mean in a text composed of earth and sky

What reason to believe this, any more
Than that I am myself a metaphor
That's noticed in the researches of a rose
And self-instructs a star? Time only knows
Creation's mad cross-purposes and will
Destroy the evidence to keep them secret still.

SPATE IN WINTER MIDNIGHT

THE streams fall down and through the darkness bear
Such wild and shaking hair,
Such looks beyond a cool surmise,
Such lamentable uproar from night skies
As turn the owl from honey of blood and make
Great stags stand still to hear the darkness shake.

Through Troys of bracken and Babel towers of rocks
Shrinks now the looting fox,
Fearful to touch the thudding ground
And flattened to it by the mastering sound.
And roebuck stilt and leap sideways; their skin
Twitches like water on the fear within.

Black hills are slashed white with this falling grace
Whose violence buckles space
To a sheet-iron thunder. This
Is noise made universe, whose still centre is
Where the cold adder sleeps in his small bed,
Curled neatly round his neat and evil head.

DEMETRIOS CAPETANAKIS

1912–1944

ABEL

MY brother Cain, the wounded, liked to sit
Brushing my shoulder, by the staring water
Of life, or death, in cinemas half-lit
By scenes of peace that always turned to slaughter.

He liked to talk to me. His eager voice
Whispered the puzzle of his bleeding thirst,
Or prayed me not to make my final choice,
Unless we had a chat about it first.

CAPETANAKIS

And then he chose the final pain for me.
I do not blame his nature: he's my brother;
Nor what you call the times: our love was free,
Would be the same at any time; but rather

The ageless ambiguity of things
Which makes our life mean death, our love be hate.
My blood that streams across the bedroom sings:
'I am my brother opening the gate!'

THE ISLES OF GREECE

THE sun is not in love with us,
Nor the corrosive sea;
Yet both will burn our dried-up flesh
In deep intimacy

With stubborn tongues of briny death
And heavy snakes of fire,
Which writhe and hiss and crack the Greek
Myth of the singing lyre.

The dusty fig-tree cries for help,
Two peasants kill one snake,
While in our rocky heart the gods
Of marble hush and break.

After long ages all our love
Became a barren fever,
Which makes us glow in martyrdom
More beautiful than ever.

Yet when the burning horses force
Apollo to dismount
And rest with us at last, he says
That beauty does not count.

LAWRENCE DURRELL

b. 1912

NEMEA

A song in the valley of Nemea:
Sing quiet, quite quiet here.

Song for the brides of Argos
Combing the swarms of golden hair:
Quite quiet, quiet there.

Under the rolling comb of grass,
The sword outrusts the golden helm.

Agamemnon under tumulus serene
Outsmiles the jury of skeletons:
Cool under cumulus the lion queen:

Only the drum can celebrate,
Only the adjective outlive them.

A song in the valley of Nemea:
Sing quiet, quiet, quiet here.

Tone of the frog in the empty well,
Drone of the bald bee on the cold skull,

Quiet, Quiet, Quiet.

SARAJEVO

BOSNIA. November. And the mountain roads
Earthbound but matching perfectly these long
And passionate self-communings counter-march,
Balanced on scarps of trap, ramble or blunder
Over traverses of cloud: and here they move,
Mule-teams like insects harnessed by a bell
Upon the leaf-edge of a winter sky,

And down at last into this lap of stone
Between four cataracts of rock: a town
Peopled by sleepy eagles, whispering only
Of the sunburnt herdsman's hopeless ploy:
A sterile earth quickened by shards of rock
Where nothing grows, not even in his sleep,

Where minarets have twisted up like sugar
And a river, curdled with blond ice, drives on
Tinkling among the mule-teams and the mountaineers,
Under the bridges and the wooden trellises
Which tame the air and promise us a peace
Harmless with nightingales. None are singing now.

No history much? Perhaps. Only this ominous
Dark beauty flowering under veils,
Trapped in the spectrum of a dying style:
A village like an instinct left to rust,
Composed around the echo of a pistol-shot.

ROY FULLER

b. 1912

THE IMAGE

A SPIDER in the bath. The image noted:
Significant maybe but surely cryptic.
A creature motionless and rather bloated,
The barriers shining, vertical and white:
Passing concern, and pity mixed with spite.

Next day with some surprise one finds it there.
It seems to have moved an inch or two, perhaps.
It starts to take on that familiar air
Of prisoners for whom time is erratic:
The filthy aunt forgotten in the attic.

FULLER

Quite obviously it came up through the waste,
Rejects through ignorance or apathy
That passage back. The problem must be faced;
And life go on though strange intruders stir
Among its ordinary furniture.

One jibs at murder, so a sheet of paper
Is slipped beneath the accommodating legs.
The bathroom window shows for the escaper
The lighted lanterns of laburnum hung
In copper beeches—on which scene it's flung.

We certainly would like thus easily
To cast out of the house all suffering things.
But sadness and responsibility
For our own kind lives in the image noted:
A half-loved creature, motionless and bloated.

From MYTHOLOGICAL SONNETS

VIII

SUNS in a skein, the uncut stones of night,
Calm planets rising, violet, golden, red—
Bear names evolved from man's enormous head
Of gods who govern battle, rivers, flight,
And goddesses of science and delight;
Arranged in the mortal shapes of those who bled
To found a dynasty or in great dread
Slept with their destiny, full-breasted, white.

But long before stout Venus, clanking Mars,
What appellations had the eternal stars?
When, cheek by jowl with burial pits, rank dens
Lay open to the dark, and dwarfish men
Stared under huge brow-ridges, wits awry,
What fearful monsters slouched about the sky?

F. T. PRINCE

b. 1912

THE QUESTION

AND so we two came where the rest have come,
To where each dreamed, each drew, the other home
From all distractions to the other's breast,
Where each had found, each was, the wild bird's nest.
For that we came, and knew that we must know
The thing we knew of but we did not know.

We said then, What if this were now no more
Than a faint shade of what we dreamed before?
If love should here find little joy or none,
And done, it were as if it were not done;
Would we not love still? What if none can know
The thing we know of but we do not know?

For we know nothing but that, long ago,
We learnt to love God whom we cannot know.
I touch your eyelids that one day must close,
Your lips as perishable as a rose:
And say that all must fade, before we know
The thing we know of but we do not know.

SOLDIERS BATHING

THE sea at evening moves across the sand.
Under a reddening sky I watch the freedom of a band
Of soldiers who belong to me. Stripped bare
For bathing in the sea, they shout and run in the warm air;
Their flesh, worn by the trade of war, revives
And my mind towards the meaning of it strives.

All's pathos now. The body that was gross,
Rank, ravenous, disgusting in the act or in repose,
All fever, filth and sweat, its bestial strength
And bestial decay, by pain and labour grows at length

528

Fragile and luminous. 'Poor bare forked animal,'
Conscious of his desires and needs and flesh that rise and fall,
Stands in the soft air, tasting after toil
The sweetness of his nakedness: letting the sea-waves coil
Their frothy tongues about his feet, forgets
His hatred of the war, its terrible pressure that begets
A machinery of death and slavery,
Each being a slave and making slaves of others: finds that he
Remembers lovely freedom in a game,
Mocking himself, and comically mimics fear and shame.

He plays with death and animality;
And reading in the shadows of his pallid flesh, I see
The idea of Michelangelo's cartoon
Of soldiers bathing, breaking off before they were half done
At some sortie of the enemy, an episode
Of the Pisan wars with Florence. I remember how he showed
Their muscular limbs that clamber from the water,
And heads that turn across the shoulder, eager for the
    slaughter,
Forgetful of their bodies that are bare,
And hot to buckle on and use the weapons that are lying
    there.
—And I think too of the theme another found
When, shadowing men's bodies on a sinister red ground,
Another Florentine, Pollaiuolo,
Painted a naked battle: warriors straddled, hacked the foe,
Dug their bare toes into the ground and slew
The brother-naked man who lay between their feet and drew
His lips back from his teeth in a grimace.

They were Italians who knew war's sorrow and disgrace
And showed the thing suspended, stripped: a theme
Born out of the experience of war's horrible extreme
Beneath a sky where even the air flows
With lacrimae Christi. For that rage, that bitterness, those
    blows,
That hatred of the slain, what could they be
But indirectly or directly a commentary

On the Crucifixion? And the picture burns
With indignation and pity and despair by turns,
Because it is the obverse of the scene
Where Christ hangs murdered, stripped, upon the Cross.
  I mean,
That is the explanation of its rage.

And we too have our bitterness and pity that engage
Blood, spirit, in this war. But night begins,
Night of the mind: who nowadays is conscious of our sins?
Though every human deed concerns our blood,
And even we must know, what nobody has understood,
That some great love is over all we do,
And that is what has driven us to this fury, for so few
Can suffer all the terror of that love:
The terror of that love has set us spinning in this groove
Greased with our blood.
     These dry themselves and dress,
Combing their hair, forget the fear and shame of nakedness.
Because to love is frightening we prefer
The freedom of our crimes. Yet, as I drink the dusky air,
I feel a strange delight that fills me full,
Strange gratitude, as if evil itself were beautiful,
And kiss the wound in thought, while in the west
I watch a streak of red that might have issued from Christ's
  breast.

W. R. RODGERS

1912–1969

LIFE'S CIRCUMNAVIGATORS

HERE, where the taut wave hangs
Its tented tons, we steer
Through rocking arch of eye
And creaking reach of ear,
Anchored to flying sky,
And chained to changing fear.

O when shall we, all spent,
Row in to some far strand,
And find, to our content,
The original land
From which our boat once went,
Though not the one we planned.

Us on that happy day
This fierce sea will release,
On our rough face of clay,
The final glaze of peace.
Our oars we will all lay
Down, and desire will cease.

LAURENCE WHISTLER

b. 1912

A PORTRAIT IN THE GUARDS

So these two faced each other there,
The artist and his model. Both
In uniform. Years back. In training.
Not combatant yet. But both aware
Of what the word meant. Not complaining,
But, inwardly, how loth.

They talked of this, perhaps. Each knew
The other, or himself, might be
Unlucky. But each knew this true
Of anyone at all. And so
There was no thrill in it. A knee
Jigged to the hit-tune of some show.

Each scrutinized the other frankly,
As only painter and sitter do:
Objectively and at leisure. Face
That must not, please, relax too blankly
Into repose. And face that threw
Glances, the brush being poised in space.

WHISTLER

So both, it may be, had the sense
Of seeing suddenly very plain
A very obvious thing: the immense
Thereness of someone else: a man
Once only, since the world began.
Never before, and never again.

It could be, while a cigarette
Hung grey, each recognized the other
As valid utterly and brother.
It should be so. Because, of all
Who in that mess-tent shortly met,
These would be first to fall.

A FORM OF EPITAPH

NAME in block letters   *None that signified*
Purpose of visit   *Barely ascertained*
Reasons for persevering   *Hope—or pride*
Status before admission here   *Regained*
Previous experience   *Nil, or records lost*
Requirements   *Few in fact, not all unmet*
Knowledge accumulated   *At a cost*
Plans   *Vague*   Sworn declaration   *Not in debt*

Evidence of departure   *Orthodox*
Country of origin   *Stateless then, as now*
Securities where held   *In one wood box*
Address for future reference   *Below*

Is further time desired?   *Not the clock's*
Was permit of return petitioned?   *No*

GEORGE BARKER

b. 1913

CHANNEL CROSSING

AND just by crossing the short sea
To find the answer sitting there
Combing out its snaky hair
And with a smile regarding me
Because it knows only too well
That I shall never recognize
The axioms that I should prize
Or the lies that I should tell.

I saw the question in the sky
Ride like a gull to fool me, as
The squat boat butted at the seas
As grossly as through ultimates I
Churn up a frothy wake of verbs
Or stir up a muddy residue
Looking for that answer who
Sanctifies where she perturbs.

The horror of the questionmark
I looked back and saw stand over
The white and open page of Dover
Huge as the horn of a scapegoat. Dark
It stood up in the English day
Interrogating Destiny
With the old lip of the sea:
'What can a dead nation say?'

As these words wailed in the air
I looked at Europe and I saw
The glittering instruments of war
Grow paler but not go from where
Like a Caesarian sunset on
The cold slab of the horizon
They lay foretelling for tomorrow
Another day of human sorrow.

But when I turned and looked into
The silent chambers of the sea
I saw the displaced fishes flee
From nowhere into nowhere through
Their continent of liberty.
O skipping porpoise of the tide
No longer shall the sailors ride
You cheering out to sea.

I thought of Britain in its cloud
Chained to the economic rocks
Dying behind me. I saw the flocks
Of great and grieving omens crowd
About the lion on the stone.
And I heard Milton's eagle mewing
Her desolation in the ruin
Of a great nation, alone.

That granite and gigantic sigh
Of the proud man beaten by
Those victories from which we die;
The gentle and defeated grief
Of the gale that groans among
Trees that are a day too strong
And, victorious by a leaf,
Show the winner he was wrong.

The continent of discontent
Rose up before me as I stood
Above the happy fish. Endued
With hotter and unhappier blood
Contented in my discontent,
I saw that every man's a soul
Caught in the glass wishing bowl:
To live at peace in discontent.

O somewhere in the seven leagues
That separate us from the stricken
Amphitheatre of the spirit,
O somewhere in that baleful sea

The answer of sad Europe lodges,
The clue that causes us to sicken
Because we cannot find and share it,
Or, finding, cannot see.

So in the sky the monstrous sun
Mocked like a punishment to be,
Extending now, to you and me
The vision of what we have done:
And as the boat drew to the quay
I thought, by crossing the short water
I shall not find, in its place,
The answer with a silent face.

EDWARD LOWBURY

b. 1913

SWAN

From bill to breast a snake,
From nape to tail a cloud
Resting upon the lake,

Puffed up rather than proud
The swan in any place
Attracts a little crowd;

Who ever saw such grace?
But now I chiefly see,
With wonder on my face,

His mixed identity—
A metamorphosis
That is no fantasy;

Now hear that song of his
From heavy wings in flight—
The very voice of bliss;

And watch him now alight,
Allaying wave and wind,
Restoring second sight:

God must have changed His mind
And pardoned, after all,
The serpent and its kind

For plotting Adam's fall.

R. S. THOMAS

b. 1913

THE HILL FARMER SPEAKS

I AM the farmer, stripped of love
And thought and grace by the land's hardness;
But what I am saying over the fields'
Desolate acres, rough with dew,
Is, Listen, listen, I am a man like you.

The wind goes over the hill pastures
Year after year, and the ewes starve,
Milkless, for want of the new grass.
And I starve, too, for something the spring
Can never foster in veins run dry.

The pig is a friend, the cattle's breath
Mingles with mine in the still lanes;
I wear it willingly like a cloak
To shelter me from your curious gaze.

The hens go in and out at the door
From sun to shadow, as stray thoughts pass
Over the floor of my wide skull.
The dirt is under my cracked nails;
The tale of my life is smirched with dung;
The phlegm rattles. But what I am saying
Over the grasses rough with dew
Is, Listen, listen, I am a man like you.

R. S. THOMAS

THE COUNTRY CLERGY

I SEE them working in old rectories
By the sun's light, by candlelight,
Venerable men, their black cloth
A little dusty, a little green
With holy mildew. And yet their skulls,
Ripening over so many prayers,
Toppled into the same grave
With oafs and yokels. They left no books,
Memorial to their lonely thought
In grey parishes; rather they wrote
On men's hearts and in the minds
Of young children sublime words
Too soon forgotten. God in his time
Or out of time will correct this.

HERE

I AM a man now.
Pass your hand over my brow,
You can feel the place where the brains grow.

I am like a tree,
From my top boughs I can see
The footprints that led up to me.

There is blood in my veins
That has run clear of the stain
Contracted in so many loins.

Why, then, are my hands red
With the blood of so many dead?
Is this where I was misled?

Why are my hands this way
That they will not do as I say?
Does no God hear when I pray?

R. S. THOMAS

I have nowhere to go.
The swift satellites show
The clock of my whole being is slow.

It is too late to start
For destinations not of the heart.
I must stay here with my hurt.

HENRY REED

b. 1914

LESSONS OF THE WAR

TO ALAN MICHELL

*Vixi duellis nuper idoneus
Et militavi non sine gloria.*

II. JUDGING DISTANCES

NOT only how far away, but the way that you say it
Is very important. Perhaps you may never get
The knack of judging a distance, but at least you know
How to report on a landscape: the central sector,
The right of arc and that, which we had last Tuesday,
    And at least you know

That maps are of time, not place, so far as the army
Happens to be concerned—the reason being,
Is one which need not delay us. Again, you know
There are three kinds of tree, three only, the fir and the
        poplar,
And those which have bushy tops to; and lastly
    That things only seem to be things.

A barn is not called a barn, to put it more plainly,
Or a field in the distance, where sheep may be safely grazing.
You must never be over-sure. You must say, when reporting:

538

At five o'clock in the central sector is a dozen
Of what appear to be animals; whatever you do,
    Don't call the bleeders *sheep.*

I am sure that's quite clear; and suppose, for the sake of
    example,
The one at the end, asleep, endeavours to tell us
What he sees over there to the west, and how far away,
After first having come to attention. There to the west,
On the fields of summer the sun and the shadows bestow
    Vestments of purple and gold.

The still white dwellings are like a mirage in the heat,
And under the swaying elms a man and a woman
Lie gently together. Which is, perhaps, only to say
That there is a row of houses to the left of arc,
And that under some poplars a pair of what appear to be
    humans
    Appear to be loving.

Well that, for an answer, is what we might rightly call
Moderately satisfactory only, the reason being,
Is that two things have been omitted, and those are impor-
    tant.
The human beings, now: in what direction are they,
And how far away, would you say? And do not forget
    There may be dead ground in between.

There may be dead ground in between; and I may not have
    got
The knack of judging a distance; I will only venture
A guess that perhaps between me and the apparent lovers,
(Who, incidentally, appear by now to have finished,)
At seven o'clock from the houses, is roughly a distance
    Of about one year and a half.

DYLAN THOMAS

1914-1953

THE CONVERSATION OF PRAYER

THE conversation of prayers about to be said
By the child going to bed and the man on the stairs
Who climbs to his dying love in her high room,
The one not caring to whom in his sleep he will move
And the other full of tears that she will be dead,

Turns in the dark on the sound they know will arise
Into the answering skies from the green ground,
From the man on the stairs and the child by his bed.
The sound about to be said in the two prayers
For the sleep in a safe land and the love who dies

Will be the same grief flying. Whom shall they calm?
Shall the child sleep unharmed or the man be crying?
The conversation of prayers about to be said
Turns on the quick and the dead, and the man on the stairs
To-night shall find no dying but alive and warm

In the fire of his care his love in the high room.
And the child not caring to whom he climbs his prayer
Shall drown in a grief as deep as his true grave,
And mark the dark eyed wave, through the eyes of sleep,
Dragging him up the stairs to one who lies dead.

A REFUSAL TO MOURN THE DEATH, BY FIRE, OF A CHILD IN LONDON

NEVER until the mankind making
Bird beast and flower
Fathering and all humbling darkness
Tells with silence the last light breaking
And the still hour
Is come of the sea tumbling in harness

540

And I must enter again the round
Zion of the water bead
And the synagogue of the ear of corn
Shall I let pray the shadow of a sound
Or sow my salt seed
In the least valley of sackcloth to mourn

The majesty and burning of the child's death.
I shall not murder
The mankind of her going with a grave truth
Nor blaspheme down the stations of the breath
With any further
Elegy of innocence and youth.

Deep with the first dead lies London's daughter,
Robed in the long friends,
The grains beyond age, the dark veins of her mother,
Secret by the unmourning water
Of the riding Thames.
After the first death, there is no other.

IN MY CRAFT OR SULLEN ART

In my craft or sullen art
Exercised in the still night
When only the moon rages
And the lovers lie abed
With all their griefs in their arms,
I labour by singing light
Not for ambition or bread
Or the strut and trade of charms
On the ivory stages
But for the common wages
Of their most secret heart.

Not for the proud man apart
From the raging moon I write
On these spindrift pages
Nor for the towering dead

With their nightingales and psalms
But for the lovers, their arms
Round the griefs of the ages,
Who pay no praise or wages
Nor heed my craft or art.

FERN HILL

Now as I was young and easy under the apple boughs
About the lilting house and happy as the grass was green,
        The night above the dingle starry,
            Time let me hail and climb
        Golden in the heydays of his eyes,
And honoured among wagons I was prince of the apple towns
And once below a time I lordly had the trees and leaves
            Trail with daisies and barley
        Down the rivers of the windfall light.

And as I was green and carefree, famous among the barns
About the happy yard and singing as the farm was home,
        In the sun that is young once only,
            Time let me play and be
        Golden in the mercy of his means,
And green and golden I was huntsman and herdsman, the
            calves
Sang to my horn, the foxes on the hills barked clear and cold,
        And the sabbath rang slowly
        In the pebbles of the holy streams.

All the sun long it was running, it was lovely, the hay
Fields high as the house, the tunes from the chimneys, it
            was air
        And playing, lovely and watery
            And fire green as grass.
        And nightly under the simple stars
As I rode to sleep the owls were bearing the farm away,
All the moon long I heard, blessed among stables, the night-
            jars
        Flying with the ricks, and the horses
            Flashing into the dark.

And then to awake, and the farm, like a wanderer white
With the dew, come back, the cock on his shoulder: it was all
    Shining, it was Adam and maiden,
        The sky gathered again
      And the sun grew round that very day.
So it must have been after the birth of the simple light
In the first, spinning place, the spellbound horses walking
        warm
    Out of the whinnying green stable
     On to the fields of praise.

And honoured among foxes and pheasants by the gay house
Under the new made clouds and happy as the heart was long,
    In the sun born over and over,
      I ran my heedless ways,
    My wishes raced through the house high hay
And nothing I cared, at my sky blue trades, that time allows
In all his tuneful turning so few and such morning songs
    Before the children green and golden
     Follow him out of grace,

Nothing I cared, in the lamb white days, that time would
      take me
Up to the swallow thronged loft by the shadow of my hand,
    In the moon that is always rising,
     Nor that riding to sleep
    I should hear him fly with the high fields
And wake to the farm forever fled from the childless land.
Oh as I was young and easy in the mercy of his means,
     Time held me green and dying
    Though I sang in my chains like the sea.

ALUN LEWIS

1916–1944

ALL DAY IT HAS RAINED

ALL day it has rained, and we on the edge of the moors
Have sprawled in our bell-tents, moody and dull as boors,
Groundsheets and blankets spread on the muddy ground.
And from the first grey wakening we have found

No refuge from the skirmishing fine rain
And the wind that made the bell-tents heave and flap
And the taut wet guy ropes ravel out and snap.
All day the rain has glided, wave and mist and dream,
Drenching the gorse and heather, a gossamer stream
Too light to move the acorns that suddenly
Snatched from their cups by the wild southwesterly
Pattered against the tent and our up-turned dreaming faces.
And we stretched out, unbuttoning our braces,
Smoking a woodbine, darning dirty socks,
Reading the Sunday papers—I saw a fox
And mentioned it in the note I scribbled home—
And we talked of girls and dropping bombs on Rome
And thought of the quiet dead and the loud celebrities
Exhorting us to slaughter and the herded refugees;
Yet thought softly, morosely of them, and as indifferently
As of ourselves and those whom we for years
Have loved and will again
Tomorrow maybe love:—but now it is the rain
Possesses us, the darkness and the rain.

And I can remember nothing dearer or more to my heart
Than the children I watched in the woods on Saturday
Shaking down burning chestnuts for the school-yard's merry
      play,
Or the shaggy patient dog who followed me
Through Sheet and Steep and up the wooded scree
To the Shoulder o' Mutton where Edward Thomas brooded
      long
On death and beauty till a bullet stopped his song.

POSTSCRIPT FOR GWENO

If I should go away,
Beloved, do not say
'He has forgotten me.'
For you abide,
A singing rib within my dreaming side;
You always stay.

And in the mad tormented valley
Where blood and hunger rally
And Death the wild beast is uncaught, untamed,
Our soul withstands the terror
And has its quiet honour
Among the glittering stars your voices named.

KEITH DOUGLAS

1920–1944

VERGISSMEINNICHT

THREE weeks gone and the combatants gone,
returning over the nightmare ground
we found the place again, and found
the soldier sprawling in the sun.

The frowning barrel of his gun
overshadowing. As we came on
that day, he hit my tank with one
like the entry of a demon.

Look. Here in the gunpit spoil
the dishonoured picture of his girl
who has put: *Steffi. Vergissmeinnicht*
in a copybook gothic script.

We see him almost with content
abased, and seeming to have paid
and mocked at by his own equipment
that's hard and good when he's decayed.

But she would weep to see today
how on his skin the swart flies move;
the dust upon the paper eye
and the burst stomach like a cave.

For here the lover and killer are mingled
who had one body and one heart.
And death who had the soldier singled
has done the lover mortal hurt.

THOMAS BLACKBURN

b. 1916

THE LUCKY MARRIAGE

I OFTEN wonder as the fairy-story
Tells how the little goose-girl found her prince,
Or of the widowed queen who stopped her carriage
And threw a rose down to the gangling dunce,
What is the meaning of this lucky marriage
Which lasts forever, it is often said,
Because I know too well such consummation
Is not a question of a double bed,
Or of the wedding bells and royal procession
With twenty major-domos at its head.

At least its bride and groom must be rejected,
The fairy godmother will only call
On Cinders scrubbing tiles beside the chimney
While her proud sisters foot it at the ball;
From all but the last son without a birthright
The beggarwoman hordes her magic seed.
Well, if they'd had the good luck of their siblings
And found occasion kinder to their need,
They would have spent their breath on natural pleasures
And had no time for murmurs in the night:
They heard because they were condemned to silence,
And learnt to see because they had no light.

I mean the elder son and cherished sister
Know but the surface of each common day;
It takes the cunning eye of the rejected
To dip beneath that skin of shadow-play
And come into the meaning of a landscape.
I think that every bird and casual stone
Are syllables thrust down from some broad language
That we must ravel out and make our own.
Yet who is ever turned towards that journey
Till deprivations riddle through the heart?
And so I praise the goose-girl and the scullion
Beside a midden or a refuse cart.

And yet all images for this completion
Somehow byepass its real ghostliness
Which can't be measured by a sweating finger,
Or any salt and carnal nakedness.
Although two heads upon a single pillow
May be the metaphor that serves it best,
No lying down within a single moment
Will give the outward going any rest;
It's only when we reach beyond our pronouns
And come into ourselves that we are blest.
Is this the meaning of the lucky marriage
Which lasts forever, it is often said,
Between the goose-girl and the kitchen servant,
Who have no wedding ring or mutual bed?

HOSPITAL FOR DEFECTIVES

By your unnumbered charities
A miracle disclose,
Lord of the Images, whose love,
The eyelid and the rose,
Takes for a language, and today
Tell to me what is said
By these men in a turnip field
And their unleavened bread.

For all things seem to figure out
The stirrings of your heart,
And two men pick the turnips up
And two men pull the cart;
And yet between the four of them
No word is ever said
Because the yeast was not put in
Which makes the human bread.
But three men stare on vacancy
And one man strokes his knees;
What is the meaning to be found
In such dark vowels as these?

BLACKBURN

Lord of the Images, whose love,
The eyelid and the rose,
Takes for a metaphor, today
Beneath the warder's blows,
The unleavened man did not cry out
Or turn his face away;
Through such men in a turnip field
What is it that you say?

JACK CLEMO

b. 1916

CHRIST IN THE CLAY-PIT

WHY should I find Him here
And not in a church, nor yet
Where Nature heaves a breast like Olivet
Against the stars? I peer
Upon His footsteps in this quarried mud;
I see His blood
In rusty stains on pit-props, waggon-frames
Bristling with nails, not leaves. There were no leaves
Upon His chosen Tree,
No parasitic flowering over shames
Of Eden's primal infidelity.

Just splintered wood and nails
Were fairest blossoming for Him Who speaks
Where mica-silt outbreaks
Like water from the side of His own clay
In that strange day
When He was pierced. Here still the earth-face pales
And rends in earthquake roarings of a blast
With tainted rock outcast
While fields and woods lie dreaming yet of peace
'Twixt God and His creation, of release
From potent wrath—a faith that waxes bold
In churches nestling snugly in the fold

Of scented hillsides where mild shadows brood.
The dark and stubborn mood
Of Him Whose feet are bare upon this mire,
And in the furnace fire
Which hardens all the clay that has escaped,
Would not be understood
By worshippers of beauty toned and shaped
To flower or hymn. I know their facile praise
False to the heart of me, which like this pit
Must still be disembowelled of Nature's stain,
And rendered fit
By violent mouldings through the tunnelled ways
Of all He would regain.

DAVID GASCOYNE

b. 1916

EX NIHILO

HERE am I now cast down
Beneath the black glare of a netherworld's
Dead suns, dust in my mouth, among
Dun tiers no tears refresh: am cast
Down by a lofty hand,

Hand that I love! Lord Light,
How dark is thy arm's will and ironlike
Thy ruler's finger that has sent me here!
Far from Thy face I nothing understand,
But kiss the Hand that has consigned

Me to these latter years where I must learn
The revelation of despair, and find
Among the debris of all certainties
The hardest stone on which to found
Altar and shelter for Eternity.

WINTER GARDEN

THE season's anguish, crashing whirlwind, ice,
Have passed, and cleansed the trodden paths
That silent gardeners have strewn with ash.

GASCOYNE

The iron circles of the sky
Are worn away by tempest;
Yet in this garden there is no more strife:
The Winter's knife is buried in the earth.
Pure music is the cry that tears
The birdless branches in the wind.
No blossom is reborn. The blue
Stare of the pond is blind.

And no-one sees
A restless stranger through the morning stray
Across the sodden lawn, whose eyes
Are tired of weeping, in whose breast
A savage sun consumes its hidden day.

EVE

PROFOUND the radiance issuing
From the all-inhaling mouth among
The blonde and stifling hair which falls
In heavy rivers from the high-crowned head,
While in the tension of her heat and light
The upward creeping blood whispers her name:
Insurgent, wounded and avenging one,
In whose black sex
Our ancient culpability like a pearl is set.

TERENCE TILLER

b. 1916

READING A MEDAL

who, minter of medallions,
casting or striking, caused me so
to speak with double voice in bronze,
I may not help and cannot know.
But I am Pallas, and I bear
the mask of war by wisdom; you
shall spin my olives to despair:
all my reverse will say is true.

TILLER

(Turn me, and read that other side;
you must return: for, mask and coin,
I give no rest unless you ride
the felloe where my faces join.)

My face is Aphrodite's—she
that rules by myrtle and by dove;
I loose my zone to let you see
the end of reasoning by love.
Nothing my obverse tells is true:
turn till you read me as it was;
turn till you know me, and renew
my helpless paradox—because

STREET PERFORMERS, 1851

Street performers . . . admit of being classified into:
(a) mountebanks—or those who enact puppet-shows, as Punch
*   and Judy, the fantoccini, and the Chinese shades . . .*
(b) the street-performers of feats of strength and dexterity,
*   as . . . stiff and bending tumblers, salamanders, swords-*
*   men, &c. . . .*
(c) the street-performers with trained animals—as sapient pigs,
*   dancing bears, and tame camels.*
   Henry Mayhew, *London Labour and the London Poor*, 1851

LONDON is painted round them: burly railings
and grey rich inaccessible houses; squares—
laurelled and priveted, flowered, and fast in palings—
where the grave children move and are not theirs
and are more bright and distant than the sun
whose wan dry wine shines in the windows—squares
and heavy curtains, curtains and steps of stone:
these are their coloured cards, their theatres.

Hooked nose and hump, the Black Man, the police,
the hangman's shadow by the prison wall,
the wandering misery in the courts of peace:
the mad voice like a wire will draw them all—
the puppets and the puppet-masters. Watch:
who is to tell, seeing no showmen's heads,
which are the audience, penny-foolish, which
the fantoccini and the Chinese shades?

551

TILLER

Now (scarlet plush and gilt) the lights go on;
cold smoky curtains fold the stage away;
and all but shadows, penny plain, are gone.
Flare-cast from vehement oil, great blurs of grey
upon the gold and indigo, their dole
habit's iniquity and ungiven bread,
they drift before the rainy street; they roll
on sad wheels rags to be inherited.

The salamander and the swordsman, and
the maypole-ribboned bear: from dark they pass
to dark, through blazing islands—as if stained
in mockery upon hot slips of glass.
And the flame dies; the fingers are withdrawn;
the puppets tumble; there are no more slides;
the paints are in their boxes: they have gone,
the fantoccini and the Chinese shades.

CHARLES CAUSLEY

b. 1917

INNOCENT'S SONG

Who's that knocking on the window,
Who's that standing at the door,
What are all those presents
Lying on the kitchen floor?

Who is the smiling stranger
With hair as white as gin,
What is he doing with the children
And who could have let him in?

Why has he rubies on his fingers,
A cold, cold crown on his head,
Why, when he caws his carol,
Does the salty snow run red?

Why does he ferry my fireside
As a spider on a thread,
His fingers made of fuses
And his tongue of gingerbread?

Why does the world before him
Melt in a million suns,
Why do his yellow, yearning eyes
Burn like saffron buns?

Watch where he comes walking
Out of the Christmas flame,
Dancing, double-talking:

Herod is his name.

JOHN HEATH-STUBBS

b. 1918

TITUS AND BERENICE

'TURN to me in the darkness,
    Asia with your cool
Gardens beyond the desert,
    Your clear, frog-haunted pool;
I seek your reassurance—
    Forget, as I would forget,
Your holy city cast down, the Temple
    That still I desecrate.'
'Buzz!' said the blue-fly in his head.

'In darkness master me,
    Rome with your seven hills,
Roads, rhetorical aqueducts,
    And ravaging eagles;
Worlds are at bitter odds, yet we
    Can find our love at least—
Not expedient to the Senate,
    Abominable to the priest.'
'Buzz!' said the blue-fly in his head.

Titus the clement Emperor
    And she of Herod's house
Slobbered and clawed each other
    Like creatures of the stews;
Lay together, then lay apart
    And knew they had not subdued—
She the insect in his brain,
    Nor he her angry God.

NOTE. *According to a Jewish tradition Titus was afflicted with an insect in his brain as a punishment for his destruction of the Temple.*

DONALD DAVIE

b. 1922

THE FOUNTAIN

FEATHERS up fast, and steeples; then in clods
Thuds into its first basin; thence as surf
Smokes up and hangs; irregularly slops
Into its second, tattered like a shawl;
There, chill as rain, stipples a danker green,
Where urgent tritons lob their heavy jets.

For Berkeley this was human thought, that mounts
From bland assumptions to inquiring skies,
There glints with wit, fumes into fancies, plays
With its negations, and at last descends,
As by a law of nature, to its bowl
Of thus enlightened but still common sense.

We who have no such confidence must gaze
With all the more affection on these forms,
These spires, these plumes, these calm reflections, these
Similitudes of surf and turf and shawl,
Graceful returns upon acceptances.
We ask of fountains only that they play,

Though that was not what Berkeley meant at all.

HEARING RUSSIAN SPOKEN

UNSETTLED again and hearing Russian spoken
I think of brokenness perversely planned
By Dostoievsky's debauchees; recall
The 'visible brokenness' that is the token
Of the true believer; and connect it all
With speaking a language I cannot command.

If broken means unmusical I speak
Even in English brokenly, a man
Wretched enough, yet one who cannot borrow
Their hunger for indignity nor, weak,
Abet my weakness, drink to drown a sorrow
Or write in metres that I cannot scan.

Unsettled again at hearing Russian spoken,
'Abjure politic brokenness for good',
I tell myself. 'Recall what menaces,
What self-loathings must be re-awoken:
This girl and that, and all your promises
Your pidgin that they too well understood.'

Not just in Russian but in any tongue
Abandonment, morality's soubrette
Of lyrical surrender and excess,
Knows the weak endings equal to the strong;
She trades on broken English with success
And, disenchanted, I'm enamoured yet.

PHILIP LARKIN

b. 1922

WANTS

Beyond all this, the wish to be alone:
However the sky grows dark with invitation-cards
However we follow the printed directions of sex
However the family is photographed under the flagstaff—
Beyond all this, the wish to be alone.

Beneath it all, desire of oblivion runs:
Despite the artful tensions of the calendar,
The life insurance, the tabled fertility rites,
The costly aversion of the eyes from death—
Beneath it all, desire of oblivion runs.

MAIDEN NAME

Marrying left your maiden name disused.
Its five light sounds no longer mean your face,
Your voice, and all your variants of grace;
For since you were so thankfully confused
By law with someone else, you cannot be
Semantically the same as that young beauty:
It was of her that these two words were used.

Now it's a phrase applicable to no one,
Lying just where you left it, scattered through
Old lists, old programmes, a school prize or two,
Packets of letters tied with tartan ribbon—
Then is it scentless, weightless, strengthless, wholly
Untruthful? Try whispering it slowly.
No, it means you. Or, since you're past and gone,

It means what we feel now about you then:
How beautiful you were, and near, and young,
So vivid, you might still be there among
Those first few days, unfingermarked again.
So your old name shelters our faithfulness,
Instead of losing shape and meaning less
With your depreciating luggage laden.

DECEPTIONS

*'Of course I was drugged, and so heavily I did not regain my
consciousness till the next morning. I was horrified to discover
that I had been ruined, and for some days I was inconsolable,
and cried like a child to be killed or sent back to my aunt.'*
Henry Mayhew, *London Labour and the London Poor*, 1851

EVEN so distant, I can taste the grief,
Bitter and sharp with stalks, he made you gulp.
The sun's occasional print, the brisk brief
Worry of wheels along the street outside
Where bridal London bows the other way,
And light, unanswerable and tall and wide,
Forbids the scar to heal, and drives
Shame out of hiding. All the unhurried day
Your mind lay open like a drawer of knives.

Slums, years, have buried you. I would not dare
Console you if I could. What can be said,
Except that suffering is exact, but where
Desire takes charge, readings will grow erratic?
For you would hardly care
That you were less deceived, out on that bed,
Than he was, stumbling up the breathless stair
To burst into fulfilment's desolate attic.

CHURCH GOING

ONCE I am sure there's nothing going on
I step inside, letting the door thud shut.
Another church: matting, seats, and stone,
And little books; sprawlings of flowers, cut
For Sunday, brownish now; some brass and stuff
Up at the holy end; the small neat organ;
And a tense, musty, unignorable silence,
Brewed God knows how long. Hatless, I take off
My cycle-clips in awkward reverence,

Move forward, run my hand around the font.
From where I stand, the roof looks almost new—
Cleaned, or restored? Someone would know: I don't.
Mounting the lectern, I peruse a few
Hectoring large-scale verses, and pronounce
'Here endeth' much more loudly than I'd meant.
The echoes snigger briefly. Back at the door
I sign the book, donate an Irish sixpence,
Reflect the place was not worth stopping for.

Yet stop I did: in fact I often do,
And always end much at a loss like this,
Wondering what to look for; wondering, too,
When churches fall completely out of use
What we shall turn them into, if we shall keep
A few cathedrals chronically on show,
Their parchment, plate and pyx in locked cases,
And let the rest rent-free to rain and sheep.
Shall we avoid them as unlucky places?

Or, after dark, will dubious women come
To make their children touch a particular stone;
Pick simples for a cancer; or on some
Advised night see walking a dead one?
Power of some sort or other will go on
In games, in riddles, seemingly at random;
But superstition, like belief, must die,
And what remains when disbelief has gone?
Grass, weedy pavement, brambles, buttress, sky,

A shape less recognisable each week,
A purpose more obscure. I wonder who
Will be the last, the very last, to seek
This place for what it was; one of the crew
That tap and jot and know what rood-lofts were?
Some ruin-bibber, randy for antique,
Or Christmas-addict, counting on a whiff
Of gown-and-bands and organ-pipes and myrrh?
Or will he be my representative,

Bored, uninformed, knowing the ghostly silt
Dispersed, yet tending to this cross of ground
Through suburb scrub because it held unspilt
So long and equably what since is found
Only in separation—marriage, and birth,
And death, and thoughts of these—for whom was built
This special shell? For, though I've no idea
What this accoutred frowsty barn is worth,
It pleases me to stand in silence here;

A serious house on serious earth it is,
In whose blent air all our compulsions meet,
Are recognised, and robed as destinies.
And that much never can be obsolete,
Since someone will forever be surprising
A hunger in himself to be more serious,
And gravitating with it to this ground,
Which, he once heard, was proper to grow wise in,
If only that so many dead lie round.

CHARLES TOMLINSON

b. 1927

ICOS

WHITE, a shingled path
Climbs among dusted olives
To where at the hill-crest
Stare houses, whiter
Than either dust or shingle.
The view, held from this vantage
Unsoftened by distance, because
Scoured by a full light,
Draws lucid across its depth
The willing eye: a beach,
A surf-line, broken
Where reefs meet it, into the heaving
Blanched rims of bay-arcs;

Above, piercing the empty blue,
A gull would convey whiteness
Through the sole space which lacks it
But, there, scanning the shore,
Hangs only the eagle, depth
Measured within its level gaze.

TRAMONTANA AT LERICI

TODAY, should you let fall a glass it would
   Disintegrate, played off with such keenness
Against the cold's resonance (the sounds
   Hard, separate and distinct, dropping away
In a diminishing cadence) that you might swear
   This was the imitation of glass falling.

Leaf-dapples sharpen. Emboldened by this clarity
   The minds of artificers would turn prismatic,
Running on lace perforated in crisp wafers
   That could cut like steel. Constitutions,
Drafted under this fecund chill, would be annulled
   For the strictness of their equity, the moderation of their
      pity.

At evening, one is alarmed by such definition
   In as many lost greens as one will give glances to recover,
As many again which the landscape
   Absorbing into the steady dusk, condenses
From aquamarine to that slow indigo-pitch
   Where the light and twilight abandon themselves.

And the chill grows. In this air
   Unfit for politicians and romantics
Dark hardens from blue, effacing the windows:
   A tangible block, it will be no accessory
To that which does not concern it. One is ignored
   By so much cold suspended in so much night.

FAREWELL TO VAN GOGH

THE quiet deepens. You will not persuade
    One leaf of the accomplished, steady, darkening
Chestnut-tower to displace itself
    With more of violence than the air supplies
When, gathering dusk, the pond brims evenly
    And we must be content with stillness.

Unhastening, daylight withdraws from us its shapes
    Into their central calm. Stone by stone
Your rhetoric is dispersed until the earth
    Becomes once more the earth, the leaves
A sharp partition against cooling blue.

Farewell, and for your instructive frenzy
    Gratitude. The world does not end tonight
And the fruit that we shall pick tomorrow
    Await us, weighing the unstripped bough.

THOMAS KINSELLA

b. 1928

MIRROR IN FEBRUARY

THE day dawns with scent of must and rain,
Of opened soil, dark trees, dry bedroom air.
Under the fading lamp, half dressed—my brain
Idling on some compulsive fantasy—
I towel my shaven jaw and stop, and stare,
Riveted by a dark exhausted eye,
A dry downturning mouth.

It seems again that it is time to learn,
In this untiring, crumbling place of growth
To which, for the time being, I return.
Now plainly in the mirror of my soul
I read that I have looked my last on youth
And little more; for they are not made whole
That reach the age of Christ.

Below my window the awakening trees,
Hacked clean for better bearing, stand defaced
Suffering their brute necessities,
And how should the flesh not quail that span for span
Is mutilated more? In slow distaste
I fold my towel with what grace I can,
Not young and not renewable, but man.

THOM GUNN

b. 1929

TO YVOR WINTERS, 1955

I LEAVE you in your garden.

In the yard
Behind it, run the airedales you have reared
With boxer's vigilance and poet's rigour:
Dog-generations you have trained the vigour
That few can breed to train and fewer still
Control with the deliberate human will.
And in the house there rest, piled shelf on shelf,
The accumulations that compose the self—
Poem and history: for if we use
Words to maintain the actions that we choose,
Our words, with slow defining influence,
Stay to mark out our chosen lineaments.

Continual temptation waits on each
To renounce his empire over thought and speech,
Till he submit his passive faculties
To evening, come where no resistance is;
The unmotivated sadness of the air
Filling the human with his own despair.
Where now lies power to hold the evening back?
Implicit in the grey is total black:
Denial of the discriminating brain
Brings the neurotic vision, and the vein
Of necromancy. All as relative
For mind as for the sense, we have to live
In a half-world, not ours nor history's,
And learn the false from half-true premisses.

But sitting in the dusk—though shapes combine,
Vague mass replacing edge and flickering line,
You keep both Rule and Energy in view,
Much power in each, most in the balanced two:
Ferocity existing in the fence
Built by an exercised intelligence.
Though night is always close, complete negation
Ready to drop on wisdom and emotion,
Night from the air or the carnivorous breath,
Still it is right to know the force of death,
And, as you do, persistent, tough in will,
Raise from the excellent the better still.

IN SANTA MARIA DEL POPOLO

WAITING for when the sun an hour or less
Conveniently oblique makes visible
The painting on one wall of this recess
By Caravaggio, of the Roman School,
I see how shadow in the painting brims
With a real shadow, drowning all shapes out
But a dim horse's haunch and various limbs,
Until the very subject is in doubt.

But evening gives the act, beneath the horse
And one indifferent groom, I see him sprawl,
Foreshortened from the head, with hidden face,
Where he has fallen, Saul becoming Paul.
O wily painter, limiting the scene
From a cacophony of dusty forms
To the one convulsion, what is it you mean
In that wide gesture of the lifting arms?

No Ananias croons a mystery yet,
Casting the pain out under name of sin.
The painter saw what was, an alternate
Candour and secrecy inside the skin.
He painted, elsewhere, that firm insolent
Young whore in Venus' clothes, those pudgy cheats,
Those sharpers; and was strangled, as things went,
For money, by one such picked off the streets.

I turn, hardly enlightened, from the chapel
To the dim interior of the church instead,
In which there kneel already several people,
Mostly old women: each head closeted
In tiny fists holds comfort as it can.
Their poor arms are too tired for more than this
—For the large gesture of solitary man,
Resisting, by embracing, nothingness.

TED HUGHES

b. 1930

HAWK ROOSTING

I sit in the top of the wood, my eyes closed.
Inaction, no falsifying dream
Between my hooked head and hooked feet:
Or in sleep rehearse perfect kills and eat.

The convenience of the high trees!
The air's buoyancy and the sun's ray
Are of advantage to me;
And the earth's face upward for my inspection.

My feet are locked upon the rough bark.
It took the whole of Creation
To produce my foot, my each feather:
Now I hold Creation in my foot

Or fly up, and revolve it all slowly—
I kill where I please because it is all mine.
There is no sophistry in my body:
My manners are tearing off heads—

The allotment of death.
For the one path of my flight is direct
Through the bones of the living.
No arguments assert my right:

The sun is behind me.
Nothing has changed since I began.
My eye has permitted no change.
I am going to keep things like this.

NOVEMBER

THE month of the drowned dog. After long rain the land
Was sodden as the bed of an ancient lake,
Treed with iron and birdless. In the sunk lane
The ditch—a seep silent all summer—

Made brown foam with a big voice: that, and my boots
On the lane's scrubbed stones, in the gulleyed leaves,
Against the hill's hanging silence;
Mist silvering the droplets on the bare thorns

Slower than the change of daylight.
In a let of the ditch a tramp was bundled asleep:
Face tucked down into beard, drawn in
Under its hair like a hedgehog's. I took him for dead,

But his stillness separated from the death
Of the rotting grass and the ground. A wind chilled,
And a fresh comfort tightened through him,
Each hand stuffed deeper into the other sleeve.

His ankles, bound with sacking and hairy band,
Rubbed each other, resettling. The wind hardened;
A puff shook a glittering from the thorns,
And again the rains' dragging grey columns

Smudged the farms. In a moment
The fields were jumping and smoking; the thorns
Quivered, riddled with the glassy verticals.
I stayed on under the welding cold

Watching the tramp's face glisten and the drops on his coat
Flash and darken. I thought what strong trust
Slept in him—as the trickling furrows slept,
And the thorn-roots in their grip on darkness;

And the buried stones, taking the weight of winter;
The hill where the hare crouched with clenched teeth.
Rain plastered the land till it was shining
Like hammered lead, and I ran, and in the rushing wood

Shuttered by a black oak leaned.
The keeper's gibbet had owls and hawks
By the neck, weasels, a gang of cats, crows:
Some, stiff, weightless, twirled like dry bark bits

In the drilling rain. Some still had their shape,
Had their pride with it; hung, chins on chests,
Patient to outwait these worst days that beat
Their crowns bare and dripped from their feet.

JON SILKIN

b. 1930

DEATH OF A SON

(who died in a mental hospital aged one)

SOMETHING has ceased to come along with me.
Something like a person: something very like one.
    And there was no nobility in it
      Or anything like that.

    Something was there like a one year
Old house, dumb as a stone. While the near buildings
    Sang like birds and laughed
      Understanding the pact

    They were to have with silence. But he
Neither sang nor laughed. He did not bless silence
    Like bread, with words.
      He did not forsake silence.

    But rather, like a house in mourning
Kept the eye turned in to watch the silence while
    The other houses like birds
      Sang around him.

And the breathing silence neither
Moved nor was still.

   I have seen stones: I have seen brick
But this house was made up of neither bricks nor stone
      But a house of flesh and blood
        With flesh of stone

   And bricks for blood. A house
Of stones and blood in breathing silence with the other
      Birds singing crazy on its chimneys.
        But this was silence,

   This was something else, this was
Hearing and speaking though he was a house drawn
      Into silence, this was
        Something religious in his silence,

   Something shining in his quiet,
This was different this was altogether something else:
      Though he never spoke, this
        Was something to do with death.

   And then slowly the eye stopped looking
Inward. The silence rose and became still.
The look turned to the outer place and stopped,
      With the birds still shrilling around him.
        And as if he could speak

He turned over on his side with his one year
Red as a wound
He turned over as if he could be sorry for this
And out of his eyes two great tears rolled, like stones,
        and he died.

STEVIE SMITH

1903–1971

NOT WAVING BUT DROWNING

Nobody heard him, the dead man,
But still he lay moaning:
I was much further out than you thought
And not waving but drowning.

Poor chap, he always loved larking
And now he's dead
It must have been too cold for him his heart gave way,
They said.

Oh, no no no, it was too cold always
(Still the dead one lay moaning)
I was much too far out all my life
And not waving but drowning.

NOTES TO
THE GOLDEN TREASURY

By FRANCIS TURNER PALGRAVE

Summary of Book First

THE Elizabethan Poetry, as it is rather vaguely termed, forms the substance of this Book, which contains pieces from Wyat under Henry VIII to Shakespeare midway through the reign of James I, and Drummond who carried on the early manner to a still later period. There is here a wide range of style;—from simplicity expressed in a language hardly yet broken in to verse,—through the pastoral fancies and Italian conceits of the strictly Elizabethan time,—to the passionate reality of Shakespeare: yet a general uniformity of tone prevails. Few readers can fail to observe the natural sweetness of the verse, the single-hearted straightforwardness of the thoughts:—nor less, the limitation of subject to the many phases of one passion, which then characterized our lyrical poetry,—unless when, as with Drummond and Shakespeare, the 'purple light of Love' is tempered by a spirit of sterner reflection.

It should be observed that this and the following Summaries apply in the main to the Collection here presented, in which (besides its restriction to Lyrical Poetry) a strictly representative or historical Anthology has not been aimed at. Great excellence, in human art as in human character, has from the beginning of things been even more uniform than Mediocrity, by virtue of the closeness of its approach to Nature:—and so far as the standard of Excellence kept in view has been attained in this volume, a comparative absence of extreme or temporary phases in style, a similarity of tone and manner, will be found throughout:—something neither modern nor ancient, but true in all ages, and like the works of Creation, perfect as on the first day.

Page No.		
1	2	l. 4. *Rouse Memnon's mother:* Awaken the Dawn from the dark Earth and the clouds where she is resting. Aurora in the old mythology is mother of Memnon (the East), and wife of Tithonus (the appearances of Earth and Sky during the last hours of Night). She leaves him every morning in renewed youth, to prepare the way for Phoebus (the Sun), whilst Tithonus remains in perpetual old age and greyness.
2	—	l. 21 *by Peneus' streams:* Phoebus loved the Nymph Daphne whom he met by the river Peneus in the vale of Tempe. This legend expressed the attachment of the Laurel (Daphne) to the Sun, under whose heat the tree both fades and flourishes.

It has been thought worth while to explain these allusions, because they illustrate the character of the Grecian

NOTES

Mythology, which arose in the Personification of natural phenomena, and was totally free from those debasing and ludicrous ideas with which, through Roman and later misunderstanding or perversion, it has been associated.

2   2   l. 25 *Amphion's lyre:* He was said to have built the walls of Thebes to the sound of his music.

—   —   l. 33 *Night like a drunkard reels:* Compare *Romeo and Juliet,* Act II, Scene 3: 'The grey-eyed morn smiles,' &c.— It should be added that three lines, which appeared hopelessly misprinted, have been omitted in this Poem.

3   4   l. 10 *Time's chest:* in which he is figuratively supposed to lay up past treasures. So in *Troilus,* Act III, Scene 3, 'Time hath . . . a wallet at his back,' &c.

4   5   A fine example of the high-wrought and conventional Elizabethan Pastoralism, which it would be ludicrous to criticize on the ground of the unshepherdlike or unreal character of some images suggested. Stanza 6 was probably inserted by Izaak Walton.

6   9   This Poem, with 25 and 94, is taken from Davison's *Rhapsody,* first published in 1602. One stanza has been here omitted, in accordance with the principle noticed in the Preface. Similar omissions occur in 45, 87, 100, 128, 160, 165, 227, 235. The more serious abbreviation by which it has been attempted to bring Crashaw's 'Wishes' and Shelley's 'Euganean Hills' within the limits of lyrical unity, is commended with much diffidence to the judgement of readers acquainted with the original pieces.

7   9   *Presence* in line 8 is here conjecturally printed for *Present.* A very few similar corrections of (it is presumed) misprints have been made—as *thy* for *my,* 22, 9; *men* for *me,* 41, 3; and *one* for *our,* 252, 90; *locks* for *looks,* 271, 5; *dome* for *doom,* 275, 25—with two or three more or less important.

10   15   This charming little poem, truly 'old and plain, and dallying with the innocence of love' like that spoken of in *Twelfth Night,* is taken, with 5, 17, 20, 34, and 40, from the most characteristic collection of Elizabeth's reign, *England's Helicon,* first published in 1600.

—   16   Readers who have visited Italy will be reminded of more than one picture by this gorgeous Vision of Beauty, equally sublime and pure in its Paradisaical naturalness. Lodge wrote it on a voyage to 'the Islands of Terceras and the Canaries'; and he seems to have caught, in those southern seas, no small portion of the qualities which marked the almost contemporary Art of Venice,—the glory and the glow of Veronese, or Titian, or Tintoret, when he most resembles Titian, and all but surpasses him.

—   16   l. 1 *The clear* is the crystalline or outermost heaven of the old cosmography. For *resembling* (l. 7) other copies give *refining:* the correct reading is perhaps *revealing.*

Page No.

11   16   l. 33 *for a fair there's fairer none:* If you desire a **Beauty**, there is none more beautiful than Rosaline.

13   18   l. 2 *that fair thou owest:* that beauty thou ownest.

15   23   ll. 7, 8 *the star . . . Whose worth's unknown, although his height be taken;* apparently, Whose stellar influence is un-calculated, although his angular altitude from the plane of the astrolabe or artificial horizon used by astrologers has been determined.

17   27   l. 9 *keel:* skim.

19   29   l. 4 *expense:* waste.

—   30   l. 5 *Nativity, once in the main light:* when a star has risen and entered on the full stream of light;—another of the astrological phrases no longer familiar.

l. 7 *Crooked* eclipses: as coming athwart the Sun's ap-parent course.

Wordsworth, thinking probably of the *Venus* and the *Lucrece*, said finely of Shakespeare: 'Shakespeare *could* not have written an Epic; he would have died of plethora of thought.' This prodigality of nature is exemplified equally in his Sonnets. The copious selection here given (which, from the wealth of the material, required greater considera-tion than any other portion of the Editor's task) contains many that will not be fully felt and understood without some earnestness of thought on the reader's part. But he is not likely to regret the labour.

20   31   l. 7 *upon misprision growing:* either, granted in error, or, on the growth of contempt.

—   32   With the tone of this Sonnet compare Hamlet's 'Give me that man That is not passion's slave,' &c. Shakespeare's writings show the deepest sensitiveness to passion—hence the attraction he felt in the contrasting effects of apathy.

21   33   l. 4 *grame:* sorrow. It was long before English Poetry returned to the charming simplicity of this and a few other poems by Wyat.

22   34   l. 19 Pandion in the ancient fable was father to Philomela.

24   38   l. 4 *ramage:* confused noise.

—   39   l. 4 *censures:* judges.

25   40   By its style this beautiful example of old simplicity and feeling may be referred to the early years of Elizabeth. L. 3 *late* forgot: lately.

26   41   l. 9 *haggards:* the least tameable hawks.

27   44   l. 2 *cypres* or cyprus,—used by the old writers for *crape;* whether from the French *crespe* or from the Island whence it was imported. Its accidental similarity in spelling to *cypress* has, here and in Milton's Penseroso, probably con-fused readers.

29   46, 47   'I never saw anything like this funeral dirge,' says Charles Lamb, 'except the ditty which reminds Ferdinand

Page No.

of his drowned father in *The Tempest*. As that is of the water, watery; so this is of the earth, earthy. Both have that intenseness of feeling, which seems to resolve itself into the element which it contemplates.'

31   51   l. 8 *crystal:* fairness.

32   53   This 'Spousal Verse' was written in honour of the Ladies Elizabeth and Katherine Somerset. Although beautiful, it is inferior to the *Epithalamion* on Spenser's own marriage,—omitted with great reluctance as not in harmony with modern manners.

33   —   l. 4 *feateously:* elegantly.

35   —   l. 21 *shend:* put out.

36   —   l. 7 *a noble peer:* Robert Devereux, second Lord Essex, then at the height of his brief triumph after taking Cadiz: hence the allusion following to the Pillars of Hercules, placed near Gades by ancient legend. L. 19 *Eliza:* Elizabeth. L. 35 *twins of Jove:* the stars Castor and Pollux. L. 36 *baldric,* belt; the zodiac.

38   57   A fine example of a peculiar class of Poetry;—that written by thoughtful men who practised this Art but little. Wotton's, 72, is another. Jeremy Taylor, Bishop Berkeley, Dr. Johnson, Lord Macaulay, have left similar specimens.

Summary of Book Second

THIS division, embracing the latter eighty years of the seventeenth century, contains the close of our Early poetical style and the commencement of the Modern. In Dryden we see the first master of the new: in Milton, whose genius dominates here as Shakespeare's in the former book,—the crown and consummation of the early period. Their splendid Odes are far in advance of any prior attempts, Spenser's excepted: they exhibit the wider and grander range which years and experience and the struggles of the time conferred on Poetry. Our Muses now give expression to political feeling, to religious thought, to a high philosophic statesmanship in writers such as Marvell, Herbert, and Wotton: whilst in Marvell and Milton, again, we find the first noble attempts at pure description of nature, destined in our own ages to be continued and equalled. Meanwhile the poetry of simple passion, although before 1660 often deformed by verbal fancies and conceits of thought, and afterward by levity and an artificial tone,—produced in Herrick and Waller some charming pieces of more finished art than the Elizabethan: until in the courtly compliments of Sedley it seems to exhaust itself, and lie almost dormant for the hundred years between the days of Wither and Suckling and the days of Burns and Cowper.—That the change from our early style to the modern brought with it at first a loss of nature and simplicity is undeniable: yet the far bolder and wider scope which Poetry took between 1620 and 1700, and the successful efforts then made to gain greater clearness in expression, in their results have been no slight compensation.

44 62   l. 4 *whist:* hushed. L. 29 *Pan:* used here for the Lord of all.

47 —   l. 19 *Lars and Lemurés:* household gods and spirits of relations dead. L. 22 *Flamens:* Roman priests. L. 27 *that twice-batter'd god:* Dagon.

48 —   l. 3 *Osiris,* the Egyptian god of Agriculture (here, perhaps by confusion with Apis, figured as a Bull), was torn to pieces by Typho and embalmed after death in a sacred chest. This myth, reproduced in Syria and Greece in the legends of Thammuz, Adonis, and perhaps Absyrtus, represents the annual death of the Sun or the Year under the influences of the winter darkness. Horus, the son of Osiris, as the New Year, in his turn overcomes Typho.—It suited the genius of Milton's time to regard this primeval poetry and philosophy of the seasons, which has a further reference to the contest of Good and Evil in Creation, as a malignant idolatry. Shelley's Chorus in *Hellas,* 'Worlds on worlds,' treats the subject in a larger and sweeter spirit. L. 5 *unshower'd grass:* as watered by the Nile only.

51 64   *The Late Massacre:* the Vaudois persecution, carried on in 1655 by the Duke of Savoy. This 'collect in verse,' as it has been justly named, is the most mighty Sonnet in any language known to the Editor. Readers should observe that, unlike our sonnets of the sixteenth century, it is constructed on the original Italian or Provençal model,—unquestionably far superior to the imperfect form employed by Shakespeare and Drummond.

—   65   Cromwell returned from Ireland in 1650. Hence the prophecies, not strictly fulfilled, of his deference to the Parliament, in stanzas xxi–xxiv.

This Ode, beyond doubt one of the finest in our language, and more in Milton's style than has been reached by any other poet, is occasionally obscure from imitation of the condensed Latin syntax. The meaning of st. v is 'rivalry or hostility are the same to a lofty spirit, and limitation more hateful than opposition.' The allusion in st. xi is to the old physical doctrines of the non-existence of a vacuum and the impenetrability of matter—in st. xvii to the omen traditionally connected with the foundation of the Capitol at Rome. The ancient belief that certain years in life complete natural periods and are hence peculiarly exposed to death, is introduced in st. xxvi by the word *climacteric.*

55 66   *Lycidas.* The person lamented is Milton's college friend Edward King, drowned in 1637 whilst crossing from Chester to Ireland.

Strict Pastoral Poetry was first written or perfected by the Dorian Greeks settled in Sicily: but the conventional use of it, exhibited more magnificently in *Lycidas* than in any other pastoral, is apparently of Roman origin. Milton, employing the noble freedom of a great artist, has here united ancient mythology with what may be called the modern mythology of Camus and Saint Peter,—to direct Christian images.—The metrical structure of this glorious poem is partly derived from Italian models.

55   66   l. 15 *Sisters of the sacred well*: the Muses, said to frequent the fountain Helicon on Mount Parnassus.

56   —   l. 20 *Mona*: Anglesea, called by the Welsh Inis Dowil or the Dark Island, from its dense forests. L. 21 *Deva*: the Dee, a river which probably derived its magical character from Celtic traditions: it was long the boundary of Briton and Saxon.—These places are introduced, as being near the scene of the shipwreck. L. 24 *Orpheus* was torn to pieces by Thracian women. Ll. 34, 35 *Amaryllis* and *Neaera*: names used here for the love-idols of poets: as *Damoetas* previously for a shepherd.

57   —   l. 2 *the blind Fury*: Atropos, fabled to cut the thread of life. Ll. 12, 13 *Arethuse* and *Mincius*: Sicilian and Italian waters here alluded to as synonymous with the pastoral poetry of Theocritus and Virgil. L. 15 *oat*: pipe, used here like Collins' *oaten stop*, l. 1, No. 146, for Song. L. 23 *Hippotades*: Aeolus, god of the Winds. L. 26 *Panope*: a Nereid. The names of local deities in the Hellenic mythology express generally some feature in the natural landscape, which the Greeks studied and analysed with their usual unequalled insight and feeling. *Panope* represents the boundlessness of the ocean-horizon when seen from a height, as compared with the limited horizon of the land in hilly countries such as Greece or Asia Minor. L. 30 *Camus*: the Cam; put for King's University. L. 33 *that sanguine flower*: the Hyacinth of the ancients; probably our Iris. L. 36 *The pilot*: Saint Peter, figuratively introduced as the head of the Church on earth, to foretell 'the ruin of our corrupted clergy, then in their heighth' under Laud's primacy.

58   66   l. 16 *the wolf*: Popery. L. 20 *Alpheus*: a stream in Southern Greece, supposed to flow underseas to join the Arethuse. L. 26 *swart star*: the Dogstar, called swarthy because its heliacal rising in ancient times occurred soon after midsummer.

59   —   l. 8 *moist vows*: either tearful prayers, or prayers for one at sea. L. 9 *Bellerus*: a giant, apparently created here by Milton to personify Bellerium, the ancient title of the Land's End. L. 10 *the great Vision*: the story was that the Archangel Michael had appeared on the rock by Marazion in Mount's Bay which bears his name. Milton calls on him to turn his eyes from the south homeward, and to pity Lycidas, if his body has drifted into the troubled waters off the Land's End. Finisterre being the land due south of Marazion, two places in that district (then by our trade with Corunna probably less unfamiliar to English ears), are named,—*Namancos* now Mujio in Galicia, *Bayona* north of the Minho, or

574

perhaps a fortified rock (one of the *Cies* Islands) not unlike
Saint Michael's Mount, at the entrance of Vigo Bay. L. 19
ore: rays of golden light. L. 38 *Doric lay:* Sicilian, pastoral.

62 70   *The assault* was an attack on London expected in 1642,
when the troops of Charles I reached Brentford. 'Written
on his door' was in the original title of this sonnet. Milton
was then living in Aldersgate Street.

— —   l. 10 *The Emathian conqueror:* When Thebes was de-
stroyed (335 B.C.) and the citizens massacred by thousands,
Alexander ordered the house of Pindar to be spared. He was
as incapable of appreciating the Poet as Lewis XIV of appreciating Racine: but even the narrow and barbarian mind of
Alexander could understand the advantage of a showy act
of homage to Poetry. Ll. 12–13 *the repeated air Of sad
Electra's poet:* Amongst Plutarch's vague stories, he says
that when the Spartan confederacy in 404 B.C. took Athens,
a proposal to demolish it was rejected through the effect
produced on the commanders by hearing part of a chorus
from the Electra of Euripides sung at a feast. There is however no apparent congruity between the lines quoted (167–8,
ed. Dindorf) and the result ascribed to them.

63 73   This high-toned and lovely Madrigal is quite in the style,
and worthy of, the 'pure Simonides'.

65 75   Vaughan's beautiful though quaint verses should be
compared with Wordsworth's great Ode, No. 287.

66 76   l. 6 *Favonius:* the spring wind.

— **77**   l. 2 *Themis:* the goddess of justice. Skinner was grandson
by his mother to Sir E. Coke;—hence, as pointed out by
Mr. Keightley, Milton's allusion to the *bench.* L. 8: Sweden
was then at war with Poland, and France with the Spanish
Netherlands.

68 79   l. 19 *Sidneian showers:* either in allusion to the conversa-
tions in the *Arcadia,* or to Sidney himself as a model of
'gentleness' in spirit and demeanour.

73 84   *Elizabeth of Bohemia:* daughter to James I, and ancestor
to Sophia of Hanover. These lines are a fine specimen of
gallant and courtly compliment.

— **85**   Lady M. Ley was daughter to Sir J. Ley, afterwards Earl
of Marlborough, who died March, 1628–9, coincidently
with the dissolution of the third Parliament of Charles's
reign. Hence Milton poetically compares his death to that
of the Orator Isocrates of Athens, after Philip's victory in
328 B.C.

78 92, 93   These are quite a Painter's poems.

81 99   *From Prison:* to which his active support of Charles I
twice brought the high-spirited writer.

86 105   Inserted in Book II as written in the character of a
Soldier of Fortune in the Seventeenth Century.

87 106   *waly waly:* an exclamation of sorrow, the root and the pronunciation of which are preserved in the word *caterwaul. Brae*, hillside; *burn*, brook; *busk*, adorn. *Saint Anton's Well:* at the foot of Arthur's Seat by Edinburgh. *Cramasie*, crimson.

89 107   l. 7 *burd*, maiden.

90 108   *corbies*, crows; *fail*, turf; *hause*, neck; *theek*, thatch.—If not in their origin, in their present form this and the two preceding poems appear due to the Seventeenth Century, and have therefore been placed in Book II.

92 111   The remark quoted in the note to No. 47 applies equally to these truly wonderful verses, which, like *Lycidas*, may be regarded as a test of any reader's insight into the most poetical aspects of Poetry. The general differences between them are vast: but in imaginative intensity Marvell and Shelley are closely related.—This poem is printed as a translation in Marvell's works: but the original Latin is obviously his own. The most striking verses in it, here quoted as the book is rare, answer more or less to stanzas ii and vi:

Alma Quies, teneo te! et te, germana Quietis,
Simplicitas! vos ergo diu per templa, per urbes
Quaesivi, regum perque alta palatia, frustra:
Sed vos hortorum per opaca silentia, longe
Celarunt plantae virides, et concolor umbra.

94, 98 112,   *L'Allégro* and *Il Penseroso*. It is striking proof of
        113   Milton's astonishing power, that these, the earliest pure Descriptive Lyrics in our language, should still remain the best in a style which so many great poets have since attempted. The Bright and the Thoughtful aspects of Nature are their subjects: but each is preceded by a mythological introduction in a mixed Classical and Italian manner. The meaning of the first is that Gaiety is the child of Nature; of the second, that Pensiveness is the daughter of Sorrow and Genius.

94 112   l. 2: Perverse ingenuity has conjectured that for *Cerberus* we should read *Erebus*, who in the Mythology is at once brother and husband of Night. But the issue of that union is not Sadness, but Day and Aether—completing the circle of primary Creation, as the parents are both children of Chaos, the first-begotten of all things. (Hesiod.)

95 —   l. 12 *the mountain nymph:* compare Wordsworth's Sonnet, No. 210. L. 38 is in *apposition* to the preceding, by a grammatical licence not uncommon with Milton.

96 —   l. 3 *tells his tale:* counts his flock. L. 16 *Cynosure:* the Pole Star. Ll. 19 sqq. *Corydon, Thyrsis* &c.: shepherd names from the old Idylls.

97 —   l. 28 *Jonson's learned sock:* the gaiety of our age would find little pleasure in his elaborate comedies. L. 32 *Lydian airs:* a light and festive style of ancient music.

98 113   l. 3 *bestead:* avail. L. 19 *starr'd Ethiop queen:* Cassiopeia, the legendary Queen of Ethiopia, and thence translated amongst the constellations.

99 —   l. 37 *Cynthia:* the Moon: her chariot is drawn by dragons in ancient representations.

100 —   l. 26 *Hermes,* called Trismegistus, a mystical writer of the Neo-Platonist school. L. 37 *Thebes* &c: subjects of Athenian Tragedy. L. 40 *Buskin'd:* tragic.

101 —   l. 2 *Musaeus:* a poet in Mythology. L. 7 *him that left half told:* Chaucer, in his incomplete 'Squire's Tale.' L. 14 *great bards:* Ariosto, Tasso, and Spenser are here intended. L. 21 *frounced:* curled. L. 22 *the Attic Boy:* Cephalus.

103 114   Emigrants supposed to be driven towards America by the government of Charles I. Ll. 23–24 *But apples* &c. A fine example of Marvell's imaginative hyperbole.

104 115   l. 6 *concent:* harmony.

Summary of Book Third

It is more difficult to characterize the English Poetry of the eighteenth century than that of any other. For it was an age not only of spontaneous transition, but of bold experiment: it includes not only such divergences of thought as distinguish the *Rape of the Lock* from the *Parish Register*, but such vast contemporaneous differences as lie between Pope and Collins, Burns and Cowper. Yet we may clearly trace three leading moods or tendencies: the aspects of courtly or educated life represented by Pope and carried to exhaustion by his followers; the poetry of Nature and of Man, viewed through a cultivated, and at the same time an impassioned frame of mind by Collins and Gray: lastly, the study of vivid and simple narrative, including natural description, begun by Gay and Thomson, pursued by Burns and others in the north, and established in England by Goldsmith, Percy, Crabbe, and Cowper. Great varieties in style accompanied these diversities in aim: poets could not always distinguish the manner suitable for subjects so far apart; and the union of the language of courtly and of common life, exhibited most conspicuously by Burns, has given a tone to the poetry of that century which is better explained by reference to its historical origin than by naming it, in the common criticism of our day, artificial. There is, again, a nobleness of thought, a courageous aim at high and, in a strict sense, manly excellence in many of the writers: nor can that period be justly termed tame and wanting in originality, which produced poems such as Pope's *Satires,* Gray's *Odes* and *Elegy,* the ballads of Gay and Carey, the songs of Burns and Cowper. In truth Poetry at this as at all times was a more or less unconscious mirror of the genius of the age: and the brave and admirable spirit of inquiry which made the eighteenth century the turning-time in European civilization is reflected faithfully in its verse. An intelligent reader will find the influence of Newton as markedly in the poems of Pope as of Elizabeth in the plays of

Shakespeare. On this great subject, however, these indications must here be sufficient.

115 123   *The Bard.* This Ode is founded on a fable that Edward I, after conquering Wales, put the native Poets to death.— After lamenting his comrades (st. ii, iii) the Bard prophesies the fate of Edward II and the conquests of Edward III (iv); his death and that of the Black Prince (v); of Richard II, with the wars of York and Lancaster, the murder of Henry VI (the *meek usurper*), and of Edward V and his brother (vi). He turns to the glory and prosperity following the accession of the Tudors (vii), through Elizabeth's reign (viii); and concludes with a vision of the poetry of Shakespeare and Milton.

—   —   l. 13 *Glo'ster:* Gilbert de Clare, son-in-law to Edward. L. 14 *Mortimer,* one of the Lords Marchers of Wales.

116   —   l. 13 *Arvon:* the shores of Carnarvonshire opposite Anglesey. L. 35 *She-wolf:* Isabel of France, adulterous Queen of Edward II.

117   —   l. 27 *towers of Julius:* the Tower of London, built in part, according to tradition, by Julius Caesar. L. 33 *bristled boar:* the badge of Richard III.

118   —   l. 1 *Half of thy heart:* Queen Eleanor died soon after the conquest of Wales. L. 11 *Arthur:* Henry VII named his eldest son thus, in deference to British feeling and legend.

119 125   l. 5 The Highlanders called the battle of Culloden, Drumossie.

120 126   *lilting,* singing blithely; *loaning,* broad lane; *bughts,* pens; *scorning,* rallying; *dowie,* dreary; *daffin'* and *gabbin',* joking and chatting; *leglin,* milk-pail; *shearing,* reaping; *bandsters,* sheaf-binders; *lyart,* grizzled; *runkled,* wrinkled; *fleeching,* coaxing; *gloaming,* twilight; *bogle,* ghost; *dool,* sorrow.

122 128   The Editor has found no authoritative text of this poem, in his judgement superior to any other of its class in melody and pathos. Part is probably not later than the seventeenth century: in other stanzas a more modern hand, much resembling Scott's, is traceable. Logan's poem (127) exhibits a knowledge rather of the old legend than of the old verses: *Hecht,* promised, the obsolete *hight; mavis,* thrush; *ilka,* every; *lav'rock,* lark; *haughs,* valley-meadows; *twined,* parted from; *marrow,* mate; *syne,* then.

123 129   The Royal George, of 108 guns, whilst undergoing a partial careening in Portsmouth Harbour, was overset about 10 A.M. Aug. 29, 1782. The total loss was believed to be near 1,000 souls.

126 131   A little masterpiece in a very difficult style: Catullus himself could hardly have bettered it. In grace, tenderness, simplicity, and humour it is worthy of the Ancients; and

NOTES

Page No.

even more so, from the completeness and unity of the picture presented.

130 136   Perhaps no writer who has given such strong proofs of the poetic nature has left less satisfactory poetry than Thomson. Yet he touched little which he did not beautify; and this song, with 'Rule, Britannia' and a few others, must make us regret that he did not more seriously apply himself to lyrical writing.

132 140   l. 1 *Aeolian lyre*: the Greeks ascribed the origin of their Lyrical Poetry to the colonies of Aeolis in Asia Minor. L. 17 *Thracia's hills*: supposed a favourite resort of Mars.

133 —   l. 3 *feather'd king*: the Eagle of Jupiter, admirably described by Pindar in a passage here imitated by Gray. L. 9 *Idalia* in Cyprus, where *Cytherea* (Venus) was especially worshipped. L. 35 *Hyperion*: the Sun. St. vi–viii allude to the Poets of the islands and mainland of Greece, to those of Rome and of England.

135 140   l. 21 *Theban Eagle*: Pindar.

138 141   l. 7 *chaste-eyed Queen*: Diana.

139 142   l. 5 *Attic warbler*: the nightingale.

141 144   *sleekit*, sleek; *bickering brattle*, flittering flight; *laith*, loath; *pattle*, ploughstaff; *whiles*, at times; *a daimen-icker*, a corn-ear now and then; *thrave*, shock; *lave*, rest; *foggage*, aftergrass; *snell*, biting; *but hald*, without dwelling-place; *thole*, bear; *cranreuch*, hoarfrost; *thy lane*, alone; *a-gley*, off the right line, awry.

145 147   Perhaps the noblest stanzas in our language.

149 148   *stoure*, dust-storm; *braw*, smart.

150 149   *scaith*, hurt; *tent*, guard; *steer*, molest.

151 151   *drumlie*, muddy; *birk*, birch.

153 152   *greet*, cry; *daurna*, dare not.—There can hardly exist a poem more truly tragic in the highest sense than this: nor, except Sappho, has any Poetess known to the Editor equalled it in excellence.

— 153   *fou*, merry with drink; *coost*, carried; *unco skeigh*, very proud; *gart*, forced; *abeigh*, aside; *Ailsa Craig*, a rock in the Firth of Clyde; *grat his een bleert*, cried till his eyes were bleared; *lowpin*, leaping; *linn*, waterfall; *sair*, sore; *snoor'd*, smothered; *crouse* and *canty*, blithe and gay.

154 154   Burns justly named this 'one of the most beautiful songs in the Scots or any other language.' One verse, interpolated by Beattie, is here omitted: it contains two good lines, but is quite out of harmony with the original poem. *Bigonet*, little cap; probably altered from *beguinette*; *thraw*, twist; *caller*, fresh.

156 155   *airts*, quarters; *row*, roll; *shaw*, small wood in a hollow, spinney; *knowes*, knolls.

157 156   *jo*, sweetheart; *brent*, smooth; *pow*, head.

— 157   *leal*, faithful; *fain*, happy.

NOTES

Summary of Book Fourth

I t proves sufficiently the lavish wealth of our own age in Poetry that the pieces which, without conscious departure from the standard of Excellence, render this Book by far the longest, are with very few exceptions composed during the first thirty years of the nineteenth century. Exhaustive reasons can hardly be given for the strangely sudden appearance of individual genius: but none, in the Editor's judgement, can be less adequate than that which assigns the splendid national achievements of our recent poetry to an impulse from the follies and wars that at the time disgraced our foreign neighbours. The first French Revolution was rather, in his opinion, one result, and in itself by no means the most important, of that far wider and greater spirit which through inquiry and doubt, through pain and triumph, sweeps mankind round the circles of its gradual development: and it is to this that we must trace the literature of modern Europe. But, without more detailed discussion on the motive causes of Scott,

Wordsworth, Campbell, Keats, and Shelley, we may observe that these Poets, with others, carried to further perfection the later tendencies of the century preceding, in simplicity of narrative, reverence for human Passion and Character in every sphere, and impassioned love of Nature: that, whilst maintaining on the whole the advances in art made since the Restoration, they renewed the half-forgotten melody and depth of tone which marked the best Elizabethan writers: that, lastly, to what was thus inherited they added a richness in language and a variety in metre, a force and fire in narrative, a tenderness and bloom in feeling, an insight into the finer passages of the Soul and the inner meanings of the landscape, a larger and wiser Humanity,—hitherto hardly attained, and perhaps unattainable even by predecessors of not inferior individual genius. In a word, the nation which, after the Greeks in their glory, has been the most gifted of all nations for Poetry, expressed in these men the highest strength and prodigality of its nature. They interpreted the age to itself—hence the many phases of thought and style they present: to sympathize with each, fervently and impartially, without fear and without fancifulness, is no doubtful step in the higher education of the Soul. For, as with the Affections and the Conscience, Purity in Taste is absolutely proportionate to Strength: and when once the mind has raised itself to grasp and to delight in Excellence, those who love most will be found to love most wisely.

Page No.

169	166	l. 11 *stout Cortez:* History requires here *Balbóa:* (A. T.). It may be noticed, that to find in Chapman's Homer the 'pure serene' of the original, the reader must bring with him the imagination of the youthful poet—he must be 'a Greek himself', as Shelley finely said of Keats.
173	169	The most tender and true of Byron's smaller poems.
174	170	This poem, with 236, exemplifies the peculiar skill with which Scott employs proper names: nor is there a surer sign of high poetical genius.
191	191	The Editor in this and in other instances has risked the addition (or the change) of a Title, that the aim of the verses following may be grasped more clearly and immediately.
197	198	l. 4 *Nature's Eremite:* like a solitary thing in Nature.—This beautiful Sonnet was the last word of a poet deserving the title 'marvellous boy' in a much higher sense than Chatterton. If the fulfilment may ever safely be prophesied from the promise, England appears to have lost in Keats one whose gifts in Poetry have rarely been surpassed. Shakespeare, Milton, and Wordsworth, had their lives been closed at twenty-five, would (so far as we know) have left poems of less excellence and hope than the youth who, from the petty school and the London surgery, passed at once to a place with them of 'high collateral glory'.
199	201	It is impossible not to regret that Moore has written so little in this sweet and genuinely national style.

NOTES

199 202   A masterly example of Byron's command of strong thought and close reasoning in verse: as the next is equally characteristic of Shelley's wayward intensity, and 204 of the dramatic power, the vital identification of the poet with other times and characters, in which Scott is second only to Shakespeare.

209 209   Bonnivard, a Genevese, was imprisoned by the Duke of Savoy in Chillon on the lake of Geneva for his courageous defence of his country against the tyranny with which Piedmont threatened it during the first half of the seventeenth century.—This noble Sonnet is worthy to stand near Milton's on the Vaudois massacre.

— 210   Switzerland was usurped by the French under Napoleon in 1800: Venice in 1797 (211).

212 215   This battle was fought Dec. 2, 1800, between the Austrians under Archduke John and the French under Moreau, in a forest near Munich. *Hohen Linden* means *High Lime-trees.*

216 218   After the capture of Madrid by Napoleon, Sir J. Moore retreated before Soult and Ney to Corunna, and was killed whilst covering the embarkation of his troops. His tomb, built by Ney, bears this inscription—'John Moore, leader of the English armies, slain in battle, 1809.'

229 229   The Mermaid was the club-house of Shakespeare, Ben Jonson, and other choice spirits of that age.

— 230   l. 1 *Maisie:* Mary. Scott has given us nothing more complete and lovely than this little song, which unites simplicity and dramatic power to a wildwood music of the rarest quality. No moral is drawn, far less any conscious analysis of feeling attempted: the pathetic meaning is left to be suggested by the mere presentment of the situation. Inexperienced critics have often named this, which may be called the Homeric manner, superficial, from its apparent simple facility: but first-rate excellence in it (as shown here, in 196, 156, and 129) is in truth one of the least common triumphs of Poetry.—This style should be compared with what is not less perfect in its way, the searching out of inner feeling, the expression of hidden meanings, the revelation of the heart of Nature and of the Soul within the Soul,—the Analytical method, in short,—most completely represented by Wordsworth and by Shelley.

235 234   *correi:* covert on a hillside. *Cumber:* trouble.

— 235   Two intermediate stanzas have been here omitted. They are very ingenious, but, of all poetical qualities, ingenuity is least in accordance with pathos.

247 243   This poem has an exaltation and a glory, joined with an exquisiteness of expression, which place it in the highest rank amongst the many masterpieces of its illustrious Author.

257 252   l. 24 *interlunar swoon:* interval of the Moon's invisibility.

NOTES

INDEX OF WRITERS

INDEX OF WRITERS

585

INDEX OF WRITERS

589

INDEX OF WRITERS

INDEX OF WRITERS

INDEX OF WRITERS

INDEX OF WRITERS

INDEX OF FIRST LINES

INDEX OF FIRST LINES

INDEX OF FIRST LINES

INDEX OF FIRST LINES

INDEX OF FIRST LINES

INDEX OF FIRST LINES

INDEX OF FIRST LINES

611

INDEX OF FIRST LINES

INDEX OF FIRST LINES

INDEX OF FIRST LINES